WICCA

LIVING WICCA

THE COMPLETE BOOK OF INCENSE, OILS & BREWS

WICCA

LIVING WICCA

THE COMPLETE BOOK OF INCENSE, OILS & BREWS

SCOTT CUNNINGHAM

ONE SPIRIT
NEW YORK

WICCA

*This book is dedicated
to the forces that watch over
and guide us—however we may envision
or name Them*

Acknowledgements

To deTraci Regula, Marilee, Juanita, and Mark and Kyri of the House of the Silver Wheel for commenting on earlier drafts of this work.

To Morgan, Morgana, Abraham, Barda and all those who have shared their knowledge and practices with me.

To all my friends at Llewellyn Publications for their years of continuing support.

Contents

Preface

This book, the result of sixteen years of practical experience and research, is a guidebook outlining basic Wiccan theory and practice. It is written with the solitary student or practitioner in mind; there are no coven rituals or magical group dynamics described herein.

The Wicca as described here is "new." It is not a revelation of ancient rituals handed down for thousands of years. This does not invalidate it, however, for it is based on time-honored practices.

A three-thousand-year-old incantation to Inanna isn't necessarily more powerful or effective than one improvised during a private rite. The person practicing the ritual or spell determines its success.

If centuries-old incantations are nothing more to you than senseless gibberish, chances are the ritual won't work, any more than would a Shinto ceremony in the hands of a Methodist. To be effective, rituals must speak to you.

Rituals are at the heart of Wicca for some, and are pleasant adjuncts to Wicca's philosophy and way of life for others. In Wicca, as with every religion, ritual is a means of contacting the Divine. Effective ritual unites the worshipper with Deity. Ineffective ritual kills spirituality.

There are rituals in this book, yes, but they're guideposts, not holy writ. I wrote them so that others, using them as general guidelines, could create their own.

Some people might say, "But that's just your stuff. We want the *real* Wicca! *Tell us the secrets!*

There is not, and can never be, one "pure" or "true" or "genuine" form of Wicca. There are no central governing agencies, no physical leaders, no universally-recognized prophets or messengers. Although specific, structured forms of Wicca certainly exist, they aren't in agreement regarding ritual, symbolism and theology. Because of this healthy individualism, no one ritual or philosophical system has emerged to consume the others.

Wicca is varied and multi-faceted. As in every religion, the Wiccan spiritual experience is one shared with Deity alone. This book is simply one way, based on my experiences and the instruction I have received, to practice Wicca.

Although I wrote it, it didn't hatch out of thin air. The jeweler who facets rough emeralds didn't create the gemstones; nor the potter the clay. I've tried to present a blending of the major themes and ritual structures of Wicca, not to create a new form, but to present one so that others can develop their own Wiccan practices.

When I began learning Wicca there were few books, certainly no published Books of Shadows.* Wiccan rituals and magical texts are secret within many traditions of Wicca, and it wasn't until recently that any systems have "gone public." Due to this fact, few Wiccans wrote books describing the rituals and inner teachings of Wicca. Those outside the Wicca (or the Craft as it is also known) who wrote of it could necessarily report only garbled or incomplete pictures.

Within a few years of my introduction to Wicca, however, many authentic, informative books began to be published. As I continued my studies, both independently and under teachers I had met, I realized that anyone trying to learn and practice Wicca solely from published sources would gain a sadly unbalanced picture.

Most Wiccan authors tout their own form of Wicca. This makes sense: write what you know. Unfortunately, many of the foremost Wiccan authors share similar views, and so most of the published Wiccan material is repetitive.

Also, most of these books are geared toward coven (group)-oriented Wicca. This poses a problem for anyone unable to find a minimum of four or five interested, compatible persons to create a coven. It also lays a burden on those who desire private religious practice.

Perhaps my true reason for writing this book—besides numerous requests—is strictly personal. I not only wish to present an alternate to staid, structured Wiccan books, I also want to return something for the training I have received in this contemporary religion.

Although I occasionally teach, and Wicca always draws a crowd, I prefer the medium of printed words to point out some of the things I have learned. Although nothing can replace one-on-one teaching, this isn't practical for all those desiring to learn.

And so, several years ago, I began jotting down notes and chapters that eventually became this book. To avoid becoming too narrow-

---

* See glossary for unfamiliar terms.

minded (Sybil Leek once said that it was dangerous writing about your own religion—you're too close to it), I've had Wiccan friends read and comment on early drafts to ensure that the picture of Wicca presented here isn't too limited or dogmatic.

Please don't misunderstand me. Though this book's goal is a wider understanding of, and appreciation of Wicca, I'm not proselytizing. Like most Wiccans, I'm not out to change your spiritual and religious beliefs; it's none of my business.

However, with the continuing interest in non-traditional religions, concern over environmental destruction and a wide interest in the Wiccan religion, I hope this book partially answers one of the questions I'm most commonly asked:

"What *is* Wicca?"

Linguistic Note

Much disagreement concerning the exact (and original) meaning of the word "Wicca" presently exists. It's not my intention to enter into or add to such discussions, but I don't feel that I can use this term without defining it. Therefore, "Wicca" will be used within this book to describe both the religion itself (a loosely organized Pagan religion centering toward reverence for the creative forces of Nature, usually symbolized by a goddess and a god), as well as its practitioners of both sexes. The term "Warlock," though sometimes used to describe male practitioners, is virtually never used by Wiccans themselves; hence I've avoided it here. Though some use "Wicca" and "Witch" almost interchangeably, I prefer the older, less-encumbered word Wicca, and so use it almost exclusively.

Introduction

Wicca, the religion of the "Witches," has long been shrouded in secrecy. Anyone interested in learning "the Craft" had to content themselves with hints from books and articles. The Wiccans wouldn't say much, save that they weren't looking for new members.

Growing numbers today are dissatisfied with traditional religious structures. Many are searching for a personally-involving religion, one which celebrates both physical and spiritual realities, in which attunement with deity is coupled with the practice of magic.

Wicca is just such a religion, centering around reverence for nature as seen in the Goddess and the God. Its spiritual roots in antiquity, acceptance of magic and mysterious nature have made it particularly appealing. Until recently, the lack of public information concerning Wicca and its apparent exclusivity has caused much frustration among interested students.

Wicca doesn't seek new members. This has been a major stumbling block to those wishing to learn its rites and ways of magic. Wicca doesn't solicit because, unlike most Western religions, it doesn't claim to be the one true way to Deity.

With growing numbers interested in practicing Wicca, perhaps it's time to allow the full light of the dawning Aquarian Age to illuminate these ways. To do so is not to trumpet Wicca as the salvation of our planet, but simply to present it to anyone who cares to learn.

There have been many obstacles. Until recently the only way to enter Wicca was to *a:* contact an initiated Wicca, usually a coven member, and *b:* receive initiation. If you didn't know any Witches you were out of luck, for initiation was an absolute prerequisite.

Today, times are changing. We are maturing, perhaps too quickly. Our technology outpaces the wisdom to utilize it. Vast unrest spreads over the globe, and the threat of war looms over most of the more than five billion persons alive today.

Wicca as a religion is changing too. This is necessary if it is to be more than a curiosity of an earlier age. The heirs of Wicca must point their religion firmly to the future if it is to have something to offer coming generations.

Since we have arrived at the point where one mishap could end our planet as we know it, there has never been a time when Wicca as a nature-reverencing religion has had more to offer.

This book breaks many Wicca conventions. It has been structured so that anyone, anywhere in the world, can practice Wicca. No initiations are required. It is designed for the solitary practitioner, since finding others with similar interests is difficult, especially in rural areas.

Wicca is a joyous religion springing from our kinship with nature. It is a merging with the Goddesses and Gods, the universal energies which created all in existence. It is a personal, positive celebration of life.

And now it is available to all.

SECTION I:
THEORY

1

Wicca and Shamanism

Shamanism has been defined as the first religion. It existed prior to the earliest civilizations, before our ancestors took the first steps down the long journey to the present. Prior to this time the shamans were the medicine people, the power wielders, male and female. They wrought magic and spoke to the spirits of nature.

The shamans were the first humans with knowledge. They created, discovered, nurtured and used it. Knowledge is power; women and men who possessed it in those far-flung days were shamans.

How did shamans capture or discover this power? Through ecstasy—alternate states of consciousness in which they communed with the forces of the universe. Early shamans first attained this state through the use of such "tools" as fasts, thirsts, self-infliction of pain, ingestion of hallucinogenic substances, concentration and so on. Once mastered, these techniques allowed them to gain awareness of other, non-physical worlds.

Through such "awareness shifts," all magical knowledge was obtained. Conference with spirits and deities, plants and animals opened up new vistas of learning. Among their own people, the shamans often shared some of this knowledge but reserved the rest for personal use. Shamanic lore wasn't for public consumption.

Later, shamans advanced in the use of tools to facilitate these awareness shifts, marking the advent of magical ritual. Shamans around the world still use tools such as drums, rattles, reflective objects, music, chants and dance. Indeed, the most effective shamanic rites are those which utilize both natural and artificial tools—a sighing wind, roaring ocean, flickering firelight, a steady drum beat, the hiss of a rattle. These combined with darkness and chants eventually overwhelm the senses, forcing a shifting from awareness of the physical world to the vaster realm of energies. Such are shamanic rites which exist to this day.

From these primitive beginnings arose all magic and religion, including Wicca. Despite current controversy as to the "antiquity" of Wicca, it is spiritually descended from such rites. Though refined and changed for our world, Wicca still touches our souls and causes ecstasy—awareness shifts—uniting us with Deity. Many of the techniques of Wicca are shamanic in origin.

Therefore, Wicca can be described as a shamanic religion. As with shamanism, only a select few feel compelled to enter its circle of light.

Today, Wicca has dropped the ordeals of pain and the use of hallucinogens in favor of chanting, meditation, concentration, visualization, music, dance, invocation and ritual drama. With these spiritual tools the Wicca achieve a state of ritual consciousness similar to those attained by the most brutal shamanic ordeals.

I deliberately used the term "alternate states of consciousness." Such changed consciousness states aren't unnatural, a deviation from the "normal" waking consciousness. Wicca teaches that nature includes a broad spectrum of mental and spiritual states of which most of us are ignorant. Effective Wiccan ritual enables us to slip into such states, allowing communication and communion with the Goddess and God.

Unlike some religions, Wicca doesn't view Deity as distant. The Goddess and God are both within ourselves and manifest in all nature. This is the universality: there is nothing that isn't of the Gods.

A study of shamanism reveals much of the heart of magical and religious experience in general, and Wicca in particular (see Bibliography for recommended books). With ritual as a means to enter ritual consciousness, the shaman or Wicca constantly expands his or her knowledge, and knowledge is power. Wicca helps its practitioners to understand the universe and our place within it.

At present, Wicca is a religion with many variations. Because it is such a personally-structured system, I can only state generalities about its creed and form here, filtered through my experience and knowledge, to create a picture of the nature of Wicca.

Wicca, in common with many other religions, recognizes Deity as dual. It reveres both the Goddess and the God. They are equal, warm and loving, not distant or resident in "heaven" but omnipresent throughout the universe.

Wicca also teaches that the physical world is one of many realities. The physical is not the absolute highest expression, nor is the spiritual "purer" than the base. The only difference between the physical and the spiritual is that the former is denser.

As in Eastern religions, Wicca also embraces the doctrine of reincarnation, that much-misunderstood subject. Unlike some Eastern philosophies, however, Wicca doesn't teach that upon physical death our souls will reincarnate in anything other than a human body. Also, few of the Wicca believe we began our existence as rocks, trees, snails or birds before we evolved to the point where we could incarnate as human beings. Though these creatures and substances do possess a type of soul, it's not the sort we humans have.

Reincarnation is accepted as fact by many millions in the East and West. It answers many questions: what happens after death? Why do we seem to remember things we've never done in this life? Why are we sometimes strangely attracted to places or people who we've never before seen?

Surely reincarnation can't answer all these questions, but it is there for those who wish to study it. This isn't something that should be *believed*. Through contemplation, meditation and self-analysis many come to the point where they accept reincarnation as fact. For more information on this subject see Chapter Ten: The Spiral of Rebirth.

The Wiccan ideal of morality is simple: do what you want, as long as you harm none. This rule contains another unwritten condition: do nothing that will harm yourself. Thus, if you as a Wicca abuse your body, deny it the necessities of life or otherwise harm yourself, you're in violation of this principle.

This is more than survival. It also ensures that you'll be in good condition to take on the tasks of preserving and bettering our world, for concern and love for our planet play major roles in Wicca.

Wicca is a religion that utilizes magic. This is one of its most appealing and unique features. Religious magic? This isn't as strange as it might seem. Catholic priests use "magic" to transform a piece of bread into the body of a long-deceased "savior." Prayer—a common tool in many religions—is simply a form of concentration and communication with Deity. If the concentration is extended, energies are sent out with the thoughts which may in time make the prayer come true. Prayer is a form of religious magic.

Magic is the practice of moving natural (though little-understood) energies to effect needed change. In Wicca, magic is used as a tool to sanctify ritual areas, to improve ourselves and the world in which we live.

Many people confuse Wicca and magic as if the two words were interchangeable. Wicca is a religion that embraces magic. If you seek only to practice magic, Wicca probably isn't the answer for you.

Another fundamental point: magic isn't a means of forcing nature to do your will. This is a completely erroneous idea, fostered by the belief that magic is somehow supernatural, as if anything that exists can be outside of nature. *Magic is natural.* It is a harmonious movement of energies to create needed change. If you wish to practice magic, all thoughts of it being paranormal or supernatural must be forgotten.

Most Wiccans don't believe in predestination. Although we honor and revere the Goddess and God, we know that we're free souls with full control and responsibility of our lives. We can't point at an image of an evil god, such as Satan, and blame it for our faults and weaknesses. We can't blame fate. Every second of each day we're creating our futures, shaping the courses of our lives. Once a Wiccan takes full responsibility for all that she or he has done (in this life and past ones) and determines that future actions will be in accord with higher ideals and goals, magic will blossom and life will be a joy.

That perhaps is at the core of Wicca—it is a joyous union with nature. The Earth is a manifestation of divine energy. Wicca's temples are flower-splashed meadows, forests, beaches and deserts. When a Wicca is outdoors she or he is actually surrounded by sanctity, much as is a Christian when entering a church or cathedral.

Additionally, all nature is constantly singing to us, revealing Her secrets. Wiccans listen to the Earth. They don't shut out the lessons that She is so desperately trying to teach us. When we lose touch with our blessed planet, we lose touch with Deity.

These have been some of the basic principles of Wicca. They are the *true* Wicca; the rituals and myths are secondary to these ideals and serve to celebrate them.

The Complete Book of Shadows (ritual book) included in Section III is a guide to constructing your own. Because these rituals are outer form only, you needn't be chained to them. Change rites as the mood strikes you. As long as the rite attunes you with the Deities, all is fine.

Don't shut out the physical world in favor of the spiritual or magical realms, for only through nature can we experience these realities. We are here on the Earth for a reason. Do, however, use ritual to expand your awareness so that you are truly at one with all creation.

The way is open. The ancient Goddess and God await within and around you.

May They bless you with wisdom and power.

2

The Deities

All religions are structures built upon reverence of Deity. Wicca is no exception. The Wicca acknowledge a supreme divine power, unknowable, ultimate, from which the entire universe sprang.

The concept of this power, far beyond our comprehension, has nearly been lost in Wicca because of our difficulty in relating to it. However, Wiccans link with this force through their deities. In accordance with the principles of nature, the supreme power was personified into two basic beings: the Goddess and the God.

Every deity that has received worship upon this planet exists with the archetypal God and Goddess. The complex pantheons of deities which arose in many parts of the world are simply *aspects* of the two. Every Goddess is resident within the concept of the Goddess; every God in the God.

Wicca reveres these twin deities because of its links with nature. Since most (but certainly not all) nature is divided into gender, the deities embodying it are similarly conceived.

In the past, when the Goddess and God were as real as the Moon and Sun, rites of worship and adoration were unstructured—spontaneous, joyous union with the divine. Later, rituals followed the course of the Sun through its astronomical year (and thusly the seasons) as well as the monthly waxing and waning of the Moon.

Today similar rites are observed by the Wicca, and their regular performance creates a truly magical closeness with these deities and the powers behind them.

Fortunately, we needn't wait for ritual occasions to be reminded of the Gods' presence. The sight of a perfect blossom in a field of bare earth can instill feelings rivaling those of the most powerful formal rite. Living in nature makes every moment a ritual. The Wiccans are comfortable in communicating with animals, plants and trees. They feel energies within stones and sand, and cause fossils to speak of their primeval beginnings. For some Wiccans, watching the Sun or Moon rise and set each day is a ritual unto itself, for these are the heavenly symbols of the God and Goddess.

Because the Wicca see Deity inherent in nature, many of us are involved in ecology—saving the Earth from utter destruction by our own hands. The Goddess and God still exist, as they have always existed, and to honor them we honor and preserve our precious planet.

In Wiccan thought, the Deities didn't exist before our spiritual ancestor's acknowledgement of them. However, the *energies* behind them did; they created us. Early worshippers recognized these forces as the Goddess and God, personifying them in an attempt to understand them.

The Old Ones didn't die when the ancient Pagan religions fell to upstart Christianity in Europe. Most of the rites vanished, but they weren't the only effective ones. Wicca is alive and well and the Deities respond to our calls and invocations.

When envisioning the Goddess and God, many of the Wicca see Them as well-known deities from ancient religions. Diana, Pan, Isis, Hermes, Hina, Tammuz, Hecate, Ishtar, Cerridwen, Thoth, Tara, Aradia, Artemis, Pele, Apollo, Kanaloa, Bridget, Helios, Bran, Lugh, Hera, Cybele, Inanna, Maui, Ea, Athena, Lono, Marduk—the list is virtually endless. Many of these deities, with their corresponding histories, rites and mythic information, furnish the concept of deity for Wiccans.

Some feel comfortable associating such names and forms with the Goddess and God, feeling that they can't possibly revere nameless divine beings. Others find a lack of names and costumes a comforting lack of limitations.

As stated earlier, the Wicca as outlined in this book is "new," although built upon established rituals and myths, firmly rooted within the earliest religious feelings which nature aroused within our species. In these rituals I've used the words "the God" and "the Goddess" rather than specific names such as Diana and Pan. Anyone with a special affinity with particular deities should feel free to adapt the rituals in Section III: *The Standing Stones Book of Shadows* to include them.

If you haven't studied non-Western polytheistic religions or developed a rapport with divinities other than those with which you were raised, start by accepting this premise (if only for the moment): deity is twin, consisting of the Goddess and the God.

They have been given so many names they have been called the Nameless Ones. In appearance they look exactly as we wish them to, for they're all the Deities that ever were. The Goddess and God are all-powerful because they are the creators of all manifest and unmanifest existence. We can contact and communicate with them because a part of us is in them and they are within us.

The Goddess and God are equal; neither is higher or more deserving of respect. Though some Wiccans focus their rituals toward the Goddess and seem to forget the God entirely, this is a reaction to centuries of stifling patriarchal religion, and the loss of acknowledgement of the feminine aspect of Divinity. Religion based entirely on feminine energy, however, is as unbalanced and unnatural as one totally masculine in focus. The ideal is a perfect balance of the two. The Goddess and God are equal, complementary.

The Goddess

The Goddess is the universal mother. She is the source of fertility, endless wisdom and loving caresses. As the Wicca know Her, She is often of three aspects: the Maiden, the Mother and the Crone, symbolized in the waxing, full and waning of the Moon. She is at once the unploughed field, the full harvest and the dormant, frost-covered Earth. She gives birth to abundance. But as life is Her gift, She lends it with the promise of death. This is not darkness and oblivion, but rest from the toils of physical existence. It is human existence between incarnations.

Since the Goddess is nature, all nature, She is both the Temptress and the Crone; the tornado and the fresh spring rain; the cradle and the grave.

But though She is possessed of both natures, the Wicca revere Her as the giver of fertility, love and abundance, though they acknowledge Her darker side as well. We see Her in the Moon, the soundless, ever-moving sea, and in the green growth of the first spring. She is the embodiment of fertility and love.

The Goddess has been known as the Queen of Heaven, Mother of the Gods that Made the Gods, the Divine Source, the Universal Matrix, the Great Mother, and by countless other titles.

Many symbols are used in Wicca to honor Her, such as the cauldron, cup, labrys, five-petalled flowers, the mirror, necklace, seashell, pearl, silver, emerald . . . to name a few.

As She has dominion over the Earth, sea and Moon, Her creatures are varied and numerous. A few include the rabbit, the bear, the owl, the cat, dog, bat, goose, cow, dolphin, lion, horse, wren, scorpion, spider and bee. All are sacred to the Goddess.

The Goddess has been depicted as a huntress running with Her hounds; a celestial deity striding across the sky with stardust falling from Her heels; the eternal Mother heavy with child; the weaver of our lives and deaths; a Crone walking by waning moonlight seeking out the weak and forlorn, and as many other beings. But no matter how we envision Her, She is omnipresent, changeless, eternal.

The God

The God has been revered for eons. He is neither the stern, all-powerful deity of Christianity and Judaism, nor is He simply the consort of the Goddess. God or Goddess, they are equal, one.

We see the God in the Sun, brilliantly shining overhead during the day, rising and setting in the endless cycle which governs our lives. Without the Sun we could not exist; therefore it has been revered as the source of all life, the warmth that bursts the dormant seeds into life and hastens the greening of the Earth after the cold snows of winter.

The God is also tender of the wild animals. As the Horned God He is sometimes seen wearing horns on His head, symbolizing His connection with these beasts. In earlier times, hunting was one of the activities thought to be ruled by the God, while the domestication of animals was seen to be Goddess-oriented.

The God's domains include forests untouched by human hands, burning deserts and towering mountains. The stars, since they are but distant suns, are sometimes thought to be under His domain.

The yearly cycle of greening, maturation and harvest has long been associated with the Sun, hence the solar festivals of Europe (further discussed in Chapter Eight: The Days of Power) which are still observed in Wicca.

The God is the fully ripened harvest, intoxicating wine pressed from grapes, golden grain waving in a lone field, shimmering apples hanging from verdant boughs on October afternoons.

With the Goddess He also celebrates and rules sex. The Wicca don't avoid sex or speak of it in hushed words. It's a part of nature and is accepted as such. Since it brings pleasure, shifts our awareness away from the everyday world and perpetuates our species, it is thought to be sacred. The God lustily imbues us with the urge that ensures our species' biological future.

Symbols often used to depict or to worship the God include the sword, horns, spear, candle, gold, brass, diamond, the sickle, arrow, magical wand, trident, knife and others. Creatures sacred to Him include the bull, dog, snake, fish, stag, dragon, wolf, boar, eagle, falcon, shark, lizard and many others.

Of old, the God was the Sky Father, and the Goddess, the Earth Mother. The God of the sky, of rain and lightning, descended upon and united with the Goddess, spreading seed upon the land, celebrating Her fertility.

Today the deities of Wicca are still firmly associated with fertility, but every aspect of human existence can be linked with the Goddess and God. They can be called upon to help us sort through the vicissitudes of our existences and bring joy into our often spiritually-bereft lives.

This doesn't mean that when problems occur we should leave them in the hands of the Goddess. This is a stalling maneuver, an avoidance of dealing with the bumps on the road of life. However, as Wiccans we can call on the Goddess and God to clear our minds and to *help us help ourselves*. Magic is an excellent means of accomplishing this. After attuning with the Goddess and God, Wiccans ask Their assistance during the magical rite that usually follows.

Beyond this, the Goddess and God can help us change our lives. Because the Deities *are* the creative forces of the universe (not just symbols), we can call upon Them to empower our rites and to bless our magic. Again, this is in direct opposition to most religions. The power is in the hands of every practitioner, not specialized priests or priestesses who perform these feats for the masses. This is what makes Wicca a truly satisfying way of life. We have direct links with the Deities. No intermediaries are needed; no priests or confessors or shamans. *We are the shamans.*

To develop a rapport with the Goddess and God, a necessity for those who desire to practice Wicca, you might wish to follow these simple rituals.

At night, stand or sit facing the Moon, if it is visible. If not, imagine the fullest Moon you've ever seen glowing silver-white in the inky blackness, directly above and before you.

Feel the soft lunar light streaming onto your skin. Sense it touching and mixing with your own energies, commingling and forming new patterns.

See the Goddess in any form that you will. Call to Her, chanting old names if you wish: Diana, Lucina, Selena (pronouncing them as : Dee-AH-nah, Loo-CHEE-nah, Say-LEE-nah). Open your heart and mind to the aspect of Goddess-energy manifested in the Moon's light.

Repeat this daily for one week, preferably at the same time each night.

Concurrently with this exercise, attune with the God. Upon rising in the morning, no matter how late it is, stand before the Sun (through a window if necessary; outside if possible) and soak in its energies. Think about the God. Visualize Him as you wish. It might be as a mighty warrior rippling with muscles, a spear upraised in one hand, the other cradling a child or a bunch of dew-dripping grapes.

You may want to chant God names, such as Kernunnos, Osiris, Apollo (Care-NOON-nos, Oh-SIGH-rus, Ah-PALL-low) as with the Goddess.

If you don't wish to visualize the God (for visualization can impose limitations), simply attune to the energies pouring down from the Sun. Even if clouds fill the sky, the God's energies will still reach you. Feel them with all your magical imagination. (See Chapter 11: Exercises and Magical Techniques.)

Let no thoughts but those of the God disturb your revery. Reach out with your feelings; open your awareness to higher things. Call upon the God in any words. Express your desire to attune with Him.

Practice these exercises daily for one week. If you wish to explore the concepts of the Goddess and God, read books on mythology from any country in the world. Read the myths but look for their underlying themes. The more you read, the more information you'll have at your fingertips; eventually it will merge into a non-structured but extremely complex knowledge bank concerning the deities. In other words, you'll begin to know them.

If after seven days you feel the need (or the desire), continue these exercises until you feel comfortable with the Goddess and God. They've been in us and around us all the time; we need only open ourselves to this awareness. This is one of the secrets of Wicca—Deity dwells within.

In your quest to know the Gods, take long walks beneath trees. Study flowers and plants. Visit wild, natural places and feel the energies of the Goddess and God directly—through the rush of a stream, the pulse of energy from an old oak's trunk, the heat of a Sun-warmed rock. Familiarizing yourself with the existence of the Deities comes more easily through actual contact with such power sources.

Next, when you've achieved this state, you may wish to set up a temporary or permanent shrine or altar to the Goddess and God. This needn't be more than a small table, two candles, an incense burner and a plate or bowl to hold offerings of flowers, fruit, grain, seed, wine or milk.

Goddess *Candle*	*Flowers*	*God* *Candle*
	Censer	
	Offering *Plate*	

Layout of the Shrine

Place the two candles in their holders to the rear of the shrine. The candle on the left represents the Goddess; that on the right the God. Colors are often used to distinguish between the two; a red candle for the God and a green one to honor the Goddess. This ties in with the nature-associations of Wicca, for green and red are ancient magical colors linked with life and death. Other colors can be used— yellow or gold to honor the God, and white or silver for the Goddess.

Before and between these candles place the incense burner, and in front of this the plate or offering bowl. A vase of seasonal flowers can also be added, as can any personal power objects such as crystals, fossils and dried herbs.

To begin a simple ritual to the Gods at your shrine, stand before it with an offering of some kind in your hand. Light the candles and incense, place the offering in the bowl or plate, and say such words as these:

Lady of the Moon, of the restless sea and verdant Earth,
Lord of the Sun and of the wild creatures,
Accept this offering I place here in Your honor.
Grant me the wisdom to see Your presence in all nature,
    O Great Ones!

Afterward, sit or stand for a few minutes in contemplation of the deities and of your growing relationship with them. Feel them inside and around you. Then quench the flames (use your fingers, a candle snuffer, or a knife blade. Blowing them out is an affront to the element* of Fire). Allow the incense to burn itself out, and continue on with your day or night.

If you wish, go before the shrine once a day at a prescribed time. This may be upon rising, just before sleep, or after lunch. Light the candles, attune and commune with the Goddess and God. This isn't necessary, but the steady rhythm set up by this cycle is beneficial and will improve your relationship with the deities.

Return the offerings left on the shrine to the Earth at the end of each day, or when you bring more to leave.

If you cannot erect a permanent shrine, set it up each time you feel the need to use it, then store the articles away. Make the placing of the objects on the shrine a part of the ritual.

---

* See Glossary.

This simple rite belies its powers. The Goddess and God are real, viable entities, possessing the force that created the universe. Attuning with them changes us forever. It also sparks new hope for our planet and for our continued existence upon it.

If this rite is too formalized for you, change it or write your own. This is the basic thrust of this book: do it your way, not my way simply because I've set it down on paper. I can never fit my feet into someone else's footprints on the sand. There's no one true right and only way in Wicca; that thinking belongs to monotheistic religions which have largely become political and business institutions.

Discovering the deities of Wicca is a never-ending experience. They constantly reveal themselves. As the shamans say, "Be attentive." All nature is singing to us of Her secrets. The Goddess constantly draws aside Her veil; the God lights us up with inspiration and illumination. We simply don't notice.

Don't worry what others might think if they knew you were attuning with a 20,000 year-old Goddess. Their feelings and thoughts concerning your religion are of no consequence. If you feel the need to shelter your experiences from others do so, not out of fear or embarrassment, but because we're truly all on separate paths. Everyone isn't suited to Wicca.

There are some who say that we (and anyone else who won't follow their rituals or embrace their theology) are worshipping Satan. Not that we know it, of course; Satan is too tricky for that, according to these experts.

Such people can't believe that any religion but their own can be meaningful, fulfilling and true to its adherent. So if we worship the God and Goddess, they say, we're denying all good and are worshipping Satan, the embodiment of all negativity and evil.

Wiccans aren't so close-minded. Perhaps it's the greatest of all human vanities to assume that one's religion is the only way to Deity. Such beliefs have caused incalculable bloodshed and the rise of the hideous concept of holy wars.

The basis of this misconception seems to be the concept of a pristine, pure, positive being—God. If this deity is the sum of all good, worshippers believe that there must be an equally negative one as well. Thus, Satan.

The Wicca don't accept such ideas. *We acknowledge the dark aspects of the Goddess and the God as well as the bright.* All nature is composed of opposites, and this polarity is also resident within ourselves. The darkest human traits as well as the brightest are locked within our unconsciousnesses. It is only our ability to rise above destructive urges, to channel such energies into positive thoughts and actions, that separates us from mass-murderers and sociopaths.

Yes, the God and Goddess have dark aspects, but this needn't scare us off. Look at some of the manifestations of Their powers. From a ravaging flood comes rich soil in which new plants thrive. Death brings a deeper appreciation of life to the living and rest for the transcended one. "Good" and "evil" are often identical in nature, depending on one's viewpoint. Additionally, out of every evil some good is eventually born.

Any and all religions are real, the genuine article, to their practitioners. There can never be one religion, prophet or savior that will satisfy all five billion humans. Each of us must find our ideal way to attune with Deity. For some, it's Wicca.

Wiccans emphasize the bright aspects of the deities because this gives us purpose to grow and evolve to the highest realm of existence. When death, destruction, hurt, pain and anger appear in our lives (as they must), we can turn to the Goddess and God and know that this is a part of them too. We needn't blame a devil on these natural aspects of life and call upon a pure-white god to fend them off.

In truly understanding the Goddess and God, one comes to understand life, for the two are inextricably entwined. Live your earthly life fully, but try to see the spiritual aspects of your activities as well. Remember—the physical and spiritual are but reflections of each other.

When I give classes, one question seems to come up frequently: "What is the meaning of life?"

It may be asked with a laugh, but this is the one question that, if answered, satisfies any others we may have. It is the problem every religion and philosophical system has struggled to solve.

Anyone can find the answer through the simple technique of living and observing life. Though two people won't find the same answers, they can find them together.

The Goddess and God are of nature, both the delightful and the dark. We don't worship nature as such; some Wiccans probably wouldn't even say that they worship the Goddess and God. We don't bow down to the deities; we work with Them to create a better world.

This is what makes Wicca a truly participatory religion.

3

Magic

It's common knowledge even among the masses that Witches practice magic. They may have misguided ideas concerning the *type* of magic performed, but the Witch is firmly linked in popular thought with the magical arts.

Wicca is, as we have seen, a religion that embraces magic as one of its basic concepts. This isn't unusual. In fact, it's often difficult to discern where religion ends and magic begins in any faith.

Still, magic plays a special role in Wicca. It allows us to improve our lives and return energy to our ravaged planet. Wiccans also develop special relationships with the Goddess and God through magic. This doesn't mean that every spell is a prayer, nor are invocations differently worded spells. Through working with the powers which the God and the Goddess embody, we grow close to them. Calling upon their names and visualizing their presence during spells and rites creates a bond between Deity and human. Thus, in Wicca, magic is a religious practice.

I've defined magic a number of times in my books. Surprisingly, this is a difficult task. My latest, most refined definition is:

Magic is the projection of natural energies to produce needed effects.

There are three main sources of this energy—personal power, Earth power and divine power.

Personal power is the life force that sustains our earthly existences. It powers our bodies. We absorb energy from the Moon and Sun, from water and food. We release it during movement, exercise, sex and childbirth. Even exhaling releases some power, though we recoup the loss through inhaling. In magic, personal power is aroused, infused with a specific purpose, released and directed toward its goal.

Earth power is that which resides within our planet and in its natural products. Stones, trees, wind, flames, water, crystals and scents all possess unique, specific powers which can be used during magical ritual. A Wiccan may dip a quartz crystal in salt water to cleanse it and then press it against an ailing person's body to send its healing energies within. Or, herbs may be sprinkled around a candle which is burned to produce a specific magical effect. Oils are rubbed onto the body to effect internal changes.

Both personal power and Earth power are manifestations of *divine power*. This is the energy that exists within the Goddess and God—the life force, the source of universal power which created everything in existence.

Wiccans invoke the Goddess and God to bless their magic with power. During ritual they may direct personal power to the deities, asking that a specific need be met. This is truly religious magic.

And so, magic is a process in which Wiccans work in harmony with the universal power source which we envision as the Goddess and God, as well as with personal and Earth energies, to improve our lives and to lend energy to the Earth. Magic is a method whereby individuals under none but self-determined predestination take control of their lives.

Contrary to popular belief, magic isn't supernatural. True, it is an occult (hidden) practice steeped in millenia of secrecy, slander and misinformation, but it is a natural practice utilizing genuine powers that haven't yet been discovered or labeled by science.

This doesn't invalidate magic. Even scientists don't claim to know everything about our universe. If they did, the field of scientific investigation wouldn't exist. The powers the Wiccans use will eventually be documented and so lose their mystery. Such has already partially occurred to hypnotism and psychology, and may soon happen to extra-sensory perception. Magnetism, indeed, was a firmly established aspect of magic until it was "discovered" by science. But even today, magnets are used in spells and charms, and such forces as these call up strange old feelings.

Play with two magnets. See the invisible forces resisting and attracting in seemingly supernatural ways.

Magic is similar. Though it appears to be completely nonsensical, with no basis in fact, it operates along its own rules and logic. Simply because it isn't fully understood doesn't mean that it doesn't exist. Magic is effective in causing manifestations of needed change.

This isn't self-deception. Correctly performed magic works, and no amount of explaining away alters this fact.

Here's a description of a typical candle ritual. I'll use myself as an example. Say I need to pay a hundred-dollar phone bill but don't have the money. My magical goal: the means to pay the bill.

I decide to use a ritual to help focus my concentration and visualization. (See Chapter Eleven: Exercises and Magical Techniques for visualization information.) Checking my magical supplies, I discover that I have green candles, patchouly oil, a good selection of money-drawing herbs, parchment paper and green ink.

At my altar, I light the candles representing the Goddess and the God while silently invoking their presence. Next, I ignite a charcoal block and sprinkle cinnamon and sage onto the block as a magical prosperity incense.

I draw a picture of the phone bill on the paper, clearly marking the amount in numerals. While drawing, I visualize that the paper is no longer just a piece of paper; it is the bill itself.

Then I sketch a square around the bill, symbolizing my control over it, and mark a large "x" through it, effectively cancelling out its existence (as will occur when it is paid).

I now start to visualize the bill being paid in full. I might write this over the picture, making it appear to have been stamped with these words. I visualize myself looking in my checkbook, seeing that the balance will cover the check, and then writing the check itself.

Next, I rub a green candle with patchouly oil, from each end to the middle, while saying something like the following:

I call upon the powers of the Mother Goddess and the Father God; I call upon the forces of the Earth, Air, Fire and Water; I call upon the Sun, Moon and Stars to bring me the funds to pay this bill.

Still visualizing, I place the candle in the holder directly over the picture of the bill. I sprinkle herbs around the candle's base, stating (and visualizing) that each is lending its energy toward my goal:

Sage, herb of Jupiter, send your powers to my spell.
Cinnamon, herb of the Sun, send your powers to my spell.

Once this is done, still visualizing my bill as paid in full, I light the candle and, as its flame shines, release the energy I've built up into the picture.

I let the candle burn for ten, fifteen minutes or longer, depending on my ability to retain the visualization. I see the candle absorbing the energy I've put into the picture. I see the herbs streaming their energies into the candle flame, and the combined energies of the herbs, candle, patchouly oil and picture—coupled with my personal power—pouring from the flame and out to bring my magical goal toward manifestation.

When I can do no more, I remove the picture, light it in the candle, hold it as it burns for a few seconds, and then throw it into the small cauldron that sits beside my altar.

Finished, I allow the candle to burn itself out, knowing that the ritual will take effect.

Within a day or two, perhaps a week, I'll either receive unexpected (or delayed) money, or will satisfy other financial obligations in a manner which frees me to pay the bill.

How does it work? From the time I decide to do an act of magic, *I'm doing it.* Thinking about it sets personal power into motion. Throughout the whole process—gathering supplies, drawing the bill, lighting the candle, visualizing—I'm rousing and infusing personal power with my magical need. During the rite itself, I release this power into the candle. When I finally burn the picture, the last of these energies are released and free, set to work to arrange for me to pay the bill.

I may not be able to tell you exactly *how* magic works, only that it does work. Fortunately, we don't have to know this; all we must know is how to make it work.

I'm no expert in electricity, but I can plug my toaster into a wall socket and burn my whole wheat bread. Similarly, in magic we "plug into" energies that stretch, criss-cross and zip around and through us.

There are many ways to practice magic. Wiccans generally choose simple, natural forms, though some enjoy heavy ceremony, borrowing from the classical *grimoires* such as the *Key of Solomon* (see Bibliography). Usually, however, it involves herbs, crystals and rocks; the use of symbols and color; magical gestures, music, voice, dance and trance; astral projection, meditation, concentration and visualization.

There are literally thousands of magical systems, even among Wiccans themselves. For instance, numerous magical ways exist to use crystals, or herbs, or symbols, and by combining them more systems are created.

Many, many books have been published outlining magical systems, and some of these are listed in the Bibliography. In my books I've discussed the powers of the elements, crystals and herbs. In this work, the subject of rune magic is explored as an example of a self-contained magical system with hints at combining it with others.

Such systems aren't necessary to the successful practice of magic. Performing magical rituals simply by manipulating tools such as herbs and crystals will be ineffective, for the true power of magic lies within ourselves—the gift of Deity.

So no matter the magical system, personal power must be infused with the need and then released. In Wiccan magic, personal power is recognized as our direct link with the Goddess and God. Magic, therefore, is a religious act in which the Wiccans unite with their deities to better themselves and their world.

This is important—magic is a positive practice. *Wiccans don't perform destructive, manipulative or exploitive magic.* Because they recognize that the power at work in magic is, ultimately, derived from the Goddess and God, negative workings are absolutely taboo. "Evil" magic is an insult to themselves, to the human race, to the Earth, the Goddess and God, and the universe itself. The repercussions can be imagined.

The energies of magic are those of life itself.

Anyone can practice magic—within a religious context or not. If certain words or gestures pop into your mind while performing a spell, and they seem right, by all means use them. If you can't find a ritual to your liking or that fits your needs, create one. You needn't write fancy poetry or choreography for thirty singing incense bearers and thirteen singing priestesses.

If nothing else, light a candle, settle down before it, and concentrate on your magical need. Trust yourself.

If you truly desire to know the nature of magic, practice it! Many are afraid of magic. They've been taught (by non-practitioners) that it's dangerous. Don't be scared. Crossing the street is dangerous too. But if you do it properly, you're fine.

Of course, the only way you'll find this out is to cross that street. If your magic is infused with love you'll be in no danger whatsoever.

Call upon the Goddess and God to protect you and teach you the secrets of magic. Ask stones and plants to reveal their powers—and listen. Read as much as you can, discarding negative or disturbing information.

Learn by doing, and the Goddess and God will bless you with all that you truly need.

4

Tools

In common with most religions, certain objects are used in Wicca for ritual purposes. These tools invoke the Deities, banish negativity, direct energy through our touch and intention.

Some of the tools of the Witch (the broom, cauldron, and magic wand) have gained firm places in contemporary folklore and myth. Through the popularization of folk tales and the work of the Disney studios, millions know that cauldrons are used to brew up potions and that wands transform the drab into the beautiful. Most folks, however, don't know the powerful magic behind such tools and their inner symbolism within Wicca.

To practice Wicca, you may want to collect at least some of these tools. Search through antique and junk shops, swap meets and flea markets for these treasures. Or, write to occult suppliers (addresses in Appendix I). Though difficult to find, your ritual tools are well worth any efforts expended to obtain them.

These tools aren't necessary to the practice of Wicca. However, they enrich rituals and symbolize complex energies. The tools have no power save for that which we lend to them.

Some say that we should use magical tools until we no longer need them. Perhaps it's better to use them as long as you feel comfortable in doing so.

The Broom

Witches use brooms in magic and ritual. It is a tool sacred to both the Goddess and God. This is nothing new; pre-Colombian Mexico saw the worship of a type of Witch deity, Tlazelteotl, who was pictured riding naked on a broom. The Chinese worship a broom goddess who is invoked to bring clear weather in times of rain.

Then too, probably because of its phallic shape, the broom became a powerful tool against curses and practitioners of evil magic. Laid across the threshold, the broom halted all spells sent to the house or those resident within. A broom under the pillow brought pleasant dreams and guarded the sleeper.

European Witches became identified with the broom because both were infused with magic in religious and popular thought. Witches were accused of flying on broomsticks, and this was considered proof of their alliance with "dark powers." Such an act, if it could be performed, would indeed be supernatural and, therefore, of the Devil in their eyes, in contrast to the simple healing and love spells that Witches actually performed. Of course the tale was invented by Witch persecutors.*

Today the broom is still used in Wicca. A Wicca may begin a ritual by sweeping the area (indoors or out) lightly with the magic broom. After this, the altar is set up, the tools carried out, and the ritual is ready to begin. (See Chapter Thirteen, Ritual Design).

This sweeping is more than a physical cleansing. In fact, the broom's bristles needn't touch the ground. While brushing, the Wiccan visualizes the broom sweeping out the astral buildup that occurs where humans live. This purifies the area to allow smoother ritual workings.

Since it is a purifier, the broom is linked with the element of Water. Thus it as also used in all types of water spells including those of love and psychic workings.

Many Witches collect brooms, and indeed their endless variety and the exotic materials used in their manufacture make this an interesting hobby.

If you wish to make your magic broom, you might try the old magical formula of an ash staff, birch twigs and a willow binding. The

---

* Some Wiccans claim that brooms were "ridden" while hopping along the ground, much as are children's hobby-horses, to promote fertility of the fields. Then too it is believed that tales of Witches riding brooms through the air were unsophisticated explanations of astral projection.

ash is protective, the birch purifying, and the willow is sacred to the Goddesss.

Of course, a branch from any tree or bush can be used in place of the broom (while cutting it, thank the tree for its sacrifice, using such words as will be found in the "An Herbal Grimoire" section of *The Standing Stones Book of Shadows*, Section I). A tiny broom of pine needles can also be used.

In early American slave weddings, as well as Gypsy nuptials, the couple often ritually jumped a broomstick to solemnize their union. Such marriages are quite common until recent times, and even today Wiccan and pagan handfastings often include a broom leap.

There are many old spells involving brooms. In general, the broom is a purificatory and protective instrument, used to ritually cleanse the area for magic or to guard a home by laying it across the threshold, under the bed, in windowsills or on doors.

The broom used for magic, as with all magical tools, should be reserved for this purpose only. If you decide to buy a broom, try to find a round one; the flat Shaker-type brooms just don't seem to have the same effect.*

Wand

The wand is one of the prime magical tools. It has been utilized for thousands of years in magical and religious rites. It is an instrument of invocation. The Goddess and God may be called to watch the ritual with words and an uplifted wand. It is also sometimes used to direct energy, to draw magical symbols or a circle on the ground, to point toward danger while perfectly balanced on the Witch's palm or arm, or even to stir brew in a cauldron. The wand represents the element of Air to some Wiccans, and is sacred to the Gods.

There are traditional woods used for the wand, including willow, elder, oak, apple, peach, hazel, cherry and so on. Some Wiccans cut it the length from the crook of the elbow to the tip of the forefinger, but this isn't necessary. Any fairly straight piece of wood can be used; even dowels purchased from hardware stores work well, and I've seen beautifully carved and painted wands made from these.

New Age consciousness (and merchandising) has brought the wand into renewed prominence. Delightful, beautiful creations fash-

---

* More broom lore can be found in Chapter 13 of *The Magical Household* (Llewellyn, 1987).

ioned of silver and quartz crystals are now available in a wide range of sizes and prices. These certainly could be used within Wiccan ritual, though wooden wands have a longer history.

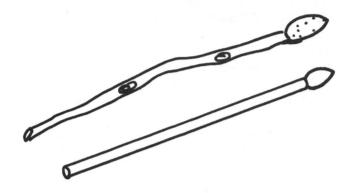

Don't worry about finding the ideal wand at first; one will come to you. I used a length of licorice root as a wand for a while and had good results with it.

Any stick you use will be infused with energy and power. Find one that feels comfortable, and it'll do just fine.

Censer

The censer is an incense burner. It can be a complex, swinging metal censer like those used in the Catholic church, or a simple seashell. The censer holds the smoldering incense during Wiccan rites.

If you cannot find a suitable censer, make one. Any bowl or cup half-filled with sand or salt will serve well. The salt or sand absorbs the heat from the charcoal or incense and prevents the bowl from cracking. Incense sticks can also be pushed into the salt, or cones placed upon its surface.

Incense use in ritual and magic is an art in and of itself. When no specific incense is called for in rituals and spells, use your own intuition and creativity in determining which blend to use.

Stick, cone or block incense can be used, but most Wiccans favor the raw or granulated incense, the type which must be burned on self-igniting charcoal briquettes, available from occult suppliers. Either is fine.

In ceremonial magic, "spirits" are sometimes commanded to appear in visible form in the smoke rising from the censer. While this isn't part of Wicca, the Goddess and God can sometimes be seen in the curling, twisting smoke. Sitting while breathing slowly and watching the smoke can be an entrancing act, and you might slip into an alternate state of consciousness.

Wiccan ritual, when performed indoors, isn't complete without incense. Outdoors a fire often substitutes, or stick-type incense is stuck into the ground. Thus, the censer is an important tool for indoor rites. To some of the Wicca, the censer represents the element of Air. It is often placed before the images of the Deities on the altar, if any.

Cauldron

The cauldron is the Witch's tool *par excellence*. It is an ancient vessel of cooking and brew making, steeped in magical tradition and mystery. The cauldron is the container in which magical transformations occur; the sacred grail, the holy spring, the sea of Primeval creation.

The Wicca see the cauldron as a symbol of the Goddess, the manifested essence of femininity and fertility. It is also symbolic of the element of Water, reincarnation, immortality and inspiration. Celtic legends concerning Kerridwen's cauldron have had a strong impact on contemporary Wicca.

The cauldron is often a focal point of ritual. During spring rites it is sometimes filled with fresh water and flowers; during winter a fire may be kindled *within* the cauldron to represent the returning heat and light of the Sun (the God) from the cauldron (the Goddess). This links in with agricultural myths wherein the God is born in winter, reaches maturity in summer, and dies after the last harvest (see Chapter Eight, The Days of Power).

Ideally speaking, the cauldron should be of iron, resting on three legs, with its opening smaller than its widest part. Cauldrons can be difficult to find, even small ones, but a thorough search usually produces some type of cauldron. A few mail-order houses stock cauldrons, but not regularly. You may wish to query these sources.

Cauldrons come in all sizes ranging from a few inches in diameter to monsters three feet across. I have collected a few, including an old one reserved for ritual purposes.

The cauldron can be an instrument of scrying (gazing) by filling it with water and staring into its inky depths. It can also serve as a container in which to brew up those infamous Wicca brews, but bear in mind that a large fire and plenty of patience are required to make liquids boil in larger cauldrons. Most Wiccans use stoves and cooking pots today.

If you have difficulty finding a cauldron, persevere and one will eventually materialize. It certainly can't hurt to ask the Goddess and God to send one your way.

Magic Knife

The magic knife (or athame) has an ancient history. It isn't used for cutting purposes in Wicca, but to direct the energy raised during rites and spells. It is seldom used to invoke or call upon the Deities for it is an instrument of commanding and power manipulation. We'd rather *invoke* the Goddess and God.

The knife is often dull, usually double-edged with a black or dark handle. Black absorbs power. When the knife is used in ritual (see *The Standing Stones Book of Shadows*) to direct energy, some of this power is absorbed into the handle—only a tiny amount—which can be called upon later. Then again sometimes energy raised within Wiccan ritual is channeled into the knife for later use. The stories of swords with magical powers and names are quite common in mythic literature, and swords are nothing more than large knives.

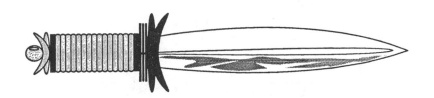

Some Wiccans engrave their knives with magical symbols, usually taken from *The Key of Solomon*, but this isn't necessary. As with most magical tools, the knife becomes powerful by your touch and usage. However, if you so desire, scratch words, symbols or runes onto its blade or handle.

A sword is sometimes used in Wicca, as it has all the properties of the knife, but can be difficult for indoor rituals due to its size.

Because of the symbolism of the knife, which is a tool that causes change, it is commonly linked with the element of Fire. Its phallic nature links it with the God.

White-Handled Knife

The white-handled knife (sometimes called a *bolline*) is simply a practical, working knife as opposed to the purely ritualistic magic knife. It is used to cut wands or sacred herbs, inscribe symbols onto candles or on wood, clay, or wax, and in cutting cords for use in magic.

It is usually white-handled to distinguish it from the magic knife.

Some Wiccan traditions dictate that the white-handled knife be used only within the magic circle. This would, of course, limit its usefulness. It seems to me that using it solely for ritual purposes (such as harvesting flowers from the garden to place on the altar during ritual) confirms the tool's sacralness and so allows its use out of "sacred space."

Crystal Sphere

Quartz crystals are extremely popular today, but the quartz crystal sphere is an ancient magical tool. It is exquisitely expensive, selling for twenty dollars to thousands of dollars, depending on size. Most crystal balls on the market today are glass, leaded glass, or even plastic. Genuine quartz crystal spheres can be determined by their high prices and inclusions or irregularities.

The crystal has long been used in contemplative divination. The diviner gazes into the ball until the psychic faculties blossom, and images, seen in the mind or projected by it into the depths of the crystal, reveal the necessary information.

In Wiccan ritual, the crystal is sometimes placed on the altar to represent the Goddess. Its shape (spheroid) is Goddess-symbolic, as are all circles and rounds, and its icy cold temperature (another way to determine genuine rock crystal) is symbolic of the depths of the sea, the Goddess' domain.

Then too the crystal may be used to receive messages from the Gods, or to store energy raised in ritual. Some Wiccans scry in the crystal to call up images of the Goddess or of past lives. It is a magical object touched with the divine, and if you find one, guard it carefully.

Periodic exposure to moonlight, or rubbing the crystal with fresh mugwort, will increase its ability to spark our psychic powers. It may be the center of Full Moon rituals.

Cup

The cup is simply a cauldron on a stem. It symbolizes the Goddess and fertility, and is related to the element of Water. Though it can be used to hold water (which is often present on the altar), it may also contain the ritual beverage imbibed during the rite.

The cup can be made of nearly any substance: silver, brass, gold, earthenware, soapstone, alabaster, crystal and other materials.

Pentacle

The pentacle is usually a flat piece of brass, gold, silver, wood, wax or clay, inscribed with certain symbols. The most common, and indeed the only necessary one, is the pentagram, the five-pointed star which has been used in magic for millenia.

The pentacle was "borrowed" from ceremonial magic. In this ancient art it was often an instrument of protection, or a tool used to evoke spirits. In Wicca, the pentacle represents the element of Earth and is a convenient tool upon which to place amulets, charms or other objects to be ritually consecrated. It is sometimes used to summon the Gods and Goddesses.

Pentacles are also hung over doors and windows to act as protective devices, or are ritually manipulated to draw money owing to the pentacle's Earth associations.

The Book of Shadows

The Book of Shadows is a Wiccan workbook containing invocations, ritual patterns, spells, runes, rules governing magic, and so on. Some Books of Shadows are passed from one Wiccan to another, usually upon initiation, but the vast majority of Books today are composed by each individual Wiccan.

Don't believe the stories in most other Wiccan books that one single Book of Shadows has been handed down from antiquity, for each sect of Wicca seems to claim that their own is the original, and they're all different.

Although until recently a Book of Shadows was usually handwritten, today typed or even photocopied versions are quite common. Some Wiccans are even computerizing their books—to create, as friends of mine call it, the "Floppy Disc of Shadows."

To make your own Book of Shadows, begin with any blank book—these are available in most art stores and bookshops. If you cannot find a bound blank book, any lined exercise book will do. Simply write in this book any rituals, spells, invocations and magical information that you have either composed or found elsewhere and would like to preserve.

Remember—all Books of Shadows (including the one in Section III) are suggestions as to ritual, not "holy writ." Never feel tied down to these words. In fact, many Witches use three-ring binders, shuffling around pages, adding or subtracting information from their Book of Shadow at will.

It is a good idea to copy your spells and rites by hand. Not only does this ensure that you've read the work completely, it also allows easier reading by candlelight. Ideally, all rites are memorized (there's nothing more distracting than having to read or glance at the book), or created spontaneously, but if you would read your rites, be sure your copies are legible by flickering firelight.

Bell

The bell is a ritual instrument of incredible antiquity. Ringing a bell unleashes vibrations which have powerful effects according to its volume, tone and material of construction.

The bell is a feminine symbol and so is often used to invoke the Goddess in ritual. It is also rung to ward off evil spells and spirits, to halt storms, or to evoke good energies. Placed in cupboards or hung on the door, it guards the home. Bells are sometimes rung in ritual to mark various sections and to signal a spell's beginning or end.

Any type of bell can be used.

These are some of the tools used in Wiccan ritual. Working with them, familiarizing yourself with their powers and pouring your own energy into them, you may find their use becoming second nature. Gathering them is a problem, but this can be seen as a magical test of the seriousness of your Wiccan interest.

As you collect each tool, you can prepare it for ritual. If old, it should be stripped of all associations and energies; you don't know who owned the tool, nor to what purposes it may have been used.

To begin this process, clean the tool physically using the appropriate method. When the object is clean and dry, bury it (in the Earth or a bowlful of sand or salt) for a few days, allowing the energies to disperse. An alternate method consists of plunging the tool into the sea, river or lake, or even your own bathtub after purifying the water by adding a few pinches of salt.

Don't ruin a good piece of wood by wetting it; similarly don't mar the finish of some other object by allowing it to contact salt. Use the most appropriate method for each tool.

After a few days, dig up the tool, wipe it clean, and it is ready for magic. If you use the water method, leave the object submerged for a few hours, then dry it. If desired, repeat until the tool is clean, refreshed, new.

There are consecration ceremonies for the Wiccan tools in Section III, as well as preparation rites in the Herbal Grimoire section there. Both are optional; use as your intuition dictates.

5

Music, Dance and Gesture

Wicca understands that what we perceive to be the difference between the physical and the non-physical is due to our limitations as materially-based beings. Some of the tools used in the practice of religion are indeed non-physical. Three of the most effective of these are music, dance and gesture.*

These techniques are used to raise power, alter consciousness and to unite with the Goddess and God—to achieve ecstasy. These tools are often part and parcel of ritual, and indeed the most effective, powerful rites can be those exclusively utilizing such tools. (A ritual comprised entirely of gestures can be found in Section III: *The Standing Stones Book of Shadows*.)

Music and dance were among the earliest magical and religious acts. Our ancestors probably utilized the magic of hand signals and bodily postures before speech was fully developed. The simple gesture of pointing still has powerful emotional effects, from a witness singling out the defendant as the person involved in the crime, to a hopeful at an audition being selected among a sea of her or his peers.

The first music was probably rhythmic. Humans soon discovered that pleasing rhythms and sounds could be produced by slapping various parts of the body, especially the thighs and chest.

---

* Music is, technically speaking, comprised of sound waves which are physically measurable. However, we can't hold music in our hands—merely the instruments which produce it.

Clapping creates a distinctive, clean sound which is still used by some Wiccans to release personal power during magical ritual.*

Rhythmic instruments such as log drums were later used to produce fuller sounds. Some rocks ring when struck, and so another type of instrument was born. Reeds, bones and some shells produce whistling sounds when correctly blown. Shamanic systems still in existence use these tools.

Less intellectual rituals can be more effective precisely because they bypass the conscious mind and speak to the deep consciousness, the psychic awareness. Music and dance emotionally involve us in Wiccan rites.

The thought of dancing, singing or making music embarrasses some of us. This is a natural outgrowth of our increasingly repressive society. In Wicca, however, dance and music occur *before the Deities alone*. You aren't performing for a crowd, so don't worry about missing a note or tripping over your feet. *They* don't care, and no one ever need know what you do before the Gods in your rites.

Even the most unmusically inclined can bang two rocks together, shake a rattle, clap hands or walk in circles. To this day, some of the most established and effective Wiccan covens utilize a simple circular run around the altar to raise power. So much for fancy ritual choreography.

Here's some traditional lore concerning dance, music and gesture. If you find it appealing, feel free to incorporate it into your Wiccan rituals. But one suggestion: if you find your rites stuffy and unsatisfying, if they don't create a link with the deities, the problem may be a lack of emotional content. Music and dance can produce true involvement in the ritual and so open your awareness of the Goddess and God. During magic they may produce freer access to energy.

Music

Music is simply a re-creation of the sounds of nature. Wind through trees, the roar of the ocean hurling itself against jagged cliffs, pattering rain, the crackling of a lightning-produced fire, the cry of birds and roars of animals are some of the "instruments" that constitute the music of nature.

Human beings have long integrated music into religious and

---

* See Doreen Valiente's *Witchcraft For Tomorrow* (New York: St. Martin's Press, 1978), page 182.

magical rituals for its powerful effects. Shamans use a steady drum beat to induce trance, and a drum can be used to control the pace of magical dance. Then too, music has long been celebrated for calming ferocious animals—and humans as well.*

Music can be a part of Wiccan workings today. You might simply find appropriate pieces, selected from classical, ethnic, folk or contemporary sources, and play these during rituals. Musically-inclined Wiccans can create music before, during or after the ritual.

My most satisfying and vivid rituals often involve music. I remember one day I hid a small tape-recorder behind a tree in the Laguna Mountains. Strangely, the music didn't intrude on the setting of wildflowers, towering pines and ancient oaks, but heightened my solitary ritual.

If you have proficiency with an instrument, work it into your rituals. A flute, violin, recorder, guitar, folk harp and other small instruments can easily be introduced into ritual, as can drums, rattles, bells, or even glasses of water and a knife with which to strike them. Other less portable instruments can be recorded and played back during ritual.

Such musical interludes can be used directly *prior* to the rite to set the mood; *during*, as an offering to the Goddess and God or to rouse energy; and *afterward* in pure celebration and joy. Some Wiccans compose a song which is in actuality a rite, encompassing everything from the creation of sacred space and invoking the Deities to thanking them for their presence. Music magic is truly what you decide to make it.

Four distinct types of instruments have specific powers. The drum, rattle, xylophone and all percussion instruments (save for the sistrum) are ruled by the element of *Earth*. Thus, such instruments can be used to invoke fertility, increase money, find a job, and so on. They can also be used to invoke the Goddess in ritual, or to "drum up" energy to send to the Earth.

The flute, recorder and all wind instruments are under the dominion of *Air*, the intellectual element, and so can be used to increase mental powers or visualization abilities, to discover ancient wisdom or knowledge, to improve psychic faculties and to call upon the God.

Fire rules stringed instruments such as the lyre, harp (full-size or folk), guitar, mandolin, ukelele and so on. Such instruments can be

---

* A fine (if fictional) account of music magic can be found in Chapter XI of Gerald Gardner's novel *High Magic's Aid* (New York: Weiser, 1975).

used in spells or rites involving sexuality, health and bodily strength, passion and will power, change, evolution, courage and the destruction of harmful habits.

They are also excellent tools to use before ritual to purify the area in question, and also the celebrant. Play a particular song, sing with the instrument, or just strum around the area in a clockwise circle until the place is humming with your vibrations. Strings can also be used to invoke the God.

Resonant metal such as the cymbal, sistrum, bell and gong are symbolic of the element of *Water*. Since water encompasses healing, fertility, friendship, psychic powers, spiritual love, beauty, compassion, happiness and other similar energies, bells, gongs or cymbals can be featured in such spells and rites. The sistrum of Isis reminds us that resonant metal invokes the Goddess.

Musical spells (as opposed to purely verbal spells) can be simple and effective. Need money? Sit quietly dressed in green and slowly thump a drum, visualizing yourself bursting with cash while invoking the Goddess in Her aspect of provider-of-abundance.

If you're depressed, find a bell with a pleasant tone and ritually strike or ring it, feeling the sound's vibrations cleansing you of the depression and lifting your spirits. Or, wear a small bell.

When you're afraid, play a six-string or listen to pre-recorded guitar music while visualizing yourself as confident and courageous. Invoke the God in his Horned, aggressive, protective aspect.

Singing, a combination of speech and music, can be readily integrated into Wiccan rituals. Some Wiccans set chants and invocations to music or sing as they feel compelled to during ritual.

Many Wiccans never pursue the subject of music magic and simply play recorded tunes as backgrounds to their rituals. This is fine, but self-created music (however simple) integrated into your rituals can be more effective, as long as you like the piece.

Today a number of pre-recorded Wiccan and Pagan cassette tapes are available. While widely varying in quality, it's worthwhile to pick up a few tapes by mail (see Appendix I: Occult Suppliers for mail-order information). Some songs can be used in ritual, but most are best played while preparing for ritual, or afterwards when relaxing.

Appropriate music incorporated into ritual can greatly enhance the Wiccan experience.

Dance

Dance is certainly an ancient ritual practice. It's also a magical act, for physical movement releases energy from the body, the same energy used in magic. This "secret" was discovered early, and so dance was incorporated into magic and ritual to raise energy, to alter consciousness or simply to honor the Goddess and God with ritual performances.

Group dances, such as the spiral dance, are often performed in coven workings. In individual workings, however, you're bound by no tradition or choreographed steps. Feel free to move in any manner you wish, no matter how child-like or "savage" it may seem.

In magic, many Wiccans perform a short spell or ritual manipulation of some kind (inscribing runes, tying knots, tracing pictures in sand or powdered herbs, chanting deity names) and then perform the real magic: raising and channeling magical energy. They often move in an increasingly faster clockwise circle around the altar, either alone or with a coven, watching the candles flaming on the altar, smelling the incense, overwhelming themselves with chanting and intense visualization. When the practitioner has reached the point of no return, the exact moment when the body can raise and channel no more energy, the power is released toward the magical goal. To do this, some Wicca collapse to the ground, signaling the end of what is rather peculiarly called "The Dance."

Dancing is used to raise energy as well as to facilitate attunement with the Deities of nature. Dance as the wild wind; as the stream rushing down a mountain, a flame flickering from a lightning-struck tree, as grains of sand bouncing off each other in a gale, as flowers unfolding their brilliance on a sunny summer afternoon. As you dance, using whatever movements you wish, open yourself to the God and Goddess.

Think for a moment of the whirling dervishes, the untamed Gypsy dances of Europe, the sensuous belly dancing of the Middle East, and the sacred hula of old Hawaii. Dance is one of the paths to Deity.

Gesture

Gestures are silent counterparts to words. Gestures can enhance Wiccan rituals when performed in conjunction with invocations or dance, or can be used alone for their real power. Pointing (as mentioned above), the use of the first and middle fingers splayed to create a "v," and the vulgar presentation of an upraised middle finger demonstrate the variety of messages that can be conveyed through gesture, as well as the range of our emotional responses to them.

My introduction to Wicca happened to include some of these old gestures. In 1971 I saw some photographs* of magical protective gestures such as the *mano figa* (a hand clenched into a fist, the thumb jutting out between the first and middle fingers) and the *mano cornuta*, a "v" formed by the first and little fingers and held upside down. Both have long been used to avert the evil eye and negativity, and the latter is used in Wicca, with points up, to represent the God in his Horned aspect.

A few days later, in my first year in high school, I flashed these two gestures to a girl I'd just met. There was no logical reason to do this; it just felt right. She looked at me, smiled and asked me if I was a Witch. I said no, but I'd like to be. She began training me.

The magical significance of gestures is complex, and stems from the powers of the hand. The hand can heal or kill, caress or stab. It is a channel through which energies are sent from the body or received from others. Our hands set up our magical altars, grasp wands and athames, and pinch out candle flames at the conclusion of magical rites.

Hands, as the means by which most of us earn our livings, are symbolic of the physical world. But in their five digits lie the pentagram, the supreme protective magical symbol; the sum of the four elements coupled with *akasha*, the spiritual power of the universe.

The lines on our hands can, to the trained, be used to link into the deep consciousnesses and reveal things to the conscious minds that we would otherwise have difficulty knowing. The palmist doesn't read these lines as streets on a roadmap; they are a key to our souls, a fleshly mandala revealing our innermost depths.

Hands were used as the first counting devices. They were seen to have both male and female qualities and symbolism, and images of hands were used around the world as amulets.

Gestures in Wiccan ritual can easily become second nature. When invoking the Goddess and God, the hands can be held uplifted with the fingers spread to receive their power. The Goddess can be individually invoked with the left hand, the thumb and first finger

---

* Included in Douglas Hill and Pat William's *The Supernatural* (New York: Hawthorn Books, 1965), page 200.

Invoking the Goddess

held up and curled into a half-circle, while the rest of the fingers are tucked against the palm. This represents the crescent Moon. The God is invoked with the first and middle fingers of the right hand raised, or with the first and fourth fingers up, the thumb holding down the others against the palm, to represent horns.

The elements can be invoked with individual gestures when approaching the four directions: a flat hand held parallel with the ground to invoke Earth at the North; an upraised hand, fingers spread wide apart, to invoke Air at the East; an upraised fist for the South to invite Fire, and a cupped hand to the West to invoke Water.

Two gestures, together with postures, have long been used to invoke the Goddess and God, and are named after them. The Goddess position is assumed by placing the feet about two feet apart on the ground, holding the hands out palms away from you, elbows bent slightly. This position can be used to call the Goddess or to attune with her energies.

The God position consists of the feet together on the floor, body held rigidly upright, arms crossed on the chest (right over left, usually), hands held in fists. Tools such as the wand and magic knife (athame) are sometimes held in the fists, echoing the practice of pharaohs of ancient Egypt who held a crook and flail in a similar position while trying disputes.

In coven work, the High Priestess and High Priest often assume these positions when invoking the Goddess and God. In solo workings they can be used to identify with the aspects of the Goddess and God within us, and also during separate invocatory rites.

Gestures are also used in magic. Each of the fingers relates to a specific planet as well as an ancient deity. Since pointing is a magical act and is a part of many spells, the finger can be chosen by its symbolism.

The thumb relates to Venus and to the planet Earth. Jupiter (both the planet and the god) rules the forefinger. The middle finger is ruled by the god and planet Saturn, the fourth finger the Sun and Apollo, and the little finger by the planet Mercury as well as the god after which it is named.

Many spells involve pointing with the Jupiter and Saturn fingers, usually at an object to be charged or imbued with magical energy. The power is visualized as traveling straight out through the fingers and into the object.

Other ritual gestures used in Wiccan rites include the "cutting" of pentagrams at the four quarters by drawing them in the air with the magic knife, wand or index finger. This is done to alternately banish or invoke elemental powers. It is, of course, performed with visualization.

The hand can be seen as a cauldron, since it can cup and contain water; an athame, since it is used to direct magical energy, and a wand since it can also invoke.

Gestures are magical tools as potent as any other, ones we can always take with us, to be used when needed.

6

Ritual and Preparation for Ritual

I have defined ritual as: "A specific form of movement, manipulation of objects or series of inner processes designed to produce desired effects" (see Glossary). In Wicca, rituals are ceremonies which celebrate and strengthen our relationships with the Goddess, the God and the Earth.

These rituals need not be pre-planned, rehearsed or traditional, nor must they slavishly adhere to one particular pattern or form. Indeed, Wiccans I've spoken with on the subject agree that spontaneously created rituals can be the most powerful and effective.

A Wiccan rite may consist of a lone celebrant lighting a fire, chanting sacred names, and watching the moonrise. Or it may involve ten or more people, some of whom assume various roles in mythic plays, or speak long passages in honor of the Gods. The rite may be ancient or newly-written. Its outer form isn't important as long as it is successful in achieving an awareness of the deities within the Wiccan.

Wiccan ritual usually occurs on the nights of the Full Moon and the eight Days of Power, the old agricultural and seasonal festivals of Europe. Rituals are usually spiritual in nature but may also include magical workings.

In Section III you'll find a complete book of rituals, *The Standing Stones Book of Shadows*. The best way to learn Wicca is to practice it; thus through the course of time, by performing rituals such as those in this book or the ones you write yourself, you'll gain an understanding

47

of the true nature of Wicca.

Many people say they want to practice Wicca, but sit back and tell themselves that they can't observe the Full Moon with ritual because they don't have a teacher, aren't initiated, or don't know what to do. These are merely excuses. If you're interested in practicing Wicca, simply do so.

To the lone Wiccan, the creation of new rituals can be an exciting practice. You might spend nights with reference works, piecing together bits of ritual and invocation, or simply allow the spirit of the moment and the wisdom of the Deities to fill you with inspiration. No matter how they're created, all rituals should be done out of joy, not obligation.

If you wish, time your rites with the seasons, Pagan feast days, and phases of the Moon. (For more on the subject, see Chapter Eight: The Days of Power.) If you feel particularly attracted to other sacred calendars, feel free to adapt them. There have been highly successful adaptations of Wicca utilizing ancient Egyptian, American Indian, Hawaiian, Babylonian and other religio-magical systems. Though most of Wicca has, until recently, been primarily European and British-based, this needn't limit us. We're free to do what we will as solitary Wiccans. So long as the rituals are fulfilling and effective, why worry?

Instructions on designing your own rituals are included in Chapter Thirteen, but some words regarding preparation for ritual are appropriate here.

First off, make sure you won't be interrupted during your religious (or magical) rite. If you're at home, tell your family that you'll be busy and aren't to be disturbed. If alone, take the phone off the hook, lock the doors and pull the blinds, if you wish. It's best if you can ensure that you will be alone and undisturbed for some time.

A ritual bath commonly follows. For some time I almost couldn't bring myself to do a rite without having a quick dip first. This is partly psychological: if you feel clean and refreshed from the day's worries, you'll feel comfortable contacting the Goddess and God.

Ritual purification is a common feature among many religions. In Wicca, we see water as a purifying substance that strips off the disturbing vibrations of everyday tensions and allows us to stand before the Deities with purity of body as well as purity of thought.

On a deeper level, immersion in water links us with our most primal memories. Bathing in a tub of cool, salted water is akin to walking into the waves of the ever-welcoming ocean, the domain of the

Goddess. It prepares us spiritually and physically (have you ever felt different in the tub?) for the coming experience. The bath often becomes a ritual itself. Candles can be burned in the bathroom, along with incense. Fragrant oils or herbal sachets can be added to the water. My favorite purification bath sachet consists of equal parts of rosemary, fennel, lavender, basil, thyme, hyssop, vervain, mint, with a touch of ground valerian root. (This formula is derived from *The Key of Solomon*.) Place this in a cloth, tie the ends up to trap the herbs inside, and pop it into the tub.

Outdoor rituals near the ocean or lakes and streams can begin with a quick swim. Of course, bathing isn't possible prior to spontaneous rituals. Even the necessity of ritual bathing is questioned by some. If you feel comfortable bathing, do so. If you don't feel it's necessary, it isn't.

Once bathed, it's time to dress for ritual. Among many Wiccans today (particularly those influenced by the writings and ideals of Gerald Gardner, or one of his students—see Bibliography), nudity is a preferable state in which to invoke the deities of nature. It is certainly true that this is the most natural condition in which the human body can be, but ritual nudity isn't for everyone. The Church did much to instill shameful feelings regarding the undraped human figure. These distorted, unnatural emotions survive today.

Many reasons are given for this insistence on ritual nudity.* Some Wiccans state that the clothed body can't emit personal power as effectively as can a naked body, but then go on to say that when necessary, clothed rituals performed indoors are as effective as nude outdoor rites.

If clothed, Wiccans produce magic just as effective as that produced by naked Wiccans. Clothing is no barrier to the transference of power.

A more convincing explanation of Wiccan ritual nudity is that it is used for its symbolic value: mental, spiritual as well as physical nudity before the Goddess and God symbolize the Wiccan's honesty and openness. Ritual nudity was practiced in many ancient religions and can be found today in scattered areas of the world, so this isn't really a new idea, except to some Westerners.

---

* One of these which usually isn't stated is the most obvious: people like to look at naked bodies. Some unscrupulous persons form covens with the sole purpose of practicing social nudity. Such groups, it is readily apparent, aren't promoting the aims of Wicca: union with the Goddess and God and reverence for nature. I hasten to add that the majority of covens that practice ritual nudity aren't of this type. However, some are.

Though many covens insist on ritual nudity, you needn't worry about that. As a solitary practitioner the choice is yours. If you don't feel comfortable with ritual nudity, even in private, don't use it. There are many options.

Specialized dress, such as robes and tabards, are quite popular among some Wiccans. Various reasons are given for the use of robes, one of which is that slipping into garments worn only for magic lends a mystic atmosphere to such rituals and shifts your awareness to the coming proceedings, thereby promoting ritual consciousness.

Colors are also used for their specific vibrations. The listing below is a good sampling of robe colors. If I was especially interested in herb magic or performed rituals designed to halt the proliferation of nuclear power plants and weapons, I might wear a green robe to help key my rituals into Earth energies. Specific robes can also be made and worn by the industrious for certain spells or cycles of spells, according to the below descriptions.

Yellow is an excellent color for those involved with divination.

Purple is favored for those who work with pure divine power (magicians) or who wish to deepen their spiritual awareness of the Goddess and God.

Blue is suited for healers and those who work with their psychic awareness or for attuning with the Goddess in Her oceanic aspect.

Green empowers herbalists and magical ecologists.

Brown is worn by those who attune with animals or who cast spells for them.

White symbolizes purification and pure spirituality, and also is perfect for meditation and cleansing rituals. It is worn for Full Moon celebrations, or to attune with the Goddess.

Orange or **Red** robes can be worn to Sabbats, for protective rites or when attuning with the God in His fiery Solar aspect.

Black robes are quite popular. Contrary to popular misconceptions, black doesn't symbolize evil. It is the absence of color. It is a protective hue and symbolizes the night, the universe and a lack of falsehood. When a Wiccan wears a black robe, she or he is donning the blackness of outer space—symbolically, the ultimate source of divine energy.

If this is too complicated for you, simply make or buy one robe and wear it for every ritual.

Robes range from simple bath-type designs to fully hooded and lined monkish creations, complete with bell sleeves guaranteed to go up in flames if waved too close to candles. Some Wiccans wear robes with hoods, to shut off outside interference and to control sensory stimulation during ritual. This is a fine idea for magic or meditation but not for Wiccan religious rites, when we should be opening ourselves to nature rather than cutting off our connections with the physical world.

If you don't wish to dress in such a garment, are unable to sew or simply can't find anyone to make one for you, just wear clean clothing of natural fibers such as cotton, wool and silk.* So long as you're comfortable with what you are (or aren't) wearing, you're doing fine. Why not experiment to see what "suits" you best?

Selecting and donning ritual jewelry naturally follows dressing. Many Wiccans have collections of exotic pieces with religious or magical designs. Then too amulets and talismans (devices made to ward off or to attract forces) often double as ritual jewelry. Such wonders as necklaces of amber and jet, silver or gold bands worn on the wrists, crowns of silver set with crescent moons, rings of emeralds and pearls, even ritual garters set with tiny silver buckles are often part of Wiccan regalia.

But you needn't purchase or make such extravagances. Keep it simple for now. If you feel comfortable wearing one or two pieces of jewelry during ritual, fine! Choose designs incorporating crescents, ankhs, five-pointed stars (pentagrams), and so on. Many mail-order suppliers carry occult jewelry. If you wish to reserve such pieces for ritual wear, fine. Many do.

I'm often asked if I have a good luck charm, a piece of jewelry, an amulet or some other power object which I always have in my possession. I don't.

This often comes as a surprise, but it is part of my magical

---

* I realize that this is a heretical statement. Many Wiccans become quite angry when I suggest this. Such a reaction is the product of traditional Wiccan training. I feel, however, that wearing clean street clothing during ritual is no more absurd than is donning the ubiquitous, hot and uncomfortable robes that so many Wiccans seem to love. To each their own.

philosophy. If I determined that one piece of jewelry (a ring, pendant, quartz crystal point, etc.) was my power object, my link with the Gods, my assurance of good luck, I'd be crushed if it was stolen, lost, misplaced or otherwise parted company with me.

I could say that the power had gone out of it, that it was a magical lemon, taken by higher beings, or that I'm not as aware as I think. But I'd still be devastated.

It isn't wise to put our hopes, dreams and energies into physical objects. This is a limitation, a direct product of the materialism fostered upon us all our lives. It's easy to say, "I can't do a thing since I lost my lucky moonstone necklace." It's also tempting to think, "Nothing's gone right since my Horned God ring disappeared."

What *isn't* easy to see is that *all the power and luck we need is within ourselves*. It isn't wrapped up in exterior objects unless we allow it to be. If we do this, we leave ourselves open to losing that part of our personal power and good fortune, something I won't willingly do.

Power objects and ritual jewelry can indeed be reminders of the Goddess and God, and symbols of our own abilities. But I feel they shouldn't be allowed to become more than that.

Still, I do have a few pieces (a silver pentagram, an image of the Goddess, an Egyptian ankh, a Hawaiian fishhook that symbolizes the god Maui) that I sometimes wear during ritual. Donning such objects triggers the mind and produces that state of consciousness which is necessary for effective ritual.

I'm not saying that power shouldn't be sent into objects: indeed this is the way magically-charged talismans and amulets are made. I simply prefer not to do so with personal and ritual jewelry.

Certain natural objects, such as quartz crystals, are worn to invite their energies within ourselves to effect specific changes. This type of "power object" is a fine adjunct to personal energies—but it's dangerous to rely on them *exclusively*.

If wearing specific pieces puts you into a magical mood, or if wearing an image of the Goddess or one of Her sacred symbols draws you closer to Her, fine.

Your goal, however, should perhaps be the ability to constantly tune in on the hidden world around us and the reality of the Goddess and God, even in the midst of the most grounding, debasing follies of the human experience.

So, now you're bathed, clothed, adorned and ready for ritual. Any other considerations? Yes, a big one—company.

Do you wish to worship the Old Gods of Wicca privately, or with others? If you have interested friends you may want to invite them to join you.

If not, no problem. Solo ritual is fine when starting out on the Wiccan way. The presence of like-minded people is wonderful, but can be inhibiting as well.

There are certainly rituals at which others can't be present. An unexpected glimpse of the Full Moon half-shrouded in clouds calls for a few moments of silence or attunement, an invocation, or meditation. These are all rituals shared with the Goddess and God alone. Deities don't stand on ceremony; they're as unpredictable and flowing as Nature Herself.

If you wish to gather with friends for your rituals, do so only with those who are truly in tune with your feelings concerning Wicca. Snickers and wandering thoughts will do nothing to further your Wiccan progress.

Also beware the love interest—the boyfriend or girlfriend, husband or wife who takes an interest only because you're interested. They may seem to be genuine, but after a while you may realize they're not contributing to the rituals.

There are many wonderful aspects to coven workings; I've experienced them. Most of the best of Wicca can be found in a good coven (and the worst in a bad one), but most people can't contact covens. They may also lack friends who are interested in practicing with them. This is the reason why I've written this book for solitary practitioners. If you wish, continue searching for a teacher or coven with which to train while working with this and other Wiccan guides. If you do meet someone you'll be able to approach them with a practical knowledge of Wicca from personal experience, rather than mere book learning.

In spite of the emphasis placed on initiations and group workings in the vast majority of books on Wicca, solitary Wicca shouldn't be viewed as second best to the real thing. There are far more individuals worshipping the Old Ones today than there are coven members, and a surprising number of these work solo out of choice. Save for a few group meetings I attend each year, I'm one of them.

Never feel inferior because you're not working under the guidance of a teacher or an established coven. Don't worry that you won't be recognized as a true Wiccan. Such recognition is important only in the eyes of those giving or withholding it, otherwise it is meaningless.

You only need worry about pleasing yourself and developing a rapport with the Goddess and God. Feel free to write your own rituals. Break off the handcuffs of rigid conformity and the idea of "revealed books" which must be slavishly followed. Wicca is an evolving religion. A love of nature and the Goddess and God are at its heart, not unending tradition and ancient rites.

I'm not saying that traditional Wicca is bad. Far from it. Indeed, I've received initiation into several Wiccan traditions, each with their own rituals of initiation, Sabbat and Esbat observances (see Chapter Eight: The Days of Power), names for the Goddess and God, legends and magical lore. But after receiving these "secrets" I've come to realize that they're all the same, and the greatest secrets of all are available to anyone who takes the time to view nature as a manifestation of the Goddess and God.

Each tradition (expression) of Wicca, whether passed down or intuitively performed, is akin to a petal of a flower. No one petal constitutes the whole; all are necessary to the flower's existence. The solitary path is as much a part of Wicca as is any other.

7

The Magic Circle and the Altar

The circle, magic circle or sphere is a well-defined though non-physical temple. In much of Wicca today, rituals and magical workings take place within such a construction of personal power.

The magic circle is of ancient origin. Forms of it were used in old Babylonian magic. Ceremonial magicians of the Middle Ages and the Renaissance also utilized them, as did various American Indian tribes, though not, perhaps, for the same reasons.

There are two main types of magic circles. Those used by ceremonial magicians of yesterday (and today) are designed to protect the magician from the forces which he or she raises. In Wicca, the circle is used to create a sacred space in which humans meet with the Goddess and God.

In pre-Christian Europe, most Pagan religious festivals occurred outdoors. These were celebrations of the Sun, Moon, the stars and of the Earth's fertility. The standing stones, stone circles, sacred groves and revered springs of Europe are remnants of those ancient days.

The Pagan rites went underground when they were outlawed by the newly powerful Church. No longer did meadows know the sounds of voices chanting the old names of the Sun gods, and the Moon hung unadored in the nighttime skies.

The Pagans grew secretive about their rites. Some practiced them outside only under the cover of darkness. Others brought them indoors.

Wicca has, unfortunately, inherited this last practice. Among many Wiccans, outdoor ritual is a novelty, a pleasant break from stuffy house-bound rites. I call this syndrome "living room Wicca." Though most Wiccans practice their religion indoors, it's ideal to run the rites outside beneath the Sun and Moon, in wild and lonely places far from the haunts of humans.

Such Wiccan rites are difficult to perform today. Traditional Wiccan rituals are complex and usually require a large number of tools. Privacy is also hard to find, and fear of merely being seen is another. Why this fear?

There are otherwise responsible, intelligent adults who would rather see us dead than practicing our religion. Such "Christians"* are few but they certainly do exist, and even today Wiccans are exposed to psychological harassment and physical violence at the hands of those who misunderstand their religion.

Don't let this scare you off. Rituals can be done outdoors, if they're modified so as to attract a minimum of attention. Wearing a black, hooded robe, stirring a cauldron and flashing knives through the air in a public park isn't the best way to avoid undue notice.

Street clothing is advisable in the case of outdoor rituals in areas where you may be seen. Tools can be used, but remember that they're accessories, not necessities. Leave them at home if you feel that they'll become problems.

On a 1987 trip to Maui, I rose at dawn and walked to the beach. The Sun was just rising behind Haleakala, tinting the ocean with pinks and reds. I wandered along the coral sand to a place where the warm water crashed against lava rocks.

There I set up a small stone in the sand in honor of the ancient Hawaiian deities. Sitting before it I opened myself to the presence of the *akua* (gods and goddesses) around me. Afterward I walked into the ocean and threw a plumeria lei onto the water, offering it to Hina, Pele, Laka, Kane, Lono, Kanaloa and all Their kin.†

I used no lengthy speeches and brandished no tools in the air. Still, the deities were there, all around, as the waves splashed against my legs and the sunrise broke fully over the ancient volcano, touching the sea with emerald light.

---

* I put quotes around this word for obvious reasons: *such violent, crazed individuals certainly aren't Christians.* Even Fundamentalists usually limit their activities to preaching and picketing—not violence, fire-bombing and beatings.

† Or, as the Hawaiians would term them, the 4,000 gods, the 40,000 gods, the 400,000 gods. "Gods" here refers to deities and semi-divine beings of both genders.

Outdoor rituals such as this can be a thousand times more effective *because they are outdoors,* not in a room filled with steel and plastic and the trappings of our technological age.

When these aren't possible (weather is certainly a factor), Wiccans transform their living rooms and bedrooms into places of power. They do this by creating sacred space, a magical environment in which the Deities are welcomed and celebrated, and in which Wiccans become newly aware of the aspects of the God and Goddess within. Magic may also be practiced there. This sacred space is the magic circle.

It is practically a prerequisite for indoor workings. The circle defines the ritual area, holds in personal power, shuts out distracting energies—in essence, it creates the proper atmosphere for the rites. Standing within a magic circle, looking at the candles shining on the altar, smelling the incense and chanting ancient names is a wonderfully evocative experience. When properly formed and visualized, the magic circle performs its function of bringing us closer to the Goddess and God.

The circle is constructed with personal power which is felt (and visualized) as streaming from the body, through the magic knife (athame) and out into the air. When completed, the circle is a sphere of energy which encompasses the entire working area. The word circle is a misnomer; a *sphere* of energy is actually created. The circle simply marks the ring where the sphere touches the Earth (or floor) and continues on through it to form the other half.

Some kind of marking is often placed on the ground to show where the circle bisects the Earth. This might be a cord lain in a roughly circular shape, a lightly-drawn circle of chalk, or objects situated to show its outlines. These include flowers (ideal for spring and summer rites); pine boughs (winter festivals), stones or shells; quartz crystals, even tarot cards. Use objects that spark your imagination and are in tune with the ritual. (See Chapter Thirteen: Ritual Design for more information regarding the magic circle.)

The circle is usually nine feet in diameter,* though any comfortable size is fine. The cardinal points are often marked with lit candles, or the ritual tools assigned to each point.

The pentacle, a bowl of salt or earth may be placed to the North. This is the realm of Earth, the stabilizing, fertile and nourishing element

---

* Nine is a number of the Goddess.

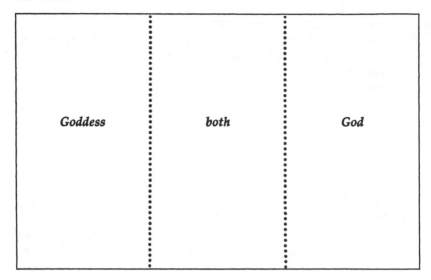

| Goddess | both | God |

Symbolic Divine Areas of the Altar

which is the foundation of the other three.

The censer with smoldering incense is assigned to the East, the home of the intellectual element, Air. Fresh flowers or stick incense can also be used. Air is the element of the mind, of communication, movement, divination and ascetic spirituality.

To the South, a candle often represents Fire, the element of transformation, of passion and change, success, health and strength. An oil lamp or piece of lava rock may be used as well.

A cup or bowl of water can be placed in the West of the circle to represent Water, the last of the four elements. Water is the realm of the emotions, of the psychic mind, love, healing, beauty and emotional spirituality.

Then again, these four objects may be placed on the altar, their positions corresponding to the directions and their elemental attributes.

Once the circle has been formed around the working space, rituals begin. During magical workings the air within the circle can grow uncomfortably hot and close—it will truly feel different from the outside world, charged with energy and alive with power.

The circle is a product of energy, a palpable construction which can be sensed and felt with experience. It isn't just a ring of flowers or cord but a solid, viable barrier.

In Wiccan thought the circle represents the Goddess, the spiritual aspects of nature, fertility, infinity, eternity. It also symbolizes the Earth itself.

The altar, bearing the tools, stands in the center of the circle. It can be made of any substance, though wood is preferred. Oak is especially recommended for its power and strength, as is willow which is sacred to the Goddess.

The Wicca don't believe that the Goddess and God inhabit the altar itself. It is a place of power and magic, but it isn't sacrosanct. Though the altar is usually set up and dismantled for each magical ritual, some Wiccans have permanent home altars as well. Your shrine can grow into such an altar.

The altar is sometimes round, to represent the Goddess and spirituality, though it may also be square, symbolic of the elements. It may be nothing more than an area of ground, a cardboard box covered with cloth, two cinder blocks with a board lying on top, a coffee table, an old sawed-off tree stump in the wild, or a large, flat rock. During outdoor rituals a fire may substitute for the altar. Stick incense may be used to outline the circle. The tools used are the powers of the mind.

The Wiccan tools are usually arranged upon the altar in a pleasing pattern. Generally, the altar is set in the center of the circle facing North. North is a direction of power. It is associated with the Earth, and because this is our home we may feel more comfortable with this alignment. Then too, some Wiccans place their altars facing East, where the Sun and Moon rise.

The left half of the altar is usually dedicated to the Goddess. Tools sacred to Her are placed there: the cup, the pentacle, bell, crystal and cauldron. An image of the Goddess may also stand there, and a broom might be laid against the left side of the altar.*

If you can't find an appropriate Goddess image (or, simply, if you don't desire one), a green, silver or white candle can be substituted. The cauldron is also sometimes placed on the floor to the left side of the altar if it is too large to fit on top.

To the right side, the emphasis is on the God. A red, yellow or gold candle, or an appropriate figure, is usually placed there, as are the censer, wand, athame (magic knife) and white-handled knife.

Flowers may be set in the middle, perhaps in a vase or small

---

* Some Wiccans—particularly those reclaiming women's spirituality—may also place a labrys (double-headed axe) there as well. The labrys is symbolic of the phases of the Moon and of the Goddess. It was extensively used in Crete.

Goddess Symbol or Candle	**Censer**	**God Symbol or Candle**
Bowl of Water	**Red Candle**	**Bowl of Salt**
Cup	**Pentacle**	**Incense**
Crystal	**Cauldron, or Spell Materials**	**Knife/Wand**
Bell		**Bolline**

Suggested Altar Layout

cauldron. Then too, the censer is often centrally situated so that its smoke is offered up to both the Goddess and the God, and the pentacle might be placed before the censer.

Some Wiccans follow a more primitive, nature-oriented altar plan. To represent the Goddess, a round stone (pierced with a hole if available), a corn dolly, or a seashell work well. Pine cones, tapered stones and acorns can be used to represent the God. Use your imagination in setting up the altar.

If you're working magic in the Circle, all necessary items should be within it before you begin, either on the altar or beneath it. Never forget to have matches handy, and a small bowl to hold the used ones (it's impolite to throw them into the censer or cauldron).

Though we may set up images of the Goddess and God, we're not idol worshippers. We don't believe that a given statue or pile of rocks actually *is* the deity represented. And although we reverence nature, we don't worship trees or birds or stones. We simply delight in seeing them as manifestations of the universal creative forces—the Goddess and God.

The altar and the magic circle in which it stands is a personal construction and it should be pleasing to you. My first Wiccan teacher laid out elaborate altars attuned with the occasion—if we couldn't practice outdoors. For one Full Moon rite she draped the altar with white satin, placed white candles in crystal holders, added a silver chalice, white roses and snowy-leafed dusty miller. An incense composed of white roses, sandalwood and gardenias drifted through the air. The glowing altar suffused the room with lunar energies. Our ritual that night was one to remember.

May yours be the same.

8

The Days of Power

In the past, when people lived with nature, the turning of the seasons and the monthly cycle of the Moon had a profound impact on religious ceremonies. Because the Moon was seen as a symbol of the Goddess, ceremonies of adoration and magic took place in its light. The coming of winter, the first stirrings of spring, the warm summer and the advent of fall were also marked with rituals.

The Wiccans, heirs of the pre-Christian folk religions of Europe, still celebrate the Full Moon and observe the changing of the seasons. The Wiccan religious calendar contains 13 Full Moon celebrations and eight Sabbats or days of power.

Four of these days (or, more properly, nights) are determined by the Solstices and Equinoxes,* the astronomical beginnings of the seasons. The other four ritual occasions are based on old folk festivals (and, to some extent, those of the ancient Near East). The rituals give structure and order to the Wiccan year, and also remind us of the endless cycle that will continue long after we're gone.

Four of the Sabbats—perhaps those that have been observed for the longest time—were probably associated with agriculture and the bearing cycles of animals. These are *Imbolc* (February 2), *Beltane* (April 30), *Lughnasadh* (August 1) and *Samhain* (October 31). These names are Celtic and are quite common among Wiccans, though many

---

* Traces of this old custom are even found in Christianity. Easter, for example, is placed on the Sunday following the first Full Moon after the spring equinox, a rather "Pagan" way to organize religious rites.

others exist.

When careful observation of the skies led to common knowledge of the astronomical year, the Solstices and Equinoxes (*circa* March 21, June 21, September 21 and December 21; the actual dates vary from year to year) were brought into this religious structure.*

Who first began worshipping and raising energy at these times? That question cannot be answered. However, these sacred days and nights are the origins of the 21 Wiccan ritual occasions.

Many of these survive today in both secular and religious forms. May Day celebrations, Halloween, Ground-hog Day and even Thanksgiving, to name some popular American holidays, are all connected with ancient Pagan worship. Heavily Christianized versions of the Sabbats have also been preserved within the Catholic Church

The Sabbats are solar rituals, marking the points of the Sun's yearly cycle, and are but half of the Wiccan ritual year. The Esbats are the Wiccan Full Moon celebrations. At this time we gather to worship She Who Is. Not that Wiccans omit the God at Esbats—both are usually revered on all ritual occasions.

There are 12 to 13 Full Moons yearly, or one every 28¼ days. The Moon is a symbol of the Goddess as well as a source of energy. Thus, after the religious aspects of the Esbats, Wiccans often practice magic, tapping into the larger amounts of energy which are thought to exist at these times.

Some of the old Pagan festivals, stripped of their once sacred qualities by the dominance of Christianity, have degenerated. Samhain seems to have been taken over by candy manufacturers in the United States, while Yule has been transformed from one of the most holy Pagan days to a time of gross commercialism. Even the later echoes of a Christian savior's birth are hardly audible above the electronic hum of cash registers.

But the old magic remains on these days and nights, and the Wicca celebrate them. Rituals vary greatly, but all relate to the Goddess and God and to our home, the Earth. Most rites are held at night for practical purposes as well as to lend a sense of mystery. The Sabbats, being solar-oriented, are more naturally celebrated at noon or at dawn, but this is rare today.

The Sabbats tell us one of the stories of the Goddess and God, of their relationship and the effects this has on the fruitfulness of the

---

* Solstices, Equinoxes and the Sabbats are listed in *Llewellyn's Astrological Calendar*.

Earth. There are many variations on these myths, but here's a fairly common one, woven into basic descriptions of the Sabbats.

The Goddess gives birth to a son, the God, at Yule (*circa* December 21). This is in no way an adaptation of Christianity. The Winter Solstice has long been viewed as a time of divine births. Mithras was said to have been born at this time. The Christians simply adopted it for *their* use in 273 C.E. (Common Era).

Yule is a time of the greatest darkness and is the shortest day of the year. Earlier peoples noticed such phenomena and supplicated the forces of nature to lengthen the days and shorten the nights. Wiccans sometimes celebrate Yule just before dawn, then watch the Sun rise as a fitting finale to their efforts.

Since the God is also the Sun, this marks the point of the year when the Sun is reborn as well. Thus, the Wicca light fires or candles to welcome the Sun's returning light. The Goddess, slumbering through the winter of Her labor, rests after Her delivery.

Yule is the remnant of early rituals celebrated to hurry the end of winter and the bounty of spring, when food was once again readily available. To contemporary Wiccans it is a reminder that the ultimate product of death is rebirth, a comforting thought in these days of unrest. (See Chapter Nine: The Spiral of Rebirth.)

Imbolc (February 2) marks the recovery of the Goddess after giving birth to the God. The lengthening periods of light awaken Her. The God is a young, lusty boy, but His power is felt in the longer days. The warmth fertilizes the Earth (the Goddess), causes seeds to germinate and sprout. And so the earliest beginnings of spring occur.

This is a Sabbat of purification after the shut-in life of winter, through the renewing power of the Sun. It is also a festival of light and of fertility, once marked in Europe with huge blazes, torches and fire in every form. Fire here represents our own illumination and inspiration as much as light and warmth.

Imbolc is also known as Feast of Torches, Oimelc, Lupercalia, Feast of Pan, Snowdrop Festival, Feast of the Waxing Light, Brigid's day, and probably by many other names. Some female Wiccans follow the old Scandinavian custom of wearing crowns of lit candles,* but many more carry tapers during their invocations.

---

* See page 72 of *Buckland's Complete Book of Witchcraft* (Llewellyn, 1986) for details.

This is one of the traditional times for initiations into covens, and so self-dedication rituals, such as the one outlined in Chapter Twelve, can be performed or renewed at this time.

Ostara (*circa* March 21), the Spring Equinox, also known as Spring, Rites of Spring and Eostra's Day, marks the first day of true spring. The energies of nature subtly shift from the sluggishness of winter to the exhuberant expansion of spring. The Goddess blankets the Earth with fertility, bursting forth from Her sleep, as the God stretches and grows to maturity. He walks the greening fields and delights in the abundance of nature.

On Ostara the hours of day and night are equal. Light is overtaking darkness; the Goddess and God impel the wild creatures of the Earth to reproduce.

This is a time of beginnings, of action, of planting spells for future gains, and of tending ritual gardens.

Beltane (April 30) marks the emergence of the young God into manhood. Stirred by the energies at work in nature, He desires the Goddess. They fall in love, lie among the grasses and blossoms, and unite. The Goddess becomes pregnant of the God. The Wiccans celebrate the symbol of Her fertility in ritual.

Beltane (also known as May Day) has long been marked with feasts and rituals. May poles, supremely phallic symbols, were the focal point of old English village rituals. Many persons rose at dawn to gather flowers and green branches from the fields and gardens, using them to decorate the May pole, their homes and themselves.

The flowers and greenery symbolize the Goddess; the May pole the God. Beltane marks the return of vitality, of passion and hopes consummated.

May poles are sometimes used by Wiccans today during Beltane rituals, but the cauldron is a more common focal point of ceremony. It represents, of course, the Goddess—the essence of womanhood, the end of all desire, the equal but opposite of the May pole, symbolic of the God.

Midsummer, the Summer Solstice (*circa* June 21), also known as Litha, arrives when the powers of nature reach their highest point. The Earth is awash in the fertility of the Goddess and God.

In the past, bonfires were leapt to encourage fertility, purification, health and love. The fire once again represents the Sun, feted on this time of the longest daylight hours.

Midsummer is a classic time for magic of all kinds.

Lughnasadh (August 1) is the time of the first harvest, when the plants of spring wither and drop their fruits or seeds for our use as well as to ensure future crops. Mystically, so too does the God lose His strength as the Sun rises farther in the South each day and the nights grow longer. The Goddess watches in sorrow and joy as She realizes that the God is dying, and yet lives on inside Her as Her child.

Lughnasadh, also known as August Eve, Feast of Bread, Harvest Home and Lammas, wasn't necessarily observed on this day. It originally coincided with the first reapings.

As summer passes, Wiccans remember its warmth and bounty in the food we eat. Every meal is an act of attunement with nature, and we are reminded that nothing in the universe is constant.

Mabon (*circa* September 21), the Autumn Equinox, is the completion of the harvest begun at Lughnasadh. Once again day and night are equal, poised as the God prepares to leave His physical body and begin the great adventure into the unseen, toward renewal and rebirth of the Goddess.

Nature declines, draws back its bounty, readying for winter and its time of rest. The Goddess nods in the weakening Sun, though fire burns within Her womb. She feels the presence of the God even as He wanes.

At Samhain (October 31), the Wicca say farewell to the God. This is a temporary farewell. He isn't wrapped in eternal darkness, but readies to be reborn of the Goddess at Yule.

Samhain, also known as November Eve, Feast of the Dead, Feast of Apples, Hallows and All Hallows, once marked the time of sacrifice. In some places this was the time when animals were slaughtered to ensure food throughout the depths of winter. The God—identified with the animals—fell as well to ensure our continuing existence.*

Samhain is a time of reflection, of looking back over the last year, of coming to terms with the one phenomenon of life over which we

---

* Vegetarian Wiccans probably don't like this part of Samhain symbolism, but it is traditional. We don't, of course, sacrifice animals in ritual. This is symbolic of the God's passing.

have no control—death.

The Wicca feel that on this night the separation between the physical and spiritual realities is thin. Wiccans remember their ancestors and all those who have gone before.

After Samhain, Wiccans celebrate Yule, and so the wheel of the year is complete.

Surely there are mysteries buried here. Why is the God the son and then the lover of the Goddess? This isn't incest, this is symbolism. In this agricultural story (one of many Wiccan myths) the ever-changing fertility of the Earth is represented by the Goddess and God. This myth speaks of the mysteries of birth, death and rebirth. It celebrates the wondrous aspects and beautiful effects of love, and honors women who perpetuate our species. It also points out the very real dependence that humans have on the Earth, the Sun and the Moon and of the effects of the seasons on our daily lives.

To agricultural peoples, the major thrust of this myth cycle is the production of food through the interplay between the Goddess and God. Food—without which we would all die—is intimately connected with the deities. Indeed, Wiccans see food as yet another manifestation of divine energy.

And so, by observing the Sabbats, Wiccans attune themselves to the Earth and to the deities. They reaffirm their Earth roots. Performing rituals on the nights of the Full Moon also strengthens their connections with the Goddess in particular.

It is the wise Wiccan who celebrates on the Sabbats and Esbats, for these are times of real as well as symbolic power. Honoring them in some fashion—perhaps with rites similar to those suggested in *The Standing Stones Book of Shadows*—is an integral part of Wicca.

9

The Spiral of Rebirth

Reincarnation seems to be one of the most controversial spiritual topics of our time. Hundreds of books are being published on the subject as if the Western world had only recently discovered this ancient doctrine.

Reincarnation is one of Wicca's most valuable lessons. The knowledge that this life is but one of many, that when the physical body dies we do not cease to exist but are reborn in another body answers many questions, but raises a few more.

Why? Why are we reincarnated? In common with many other religions, Wicca teaches that reincarnation is the instrument through which our souls are perfected. One lifetime isn't sufficient to attain this goal; hence, the consciousness (soul) is reborn many times, each life encompassing a different set of lessons, until perfection is achieved.

No one can say how many lives are required before this is accomplished. We are human and it's easy to fall into non-evolutionary behavior. Greed, anger, jealousy, obsession and all our negative emotions inhibit our growth.

In Wicca, we seek to strengthen our bodies, minds and souls. We certainly live full, productive earthly lives, but we try to do so while harming none, the antithesis of competition, intimidation and looking out for number one.

The soul is ageless, sexless, non-physical, possessed of the divine spark of the Goddess and God. Each manifestation of the soul (i.e., each body it inhabits on Earth) is different. No two bodies or lives are the same. If this wasn't so, the soul would stagnate. The sex, race, place of birth, economic class and every other individuality of the soul is determined by its actions in past lives and the lessons necessary to the present.

This is of utmost importance in Wiccan thought: *we* decide the lay of our lives. There's no god or curse or mysterious force of fate upon which we can thrust the responsibility for the trials in our lives. We decide what we need to learn in order to evolve, and then, it is hoped, during incarnation, work toward this progress. If not, we regress into darkness.

As an aid in learning the lessons of each life, a phenomenon exists which has been called karma. Karma is often misunderstood. It is not a system of rewards and punishments, but a phenomenon that guides the soul toward evolving actions. Thusly, if a person performs negative actions, negative actions will be returned. Good brings good. With this in mind, there's little reason to act negatively.

Karma means action, and that's how it works. It is a tool, not a punishment. There's no way one can "wipe out" karma, and neither is every seemingly terrible event in our lives a byproduct of karma.

We learn from karma only when we're aware of it. Many look into their past lives to discover their mistakes, to uncover the problems inhibiting progress in this one. Trance and meditation techniques can help here, but true *self-knowledge* is the best means of accomplishing this.

Past-life regression can be a dangerous thing, for much self-delusion exists here. I can't tell you how many Cleopatras, King Arthurs, Merlins, Marys, Nefertitis and other famous persons of the past I've met walking around in high-top tennis shoes and jeans. Our conscious minds, seeking past incarnations, easily hold onto such romantic ideals.

If this becomes a problem; if you don't wish to know your past lives, or lack the means to discover them, look at this life. You can learn everything of relevance about your past lives by examining this life. If you've cleared up problems in previous existences, they're of no concern to you today. If you haven't, the same problems will reappear, so look at this life.

At night, study your day's action, noting both positive, helpful actions and thoughts as well as the negative. Then look at the past week, the past year, the past decade. Refer to diaries, journals or old letters if you've kept them to refresh your memory. Do you continually make the same mistakes? If so, vow to never repeat them in a ritual of your own design.

At your altar or shrine, you might write such mistakes on a piece of paper. Your entries could include negative emotions, fear, indulgence without balance, allowing others to control your life, endless love-obsessions with men or women who are indifferent to your feelings. As you write these, visualize yourself doing these things *in the past*, not the present.

Then, light a red candle. Hold the paper in its flame and throw it into a cauldron or some other heat-proof container. Scream or shout— or simply affirm to yourself—that such past actions are no longer a part of you. Visualize your future life devoid of such harmful, limiting, inhibiting behavior. Repeat the spell as necessary, perhaps on nights of the waning Moon, to finalize the destruction of these negative aspects of your life.

If you ritualize your determination to progress in this life, your vow will vibrate with strength. When you're tempted to fall into your old, negative modes of thinking or action, recall the ritual and overcome the urge with its power.

What happens after death? Only the body dies. The soul lives on. Some Wiccans say that it journeys to a realm variously known as the Land of the Faerie, the Shining Land, and the Land of the Young.* This realm is neither in heaven nor the underworld. It simply *is*—a nonphysical reality much less dense than ours. Some Wiccan traditions describe it as a land of eternal summer, with grassy fields and sweet flowing rivers, perhaps the Earth before the advent of humans. Others see it vaguely as a realm without forms, where energy swirls coexist with the greatest energies—the Goddess and God in their celestial identities.

The soul is said to review the past life, perhaps through some mysterious way with the deities. This isn't a judgment, a weighing of one's soul, but an incarnational review. Lessons learned or ignored are brought to light.

After the proper time, when the conditions on Earth are correct, the soul is reincarnated and life begins again.

The final question—what happens after the last incarnation?

---

* These are Celtic terms. Some Wiccans call this place the Summerland, which is a Theosophical term.

Wiccan teachings have always been vague on this. Basically, the Wiccans say that after rising upon the spiral of life and death and rebirth, those souls who have attained perfection break away from the cycle forever and dwell with the Goddess and God. Nothing is ever lost. The energies resident in our souls return to the divine source from which they originally emanated.

Because of their acceptance of reincarnation, the Wicca don't fear death as a final plunge into oblivion, the days of life on Earth forever behind them. It is seen as the door to birth. Thus our very lives are symbolically linked with the endless cycles of the seasons which shape our planet.

Don't try to force yourself to believe in reincarnation. Knowledge is far superior to belief, for belief is the way of the uninformed. It isn't wise to accept a doctrine as important as reincarnation without a great deal of study to see if it speaks to you.

Also, though there may be strong connections with loved ones, be wary of the idea of soul mates, i.e. people you've loved in other lives and are destined to love again. Though your feelings and beliefs may be sincere, they aren't always based on fact. In the course of your life you might meet five or six other people with whom you feel the same tie, despite your current involvement. Can they all be soul mates?

One of the difficulties of this concept is that if we're all inextricably tied up with other persons' souls, if we continue to incarnate with them, we're learning absolutely nothing. Therefore, announcing that you've found your soul mate is rather akin to stating that you're not progressing on the incarnational spiral.*

One day you may *know*, not believe, that reincarnation is as real as a plant that buds, flowers, drops its seed, withers and creates a new plant in its image. Reincarnation was probably first intuited by earlier peoples watching nature.

Until you've decided for yourself, you may wish to reflect upon and consider the doctrine of reincarnation.

---

* I realize I'm in dangerous water here again. Still, I've met many, many people who've made such announcements—only to later tell me privately, "Boy, was I wrong."

10

Concerning Initiation

Most shamanic and magical religions utilize some sort of initiation ceremony whereby an outsider becomes a recognized member of the religion, society, group or coven. Such rites also mark the new direction which the initiate's life is taking.

Much has been made, publicly and privately, of Wiccan initiations. Each Wiccan tradition uses their own initiation ceremonies, which may or may not be recognized by other Wiccans. On one point, however, most initiates agree: a person can be a Wiccan only if she or he has received such an initiation.

This brings up an interesting question: Who initiated the first Wiccan?

Most initiation ceremonies are nothing more than rites marking the acceptance of the person into a coven, and her or his dedication to the Goddess and God. Sometimes "power is passed" between the initiator and neophyte as well.

To a non-Wiccan, the initiation might seem to be a rite of conversion. This isn't the case. Wicca has no need for such rites. We don't condemn the deities with which we may have attuned before practicing Wicca, nor need we turn our backs on them.

The initiation ceremony (or ceremonies, since in many groups three successive rites are performed) is held to be of utmost importance to those Wiccan groups still practicing ritual secrecy. Surely anyone entering such a group should undergo an initiation, part of which consists of swearing never to reveal their secrets. This makes sense, and is a part of many coven initiations. But it isn't the *essence* of initiation.

Many people have told me that they desperately need to undergo Wiccan initiation. They seem to believe that one cannot practice Wicca without this stamp of approval. If you've read this far, you know that such isn't the case.

Wicca has been, up until the past decade or so, a closed religion, but no more. The inner components of Wicca are available to anyone who can read and has the proper wit to understand the material. Wicca's only secrets are its individual ritual forms, spells, names of deities and so on.

This needn't bother you. For every secret Wiccan ritual or Goddess name there are dozens (if not hundreds) of others published and readily available. At this moment, more Wiccan information has been released than ever before. While it once may have been a secret religion, today Wicca is a religion with few secrets.*

Still, many cling to the idea of the necessity of initiation, probably thinking that with this magical act they'll be granted the *secrets of the universe* and *untold power*. To make things worse, some particularly narrow-minded Wiccans say that the Goddess and God won't listen to anyone who isn't an athame-carrying member of a coven. Many would-be Wiccans believe this.

It doesn't work this way.

True initiation isn't a rite performed by one human being upon another. Even if you accept the concept that the initiator is suffused with deity during initiation, it's still just a ritual.

Initiation is a process, gradual or instantaneous, of the individual's attunement with the Goddess and God. Many of the Wicca readily admit that the ritual initiation is the outer form only. True initiation will often occur weeks or months later, or prior to, the physical ritual.

Since this is so, "real" Wiccan initiation may take place years before the student contacts a Wiccan coven or teacher. Is this initiation less effective or less genuine because the person hasn't gone through a formal ritual at the hands of another human being? Of course not.

Rest assured, it's quite possible to experience a true Wiccan initiation without ever meeting another soul involved in the religion.

---

* Some groups simply write their own "secret" Books of Shadows and restrict access to them. This does, indeed, ensure that they're secret—but not older or better than any other.

You may even be unaware of it. Your life may gradually shift in focus until you realize that you notice the birds and clouds. You may gaze at the Moon on lonely nights and talk to plants and animals. Sunset might bring a time of quiet contemplation.

Or you may change as the seasons change, adapting your body's energies to match those of the natural world around you. The Goddess and God may sing in your thoughts, and you may perform rituals before actually realizing what you're doing.

When the Old Ways have become a part of your life and your relationship with the Goddess and God is strong, when you have gathered your tools and performed the rites and magic out of joy, you are truly of the spirit and can rightly call yourself "Wiccan."

This may be your goal, or you may wish to stretch yourself further, perhaps continuing your search for an instructor. This is fine. But if you never find one, you'll have the satisfaction of knowing that you didn't sit around waiting for the mysteries to fall into your lap. You'll have worked the old magics and talked to the Goddess and God, reaffirming your commitment to the Earth for spiritual evolvement, and transformed the lack of physical initiation into a positive stimulus to change your life and modes of thinkings.

If you contact a teacher or coven, they'll probably find you're a student worthy of acceptance. But if you discover that you're not suited to their style of Wicca, or if your personalities clash, don't be crushed. You've still got your own Wicca to fall back upon as you continue your search.

This can be a lonely path, because so few of us follow the Old Ways. It's disheartening to spend your time reverencing nature and watching the Earth suffocating under tons of concrete while nobody seems to care.

To contact others of like mind, you may wish to subscribe to Wiccan publications and start correspondence with Wiccans around the country. Continue to read new books as they're published on both Wicca and the Goddess. Keep up on the happenings in the Wiccan world. Collect and write new rituals and spells. Wicca need never grow stale.

Many wish to formalize their life within Wicca with a self-initiation ceremony. I've included one in Section II for those who feel the need for it. Again, this is simply one way to do this. Improvise if you so desire.

If you decide to invite friends and interested people to join your rites, don't make them hang back and watch while you play "priest-ess" or "Witch." Involve them. Make them a part of the rites and magic. Use your imagination and practical experience to integrate them into the rituals.

When you feel an insurmountable joy in watching the sunset or the moon rise, when you see the Goddess and God in trees marching along mountains or streams meandering through fields, when you feel the pulsating energies of the Earth amidst a noisy city, you have received true initiation and are linked with the ancient powers and ways of the deities.

Some say, "Only a Wiccan can make a Wiccan." I say only the Goddess and God can make a Wiccan.

Who's better qualified?

SECTION II:
PRACTICE

11

Exercises and Magical Techniques

Following are short sections on various exercises and procedures which are vital to your growth in Wicca and magic. Such activities, which consume no more than a few minutes of each day, shouldn't be underestimated. They're the building blocks upon which fluency in all Wiccan and magical rites will be gained.

Making them a part of your everyday schedule allows you to grow day by day.

The Mirror Book

Right now, as soon as you finish reading this perhaps, begin a "mirror book." This is a magical record of your progress in Wicca. It can be anything from a locked diary to a spiral-bound notebook. In it, record all thoughts and feelings about Wicca, the results of your readings, magical successes and failures, doubts and fears, significant dreams—even mundane concerns. This book is for your eyes only. No one else need ever read it.

This book is a mirror of your spiritual life. As such it is quite valuable in assessing your progress in Wicca and life itself. Thus, when reading over the book, you become your own teacher. Notice problem areas and take steps to resolve them.

I've found the best time to record such information is directly before sleep. Date each entry and, if you wish, also include the moon's phase and any astronomical information which might be pertinent (lunar phases, eclipses, weather).

One of the goals of the Wicca is self-knowledge; the Mirror Book is a valuable tool in achieving this.

Breathing

Breathing is usually an unconscious act which we perform continuously throughout our lives. In magic and Wicca, however, breath can also be a tool for disciplining our bodies and entering into alternate states of consciousness.

In order to meditate correctly, you must breathe correctly. This is the most basic of exercises and, fortunately, is also the easiest.

Deep breathing techniques require the full use of the lungs as well as of the diaphragm. The diaphragm is located about two finger-widths below the rib cage. As you breath in, push out with this region. Notice how much more air you can intake.

For breathing exercises, assume a comfortable position, either sitting or lying down (although deep breathing is possible in nearly every position). Relax your body slightly. Inhale through your nose to a slow count of three, four or five—whatever is comfortable. Remember to allow the air to fill your diaphragm as well as your lungs. Retain the air, then exhale to the same slow count.

Repeat this several times, gradually slowing your breath rate. Never hold your breath past the level of comfort. The inhalation, retaining and exhalation should be controlled, calm, free of tension.

Concentrate on your breathing process while doing this. As you inhale, breathe in love, health, tranquillity, perhaps visualizing (see this section in this chapter) these positive energies as golden flecked air. In exhaling, breathe out hate, disease, anger, maybe visualizing black smoke exiting your lungs.

Oxygen is the breath of life and is necessary to our existence. Breathe properly and you'll be a better person and a better Wiccan. Deep breathing is used before every act of worship or magic, and is a part of concentration and visualization exercises. Breathe deeply when you feel anger exploding within you. Exhale the fury and inhale peace. It works every time—if you allow it to.

Practice deep breathing exercises daily, and gradually increase your capacity to retain air. It is wise, if possible, to occasionally practice this near the sea or in a forest, far from the polluted air of our cities. Deep breathing in these natural settings is not only more peaceful—it's also healthier.

Meditation

Meditation is an important art for inducing total relaxation. Too few of us find a moment of freedom from tensions and worries, so meditation is a welcome relief from the cares and frustrations of everyday living. More importantly, it's a quiet time in which we commune with the Goddess, the God and ourselves, relaxing the conscious mind's hold on our psychic awareness. Meditation usually precedes every magical act and rite of worship.

Sitting is the ideal position for meditation, especially for those who tend to fall asleep during this practice.

Sit in a straight-backed chair, supporting your lower back with a pillow if necessary. Your chin should be level with the floor, eyes closed, back straight, hands resting on your knees, palms up and fingers relaxed. In this position you should be comfortable and relaxed, the spine straight and the torso erect. If you have poor posture, it may be some time before this position becomes comfortable. Persevere.

Breathe deeply for several minutes. Relax. Forget. Visualize the multitude of tensions and worries of your everyday life exiting your body with your breath. Relax into the chair.

Now open your consciousness. Allow your conscious mind to be receptive and alert. Commune and talk with the deities. Toss around symbols in your head. If you wish, chant one of the names of the Goddess or God, or a group of them. This is an excellent tool for slipping into the twilight world.

Select your time and place for meditation with care. Light should be subdued; candlelight is excellent. Burn white or blue candles if you wish. A bit of incense is fine too, but too much smoke can (obviously) cause problems during deep breathing.

Immediately after each meditation, record all images, thoughts and sensations in your mirror book.

Visualization

This is the most basic and yet advanced technique called for in magic and Wicca. The art of using our brains to "see" what is not physically present is a powerful magical tool used in many Wiccan rituals. For instance, the forming of the magic circle relies in part on the Wiccan's ability to visualize personal power flowing out to form a sphere of glowing light around the ritual area. This visualization, then, directs the power that actually creates the circle; it doesn't create it alone

Because of its usefulness in changing our attitudes and lives, many books are being written on visualization today. Each book promises to show the secrets of visualization.

Fortunately, nearly all of us already possess this ability. It may not be fine-tuned, but practice makes perfect.

Can you, at this moment, see in your mind your best friend's face, or your least favorite actor? What about the piece of clothing you most often wear, the exterior of your home, your car or your bathroom?

That's visualization. Visualization is the act of seeing with the mind, not the eyes. Magical visualization is seeing something which is presently non-existent. It may be a magic circle, a healed friend, an empowered talisman.

We can raise energy from our bodies, visualize it streaming out from our palms, and then form it into a small glowing sphere, fashioning it *physcially* as if into a snowball, and *mentally* by seeing it as we desire.

In magic, I might raise energy and, while doing this, hold an image in my mind of something I need—a new car, for example. I visualize the car, see myself signing the contract to buy it, driving it on the road, pumping gas into its tank and making payments. Then I direct energy to empower the visualization—to bring it into manifestation.

In other words, visualization "programs" the power. This could be explained as a form of mental sympathetic magic. Instead of creating a physical image, we create pictures in our heads.

Thoughts are definitely things. Our thoughts affect the quality of our lives. If we constantly moan about being broke, then do a fifteen-minute visualization to bring money into our lives, that fifteen minutes of energy will have to counteract 23 hours and 45 minutes of daily, self-induced, negative programming. Thus we must keep our thoughts in order and in line with our desires and needs.

Visualization can help here.

To hone this tool, try these simple exercises, widely known within Wicca.

Exercise One: Sit or lie comfortably with your eyes shut. Relax your body. Breathe deeply and still your mind. Pictures will contiue to pop into your head. Choose one of thse and stick with it. Let no images intrude other than the one you've chosen. Keep all thoughts revolving around the image. Retain this picture for as long as you can, then let it go and end the exercise. When you can retain one picture for more than a few minutes, move on to the next step.

Exercise Two: Decide upon an image to hold and retain it within your mind. You might wish to have it physically present and study it first, memorizing each detail—the way shadows play on it, its textures, colors, perhaps even a scent. You might choose a small three-dimensional shape, such as a pyramid, or something more complex such as an image of Aphrodite rising from the sea or a ripe apple.

After studying it thoroughly, close your eyes and see the object before them—just as if your eyes were open. Don't look at the object again with your physical eyes but with your magical imagination—with your powers of visualization.

When you can hold this image perfectly for five minutes, move on.

Exercise Three: This is more difficult, and is truly magical in nature. Visualize something, anything, but preferably something you've never seen. For instance, let's use a vegetable from Jupiter. It's purple, square, a foot across, covered with quarter-inch green hairs and half-inch yellow dots.

This is just an example. of course.

Now close your eyes and see—*really see* this vegetable in your mind. It's never existed. You're creating it with your visualization, your magical imagination. Make the vegetable real. Turn it over in your mind so that you can see it from all angles. Then let it vanish.

When you can hold any such self-created image for about five minutes or so, continue on to the next exercise.

Exercise Four: This is the most difficult. Hold a self-created image (such as the Jupiterian vegetable) in your mind *with your eyes open.* Work at keeping it visible, real, a palpable thing. Stare at a wall, look at the sky, or gaze at a busy street, but see that vegetable there. Make it so real you can touch it. Try having it resting on a table or sitting on the grass beneath a tree.

If we're to use visualization to create changes in this world, not in the shadowy realm that exists behind our eyelids, we must practice such techniques with our eyes open. The true test of visualization lies in our ability to make the visualized object (or structure) real and a part of our world.

When you've perfected this exercise, you're well on the way.

Energy Play

The energy and magical powers at work in Wicca are real. They aren't of some astral plane. They're within the Earth and ourselves. They maintain life. We daily deplete our store of energy and replenish it through the air we breathe, the food we eat, and the powers that stream down from the Sun and Moon.

Know that this power is physical. Yes, it's mysterious, but only because so few investigate it in magical ways. Following are some exercises to help you do just that. (You might wish to re-read Chapter Three: Magic.)

Calm yourself. Breathe deeply. Rub your palms together for twenty seconds. Start slowly and rub faster and faster. Feel your muscles tense. Feel your palms grow warm. Then, suddenly, stop and hold your palms about two inches from each other. Feel them tingling? That's a manifestation of power. By rubbing your palms together and using the muscles in your arms and shoulders you're raising energy—magical power. It's flowing out from your palms as you hold them apart.

If you don't feel anything, practice this once or twice a day until you have success. Remember, don't force yourself to feel the power. Trying harder won't accomplish anything. Relax and *allow* yourself to feel what's been there all the time.

After you've actually sensed this energy, begin to fashion it into shapes. Use your visualization to do this. Directly after rubbing your hands, while they're still tingling, visualize jolts of energy—perhaps electric blue or purple—passing from your right (projective) palm to your left (receptive) palm. If you're left-handed, reverse the directions.*

---

* Remember the science fiction and fantasy movies you've seen wherein a magician sends power from his or her hands? Remember what it looked like in cinematic form. If you wish, use a similar image to visualize personal power streaming from your palms. Though that was just special effects this, of course, is *real*, and we can use the picture to actually send out that power.

Now envision this energy slowly swirling in a clockwise direction between your palms. Form it into a ball of glowing, pulsating magical energy. See its dimensions, its colors. Feel its force and heat in your palms. This is a bit of energy which you've released from your body. There's nothing supernatural about it. Cup your hands around the ball. Make it grow or decrease in size *through your visualization.* Finally push it into your stomach and absorb it back into your system.

This is not only great fun but is a valuable magical learning experience. When you've mastered the art of energy spheres, go on to feel energy fields.

Sit or stand before any plant. Herbs and plants in bloom seem to work best. In a pinch, cut flowers can be used as well.

Breathe deeply for a few moments and clear your thoughts. Hold your receptive (left) palm a few inches above the plant. Pinpoint your consciousness to your palm. Do you feel a dull throbbing, a hum, a wave of heat, or simply a shift in the energies within your palm? Do you feel the inner force of the plant?

If so, good—you've felt energy. After you've accomplished this, try sensing the energies of stones and crystals.* Place a quartz crystal, say, on a table and pass your receptive hand over the crystal. Stretch out with your feelings and become aware of the non-visible but viable energies that pulsate within the crystal.

All natural objects, remember, are manifestations of divine energy. With practice we can feel the power that resides within them.

If you have difficulty feeling these powers, rub your palms lightly together to sensitize them and try again.

This energy is the same power we're filled with when we're angry, nervous, terrified, joyous or sexually aroused. It's the energy used in magic, whether we pull it from ourselves or channel it from the Goddess and God, plants, stones and other objects. It is the stuff of creation which we utilize in magic.

Now that you've felt the power, use visualization to move it around. You needn't rub your palms together to raise energy—you can do this simply by concentrating on doing so. One of the easiest methods is to tighten up the muscles—tense your body. This raises energy, which is why we must relax in meditation. Meditation lowers our energy and allows us to drift from this world.

When you feel yourself bursting with power, hold out your right

---

* For an in-depth exercise in sensing stone energies see *Cunningham's Encyclopedia of Crystal, Gem and Metal Magic* (Llewellyn, 1988).

(projective) hand and direct energy from your body, through your arm and out your fingers. Use your visualization. Really see and feel it streaming out.

For practice, stand in your home. Build the power within you. Direct it into each room, visualizing it sinking into the cracks and walls and around doors and windows. You're not creating a psychic burglar alarm but a magical protectant, so visualize the energy forming an impenetrable barrier across which no negativity or intruders can cross.

After "sealing" the house, halt the flow of energy. You can do this by visualizing it stopping and by shaking your hand. Sense your protective-powered energy resting within the walls. A secure, safe feeling should flood through you as you stand within your now guarded home.

Yes, you've done this with your mind, but also with power. Energy is real, and your ability to manipulate energy determines the effectiveness of your circles and rituals.

Work with feeling and directing the power daily. Make this a sort of magical play until you reach the point where you won't have to stop and think, "Can I do it? Can I raise the power?"

You'll know you can.

12

Self-Dedication

If you wish to walk the Wiccan path, you may desire to dedicate yourself to the Goddess and God. This self-dedication is simply a formal ritual marking your conscious decision to embark on a new way of life—for that is the essence of Wicca.

At first I hesitated including a ritual of this sort here, feeling that the best dedicatory rituals were self-created. I've read and heard numerous stories of women and men who, drawn to Wicca but lacking access of covens or books, lit a candle, drank a little wine and told the Gods of their intentions. That is perhaps the best sort of self-dedication ritual: simple and from the heart.

However, many feel more comfortable with formal rituals, so I'm including one at the end of this chapter. It is far different from most other such rites that have appeared in print, for it is an outdoor ritual that concentrates on contacting the energies of the Goddess and God.

This ritual is open to all who wish to use it. However, before even considering dedicating yourself to the deities, be certain of your intentions for so doing, and that you have studied Wicca to the point where you know it is indeed the right way for you.

This means continued study. Read every book you can find on Wicca—the good ones as well as the bad. Subscribe to Wiccan and Pagan publications. Familiarize yourself with Wicca as far as you can. Though some authors feel that their tradition is the only *true* one, don't let this stop you from reading their works. Similarly, don't accept eveything you read simply because it appears in print.

In addition to reading, study nature. As you walk along the street, watch the birds flitting overhead, or bend down to gaze at an ant colony the way a mystic gazes into a crystal sphere. Celebrate the seasons and the phases of the Moon with ritual.

You may also wish to fill your soul with music. If so, order by mail some of the Wiccan music tapes now available. (See Appendix I/ Occult Suppliers.) If this is impossible, spend time each day listening to the *music of nature*—go to a place where wind blows through leaves or around tree trunks. Listen to water bubbling over stones or pounding a rocky coastline. Pinpoint your hearing to the meow of a lonely cat heralding the dawn. Create your own music too, if you are so talented.

Let your emotions be touched; whether by flute, recorder and drum, or bird, river and wind. Your decision to center Wicca shouldn't be based solely on either your intellect or emotions; it should be a smooth product of both.

This done, stay up late a few nights or rise with the dawn. Alone, write down (even in the most broken sentences) what you hope to gain from Wicca. This may include spiritual fulfillment, deeper relationships with the Goddess and God, insight into your place in the world, the power to bring order into your existence, the ability to attune with the seasons and the Earth, and so on.

Be specific, be ruthless, be complete. If you're not satisfied with this list, if it doesn't feel truthful, start over again. No one need ever see it. Copy down the final list in your mirror book, burn all other drafts, and be done with it.

Once this list has been fashioned, spend the next evening or morning creating a new one. On this, record what you feel you can *give* to Wicca.

This may surprise you, but every religion is the sum of its adherents. Unlike most orthodox religions, Wicca doesn't want your money, so don't write down "ten percent of my monthly income." This isn't because Wicca views money as debased or non-spiritual, but because money has been so abused and misused by most established religions. Wiccans don't live off Wicca.

Since Wicca doesn't condone proselytizing, has no leading figure, temples or central organizations, you may begin to wonder what you can do for Wicca.

There is much you can give. Not only your time, energy, devotion and so on, but also more concrete things. Here are some suggestions:

Join a national Wiccan or Pagan group, such as the Pagan Spirit Alliance (through Circle—See Appendix I). This helps you socialize with others of like mind, even if only through the mail or on the phone. Attend one of the public Wiccan or Pagan gatherings held each year in various parts of the country.

Donate to an ecological organization, one striving to save our planet. Every day we poison the Earth, as if we could spoil our camp and move elsewhere. If we don't take action now, there won't be anywhere to move. Financial contributions to responsible organizations dedicated to fighting pollution, saving endangered species and bringing mindless development under control are examples of things you can give to Wicca.

The same goes for groups fighting to feed the hungry. Remember one fundamental idea—that which sustains life is sacred.

You may wish to start recycling. For nearly a decade I've saved old newspapers, glass bottles and aluminum cans from my trash. Since I live in a large city, there are numerous recycling centers nearby. Some centers pay, but the greatest rewards are not financial. They rest in the knowledge that we're helping to save the Earth's natural resources.

If there are no recycling centers near you, be more conscious of your trash. Avoid purchasing products in plastic containers. Favor white paper products over colored ones—the dyes add to the pollution in our streams and rivers. Restrict or eliminate the use of plastic bags, food wraps and other plastic products of the "use once, throw away" variety. These plastics don't break down (i.e., aren't biodegradeable), are expensive and may retain their same basic shapes for 20,000 years or more.

If you're reading this and asking yourself what this has to do with Wicca, set this book down and put it away. Or, re-read it.

Wicca consists—in part—of *reverence for nature* as a manifestation of the Goddess and God. One way to reverence the Earth is to care for Her.

Following these suggestions, discover other ways to show your devotion to Wicca. A hint: anything you do for the Earth, or for our fellow creatures on it, you do for Wicca.

The following self-dedication rite isn't designed to make you a

Wicca—that comes with time and devotion (and not through initiation ceremonies). It is, in a mystical sense, a step toward linking your personal energies with those of the goddess and God. It is a truly magical act which, if properly done, can change your life forever.

If you're hesitant, read this book again. You'll know when you're ready.

A Self-Dedication Rite

Prepare yourself by drawing a bath of warm water. Add a tablespoon or so of salt and a few drops of a scented oil such as sandalwood.

If you have no bath, use a shower. Fill a washcloth with salt, add a few drops of essential oil, and rub your body. If you're performing this ritual at the sea or a river, bathe there if you so desire.

As you bathe, prepare for the coming rite. Open your consciousness to higher levels of awareness. Deep breathe. Cleanse your mind as well as your body.

After bathing, dry and dress for the journey. Go to a place in the wild where you feel safe. It should be a comfortable spot where you won't be disturbed by others, an area where the powers of the Earth and the elements are evident. It may be a mountain top, a desert canyon or cave, perhaps a dense forest, a rocky outcropping over the sea, a quiet island in the center of a lake. Even a lonely part of a park or garden can be used. Draw on your imagination to find the place.

You need take nothing with you but a vial of richly scented oil. Sandalwood, frankincense, cinnamon or any other scent is fine. When you arrive at the place of dedication, remove your shoes and sit quietly for a few moments. Calm your heart if you've exerted yourself during your travel. Breathe deeply to return to normal, and keep your mind free of cluttered thoughts. Open yourself to the natural energies around you.

When you're calm, rise and pivot slowly on one foot, surveying the land around you. You're seeking the ideal spot. Don't try to find it; open your awareness to the place. When you've discovered it (and you'll know when), sit, kneel or lie flat on your back. Place the oil on the Earth beside you, Don't stand—contact the Earth.

Continue deep breathing. Feel the energies around you. Call the Goddess and God in any words you like, or use the following invocation. Memorize these words before the rite so that they'll spill effortlessly from you, or improvise:

O Mother Goddess,
O Father God,
Answers to all mysteries and yet mysteries unanswered;
In this place of power I open myself
to Your Essence.
In this place and in this time I am changed;
From henceforth I walk the Wiccan path.
I dedicate myself to you, Mother Goddess and Father God.

(rest for moment, silent, still. Then continue:)

I breathe your energies into my body, commingling,
*   blending,*
mixing them with mine,
that I may see the divine in nature,
nature in the divine,
and divinity within myself and all else.
O Great Goddess,
O Great God,
Make me one with your essence
Make me one with your essence
Make me one with your essence.

You may feel bursting with power and energy, or calm and at peace. Your mind might be in a whirl. The Earth beneath you may throb and undulate with energy. Wild animals, attracted by the psychic occurrence, might grace you with their presence.

The Goddess

The God

Goddess and God Symbols

Whatever occurs, *know* that you have opened yourself and that the Goddess and God have heard you. You should feel different inside, at peace or simply powerful.

After the invocation, wet a finger with the oil and mark these two symbols somewhere on your body (see figure on previous page). It doesn't matter where; you can do this on your chest, forehead, arms, legs, anywhere. As you anoint, visualize these symbols sinking into your flesh, glowing as they enter your body and then dispersing into millions of tiny points of light.

The formal self-dedication is ended. Thank the Goddess and God for their attention. Sit and meditate before leaving the place of dedication.

Once home, celebrate in some special way.

13

Ritual Design

Section III of this book contains a complete system of Wiccan rituals. I included this so that those without access to a Book of Shadows would have one, complete and ready for practical application and study. This doesn't mean that these rituals are to be slavishly followed. This is not a tradition in the sense of something that has been handed down for years, but a viable example of a basic Wiccan Book of Shadows.

Since I want you to be free to write your own rituals, or to evolve them as the need arises, I decided that a chapter on ritual design was in order.

There's no great mystery concerning the structure of Wiccan rites, at least not anymore. Some say this is a good thing, this lessening of secrecy regarding Wicca. Others feel that it has stripped the religion of its romance. I understand this, but (as you well know by now) I also feel that Wicca should be available to all.

A chapter of this kind may seem harsh, focusing a rational, analytical light on spiritual matters. As my friend Barda once wrote to me, "Wicca is akin to a beautiful flower. If you rip off all its petals one by one to see how it's put together, you still have a flower but it's not quite as beautiful." I hope to avoid this here.

First off, while I'm going to give you an overall structure for composing your own rituals, this isn't carved in stone. Most of the following nine points are basic to Wiccan rituals, although many use only some of them. They're an excellent guide to creating your own.

These are the nine basic components of Wiccan ritual:
- Purification of Self
- Purification of Space
- Creating Sacred Space
- Invocation
- Ritual Observance (on Sabbats and Esbats)
- Energy Raising (during magic)
- Earthing the Power
- Thanking the Goddess and God
- Breaking the Circle

Purification of Self
This was covered in Chapter Six: Ritual and Preparation for Ritual. In essence, it consists of bathing, anointing your body with oil, meditation, deep breathing, and otherwise purifying your body, mind and soul and readying it for the coming rite.

This is truly a purification, an attempt to shrug off problems and thoughts of your everyday world. This is a time for calmness, for peace.

Although ritual bathing is common in Wicca, there are other methods of purifying the body. Stand in a rush of wind and visualize it carrying away negative thoughts and emotions.

Or use music: drumming softly for a few minutes is an excellent cleansing ritual (though your neighbors may have different views on it). Other instruments useful for purification include bells, gongs, sistrums (of the cleansing element of Water) and guitars, violins, harps and mandolins (instruments of the purifying element of Fire).

This emphasis on purification shouldn't be taken out of context. Our bodies aren't breeding grounds for astral entities. However, we're exposed to negativity every day—from scenes of carnage and destruction in the papers and on the news and from our own dark thoughts.

So these purifications aren't intended to chase away demons or devils; they simply free us of some of this negativity

While purifying yourself, remember to purify your thoughts as well. Prepare for the ritual. A Kahuna (an expert in the ancient Hawaiian system of magic, philosophy, religion and applied technology*) once

---

* Such as canoe building, navigation and medicinal herbalism.

told me that the moment you think about performing a ritual *you are doing so*. It is already taking place. Energies are moving, consciousness is shifting.

During your ritual purification, know that you've already lit the candles, laid the circle, and invoked the Goddess and God. Don't think of the coming ritual, for it is already in progress. This may seem a bit confusing, but it is an excellent tool to train your awareness.

Purification of Space

That is, of the area in which you'll do ritual. Outdoor ritual spaces rarely have to be purified. Indoor rituals, though, usually require it. Most living spaces accumulate "astral garbage," pockets of negativity and other eneriges which collect in human habitations. Since these energies can be disruptive, the area is ritually cleansed prior to actual workings.

There are two specifics here: indoor and outdoor rituals.

For in-home rites, if you're alone in the house, lock the door, take the phone off the hook, and close the curtains. You must be assured of absolute privacy and lack of interruptions during the ritual. If others are home, tell them you're not to be disturbed until further notice.

If this presents a problem and a mate or your family won't give you any time to yourself, work your rituals late at night or early in the morning when others are asleep.

Clean the floor physically. Sweep with a regular broom, vacuum or mop. Once clean it can be purified with the old Witch's tool, the magic broom.

You needn't actually touch the bristles to the floor. Do, however, brush briskly, visualizing the broom sweeping away negativity, ill and psychic clutter. You might visualize the broom shooting out sparks, or perhaps flaming with an intense blue or violet light that burns negativity to ashes. Visualize and know that the broom is magically cleansing the room. It will be so.

Another way to purify the ritual area is to scatter salt, either alone or mixed with a powdered herb or resin such as thyme, rosemary, frankincense, copal, sage, or dragon's blood.* Salt water is also used. The scattering action releases the energies resident within the salt and herbs and these, directed and magnified by your ritual intent and

---

* Before using any herb for magical purposes, hold it in your hands and, while visualizing, infuse it with your programmed, personal power. This increases its effectiveness.

visualization, drive away the disturbing energies. *Do this with power.* Or, play a musical instrument to the four quarters while walking clockwise around the area. In general, ascending scales purify. You might also chant, especially sounds which you feel set up protective and purifying energies. You can discover these through experimentation and heightened psychic awareness.

You can also simply burn an herb with proven "clearing" qualities as an incense, such as frankincense, myrrh, sage, thyme or rosemary, alone or in combination. Fumigate the ritual space with the smoke and visualize it driving away negativity.

Outdoor rituals require a minimum of cleansing. Most of the natural environment is far less psychically polluted than are our homes and other buildings. A traditional light sweeping with the magic broom (in this case, to actually brush away fallen leaves or pebbles *as well as* negativity), backed up with your visualization, will suffice. Sprinkling pure water is also fine but, since salt can be harmful to plants, it's best not to use it outdoors.

Creating Sacred Space

This section consists of arranging the altar (if it isn't a permanent one) and forming the magic circle. In Chapter Seven: The Magic Circle and the Altar, I discussed these topics at length, and so will limit my comments here to a few.

Though many Wiccans place their altars in the center of the area, and indeed in the center of the future magic circle, others do not. Some place it in one of the "corners " of the circle, next to its edge, usually in the North or East. This, they say, makes it easier to move around the circle. I find it to be exactly the opposite. Additionally, it restricts your possible methods of forming the circle.

It doesn't matter which you use, so try both and find out which works the best.

I use two altars. One's permanent, the other erected only for rituals. I always place the altar in the center of the circle, facing North, if only because this is familiar to me. Besides, if I put it at the northern edge of the circle I'd probably kick it over.

Now to the circle, or "sphere of power." You'll find one form of circle casting in *The Standing Stones Book of Shadows.* There are many other types, and indeed that particular form can't be used in every situation. One of these variants may be more to your liking (or better suited to your ritual space).

The first is more heavily dependent upon your visualization and magical abilities than others, for it uses no tools but your mind. To help your visualization, place a purple cord or some other object(s) on the ground to mark the circle's circumference. Stand before the altar, or in the center of the circle (during outdoor rituals you might not have an altar). Face East or the preferred direction. Build the power within you. When it has reached a fine pitch (you'll know with practice), hold your projective hand palm down, waist level. Point your fingers toward the edge of the future circle.

See and *feel* the energy flowing out from your fingertips in a stream of vibrating purplish-blue light. Slowly walk the circle, clockwise. Push the power out and form it with your visualization into a circling band of glowing magical light, the exact width of your circle (usually nine feet or less). This circle should hang around you and the altar.

When this band of light is swirling in the air, stretch it with your visualization. See it expanding and increasing in size. Form it into a dome of energy surrounding the ritual area. It should touch the Earth precisely aligned with your cord ring, if any. Now extend this energy down into the Earth until it forms a complete sphere as you stand in its center.

The circle should be a living, glowing reality. Feel its energy. Sense the edge of the circle. Sense the difference in vibration within and without it. Contrary to popular Wiccan teachings, pushing your hand into or walking through a magic sphere will cause no astral damage, any more than will walking through a protective power shield set up around your home. After all, most magic circles are so designed that if you stand near the circle's edge, your head and half your torso extend outside it. Walking through the circle, at most, will give you a jolt of energy. It will also dissipate it. If this happens, simply form it again.

When the circle seems complete and solid around you, break off the flow of energy from your projective hand by turning your palm downward and pulling it back to your body. Shut off the flow. Shake your hand if necessary to break it.

Next, you may wish to invoke the rulers of the four quarters of the circle. There are varied Wiccan teachings and ideas regarding these four rulers. Some link them with the elements; thus the "spirit" or ruler of the East is related to Air; the South, to Fire; the West, to Water; the North, to Earth.

Then again, some Wiccans don't see them as necessarily elemental in nature, but simply as anciently placed guardians or watchers of the four directions, perhaps created by the goddesses and gods of earlier times.

Still other Wiccans view them as the Mighty Ones, former humans who have spiraled up the incarnational path until they've reached perfection. This allows them to "dwell with the Goddess and God." These Mighty Ones are mythologically linked to the four directions.

Perhaps it's best to get in touch with these energies and discover them for yourself. No matter how you view these rulers, open yourself to them during invocation. Don't just say the words or visualize the colors during the circle casting; invite them to be present. Stretch out with your awareness. *Know* whether they've arrived or not.

Too many Wiccans say the words but don't check their effectiveness. The words are the least important part of a Wiccan ritual, save for their use in promoting ritual consciousness.

Words don't have to be used to invoke the rulers, but they're tools which train the attention, focus our awareness and stir up the emotions—when properly stated. You can use the invocations in the circle casting section of the Book or write your own.

To leave the circle during a ritual, cut a doorway (see Section III). This preserves the flow of energy around the circle save for a small section which you clear. Through this you can pass to the outside world without unduly disturbing the rest of the circle. Just remember to close it after returning.

Another, simpler form of circle construction uses physical activity to raise power, and is easier to do if you're not quite fluent with energy raising. Stand facing North at the edge of the future circle. Turn to the right and walk slowly, marking out the circle's edge with your feet.*

As you continue your ritual tread, you may wish to chant Goddess or God names, or perhaps both. You might think of Their presence or simply shift your awareness to the energy that your body is generating. If you've placed the altar to one side of the circle, move a few feet inward as you pass by it.

Continue to move clockwise, but gently increase your pace. The energy will slide off your body and, picked up by your momentum, will be carried around with you in your circular path.

---

* In this hemisphere, most Wiccans move clockwise within the circle, except during some banishing rituals. In Australia and in other parts of the southern hemisphere, circles may be cast counter-clockwise, as this is the apparent direction in which the Sun moves.

Move faster. Feel the energy flowing within you. You may feel a sensation such as you feel when walking in water—the energy will move with you as you release it. Sense your personal power creating a sphere of energy around the altar. When this is firmly established, invoke the four quarters and the rites can begin.

Both of the above methods are ideal for rituals wherein magic will take place, but for purely religious rites such constructions of psychic energy are not strictly necessary. Though the circle is thought of as being "between the worlds," and a meeting place with the Goddess and God, we needn't create such psychic temples to commune with the deities of nature, nor do They appear when called like pets. Wiccan ritual is used to expand our awareness of Them, not the other way around.

Therefore, complex circle castings (such as the one in Section III) aren't always necessary, especially during outdoor rites where such circles are usually impossible to construct. Fortunately, there are simpler forms which can be used.

An outdoor circle casting may entail nothing more than placing a stick of burning incense at each of the quarters. Start in the North and move clockwise around the circle. Invoke the quarters.

A circle can also be traced in the sand or dirt with a finger, a wand, or the white-handled knife. This is ideal for sea and forest rituals.

Or, you may wish to place objects to mark out the circle's perimeter. Vegetation is particularly appropriate: flowers for spring, pine and holly for winter (see The Herbal Grimoire in *The Standing Stones Book of Shadows* for other suggestions). A ring of small river-polished stones or quartz crystals are other possibilities.

Some Wiccans pour a small unbroken circle of some substance to define the ritual space. Powdered herbs, flour (as was used in ancient Middle Eastern rituals as well as in contemporary Voodoo rites), crushed colored minerals, sand or salt are poured out while moving clockwise. As mentioned above, a cord can also be laid in a ring.

For more information regarding circle construction, see *The Standing Stones Book of Shadows.*

Invocation

In some ways this is the heart of all Wiccan ritual, and indeed is the only necessary part. Wiccan rites are attunements with the powers that are the Goddess and God; all else is pageantry.*

---

* Though it should, of course, promote ritual consciousness. Outdoor rituals rarely need as much invocation because the Wiccans are already surrounded by natural manifestations of the deities.

The word "invocation" shouldn't be taken too literally. This usually refers to a spoken prayer or verse, but may also consist of music, dance, gestures and song.

There are several invocations to the Goddess and God in *The Standing Stones Book of Shadows*. Feel free to use them when designing your own rituals, but remember that impromptu invocations are often more effective than the most ancient prayers.

If you do write up your own invocations, you may wish to incorporate a rhyme. Centuries of magical tradition attest to the value of rhyme. It certainly makes invocations that much easier to memorize.

Rhyme also contacts the unconscious or psychic mind. It drowses our societally, materially and intellectually-based minds and lets us slip into ritual consciousness.

When actually invoking, don't curse if you forget a word, mispronounce something or entirely lose your train of thought. This is quite natural and is usually a manifestation of fatigue, stress or a desire to be word perfect in the circle.

Invocation requires a willingness to open yourself to the Goddess and God. It needn't be a pristine performance. As most rituals begin with invocation, this is in a sense the moment of truth. If the invocation isn't sincere it won't contact the Goddess and God within, and the ritual that follows will be nothing more than form.

Practice invoking the Goddess and God, not only in ritual but daily throughout your life. Remember: Wiccan practice isn't limited to Full Moons or Sabbats—it is a round-the-clock way of life.

In a more metaphysical sense, invocation is a dual-level act. It not only invokes the Goddess and God, it also awakens us (shifts our awareness) to that part of us which is divine—our inviolable, intransmutable essence: our link with the Old Ones.

In other words, when you invoke do so not only to higher forces but also to the deities that dwell within, to that spark of divine energy that exists inside all living creatures.

The powers behind all deities are one. They are resident within all humans. This explains why all religions merge at their cores, and why they work for their respective adherents. If only one correct way of approaching Deity were possible, there would be one religious ideal. This will never happen.

The concept of the Goddess and God dwelling within may seem egotistical (we're all divine!) but only from an unbalanced viewpoint. Yes, when some people grasp this idea they start acting as if they were indeed divine. Seeing the divinity within all other humans helps bring this idea into balance.

While we are, in a sense, immortal (our souls certainly are), we are not *the* Immortal Ones. We're not the universal, timeless, transcendent beings that are revered in all religions. Call the Goddess and God with love and sincerity, and your rituals should be blessedly successful.

Ritual Observance

This usually follows the invocation, if the ritual is held on a Sabbat or Esbat. It may also be a rite of meditation, transition, thanksgiving or simply a few moments to commune. In such cases ritual observances may or may not be appropriate.

You needn't be glum, serious or stodgy while doing these rituals. Wiccans are serious about their religion, but that doesn't mean that the Deities are.*

Laughter has its ritual and magical functions. For example, truly laughing at a curse can destroy its effects. It sets up a powerful protective energy surrounding you through which no negative energies can penetrate. Laughter releases tremendous amounts of personal power.

So when you spill the salt, tip over a candle, fail to light the incense and forget the verse, laugh and start over. Too many newcomers to Wicca bring their ideas of stern, solemn religion with them into the magic circle, but these are alien to Wicca.

Leave those thoughts behind you. Wicca is a religion of peace and happiness and yes, even laughter. Wiccan ritual needs no pomposity unless it is simply desired.

Energy Raising

In practice, this is magic—the movement of natural energies to effect needed change. You can raise energy at most Wiccan rituals, though it is rarely thought to be mandatory. However, the Full Moons, solstices and equinoxes are classic times to perform magic, for there are extra Earth energies afoot that can be utilized to enhance the effectiveness of your magic.

This doesn't mean that Wiccan rituals are simply excuses to work magic. Though it is perfectly permissible to work magic on the eight

---

* Most Wiccans have favorite stories of circle mishaps. One of mine occurred when leading a ritual. I mispronounced the name of the elemental ruler of Earth ("Goob" rather than "Ghob"); the double-headed axe fell to the floor from the altar, and I smacked my hands into the chandelier that hung over the altar during power raising. It was a funny ritual.

Days of Power (indeed, it is traditional), many Wiccans don't, prefer-ring these to be times of attunement and celebration rather than of magic.

However, one of the major differences between Wicca and most other religions is its acceptance of magic, not just in the hands of specialized priests who work miracles while others watch, but to all who practice its rituals. Therefore, magic can be worked with a clear con-science at most Wiccan rituals after invocation and ritual observance.

In magic, ensure that your need is real, that you're emotionally involved in this need, and that you know that your magic will work. Some of the simplest spells are the most effective. After all these years I often prefer to use colored candles, oils and herbs as focal points of energy. There are countless ways to practice magic; find one that's right for you (see Bibliography for related books).

As I've written elsewhere, magic is magic. It isn't religious in the usual sense of the word. However, in Wicca, magic is usually worked while invoking the Goddess and God, asking for Their presence and that They lend Their strength to the task. It is this that makes Wiccan magic religious.

The magic circle (or sphere) is formed to retain power during energy raising. When building up power for a spell in one of the old ways (dance, endless chanting, visualization and so on), Wiccans attempt to hold it inside their bodies until it has reached its peak. At this time it is released and sent toward its goal. It is difficult to retain all of this power—especially during dance—and so the circle does this job. Once you've released the power, however, the circle in no way impedes the flow of energy to its destination.

Circles aren't necessary for the practice of magic, though if you invoke the Goddess and God to help you, the presence of the circle ensures that the power you receive will be properly retained until you decide it's time to send it forth.

Ask the Goddess and God to assist you, to grant your request or to amplify your own powers, no matter what type of magic you per-form in the circle.* In doing so you're expanding your awareness of the deities within, opening a channel through which divine energy can flow. Thank the Goddess and God after the finished ritual in words, by lighting a candle, or leaving an offering of food or drink on an offering plate or in the ground.

---

* As long as it is positive.

Few words should be required here regarding "evil" magic. Needless to say, any magic that is designed to harm or control another living being—even if you feel that it's in their best interest—is negative magic. This leaves you open to receiving negativity back. Negative magic isn't Wiccan magic.

Once you've finished your magical working, pause for a few moments. Gaze at the Goddess and God candles or at their images on the altar. You might also look at the rising incense smoke or bowl of fresh flowers. Think of the deities and of your relationship with them, as well as your place in the universe. Put all thoughts of the ritual out of your mind entirely by shifting your awareness away from it.

You'll probably be drained of energy if you did indeed release power, so sink back down and relax for a few moments. This is a reflective moment. It smoothly flows into the next ritual step.

Earthing the Power

Once you've sent energy, residual power usually rushes around within you. Some traces may still exist inside the circle. This should be *earthed*, or reprogrammed to fit smoothly back within your normal energy scheme. Even if you've performed no magic, an earthing is desirable before closing down the ritual, for this step, especially when it consists of a meal, has sacred aspects as well.

Some Wiccans call this Cakes and Wine or Cakes and Ale. In *The Standing Stones Book of Shadows* I've termed it the Simple Feast. It's all the same thing—a ritual ingestion of food and drink to ease us back from ecstasy.

Eating kicks your body into a different mode. Since food is a product of the Earth, it gently returns our awareness to the physical reality. Food is a manifestation of divine energy. Eating is a form of true communion.

This meal can be a light snack. Cookies and milk, juice and bread, cheese and wine, perhaps the traditional crescent-shaped cakes (actually cookies) and wine (see Recipes—Food section in *The Standing Stones Book of Shadows*) are all fine. The food is often blessed prior to eating; you'll find sample rituals for this in the Book.

Prior to eating, make a small offering to the Goddess and God by scattering cake crumbs and pouring a few drops of liquid onto the ground. If indoors, place these things in a special libation bowl. Bury its contents in the ground outside as soon as possible after the ritual. There are other methods of earthing yourself and the power.

Tasting a bit of salt and scattering it around the circle works. You might also try visualization. See the excess energy as a kind of purplish mist hanging in the circle and within yourself. Hold up a tool of some kind (the magic knife, a rock, the pentacle, or something else) and visualize it absorbing the extra energy. (Try holding this with your receptive hand as well.) When the circle is cleared and you feel back to normal, put down the tool. When doing this with your magic knife (athame), the extra energy can later be used for spells and for forming the magic circle. There are many possibilities; some Wiccans store candles beneath the altar and send the excess energy into them.

Thanking the Gods

The next phase of Wiccan ritual consists of thanking the Goddess and God for Their presence and attendance at your circle. This can be done in specific ways, with gestures or chants or music, or can be improvised on the spot.

Some Wiccans think of this as dismissing the deities. I shudder at the very notion. Imagine some puny little Wiccan telling the Goddess and God that They can leave!*

Thank Them for Their attention and ask that They come again. That's it.

Breaking the Circle

The method in which you return an area or room to its normal state depends on your method of circle casting. If you use the one in *The Standing Stones Book of Shadows*, close with the accompanying ritual. In this section we'll look at the methods to disperse the circles described in "Creating Sacred Space" above.

The first one, in which the circle is visualized as swirling around you and the altar, is the easiest. Thank the rulers for attending the rite. Stand before the altar again. Hold out your receptive hand (it will be the right if you're left-handed). Visualize yourself absorbing the energy which created the circle. *Feel* the energy sinking back into your palm and, thusly, into your body.

You can also use the magical knife to "cut" the circle. Visualize its power surging back into the blade and handle.

The next method is one to which some Wiccans take offense, but it is based on orthodox Wiccan teachings. If you created your circle by

---

* Besides, They never leave. They exist within ourselves and inside all of nature.

treading clockwise around the altar, stand in the North and move slowly to the West, the South and the East, ending back in the North again. As you move draw the energy from the circle within yourself.* For other types of circles, "break" or disperse them in some way. If you laid stones in a ring around the altar, take them up. Remove flowers or greens if they mark the circle's perimeter and disperse or sweep up rings of herbs, salt or flour.

Whatever method you use, thank the rulers of the four quarters for their presence and ask that they watch over future rites.

When the circle is gone, put away the ritual tools. If you've used salt and water (as in the circle consecration in *The Standing Stones Book of Shadows*), save the excess salt for future use, but pour the water onto the bare Earth. Offerings in the libation bowl should be buried along with the incense ashes, though these last are sometimes saved for future spells and rites.

It isn't necessary to immediately take down the altar. Indeed, it can be left for the rest of the night or day. When you do begin putting the tools away, it's good symbolism to wait to quench the candles until last. Use a snuffer, your fingers or your white-handled knife blade (clean off the wax and soot after each use). Start with the quarter candles and any others that you might have used, then put out the God taper and finally the Goddess candle.

Your rite has ended.

---

* Those south of the equator would perform this and all circle dispersions in exactly the opposite direction. Some Wiccans believe that any counter-clockwise (widdershins) movement is negative, but it is used here for a sound reason and, indeed, this is the way the circle is broken in at least one Wiccan tradition that I know of. If you feel uncomfortable in treading widdershins, simply walk clockwise and take the energy back inside you.

SECTION III:

THE STANDING STONES
BOOK OF SHADOWS

Introduction

This is a complete Book of Shadows, ready for use. I wrote much of it several years ago for students who desired to practice Wicca but couldn't gain entrance to a coven. There is certainly nothing secret here, nor am I borrowing from other traditions except in the most general ways.

I'm limiting my remarks, notes and comments on this Book of Shadows. If you have questions while reading these rituals, or while working them, settle them as best you can. Re-read Chapter Thirteen or write to me at the publisher's address and I'll try to answer. Unfamiliar words and terms can be checked in the glossary.

Please remember that this is simply *one* Book of Shadows. There are countless others, each with both strong and weak points. Some of these have been printed, in part or in their entirety (see Bibliography).

This is not, I repeat, *not* sacred writ, nor does it consist of revealed writings. I've written it in a somewhat romantic, baroque style, hoping that this will spark your imagination. Remember, the Book of Shadows isn't changeless. Feel free to alter anything for any reason, or use this Book of Shadows as a pattern to construct your own. It isn't my intention to begin a new tradition of Wicca.

The rites are constructed for individuals. Group workings will require some alterations.

Why the "standing stones?" I've long been fascinated by the megalithic sites of Britain and Europe. Stone circles and menhirs capture my imagination, and I wonder what rites their ancient creators performed there.*

I centered this system's circle casting around the erection of a psychic circle of stones, as well as a physical one. If you feel uncomfortable with this idea, simply change the ritual! Never be afraid to do this—you won't disappear into a poof of dust. No angry deities will descend unless you use rites calling for blood or death or living sacrifices, or perform magic that harms or twists others to your will.

While working these or any other rituals, remember to visualize,

---

* These weren't the Druids; they arrived over a thousand years later and had nothing to do with the construction of such sites as Stonehenge. Sorry!

sense and move power. Feel the presence of the Goddess and God. If you don't, all rituals are only form.

It is my hope that this Book of Shadows captures your imagination and guides you on the Wiccan path.

For those who are interested, the way is open.

Blessed Be!

The Standing Stones
Book of Shadows

WORDS TO THE WISE ....

O daughters and sons of the Earth, adore the Goddess and God and be blessed with the fullness of life.

Know that They have brought you to these writings, for herein lie our ways of Wicca, to serve and fulfill the keepers of wisdom, the tenders of the sacred flame of knowledge. Run the rites with love and joy, and the Goddess and God will bless you with all that you need. But those who practice dark magics shall know Their greatest wrath.

Remember that you are of the Wicca. No more do you trod the ways of doubt. You walk the path of light, ever climbing from shadow to shadow to the highest realm of existence. But though we're the bearers of truths, others do not wish to share our knowledge, so we run our rites beneath moon filled skies enwrapped in shadows. But we are happy.

Live fully, for that is the purpose of life. Refrain not from earthly existence. From it we grow to learn and understand, until such time that we are reborn to learn more, repeating this cycle 'till we have spiralled up the path of perfection and can finally call the Goddess and God our kin.

Walk the fields and forests; be refreshed by the cool winds and the touch of a nodding flower. The Moon and Sun sing in the ancient wild places: The deserted seashore, the stark desert, the roaring waterfall. We are of the Earth and should revere Her, so do Her honor.

Celebrate the rites on the appropriate days and seasons, and call upon the Goddess and God when the time is meet, but use the Power only when necessary, never for frivolous ends. Know that using the Power for harm is a perversion of Life itself.

But for those who love and magnify love, the richness of life shall be your reward. Nature will celebrate.

So love the Goddess and God, and harm none!

THE NATURE OF OUR WAY

• As often as possible, hold the rites in forests, by the seashore, on deserted mountaintops or near tranquil lakes. If this is impossible, a garden or some chamber shall suffice, if it is readied with fumes or flowers.

• Seek out wisdom in books, rare manuscripts and cryptic poems if you will, but seek it out also in simple stones and fragile herbs and in the cries of wild birds. Listen to the whisperings of the wind and the roar of water if you would discover magic, for it is here that the old secrets are preserved.

• Books contain words; trees contain energies and wisdom books ne'er dreamt of.

• Ever remember that the Old Ways are constantly revealing themselves. Therefore be as the river willow that bends and sways with the wind. That which remains changeless shall outlive its spirit, but that which evolves and grows will shine for centuries.

• There can be no monopoly on wisdom. Therefore share what you will of our ways with others who seek them, but hide mystic lore from the eyes of those who would destroy, for to do otherwise increases their destruction.

• Mock not the rituals or spells of another, for who can say yours are greater in power or wisdom?

• Ensure that your actions are honorable, for all that you do shall return to you three-fold, good or bane.

• Be wary of one who would dominate you, who would control and manipulate your workings and reverences. True reverence for

the Goddess and God occurs within. Look with suspicion on any who would twist worship from you for their own gain and glory, but welcome those priestesses and priests who are suffused with love.
• Honor all living things, for we are of the bird, the fish, the bee. Destroy not life save it be to preserve your own.
• And this is the nature of our way.

BEFORE TIME WAS

Before time was, there was The One; The One was all, and all was The One.

And the vast expanse known as the universe was The One, all-wise, all-pervading, all-powerful, eternally changing.

And space moved. The One molded energy into twin forms, equal but opposite, fashioning the Goddess and God from The One and of The One.

The Goddess and God stretched and gave thanks to The One, but darkness surrounded them. They were alone, solitary save for The One.

So They formed energy into gasses and gasses into suns and planets and moons; They sprinkled the universe with whirling globes and so all was given shape by the hands of the Goddess and God.

Light arose and the sky was illuminated by a billion suns. And the Goddess and God, satisfied by their works, rejoiced and loved, and were one.

From their union sprang the seeds of all life, and of the human race, so that we might achieve incarnation upon the Earth.

The Goddess chose the Moon as Her symbol, and the God the Sun as His symbol, to remind the inhabitants of Earth of their fashioners.

All are born, live, die and are reborn beneath the Sun and Moon; all things come to pass thereunder, and all occurs with the blessings of The One, as has been the way of existence before time was.

SONG OF THE GODDESS
(based on an invocation by Morgan*)

I am the Great Mother, worshipped by all creation and existent prior to their consciousness. I am the primal female force, boundless and eternal.

I am the chaste Goddess of the Moon, the Lady of all magic. The winds and moving leaves sing my name. I wear the crescent Moon upon my brow and my feet rest among the starry heavens. I am mysteries yet unsolved, a path newly set upon. I am a field untouched by the plow. Rejoice in me and know the fullness of youth.

I am the blessed Mother, the gracious Lady of the harvest. I am clothed with the deep, cool wonder of the Earth and the gold of the fields heavy with grain. By me the tides of the Earth are ruled; all things come to fruition according to my season. I am refuge and healing. I am the life-giving Mother, wondrously fertile.

Worship me as the Crone, tender of the unbroken cycle of death and rebirth. I am the wheel, the shadow of the Moon. I rule the tides of women and men and give release and renewal to weary souls. Though the darkness of death is my domain, the joy of birth is my gift.

I am the Goddess of the Moon, the Earth, the Seas. My names and strengths are manifold. I pour forth magic and power, peace and wisdom. I am the eternal Maiden, Mother of all, and Crone of darkness, and I send you blessings of limitless love.

CALL OF THE GOD

I am the radiant King of the Heavens, flooding the Earth with warmth and encouraging the hidden seed of creation to burst forth into manifestation. I lift my shining spear to light the lives of all beings

---

* My first teacher and priestess. She wrote this a decade or so ago. This and the following "Call of the God" aren't necessarily meant to be spoken in ritual. They can be read for devotional purposes, meditated upon to learn more of the Goddess and God or used in ritual by inserting the words "She" and "He" and making other small changes to agree with these alterations.

and daily pour forth my gold upon the Earth, putting to flight the powers of darkness.

I am the master of the beasts wild and free. I run with the swift stag and soar as a sacred falcon against the shimmering sky. The ancient woods and wild places emanate my powers, and the birds of the air sing of my sanctity.

I am also the last harvest, offering up grain and fruits beneath the sickle of time so that all may be nourished. For without planting there can be no harvest; without winter, no spring.

Worship me as the thousand-named Sun of creation, the spirit of the horned stag in the wild, the endless harvest. See in the yearly cycle of festivals my birth, death and rebirth—and know that such is the destiny of all creation.

I am the spark of life, the radiant Sun, the giver of peace and rest, and I send my rays of blessings to warm the hearts and strengthen the minds of all.

THE CIRCLE OF STONES

The Circle of stones is used during indoor rituals, for energy raising, meditation and so on.

First cleanse the area with the ritual broom.

For this circle you will need four large, flat stones. If you have none, candles can be used to mark the four cardinal points of the circle. White or purple candles can be used, as can colors related to each direction—green for the North, yellow for East, red for South and blue for West.

Place the first stone (or candle) to the North, to represent the Spirit of the North Stone. In ritual when you invoke the Spirits of the Stones you're actually invoking all that resides in that particular direction, including the elemental energies.

After setting the North Stone (or candle), place the East, South and West stones. They should mark out a rough square, nearly encompassing the working area. This square represents the physical plane on which we exist—the Earth.

Now take a long purple or white cord* and lay it out in a circle, using the four stones or candles to guide you. It takes a bit of practice to smoothly do this. The cord should be placed so that the stones remain *inside* the circle. Now you have a square and a circle, the circle representing the spiritual reality. As such, this is a squared circle; the place of interpenetration of the physical and spiritual realms.

The size of the circle can be anything from 5 to 20 feet depending on the room and your desires.

Next, set up the altar. The following tools are recommended:

- A Goddess symbol (candle, holed stone, statue)
- A God symbol (candle, horn, acorn, statue)
- Magic knife (athame)
- Wand
- Censer
- Pentacle
- A bowl of water (spring, rain or tap)
- A bowl of salt (it can also be placed on the pentacle)
- Incense
- Flowers and greens
- One red candle in holder (if not using point candles)
- Any other tools or materials required for the ritual, spell or magical working

Set up the altar according to the plan shown here or according to your own design. Also be sure to have plenty of matches, as well as a small heat-proof container in which to place them when used. A charcoal block is also necessary to burn the incense.

Light the candles. Set the incense smoking. Lift the knife and touch its blade to the water, saying:

I consecrate and cleanse this water
that it may be purified and fit to
dwell within the sacred Circle of Stones.
In the name of the Mother Goddess and the Father God†
I consecrate this water.

---

* Fashioned, perhaps, of braided yarn.

† If you are attuning with a specific Goddess and God, substitute Their names here.

Goddess Symbol or Candle	**Censer**	**God Symbol or Candle**
Bowl of Water	**Red Candle**	**Bowl of Salt**
Cup	**Pentacle**	**Incense**
Crystal	**Cauldron, or Spell Materials**	**Knife/Wand**
Bell		**Bolline**

Suggested Altar Layout

As you do this, visualize your knife blasting away all negativity from the water.

The salt is next touched with the point of the knife while saying:

I bless this salt that it may be fit
to dwell within the sacred Circle of Stones.
In the name of the Mother Goddess and the Father God,
I bless this salt.

Now stand facing North, at the edge of the cord-marked circle. Hold your magic knife point outward at waist level. Walk slowly around the circle's perimeter clockwise, your feet just inside the cord, charging it with your words and energy. Create the circle—through your visualization—with the power flowing out from your knife's blade. As you walk, stretch the energy out until it forms a complete sphere around the working area, half above the ground, half below. As you do this say:

> Here is the boundary of the Circle of Stones.
> Naught but love shall enter in,
> Naught but love shall emerge from within.
> Charge this by Your powers, Old Ones!

When you have arrived back at the North, place the magic knife on the altar. Take up the salt and sprinkle it around the circle, beginning and ending in the North, and moving clockwise. Next, carry the smoking censer around the circle, then the Southern point candle or the lit red candle from the altar, and finally sprinkle water around the circle. Do more than carrying and walking; sense the substances purifying the circle. The Circle of Stones is now sealed.

Hold aloft the wand at the North, at the edge of the circle, and say:

> O Spirit of the North Stone,
> Ancient One of the Earth,
> I call You to attend this circle.
> Charge this by Your powers, Old Ones!

As you say this, visualize a greenish mist rising and writhing in the Northern quarter, over the stone. This is the elemental energy of Earth. When the Spirit is present, lower the wand, move to the East, raise it again and say:

> O Spirit of the East Stone,
> Ancient One of Air,
> I call You to attend this circle.
> Charge this by Your powers, Old Ones!

Visualize the yellowish mist of Air energy. Lower the wand, move to the South and repeat the following with your upraised wand, visualizing a crimson Fire mist:

O Spirit of the South Stone,
Ancient One of Fire,
I call You to attend this circle.
Charge this by Your powers, Old Ones!

Finally, to the West, say with wand held aloft:

O Spirit of the West Stone,
Ancient One of Water,
I call You to attend this circle.
Charge this by Your powers, Old Ones!

Visualize the bluish mist, the essence of Water.

The circle breathes and lives around you. The Spirits of the Stones are present. Feel the energies. Visualize the circle glowing and growing in power. Stand still, sensing for a moment.

The Circle of stones is complete. The Goddess and God may be called, and magic wrought.

CUTTING A DOORWAY

At times you may have to leave the circle. This is fine, of course, but as previously mentioned, passing through the circle dissipates it. To prevent this from occurring it's traditional to cut a doorway.

To do this, face Northeast. Hold your magic knife point downward near the ground. *See* and *sense* the circle before you. Pierce its wall of energy with the athame and trace an archway, tall enough to walk through, moving counter-clockwise along the circle for about three feet. Move the point of the magic knife up at the arch's center and down the other side until it is near the ground.

As you're doing this, visualize that area of the circle's energy being sucked back into the athame. This creates a void, allowing passage in and out of the circle. Pull the magic knife out of the circle's wall. You're free to walk outside.

Once back inside, close the door by placing the athame at the lower North-Eastern* point of the archway. With your knife trace the circle's perimeter clockwise, as if redrawing that portion of the Circle of Stones, again visualizing blue or purple energy flaring out from the blade and converging with the rest of the circle. It is done.

RELEASING THE CIRCLE

Once the rite is ended, face North, hold aloft the wand and say:

Farewell, Spirit of the North Stone.
I give thanks for your presence here.
Go in power.

Repeat this same formula to the East, South and West, substituting the proper direction in the words. Then return to the North and hold the wand aloft for a few moments.

Lay the wand on the altar. Take up the athame. Standing in the North, pierce the circle's wall with the blade at waist level. Move clockwise around the circle, visualizing its power being sucked back into the knife. Literally *pull* it back into the blade and handle. Sense the circle dissolving, shrinking; the outside world slowly regaining its dominance in the area.

When you arrive at the North again, the circle is no more.

---

* The traditional direction. In some covens, members enter and withdraw from the circle from this point.

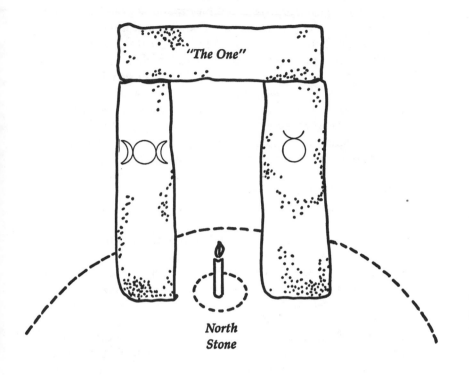

North Trilithon Visualization

VISUALIZATIONS FOR THE CIRCLE OF STONES

If you wish, you can back up the circle casting with the following visualizations as you form the circle itself:

Prepare as usual. Approach the North and set the North Stone (or the candle) on the ground. Then, visualize a stone slab standing upright two feet to the left of and behind the North Stone. Visualize this as being bluish-grey, two feet wide, two feet thick and six feet tall. This stone represents the Goddess (see figure on previous page).

When the stone is really there—in your visualization—create another stone of the same size and color two feet to the right of the North Stone. This represents the God.

Now visualize a capstone resting on top of the two upright stones. It is about two feet by two feet by five feet. This represents The One before the Goddess and God, the source of all power and magic. The Northern Trilithon is now complete.

The stones form an archway, a symbol of and gateway to the realm of the element of Earth.

Firmly visualize this, then gaze through the arch formed by the stones. See the greenish haze of Earth energy.

Repeat the entire procedure to the East, South and West. Visualize the appropriate elemental color within each trilithon.

Now purify salt and water, cast the circle as usual, and carry around the salt, censer, candle and water.

As you approach each quarter to call its Spirit of the Stone, see the trilithon firmly in your mind. Visualize it in all its Pagan splendor. See the elemental hazes within them, boiling and writhing in unmanifestedness. Stretch out with your feelings; sense the arrival of the spirit of each stone, then go on to the next.

With practice this comes easily, but such visualizations are never necessary.

THE BLESSING CHANT

May the powers of The One,
the source of all creation;
all-pervasive, omnipotent, eternal;
may the Goddess,
the Lady of the Moon;
and the God,
Horned Hunter of the Sun;
may the powers of the Spirits of the Stones,
rulers of the elemental realms;
may the powers of the stars above and the Earth below,
*bless this place, and this time, and I who am with You.**

THE SIMPLE FEAST

Hold up a cup of wine or some other liquid between your hands to the sky, and say:

Gracious Goddess of Abundance,
Bless this wine and infuse it with Your love.
In Your names, Mother Goddess and Father God,
I bless this wine (or brew, juice, etc.).

Hold up a plate of cakes (bread, biscuits) with both hands to the sky and say:

Powerful God of the Harvest,
Bless these cakes and infuse them with Your love.
In Your names, Mother Goddess and Father God,
I bless these cakes (or this bread).†

---

* The Blessing Chant can be said at the beginning of any type of ritual as a general invocation. Separate invocations of the Goddess and God may follow.

† The Simple Feast is usually held at the end of the Sabbats and Esbats, It is a sedate version of the wild feasts once held during agricultural rituals in rural Europe. Many liquids other than wine can be used; see the recipes section.

CONSECRATION OF TOOLS

Light the candles. Set the incense smoking. Cast the Circle of Stones. Place the tool on the pentacle, or a plate of salt. Touch it with the point of the magic knife (or your projective hand) and say:

> I consecrate you, O knife of steel (or wand of wood, etc.) to cleanse and purify you to serve me within the Circle of Stones. In the names of the Mother Goddess and Father God, you are consecrated.

Send projective energy into the tool, cleansing it of all negativity and past associations. Now pick it up and sprinkle with salt, pass through the incense smoke, through the candle flame and sprinkle with water, calling upon the Spirits of the Stones to consecrate it.

Then hold the tool to the sky, saying:

> I charge you by the Old Ones: By the omnipotent Goddess and God: By the virtues of the Sun, Moon and Stars: By the powers of the Earth, Air, Fire and Water, that I shall obtain all that I desire through you. Charge this by your power, Old Ones!*

The tool should immediately be put to use to strengthen and bind the consecration. For example, the athame can be used to consecrate another tool; a wand to invoke the Goddess; the pentacle to act as a resting place for a tool during its consecration.

THE FULL MOON RITE

Perform this at night, in view of the Moon if possible. It is appropriate for crescents, white flowers, silver and other lunar symbols to be present on the altar for this ritual. The quartz crystal sphere can be placed on the altar as well. Or, if you prefer, use the cauldron (or a small white or silver bowl) filled with water. Place a piece of silver into the water.

---

* The words used in this consecration rite are based on one included in *The Key of Solomon* and are similar to those used in many Wiccan traditions.

Arrange the altar, light the candles and censer, and cast the Circle of Stones.

Stand before the altar and invoke the Goddess and God, with the Blessing Chant and/or any other invocations (see Prayers, Chants and Invocations in this Book of Shadows).

Now gaze at the Moon, if possible. Feel its energies sinking into your body. Feel its cool Goddess energy wash you with power and love.

Now say these or similar words:

Wondrous Lady of the Moon
You who greets the dusk with silvered kisses;
Mistress of the night and of all magics,
who rides the clouds in blackened skies
and spills light upon the cold Earth;
O Lunar Goddess,
Crescented-One,
Shadow maker and shadow breaker;
Revealer of mysteries past and present;
Puller of seas and ruler of women;
All-wise Lunar Mother,
I greet Your celestial jewel
at the waxing of its powers
With a rite in Your honor.
I pray by the Moon,
I pray by the Moon,
I pray by the Moon.

Continue chanting "I pray by the Moon" for as long as you will. Visualize the Goddess if you so desire, perhaps as a tall, robust woman wearing silver jewelry and white, rippling, draped clothing. A crescent Moon may rest upon Her brow, or She may toss a glowing silvery white orb in Her hands. She trods the starfield of eternal night in an eternal round with Her lover, the Sun God, spreading moonrays wherever She goes. Her eyes laugh, Her skin is white and translucent. She glows.

Now is the time for magic of all types, for the full of the Moon marks the height of its powers, and all positive spells cast then are powerful.

Full Moons are also excellent times for meditation, mirror magic and psychic workings, for such are often more successful within the circle. Crystal-scrying is particularly recommended; flood the crystal with moonlight prior to the ritual. If you have no crystal sphere, use the cauldron filled with water and the piece of silver. Gaze at the water (or at the Moon glinting on the silver) to awaken your psychic awareness.

Lunar liquids such as lemonade, milk or white wine can be consumed during the Simple Feast that follows. Crescent cakes are traditional as well.

Thank the Goddess and God and release the circle. It is done.

THE SEASONAL FESTIVALS

Yule
(*circa* December 21)

The altar is adorned with evergreens such as pine, rosemary, bay, juniper and cedar, and the same can be laid to mark the Circle of Stones. Dried leaves can also be placed on the altar.

The cauldron, resting on the altar on a heat-proof surface (or placed before it if too large), should be filled with ignitable spirit (alcohol), or a red candle can be placed within it. At outdoor rites, lay a fire within the cauldron to be lit during ritual.

Arrange the altar, light the candles and incense, and cast the Circle of Stones.

Recite the Blessing Chant.

Invoke the Goddess and God.*

Stand before the cauldron and gaze within it. Say these or similar words:

I sorrow not, though the world is wrapped in sleep.
I sorrow not, though the icy winds blast.
I sorrow not, though the snow falls hard and deep.
I sorrow not; this too shall soon be past.

Ignite the cauldron (or candle), using long matches or a taper. As the flame(s) leap up say:

I light this fire in Your honor, Mother Goddess.
You have created life from death; warmth from cold;
The Sun lives once again; the time of light is
waxing. Welcome, ever-returning God of the Sun!
Hail Mother of All!

---

* Using, once again, any of the invocations found in Prayers, Chants and Invocations, or your own words.

Circle the altar and cauldron slowly, clockwise, watching the flames. Say the following chant for some time:

The wheel turns; the power burns.

Meditate upon the Sun, on the hidden energies lying dormant in winter, not only in the Earth but within ourselves. Think of birth not as the start of life but as its continuance. Welcome the return of the God.

After a time cease and stand once again before the altar and flaming cauldron. Say:

Great God of the Sun,
I welcome Your return.
May You shine brightly upon the Goddess;
May You shine brightly upon the Earth,
scattering seeds and fertilizing the land.
All blessings upon You,
Reborn One of the Sun!

Works of magic, if necessary, may follow.
Celebrate the Simple Feast.
The circle is released.

Yule Lore

One traditional Yuletide practice is the creation of a Yule tree. This can be a living, potted tree which can later be planted in the ground, or a cut one. The choice is yours.

Appropriate Wiccan decorations are fun to make, from strings of dried rosebuds and cinnamon sticks (or popcorn and cranberries) for garlands, to bags of fragrant spices which are hung from boughs. Quartz crystals can be wrapped with shiny wire and suspended from sturdy branches to resemble icicles. Apples, oranges and lemons hanging from boughs are strikingly beautiful, natural decorations, and were customary in ancient times.

Many enjoy the custom of lighting the Yule log. This is a graphic representation of the rebirth of the God within the sacred fire of the Mother Goddess. If you choose to burn one, select a proper log (traditionally of oak or pine). Carve or chalk a figure of the Sun (such as a rayed disc) or the God (a horned circle or a figure of a man) upon it, with the white-handled knife, and set it alight in the fireplace at dusk on Yule. As the log burns, visualize the Sun shining within it and think of the coming warmer days.

As to food, nuts, fruits such as apples and pears, cakes of carraways soaked in cider, and (for non-vegetarians) pork are traditional fare. Wassil, lambswool, hibiscus or ginger tea are fine drinks for the Simple Feast or Yule meals.

Imbolc
(February 2)

A symbol of the season, such as a representation of a snowflake, a white flower, or perhaps some snow in a crystal container can be placed on the altar. An orange candle anointed with musk, cinnamon, frankincense or rosemary oil, unlit, should also be there. Snow can be melted and used for the water during the circle casting.

Arrange the altar, light the candles and censer, and cast the Circle of Stones.

Recite the Blessing Chant.

Invoke the Goddess and God.

Say such words as the following:

This is the time of the feast of torches,
when every lamp blazes and shines
to welcome the rebirth of the God.
I celebrate the Goddess,
I celebrate the God;
All the Earth celebrates
Beneath its mantle of sleep.

Light the orange taper from the red candle on the altar (or at the Southern point of the circle). Slowly walk the circle clockwise, bearing the candle before you. Say these or similar words:

All the land is wrapped in winter.
The air is chilled and
frost envelopes the Earth.
But Lord of the Sun,
Horned One of animals and wild places,
Unseen you have been reborn
of the gracious Mother Goddess,
Lady of all fertility.
Hail Great God!
Hail and welcome!

Stop before the altar, holding aloft the candle. Gaze at its flame. Visualize your life blossoming with creativity, with renewed energy and strength.

If you need to look into the future or past, now is an ideal time.

Works of magic, if necessary, may follow.

Celebrate the Simple Feast.

The circle is released.

Imbolc Lore

It is traditional upon Imbolc, at sunset or just after ritual, to light every lamp in the house—if only for a few moments. Or, light candles in each room in honor of the Sun's rebirth. Alternately, light a kerosene lamp with a red chimney and place this in a prominent part of the home or in a window.

If snow lies on the ground outside, walk in it for a moment, recalling the warmth of summer. With your projective hand, trace an image of the Sun on the snow.

Foods appropriate to eat on this day include those from the dairy, since Imbolc marks the festival of calving. Sour cream dishes are fine. Spicy and full-bodied foods in honor of the Sun are equally attuned. Curries and all dishes made with peppers, onions, leeks, shallots, garlic or chives are appropriate. Spiced wines and dishes containing raisins—all foods symbolic of the Sun—are also traditional.

Ostara
(*circa* March 21)

Flowers should be laid on the altar, placed around the circle and strewn on the ground. The cauldron can be filled with spring water and flowers, and buds and blossoms may be worn as well. A small potted plant should be placed on the altar.

Arrange the altar, light the candles and incense, and cast the Circle of Stones.

Recite the Blessing Chant.

Invoke the Goddess and God in whatever words please you.

Stand before the altar and gaze upon the plant as you say:

O Great Goddess, you have freed yourself from the icy prison of winter. Now is the greening, when the fragrance of flowers drifts on the breeze. This is the beginning. Life renews itself by Your magic, Earth Goddess. The God stretches and rises, eager in His youth, and bursting with the promise of summer.

Touch the plant. Connect with its energies and, through it, all nature. Travel inside its leaves and stems through your visualization— from the center of your consciousness out through your arm and fingers and into the plant itself. Explore its inner nature; sense the miraculous processes of life at work within it.

After a time, still touching the plant, say:

I walk the earth in friendship, not in dominance.
Mother Goddess and Father God, instill within me
through this plant a warmth for all living things.
Teach me to revere the Earth and all its treasures.
May I never forget.

Meditate upon the changing of the seasons. Feel the rousing of energies around you in the Earth.

Works of magic, if necessary, may follow.
Celebrate the Simple Feast.
The circle is released.

Ostara Lore

A traditional Vernal Equinox pastime: go to a field and randomly collect wildflowers.* Or, buy some from a florist, taking one or two of those that appeal to you. Then bring them home and divine their magical meanings by the use of books, your own intuition, a pendulum or by other means. The flowers you've chosen reveal your inner thoughts and emotions.

It is important at this time of renewed life to plan a walk (or a ride) through gardens, a park, woodlands, forest and other green places. This is not simply exercise, and you should be on no other mission. It isn't even just an appreciation of nature. Make your walk *celebratory*, a ritual for nature itself.

Other traditional activities include planting seeds, working on magical gardens and practicing all forms of herb work—magical, medicinal, cosmetic, culinary and artistic.

Foods in tune with this day (linking your meals with the seasons is a fine method of attuning with nature) include those made of seeds, such as sunflower, pumpkin and sesame seeds, as well as pine nuts. Sprouts are equally appropriate, as are leafy, green vegetables. Flower dishes such as stuffed naturtiums or carnation cupcakes also find their place here.†

---

* Thank the flowers for their sacrifice before picking them, using a collection formula such as can be found in "An Herbal Grimoire" elsewhere in this Book of Shadows.

† Find a book of flower cooking or simply make spice cupcakes. Ice with pink frosting and place a fresh carnation petal on each cupcake. Stuff nasturtium blossoms with a mixture made of cream cheese, chopped nuts, chives and watercress. They're hot!

Beltane
(April 30)

If possible, celebrate Beltane in a forest or near a living tree. If this is impossible, bring a small tree within the circle, preferably potted; it can be of any type.

Create a small token or charm in honor of the wedding of the Goddess and God to hang upon the tree. You can make several if you desire. These tokens can be bags filled with fragrant flowers, strings of beads, carvings, flower garlands—whatever your talents and imagination can conjure.

Arrange the altar, light the candles and censer, and cast the Circle of Stones.

Recite the Blessing Chant.

Invoke the Goddess and God.

Stand before the altar and say, with wand upraised:

O Mother Goddess, Queen of the night and of the Earth;
O Father God, King of the day and of the forests,
I celebrate Your union as nature rejoices in a riotous
blaze of color and life. Accept my gift, Mother Goddess
and Father God, in honor of Your union.

Place the token(s) on the tree.

From Your mating shall spring forth life anew;
a profusion of living creatures shall cover the lands,
and the winds will blow pure and sweet.
O Ancient Ones, I celebrate with You!

Works of magic, if necessary, may follow.
Celebrate the Simple Feast.
The Circle is released.

Beltane Lore

Weaving and plaiting are traditional arts at this time of year, for the joining together of two substances to form a third is in the spirit of Beltane.

Foods traditionally come from the dairy, and dishes such as marigold custard (see Recipes—Food) and vanilla ice cream are fine. Oatmeal cakes are also appropriate.

Midsummer
(*circa* June 21)

Before the rite, make up a small cloth pouch filled with herbs such as lavender, chamomile, St. John's wort, vervain, or any of the Midsummer herbs listed in "An Herbal Grimoire." Mentally pour all your troubles, problems, pains, sorrows and illnesses, if any, into this petition as you construct it. Tie it shut with a red string. Place this on the altar for use during the rite. The cauldron should also be there or nearby. Even if you use candles to mark the quarters, the red candle in a holder should also be on the altar. For outdoor rituals, light a fire—however small—and drop the pouch into this.

Arrange the altar, light the candles and censer, and cast the Circle of Stones.

Recite the Blessing Chant.

Invoke the Goddess and God.

Stand before the altar and say, with wand upraised:

I celebrate the noon of summer with mystic rites.
O great Goddess and God,
all nature vibrates with your energies
and the Earth is bathed with warmth and life.
Now is the time of forgetting past cares and banes;
Now is the time for purification.
O fiery Sun,
burn away the unuseful,
the hurtful,
the bane,
in your omnipotent power.
Purify me!
Purify me!
Purify me!

Lay the wand on the altar. Take up the herbal petition and light it in the red candle on the altar (or, if outdoors, the ritual fire). When it is burning, drop it into the cauldron (or some other heat-proof container) and say:

I banish you by the powers of the Goddess and God!
I banish you by the powers of the Sun, Moon and Stars!
I banish you by the powers of Earth, Air, Fire and Water!

Pause, seeing the hurts and pains burning into nothingness.
Then say:

O Gracious Goddess, O Gracious God,
on this night of Midsummer magic
I pray that you charge my life with
wonder and joy. Help me in attuning with
the energies adrift on the enchanted night air.
I give thanks.

Reflect upon the purification you have undergone. Feel the powers of nature flowing through you, washing you clean with divine energy.
Works of magic, if necessary, may follow.
Celebrate the Simple Feast.
The circle is released.

Midsummer Lore

Midsummer is practically the classic time the perform magics of all kinds. Healings, love magic and protections are especially suitable. Herbs can be dried over the ritual fire if you're celebrating outdoors. Leap the fire for purification and renewed energy.
Fresh fruits are standard fare for Midsummer.

Lughnasadh
(August 1)

Place upon the altar sheaves of wheat, barley or oats, fruit and breads, perhaps a loaf fashioned in the figure of the Sun or a man to represent the God. Corn dollies, symbolic of the Goddess, can be present there as well.

Arrange the altar, light the candles and censer, and cast the Circle of Stones.

Recite the Blessing Chant.

Invoke the Goddess and God.

Stand before the altar, holding aloft the sheaves of grain, saying these or similar words:

Now is the time of the First Harvest,
when the bounties of nature give of themselves
so that we may survive.
O God of the ripening fields, Lord of the Grain,
grant me the understanding of sacrifice as you
prepare to deliver yourself under the sickle of the
Goddess and journey to the lands of eternal summer.
O Goddess of the Dark Moon,
teach me the secrets of rebirth
as the Sun loses its strength and the nights grow cold.

Rub the heads of the wheat with your fingers so that the grains fall onto the altar. Lift a piece of fruit and bite it, savoring its flavor, and say:

I partake of the first harvest, mixing its energies
with mine that I may continue my quest for the starry
wisdom of perfection.
O Lady of the Moon and Lord of the Sun,
gracious ones before Whom the stars halt their courses,
I offer my thanks for the continuing fertility of the Earth.

138

*May the nodding grain loose its seeds to be buried in
the Mother's breast, ensuring rebirth in the warmth
of the coming Spring.*

Consume the rest of the fruit.

Works of magic, if necessary, may follow.
Celebrate the Simple Feast.
The circle is released.

Lughnasadh Lore

It is appropriate to plant the seeds from the fruit consumed in ritual. If they sprout, grow the plant with love and as a symbol of your connection with the Goddess and God.

Wheat weaving (the making of corn dollies, etc.) is an appropriate activity for Lughnasadh. Visits to fields, orchards, lakes and wells are also traditional.

The foods of Lughnasadh include bread, blackberries and all berries, acorns (leached of their poisons first), crab apples, all grains and locally ripe produce. A cake is sometimes baked, and cider is used in place of wine.

If you do make a figure of the God from bread, it can be used for the Simple Feast.

Mabon
(*circa* September 21)

Decorate the altar with acorns, oak sprigs, pine and cypress cones, ears of corn, wheat stalks and other fruits and nuts. Also place there a small rustic basket filled with dried leaves of various colors and kinds.

Arrange the altar, light the candles and censer, and cast the Circle of Stones.

Recite the Blessing Chant.

Invoke the Goddess and God.

Stand before the altar, holding aloft the basket of leaves, and slowly scatter them so that they cascade to the ground within the circle. Say such words as these:

Leaves fall,
the days grow cold.
The Goddess pulls her mantle of Earth around Her
as You, O Great Sun God, sail toward the West
to the lands of eternal enchantment,
wrapped in the coolness of night.
Fruits ripen,
seeds drop,
the hours of day and night are balanced.
Chill winds blow in from the North wailing laments.
In this seeming extinction of nature's power, O Blessed
Goddess, I know that life continues.
For spring is impossible without the second harvest,
as surely as life is impossible without death.
Blessings upon you, O Fallen God, as you journey into
the lands of winter and into the Goddess' loving arms.

Place the basket down and say:

O Gracious Goddess of all fertility, I have sown and
reaped the fruits of my actions, good and bane.

140

*Grant me the courage to plant seeds of joy and love in
the coming year, banishing misery and hate. Teach me the secrets
of wise existence upon this planet,
O luminous one of the night!*

Works of magic, if necessary, may follow.
Celebrate the Simple Feast.
The circle is released.

Mabon Lore

A traditional practice is to walk wild places and forests, gathering
seed pods and dried plants. Some of these can be used to decorate the
home; others saved for future herbal magic.

The foods of Mabon consist of the second harvest's gleanings, so
grains, fruit and vegetables predominate, especially corn. Corn bread
is traditional fare, as are beans and baked squash.

Samhain
(October 31)

Place upon the altar apples, pomegranates, pumpkins, squashes and other late autumn fruits. Autumn flowers such as marigolds and chrysanthemums are fine too. Write on a piece of paper an aspect of your life which you wish to be free of: anger, a baneful habit, misplaced feelings, disease. The cauldron or some similar tool must be present before the altar as well, on a trivet or some other heat-proof surface (if the legs aren't long enough). A small, flat dish marked with an eight-spoked wheel symbol should also be there.*

Prior to the ritual, sit quietly and think of friends and loved ones who have passed away. Do not despair. Know that they have gone on to greater things. Keep firmly in mind that the physical isn't the absolute reality, and that souls never die.

Arrange the altar, light the candles and censer, and cast the Circle of Stones.

Recite the Blessing Chant.

Invoke the Goddess and God.

Lift one of the pomegranates and, with your freshly-washed white-handled knife, pierce the skin of the fruit. Remove several seeds and place them on the wheel-marked dish.

Raise your wand, face the altar and say:

On this night of Samhain I mark your passing,
O Sun King, through the sunset into the Land of the Young.
I mark also the passing of all who have gone before,
and all who will go after. O Gracious Goddess,
Eternal Mother, You who gives birth to the fallen,
teach me to know that in the time of the greatest
darkness there is the greatest light.

Taste the pomegranate seeds; burst them with your teeth and savor their sharp, bittersweet flavor. Look down at the eight-spoked

---

* This is just what it sounds like. On a flat plate or dish, paint a large circle. Put a dot in the center of this circle and paint eight spokes radiating out from the dot to the larger circle. Thus, you have a wheel symbol—a symbol of the Sabbats, a symbol of timelessness.

symbol on the plate; the wheel of the year, the cycle of the seasons, the end and beginning of all creation.

Light a fire within the cauldron (a candle is fine). Sit before it, holding the piece of paper, gazing at its flames. Say:

> *Wise One of the Waning Moon,*
> *Goddess of the starry night,*
> *I create this fire within Your cauldron*
> *to transform that which is plaguing me.*
> *May the energies be reversed:*
> *From darkness, light!*
> *From bane, good!*
> *From death, birth!*

Light the paper in the cauldron's flames and drop it inside. As it burns, know that your ill diminishes, lessens and finally leaves you as it is consumed within the universal fires.*

If you wish, you may attempt scrying or some other form of divination, for this is a perfect time to look into the past or future. Try to recall past lives too, if you will. But leave the dead in peace. Honor them with your memories but do not call them to you.† Release any pain and sense of loss you may feel into the cauldron's flames.

Works of magic, if necessary, may follow.

Celebrate the Simple Feast.

The circle is released.

Samhain Lore

It is traditional on Samhain night to leave a plate of food outside the home for the souls of the dead. A candle placed in the window guides them to the lands of eternal summer, and burying apples in the hard-packed earth "feeds" the passed ones on their journey.

For food, beets, turnips, apples, corn, nuts, gingerbread, cider, mulled wines and pumpkin dishes are appropriate, as are meat dishes (once again, if you're not vegetarian. If so, tofu seems ritually correct).

---

* The cauldron, seen as the Goddess.

† Many Wiccans do attempt to communicate with their deceased ancestors and friends at this time, but it seems to me that if we accept the doctrine of reincarnation, this is a rather strange practice. Perhaps the *personalities* that we knew still exist, but if the *soul* is currently incarnate in another body, communication would be difficult, to say the least. Thus, it seems best to remember them with peace and love—but not to call them up.

A Ritual of Gestures*

Stand in the ritual area. Still your thoughts. Breathe deeply for half a minute or so until composed and calm. Turn your mind to our Deities.

Face North. Lift both hands to waist height, palms down. Press your fingers together, creating two solid, flat planes. Sense solidity, foundation, fertility. Invoke the powers of *Earth* through the gesture.

Moments later, turn toward the East. Raise your hands a foot higher, your palms facing away from you (no longer parallel with the ground), and elbows slightly bent. Spread your fingers and hold this position, sensing movement and communication. Invoke the forces of *Air* through the gesture.

Face South. Lift your hands fully above your head. Keeping the elbows straight, grasp your fingers into tight fists. Feel force, power, creation and destruction. Invoke the forces of *Fire* through the gesture.

Turn to the West. Lower your hands a foot or so. Bend the elbows, turn your palms upward and cup them, pressing the thumbs against the forefingers. Sense fluidity, the ocean, liquidity. Invoke the forces of *Water* through the gesture.

Face North again. Throw your head back and raise both hands to the sky, palms up, fingers spread. Drink in the essence of The One, the unknowable, unapproachable ultimate source of all. Sense the mysteries within the universe.

Lower your projective hand but keep your receptive hand high. Pressing the third, fourth and fifth fingers against the palm, lift the forefinger and thumb to create a rough crescent shape. Sense the reality of the Goddess. Sense her love, her fertility, her compassion. Sense the powers of the Moon in the gesture; the force of the eternal seas—the presence of the Goddess.

---

* As mentioned in Chapter Five, gestures can be potent tools for slipping into ritual consciousness. After re-reading that chapter I had the idea to compose an entire ritual of gestures, using no physical tools, no words, no music or even visualizations. This is merely a suggestion as to its form, and has plenty of possibilities for expansion. It is to be used for attunement with The One, The Goddess and God, and the elemental forces, not for magic or seasonal observances.

Lower your receptive hand; lift your projective hand. Bend down the middle and fourth fingers toward the palm, and trap them with the thumb. Lift the forefinger and little finger up to the sky, creating a horned image. Sense the reality of the God. Sense the power of the Sun in the gesture; the untamed energies of the woodlands—the presence of the God.

Lower your projective hand. Lay down flat. Spread your legs and arms until you've created the pattern of a pentagram. Sense the powers of the elements running through you; merging and coalescing into your being. Sense them as emanations from The One, the Goddess and God.

Meditate. Commune. Communicate.

When finished, simply stand up. Your rite of gestures is over.

The Law of the Power

1. The Power shall not be used to bring harm, to injure or control others. But if the need rises, the Power shall be used to protect your life or the lives of others.

2. The Power is used only as need dictates.

3. The Power can be used for your own gain, as long as by doing so you harm none.

4. It is unwise to accept money for use of the Power, for it quickly controls its taker. Be not as those of other religions.

5. Use not the Power for prideful gain, for such cheapens the mysteries of Wicca and magic.

6. Ever remember that the Power is the sacred gift of the Goddess and God, and should never be misused or abused.

7. And this is the Law of the Power.

Invocation of the Elements

Air, Fire, Water, Earth,
Elements of Astral birth,
I call you now; attend to me!

In the circle, rightly cast,
Safe from psychic curse or blast,
I call you now; attend to me!

From cave and desert, sea and hill,
By wand, blade, cup and pentacle,
I call you now; attend to me!
This is my will, so mote it be!*

Prayers, Chants and Invocations
of and to the Goddess and God

These prayers can be used to invoke the Goddess and God during ritual, just after the circle casting. Of course, any which you compose or are inspired to say can be used as well.

A few chants are also included to raise energy or to commune with the deities.

Some of these invocations rhyme, and some do not. This simply speaks of my ability to compose rhyme, I suppose. But recall the power of rhyme—it links our conscious mind to the unconscious or psychic mind, thereby producing ritual consciousness.

Some of these are related to specific deities but, as Dion Fortune wrote: "All the gods are one god; and all the goddesses are one goddess, and there is one initiator.†

---

* This invocation may be chanted while moving or dancing around the altar to raise elemental energy for magical workings.

† *Aspects of Occultism.* London: Aquarian Press, 1962, page 35.

Invocation to the Goddess

Crescent One of the starry skies,
Flowered One of the fertile plain,
Flowing One of the ocean's sighs,
Blessed One of the gentle rain;
Hear *my chant 'midst the standing stones,*
Open *me to your mystic light;*
Waken *me to your silver tones,*
Be with me in my sacred rite!

Invocation to Pan

O Great God Pan,
Beast and man,
Shepherd of goats and Lord of the Land,
I call you to attend my rites
On this most magical of nights.
God of the wine,
God of the vine,
God of the fields and god of the kine,
Attend my circle with your love
And send Your blessings from above.
Help me to heal;
Help me to feel;
Help me to bring forth love and weal.
Pan of the forests, Pan of the glade,
Be with me as my magic is made!

Isis Invocation

Isis of the Moon,
You who are all that ever was,
all that is,
and all that shall be:
Come, veiled Queen of Night!
Come as the scent of the sacred lotus
Charging my circle

With love and magic.
Do descend upon my circle,
I pray,
O Blessed Isis!

Prayer to the Horned God

Horned One of the wilderness,
Winged One of the shining skies,
Rayed One of the splen'drous Sun,
Fallen One of the Samhain cries—
I call amidst the standing stones
Praying that you, O ancient One,
Will deign to bless my mystic rites—
O fiery Lord of the Blazing Sun!

New Moon Chant to Diana

Waxing, waxing, growing, growing—
Diana's power is flowing, flowing.
                        (repeat)

Call to the God

Ancient God of the forest deeps,
Master of beast and Sun;
Here where the world is hushed and sleeps
Now that the day is done.
I call You in the ancient way
Here in my circle round,
Asking that You will hear me pray
And send Your Sun force down.

Invocation to the Goddess

Gracious Goddess,
You who are the Queen of the Gods,
the lamp of night,
the creator of all that is wild and free;
Mother of woman and man;
lover of the Horned God and protectress of all the Wicca:
Descend, I pray,
with Your Lunar ray of power
upon my circle here!

Invocation to the God

Blazing God,
You Who are the King of the Gods
Lord of the Sun,
master of all that is wild and free;
Father of woman and man,
Lover of the Moon Goddess and protector of all the Wicca:
Descend, I pray,
with Your Solar ray of power
upon my circle here!

Goddess Chant

Luna, Luna, Luna, Diana
Luna, Luna, Luna, Diana
Bless me, bless me, bless me, Diana,
Luna, Luna, Luna, Diana
                    (repeat)

Evening Chant to the God

Hail fair Sun,
Ruler of day;
Rise on the morn
To light my way.
                (to be said while watching the sunset)

Evening Chant to the Goddess

Hail fair Moon,
Ruler of night;
Guard me and mine
Until the light.

     (to be said while Moon-gazing at night)

Goddess Chant

Aaaaaaaaaaaaah
Ooooooooooooooh
Uuuuuuuuuuuuu
Eeeeeeeeeeeeeeee
Iiiiiiiiiiiiiiiiiiiiii*

The Lore of Numbers

To be used in ritual and magical workings. In general, odd numbers are related to women, receptive energy and the Goddess; even numbers to men, projective energy and the God.

1. The universe; The One; the source of all.
2. The Goddess and God; The perfect duality; projective and receptive energy; the couple; personal union with deity; interpenetration of the physical and spiritual; balance.
3. The Triple Goddess; the Lunar phases; the physical, mental and spiritual aspects of our species.
4. The elements; the Spirits of the Stones; the winds; the seasons.
5. The senses; the pentagram; the elements plus Akasha; a Goddess number.
7. The planets which the ancients knew; the time of the Lunar

---

* These are, obviously, the vowels of the English language. Pronounce them as: A-"Ah," O-"O," U-"Oo," E-"E," I-"Eye." Extend the vowels as you vocalize them, stretch the sounds. This produces Goddess awareness, and rouses the psychic mind.

phase; power; protection and magic
8. The number of the Sabbats; a number of the God.
9. A number of the Goddess.
13. The number of Esbats; a fortunate number.
15. A number of good fortune.
21. The number of Sabbats and Moons in the Wiccan year; a number of the Goddess.
28. A number of the Moon; a number of the Goddess.
101. The number of fertility.

The planets are numbered thus:

Saturn, 3	Venus, 7
Jupiter, 4	Mercury, 8
Mars, 5	Moon, 9*
Sun, 6	

Thirteen Goals of a Witch

I. Know yourself
II. Know your Craft (Wicca)
III. Learn
IV. Apply knowledge with wisdom
V. Achieve balance
VI. Keep your words in good order
VII. Keep your thoughts in good order
VIII. Celebrate life
IX. Attune with the cycles of the Earth
X. Breathe and eat correctly
XI. Exercise the body
XII. Meditate
XIII. Honor the Goddess and God

---

* There are many variants of this system. This is simply the one that I use.

RECIPES

Recipes for Food

CRESCENT CAKES

    1 cup finely ground almonds
1¼ cups flour
½ cup confectioner's sugar
2 drops almond extract
½ cup butter, softened
1 egg yolk

    Combine almonds, flour, sugar and extract until thoroughly mixed. With the hands, work in butter and egg yolk until well-blended. Chill dough. Preheat oven to 325 degrees F. Pinch off pieces of dough about the size of walnuts and shape into crescents. Place on greased sheets and bake for about 20 minutes. Serve during the Simple Feast, especially at Esbats.*

---

* This is the best recipe I've been able to find. Most of the other published ones taste foul. Purists who worry about the inclusion of sugar in this recipe needn't. It's ritually related to Venus and has a long magical history. Besides, if you only eat sugar once every Full Moon, how bad can it be?

BELTANE MARIGOLD CUSTARD

2 cups milk
1 cup unsprayed marigold petals
¼ tsp. salt
3 Tbsp. sugar
1 to 2-inch piece vanilla bean
3 egg yolks, slightly beaten
⅛ tsp. allspice
⅛ tsp. nutmeg
½ tsp. rose water
whipped cream

Using a clean mortar and pestle reserved for cooking purposes, pound marigold petals. Or, crush with a spoon. Mix the salt, sugar and spices together. Scald milk with the marigolds and the vanilla bean. Remove the vanilla bean and add the slightly beaten yolks and dry ingredients. Cook on low heat. When the mixture coats a spoon, add rose water and cool.

Top with whipped cream, garnish with fresh marigold petals.

SOFT MEAD

1 quart water, preferably spring water
1 cup honey
1 sliced lemon
½ tsp. nutmeg

Boil together all ingredients in a non-metallic pot. While boiling, scrape off the rising "scum" with a wooden spoon. When no more rises add the following:

pinch salt
juice of ½ lemon
Strain and cool. Drink in place of alcoholic mead or wine during the Simple Feast.

BEVERAGES

If you wish to avoid the use of wine, which has long been utilized in religious and magical rites, there are many other beverages that can be used to toast the Goddess and God. These include (but certainly aren't limited to):

Sabbats: apple juice, grape juice, grapefruit juice, orange juice, pineapple juice, black tea, soft mead, guava nectar, cinnamon coffee, ginger tea, hibiscus tea

Full Moons: lemonade, apricot nectar, mango nectar, pear nectar, papaya nectar, peach nectar, jasmine tea, peppermint tea, rosebud tea, milk

Recipes for Incenses

To make incenses, simply grind the ingredients and mix them together. As you mix, sense their energies. Burn on charcoal blocks in the censer during ritual. See Appendix 1 for suppliers of herbs and charcoal.

CIRCLE INCENSE

4 parts Frankincense
2 parts Myrrh
2 parts Benzoin
1 part Sandalwood
½ part Cinnamon
½ part Rose petals
¼ part Vervain
¼ part Rosemary
¼ part Bay

Burn in the circle for all types of rituals and spells. Frankincense, myrrh and benzoin should definitely constitute the bulk of the mixture.

ALTAR INCENSE

3 parts Frankincense
2 parts Myrrh
1 part Cinnamon

Burn as a general incense on the altar to purify it and to promote ritual consciousness during rituals.

FULL MOON RITUAL INCENSE

2 parts Sandalwood
2 parts Frankincense
½ part Gardenia petals
¼ part Rose petals
a few drops Ambergris oil

Burn during Esbats or simply at the time of the Full Moon to attune with the Goddess.

SPRING SABBAT INCENSE

3 parts Frankincense
2 parts Sandalwood
1 part Benzoin
1 part Cinnamon
a few drops Patchouly oil

Burn during spring and summer Sabbat rituals.

FALL SABBAT INCENSE

3 parts Frankincense
2 parts Myrrh
1 part Rosemary
1 part Cedar
1 part Juniper

Burn during fall and winter Sabbat rituals.

Recipes for Oils

To create oils, simply mix them in a bottle. Wear for ritual purposes. See Appendix 1 for suppliers.

SABBAT OIL #1

3 parts Patchouli
2 parts Musk
1 part Carnation

Wear to the Sabbats to promote communion with the deities.

SABBAT OIL #2

2 parts Frankincense
1 part Myrrh
1 part Allspice
1 drop Clove

Use as the above formula.

FULL MOON OIL #1

3 parts Rose
1 part Jasmine
1 part Sandalwood

Anoint the body prior to Esbats to attune with Lunar energies.

FULL MOON OIL #2

3 parts Sandalwood
2 parts Lemon
1 part Rose

Another like the above.

GODDESS OIL

3 parts Rose
2 parts Tuberose
1 part Lemon
1 part Palmarosa
1 part Ambergris

Wear to honor the Goddess during rituals.

HORNED GOD OIL

2 parts Frankincense
2 parts Cinnamon
1 part Bay
1 part Rosemary
1 part Musk

Wear to honor the Horned God during rituals.

ALTAR OIL

4 parts Frankincense
3 parts Myrrh
1 part Galangal
1 part Vervain
1 part Lavender

Anoint the altar with this oil at regular intervals to purify and empower it.

AN HERBAL GRIMOIRE

A guide to the use of herbs and plants in Wiccan ritual.

Of Gathering Flowers, Herbs and Plants:

Before cutting with the white-handled knife, attune with the plant through visualization. Feel its energies. As you cut, say these or similar words:

O little plant of (name, such as hyssop, etc.) I ask that you give of your bounty that it may aid me in my work. Grow stronger by my stroke, stronger and more powerful, O plant of (name)!

If it is a tree, substitute the appropriate word (tree of oak). Gently cut only what you need, and never from very young plants or more than twenty-five percent of the growth. At the base of the plant leave an offering: a silver coin, a bright jewel, a bit of wine or milk, grain, a quartz crystal and so on. Cover the offering and it is done.

Of the Circle:

The magic circle may be fashioned with garlands of flowers sacred to the Goddess and God. Alternately, flowers can be scattered around the perimeter of the circle.

The point stones may be ringed with fresh flowers and herbs suitable to the elements, such as:

North: corn, cypress, fern, honeysuckle, wheat, vervain
East: acacia, bergamot, clover, dandelion, lavender, lemon

grass, mint, mistletoe, parsley, pine
South: basil, carnation, cedar, chrysanthemum, dill, ginger,
heliotrope, holly, juniper, marigold, peppermint
West: apple blossoms, lemon balm, camellia, catnip, daffodil, elder, gardenia, grape, heather, hibiscus, jasmine, orchid

Fresh flowers may be present on the altar or, if none are available,
greens such as ferns may be used.
When casting the circle around a tree, you can use the fruit,
leaves, nuts or flowers of that tree to mark out the circle, if desired.
All of these can be used in addition to the cord and stones.

Of the Balefire:

If you wish to build a fire for an outdoor ritual, it can be composed
of all or any combination of the following woods:

Rowan   Dogwood
Mesquite   Poplar
Oak   Juniper
Pine   Cedar
Apple

If these are unavailable, use native woods. Rites run on the
seashore can be illuminated with balefires of dried driftwood collected
prior to the rite.

Of the Home Circle:

Magical plants growing outside the home in containers can be
placed around the circle or on the altar during ritual. If you primarily
work indoors, choose an odd-numbered selection of sacred plants
and grow these in your ritual area. If they need more sunlight, simply
move them outdoors and bring inside during ritual. Give them energy
and love, and they'll aid you in your worship and magic.
Though any but poisonous plants can be used, such plants as
these are recommended:

African Violets	Red Geraniums
Cacti (all types)	Rose
Ferns (all types)	Rose Geranium
Holly	Rosemary
Hyssop	Ti (*Cordyline terminalis*)
Palms (all types)	Wax Plant (*Hoya carnosa*)

Of the Celebrant:

Wear fresh flowers and herbs in your hair and on your body, if you prefer, during the rites. Crowns or chaplets of flowers are always appropriate for spring and summer rites. Wear oak and pine during the winter rituals.

You may wish to wear a necklace of herbs and seeds, such as tonka beans, whole nutmegs, star anise, acorns and other seeds and nuts, strung on a natural fiber. Strings of small pine cones may also be worn.

For Full Moon rituals held at night, wear night-blooming, fragrant flowers to suffuse yourself with Lunar energies.

Of the Tools:

These are suggestions for dedicating the tools prior to their first use or formal consecration, if any. Perform these with proper visualization and ritual intent.

The Magic Knife or Sword:

Rub the blade with fresh basil, rosemary or oak leaves, at sunrise, outdoors where you will not be disturbed or seen. Lay the sword or knife on the ground with its point to the South. Walk clockwise around it thrice, scattering bay leaves (preferably fresh) over it. Take up the sword or knife, stand facing East and, holding it upward but with arms lowered, invoke the God to infuse your knife or sword with His strength. Point it to the sky, invoking the Goddess to charge your blade with Her love and power.

Wrap your knife or sword in red cloth and take it home. It may be stored in the cloth, if desired.

The White-Handled Knife:

Early in the morning, go to a forest (or park, garden, or your indoor garden). Choose the most beautiful and vibrant plants. Touch the point of the white-handled knife gently to these in turn, forging a connection between your knife and the plants (and, thusly, the Earth).

Next, sit on the Earth. Ensuring that you are quite alone, draw a pentagram with the white-handled knife's point on the ground. It is done.

The Wand:

If the wand is of wood, take it outdoors at sunset and rub it with fresh lavender, eucalyptus or mint leaves. Raise it in the air toward the East (or the Moon if it is visible) and invoke the Goddess. At sunrise, take it again outdoors, rub with the fresh, fragrant leaves and invoke the God by raising it to the East.

The Pentacle:

Place the pentacle on bare Earth. Lay upon it dried parsley, patchouly, mistletoe, or fresh jasmine or honeysuckle flowers. Sit before it facing North for several seconds, visualizing the pentacle absorbing the Earth's energies. Then pick it up and scatter the herbs or flowers to the four quarters, beginning and ending in the North.

If this must be done indoors, fill a small dish with fresh Earth and place the pentacle on this. Proceed as above, saving the herbs or flowers to be scattered outdoors at a later time.

The Censer:

Fume pure rosemary, frankincense or copal within the censer prior to its first use. Do this for about an hour.

The Cauldron:

Take the cauldron to a stream, river, lake or ocean. Gather the leaves of some plants growing nearby (at the sea, perhaps seaweed). Dip the cauldron into the water to fill it. Place the leaves in the cauldron, then set it on the water's edge where it is on both water and sand. Place your hands on the cauldron and dedicate it to the Goddess in any words you like.

Empty and dry the cauldron, and return home. The charge has been made.

If performed inside, place the cauldron in a large basin of water or the bathtub, in a candle-lit room. Add a bit of salt to the water, which should be cold. Proceed as above.

Salt water corrodes metal. Thoroughly wash the cauldron after immersion in sea or salt water.

The Cup:

Anoint the base with gardenia, rose or violet oil and fill with pure spring water. Then set afloat a sprig of ivy, a small rose, a fresh gardenia or some other appropriate flower or herb. Gaze into the cup and invoke the Goddess to bless it. You might also wish to take it outside at night, filled with water, and catch the Moon's reflection within it.

The Broom:

It can be fashioned from an ash staff, birch twigs and a willow binding. Brush the broom with chamomile, willow, lemon balm, elder or mallow stalks and branches, then bury these with due solemnity. You might also wish to carve a crescent Moon upon its handle.

The Crystal:

On the night of a Full Moon, rub the sphere with fresh (or dried) mugwort, then take it outside. Hold it up so that it drinks in the light and energies of the Moon. Gaze at the Moon through the crystal by holding it before your eyes. Repeat at least thrice yearly for the best benefits.

The Book of Shadows:

Sew into the cover of the Book leaves of the sacred herbs vervain, rue, bay, willow or others, if you wish. They should be well-dried and secretly placed by the light of the Moon. The covers of the Book of Shadows should, of course, be covered with cloth for this purpose.

The Robe:

If you choose to wear one, lay it among sachets filled with lavender, vervain and cedar when not in use. Sew a bit of rosemary or frankincense into the hem while fashioning it, if desired (and if any resulting stains won't show after washing).

Of The Herbs of the Sabbats:

To be used as decorations on the altar, around the circle, in the home.

Samhain:
Chrysanthemum, wormwood, apples, pears, hazel, thistle, pomegranates, all grains, harvested fruits and nuts, the pumpkin, corn.

Yule:
Holly, misteletoe, ivy, cedar, bay, juniper, rosemary, pine. Place offerings of apples, oranges, nutmegs, lemons and whole cinnamon sticks on the Yule tree.

Imbolc:
Snowdrop, rowan, the first flowers of the year.

Ostara:
Daffodil, woodruff, violet, gorse, olive, peony, iris, narcissus, all spring flowers.

Beltane:
Hawthorn, honeysuckle, St. John's wort, woodruff, all flowers.

Midsummer:
Mugwort, vervain, chamomile, rose, lily, oak, lavender, ivy, yarrow, fern, elder, wild thyme, daisy, carnation.

Lughnasadh:
All grains, grapes, heather, blackberries, sloe, crab apples, pears.

Mabon:
Hazel, corn, aspen, acorns, oak sprigs, autumn leaves, wheat stalks, cypress cones, pine cones, harvest gleanings.

Of the Herbs and Plants of Full Moon Rituals:

Place upon the altar all nocturnal, white or five-petaled flowers such as the white rose, night-blooming jasmine, carnation, gardenia, cereus, lily, iris; all pleasingly-scented flowers which shall call forth the Goddess. Camphor is also symbolic.

Of Offerings:

To the Goddess:

All watery and earthy flowers and seeds such as camellia, lily, water lily, willow stalks; those flowers used in Full Moon rituals; white or purple blooms such as hyacinth, magnolia, heather and lilac; sweet-scented herbs and flowers; those dedicated to Venus or to the Moon; rue, vervain and olive; or others which seem suitable.

To the God:

All fiery and airy herbs and flowers such as basil, chrysanthemum, snapdragon, clover, lavender, pine; strongly-scented, clean or citrusy herbs and flowers; those ruled by Mars or the Sun; yellow or red blooms such as sunflower, pine cones, seeds, cacti, thistles and stinging herbs; orange, heliotrope, cedar, juniper and so on.

Of the Sacred Herbs of the Goddesses:

APHRODITE: olive, cinnamon, daisy, cypress, quince, orris (iris), apple, myrtle

ARADIA: rue, vervain

ARTEMIS: silver fir, amaranth, cypress, cedar, hazel, myrtle, willow, daisy, mugwort, date palm

ASTARTE: alder, pine, cypress, myrtle, juniper

ATHENA: olive, apple

BAST: catnip, vervain

BELLONA: belladonna

BRIGIT: blackberry

CAILLEACH: wheat

CARDEA: hawthorn, bean, arbutus

CERES: willow, wheat, bay, pomegranate, poppy, leek, narcissus

CYBELE: oak, myrrh, pine

DEMETER: wheat, barley, pennyroyal, myrrh, rose, pomegranate, bean, poppy, all cultivated crops

DIANA: birch, willow, acacia, wormwood, dittany, hazel, beech, fir, apple, mugwort, plane, mulberry, rue

DRUANTIA: fir

FREYA: cowslip, daisy, primrose, maidenhair, myrrh, strawberry, mistletoe

HATHOR: myrtle, sycamore, grape, mandrake, coriander, rose
HECATE: willow, henbane, aconite, yew, mandrake, cyclamen, mint, cypress, date palm, sesame, dandelion, garlic, oak, onion
HEKAT: cypress
HERA: apple, willow, orris, pomegranate, myrrh
HINA: bamboo
HULDA: flax, rose, hellebore, elder
IRENE: olive
IRIS: wormwood, iris
ISHTAR: acacia, juniper, all grains
ISIS: fig, heather, wheat, wormwood, barley, myrrh, rose, palm, lotus, persea, onion, iris, vervain
JUNO: lily, crocus, ashpodel, quince, pomegranate, vervain, iris, lettuce, fig, mint
KERRIDWEN: vervain, acorns
MINERVA: olive, mulberry, thistle
NEFER-TUM: lotus
NEPTHYS: myrrh, lily
NUIT: sycamore
OLWEN: apple
PERSEPHONE: parsley, narcissus, willow, pomegranate
RHEA: myrrh, oak
ROWEN: clover, rowen
VENUS: cinnamon, daisy, elder, heather, anemone, apple, poppy, violet, marjoram, maidenhair fern, carnation, aster, vervain, myrtle, orchid, cedar, lily, mistletoe, pine, quince
VESTA: oak

Of the Sacred Herbs of the Gods:

ADONIS: myrrh, corn, rose, fennel, lettuce, white heather
AESCULAPIUS: bay, mustard
AJAX: delphinium
ANU: tamarisk
APOLLO: leek, hyacinth, heliotrope, cornel, bay, frankincense, date palm, cypress
ATTIS: pine, almond
ARES: buttercup

BACCHUS: grape, ivy, fig, beech, tamarisk
BALDUR: St. John's wort, daisy
BRAN: alder, all grains
CUPID: cypress, sugar, white violet, red rose
DAGDA: oak
DIANUS: fig
DIONYSUS: fig, apple, ivy, grape, pine, corn, pomegranate,
  toadstools, mushrooms, fennel, all wild and cultivated trees
DIS: cypress
EA: cedar
EROS: red rose
GWYDION: ash
HELIOS: sunflower, heliotrope
HERNE: oak
HORUS: horehound, lotus, persea
HYPNOS: poppy
JOVE: pine, cassia, houseleek, carnation, cypress
JUPITER: aloe, agrimony, sage, oak, mullein, acorn, beech, cypress,
  houseleek, date palm, violet, gorse, ox-eye daisy, vervain
KERNUNNOS: heliotrope, bay, sunflower, oak, orange
KANALOA: banana.
MARS: ash, aloe, dogwood, buttercup, witch grass, vervain
MERCURY: cinnamon, mulberry, hazel, willow
MITHRAS: cypress, violet
NEPTUNE: ash, bladderwrack, all seaweeds
ODIN: mistletoe, elm
OSIRIS: acacia, grape, ivy, tamarisk, cedar, clover, date palm,
  all grains.
PAN: fig, pine, reed, oak, fern, all meadow flowers
PLUTO: cypress, mint, pomegranate
POSEIDON: pine, ash, fig, bladderwrack, all seaweeds
PROMETHEUS: fennel
RA: acacia, frankincense, myrrh, olive
SATURN: fig, blackberry
SYLVANUS: pine
TAMMUZ: wheat, pomegranate, all grains
THOTH: almond
THOR: thistle, houseleek, vervain, hazel, ash, birch, rowan, oak,
  pomegranate, burdock, beech
URANUS: ash

WODEN: ash
ZEUS oak, olive, pine, aloe, parsley, sage, wheat, fig

As the Wicca, we will take only that which we need from the green and growing things of the Earth, never failing to attune with the plant before harvesting, nor failing to leave a token of gratitude and respect.

HERE ENDS THIS HERBAL GRIMOIRE

WICCAN CRYSTAL MAGIC

Crystals and stones are gifts of the Goddess and God. They are sacred, magical tools which can be used to enhance ritual and magic. Here are some of these ways of Earth magic.

Preparing the Circle:

The magic circle can be laid out with crystals and stones, if desired, rather than with herbs.

Beginning and ending in the North, lay 7, 9, 21 or 40 quartz crystals of any size around the circle, either inside the cord or in place of it. If the ritual to be conducted within the circle is of a usual spiritual or magical nature, place the quartz crystals with points *outward*. If of a protective nature, place with points facing *inward*.

If you use candles to mark the four quarters of the magic circle rather than large stones, ring each candle with any or all of the following stones:

> **North:** Moss Agate, Emerald, Jet, Olivine, Salt, Black
> Tourmaline
> **East:** Imperial Topaz, Citrine, Mica, Pumice
> **South:** Amber, Obsidian, Rhodochrosite, Ruby, Lava,
> Garnet
> **West:** Aquamarine, Chalcedony, Jade, Lapis Lazuli,
> Moonstone, Sugilite

A Stone Altar:

To make this altar, search through dry river beds and seashores for a variety of smoothly-shaped stones. Or check rock shops for appropriate pieces.

Create the altar itself of three large stones. Two smaller ones of even size are used as the base, while a longer, flat stone is placed on top of these to form the altar itself. On this place one stone to the left of the altar to represent the Goddess. This might be a natural, river-rounded stone, a holed stone, a quartz crystal sphere, or any of the stones related to the Goddess which are listed below.

To the right of the altar, place a stone to represent the God. This might be a piece of lava, a quartz crystal point, a long, thin or club-shaped rock or a God-symbolic stone such as those presented below.

Between these two stones place a smaller stone with a red candle affixed to it to represent the divine energy of the Goddess and God as well as the element of Fire.

Before this, place a flat stone to receive offerings of wine, honey, cakes, semi-precious stones, flowers and fruit.

A small, cupped stone (if one can be found) should be set to the left of the offering stone. Fil this with water to represent that element.

To the left of the offering stone place a flat rock. Pour salt upon this to symbolize the element of Earth.

Additionally, another flat stone can be placed before the offering stone to serve as an incense burner.

Use a long, thin, terminated quartz crystal as a wand and a flint or obsidian arrowhead for the magic knife.

Any other tools which are needed can simply be placed on the altar. Or, try to find stone alternatives to them.

This can be used for all types of Wiccan rituals.

Stones of the Goddesses:

In general, all pink, green and blue stones; those related to the Moon or Venus; Water and Earth-ruled stones, such as peridot, emerald, pink tourmaline, rose quartz, blue quartz, aquamarine, beryl, kunzite and turquoise.

Stones which are related to specific deities follow.

APHRODITE: salt
CERES: emerald
COATLICUE: jade
CYBELE: jet
DIANA: amethyst, moonstone, pearl

FREYA: pearl
GREAT MOTHER, THE: amber, coral, geodes, holed stones
HATHOR: turquoise
ISIS: coral, emerald, lapis lazuli, moonstone, pearl
KWAN YIN: jade
LAKSHMI: pearl
MAAT: jade
MARA: beryl, aquamarine
NUIT: lapis lazuli
PELE: lava, obsidian, peridot, olivine, pumice
SELENE: moonstone, selenite
TIAMAT: beryl
VENUS: emerald, lapis lazuli, pearl

Stones of the God:

Generally, all orange and red stones; stones related to the Sun and Mars; Fire and Air-ruled stones, such as carnelian, ruby, garnet, orange calcite, diamond, tiger's eye, topaz, sunstone, bloodstone, red tourmaline.

Stones which are related to specific deities follow.

AESCULAPIUS: agate
APOLLO: sapphire
BACCHUS: amethyst
CUPID: opal
DIONYSUS: amethyst
MARS: onyx, sardonyx
NEPTUNE: beryl
ODIN: holed stone
POSEIDON: beryl, pearl,* aquamarine
RA: tiger's eye
TEZCATLIPOCA: obsidian

---

* Pearl and coral have been mentioned in these lists as "stones" because they were anciently thought to be such. Our knowledge of them as the products of living creatures leaves us with the ethical question of whether or not to use them in ritual. This must be a personal decision. Save for beach-gathered coral, I have chosen not to.

Cairns:

In earlier times, throughout the world, people built mounds or piles of stones. These were sometimes formed to mark the passage of travelers, or to commemorate some historic event, but such cairns usually had ritual significance.

In magical thought, cairns are places of power. They concentrate the energies of the stones used to create them. Cairns are rooted in the Earth but lift upward to the sky, symbolically representing the interconnectedness of the physical and spiritual realms.

During outdoor circles, a small cairn, composed of no more than nine or eleven rocks, can be fashioned at each point of the Circle of Stones. This can be done prior to creating the circle itself.

The next time you're in some wild, lonely place with a profusion of stones, clear a place among them and sit. Visualize a magical need. As you visualize, grasp a near-by stone. Feel the energy beating within it—the power of the Earth, the power of nature. Place it on the cleared ground. Pick up another stone, still visualizing your need, and set it next to the first.

Still visualizing, continue to add stones, building them into a small pile. Keep adding stones until you feel them vibrating and pulsating before you. Place the last rock on top of the cairn with firm ritual intent—affirm to yourself, to the cairn and the Earth that with this final magical act you're manifesting your need.

Place your hands on either side of the pile. Give it your energy through your visualization. Nurse it. Feed it strength and see your need as being fulfilled.

Then leave the cairn alone to do its work.

A Quartz and Candle Spell:

Have a candle of the color symbolic of your magical need, according to the following list (or as your intuition tells you):

White: protection, purification, peace
Red: protection, strength, health, passion, courage
Light Blue: healing, patience, happiness
Dark Blue: change, psychism
Green: money, fertility, growth, employment

Yellow: intellect, attraction, study, divination
Brown: healing animals
Pink: love, friendships
Orange: stimulation, energy
Purple: power, healing severe diseases, spirituation, meditation

With the tip of a cleansed, terminated quartz crystal, scratch a symbol of your need onto the candle. This might be a heart for love, a dollar sign for money, a fist for strength. Alternately, use an appropriate rune* or write your need on the candle with the crystal.

As you scratch or draw, visualize your need with crystal clarity as if it had already manifested. Place the candle in a holder. Set the crystal near it and light the wick.

As the flame shines, again strongly visualize. The crystal, candle and symbol will do their work.

---

* See the following section for runic information.

SYMBOLS AND SIGNS

To be used as shorthand in magical writings, the Book of Shadows, your Mirror Book, correspondence, and so on.

The Goddess	)O(	Cup	⚱
The God	♉	Censer	
Candle		Pentacle	⛤
Broom		Wand	
Cauldron		Magic Knife/Sword	
Balefire		Altar	
Magic Circle	⊘	Salt	

Herbs, Greens

Wine

Bane, Deadly, Poison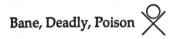

Widdershins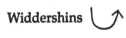

The Sun

Sunrise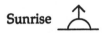

Sunset

Spring

Summer

Autumn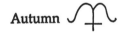

Winter

Water

Immortality

Deosil

The Moon

Moonrise

Moonset

Waxing Moon

Full Moon

Waning Moon

New Moon

RUNE MAGIC

Runes are symbols which, when drawn, painted, traced, carved or visualized, release specific energies. As such, rune magic is surprisingly easy to practice and is undergoing a renaissance today. In earlier times, runes were scratched onto birch bark, bone or wood. They were carved onto weapons to ensure accurate shots, engraved on cups and goblets to ward off poisoning, and marked on goods and the home for protective purposes.

But much confusion surrounds these figures. Some feel that runes themselves contain hidden powers. The same is also said of the pentagram and other magical symbols. The thought here is that, simply by drawing a rune, the magician unleashes supernatural powers. This isn't the case. Runes are tools of magic. *Their potency lies within their user.* If my neighbor happened to doodle a healing rune on a napkin and, later, used this to wipe his forehead, no healing energy would be transferred to him simply because he didn't put any into the rune.

Runes must be used with power to be magically effective. Carve, paint or trace away—with visualization and with personal energy.

The ways to use runes are limited only by your imagination. For example, if a friend had asked me to speed her recovery from an illness, I might draw a healing rune on a plain piece of paper and sit before it.

While concentrating on the rune, I'd visualize my friend in a healed, whole state. Then, after building up personal power, I'd send the energy to her *in the shape of the rune.* I'd see it meshing with her body, unblocking, soothing, healing.

Or, I could carve the rune on a piece of cedar wood, again visualizing perfect health, and give it to her to wear.

Runes can also be fashioned onto food—with power—and then eaten to bring that specific energy back into the body; marked on the person with oil and visualization; carved onto a candle which is then burned to release its energies; traced or visualized in a pond or

177

bathtub prior to entering it.

To draw runes on paper, specific ink colors related to each of the runes presented here can be found in their descriptions below, and can be utilized if you wish. The colors work in harmony with the runes.

Here are the runes:

GOOD FORTUNE

This is an all-purpose rune, often used to close correspondence. It is also drawn on packages, inscribed on white candles to ensure fortune in all endeavors, or engraved onto jewelry.

VICTORY

Used in legal battles as well as in general-purpose magic. Inscribe on red candles while in the midst of battles of all sorts. Draw in scarlet ink and burn during ritual or carry with you.

LOVE

This is used not only to receive and strengthen love, but also to send love to a friend. Draw with emerald or pink ink, or visualize, engrave, and so on. May also be traced in pans of cooking food with a spoon or fork to infuse the food with loving vibrations.

COMFORT

To bring relief and ease pain, and to send or induce happiness and comfort to others. If you're depressed or anxious, stand before a mirror, looking into your eyes, and visualize this rune embracing your body. Or, carve onto a pink candle and burn.

WEALTH

Draw on your business card, if you have one. Visualize in your pocket, wallet or purse. Trace with a money-attracting oil such as patchouly or cinnamon on paper money before spending to ensure its eventual return to you.

POSSESSION

Represents tangible objects. Use as a symbol to obtain a needed item. For instance, if you need furniture for your house, this rune could be manipulated magically to represent all the needed items.

TRAVEL

When you wish or need to travel, trace this rune on paper with yellow ink, visualizing yourself traveling to your desired destination. Wrap it around a feather and throw it off a high cliff or mail to your intended destination. Or, carve on a yellow candle, place the candle in its holder over a picture of the place you wish to visit, and burn the candle.

FERTILITY

If you wish to become fertile, trace this rune with oil or visualize it in the sexual region. Can also be used to induce mental fertility, and in most growth-type spells.

PHYSICAL HEALTH
To improve or strengthen health. Visualize while exercising, dieting and deep breathing.

ORDERLINESS
To maintain a structured life, or to keep thoughts in good order. Wear the rune or trace on the forehead.

HEALING
Use to aid healing of the sick. Can be drawn in blue ink on prescriptions, visualized on medicines before taking, traced above or in herbal medicinal potions. This rune can also be made into a talisman and worn.

PROTECTION
This complex sign can be marked on the home, your car or on any objects you wish safeguarded. Sewn or embroidered on clothing or robes it offers personal protection. Can also be made into an amulet and worn or carried. In times of danger when you have no access to such amulets, visualize this rune strongly.

PROTECTION
Another like the last.

A MAN
Use in conjunction with other runes to represent the subject of the spell. For example, if I wake up and can't seem to get my thoughts together, I might draw this rune with power on a piece of paper in yellow ink to represent myself. Then I'd draw the orderliness rune directly on top of the man rune, while visualizing myself attaining this state.

A WOMAN
Another like the last. Use in conjunction with other runes for spells.

FRIENDSHIP
The man and woman runes can be drawn together for a variety of purposes; experiment.

RUNIC SPELLS

A Money Rune Spell
With clove or cinnamon oil, trace the money rune on the largest denomination bill you have. Put this in your wallet or purse and resist spending it for as long as possible. Every time you look at the bill, visualize the rune to reinforce its power. This will draw money to you.

A Rune Love Spell

On an orris root or a piece of apple wood, carve the rune for love. As you do so, visualize the type of person you wish to meet. Carry the rune with you for three days, placing it in your bed at night. On the evening of the third day, toss the root or wood into a river, stream, lake, spring or ocean.

A Rune Petition

At your altar, take a piece of clean, white paper. Draw the rune appropriate to your need in the center of the paper. If you wish, add a pinch of herbs symbolic of your desire, or anoint the paper with an appropriate magical oil. Fold up the paper and hold it tightly while visualizing your need. Now take it to a fire and throw it on the flames. Or, light a red candle and hold the edge of the petition in the flame, then throw it into the cauldron or other heat-proof container to burn. If the paper isn't completely consumed by the flames, re-light it and repeat the spell another day.

To Destroy Negativity or a Baneful Situation

Draw a rune representative of the negativity (disordered thoughts, war, poison—see below) on a piece of paper with black ink. Gaze at it, visualizing the baneful influence, habit or situation. Then, all at once, blot the rune completely from sight with a jar of white ink or paint, completely destroying the rune. While the ink or paint dries, visualize a good fortune, orderliness or comfort rune over the paper and blot out all thoughts of the problem.

Casting the Runes

As mentioned above, runes can be used to glimpse possible future events or unknown circumstances. Perhaps the oldest method entails marking each of the twelve runes below on flat wooden sticks or small branches of a tree (gathered, of course, with the collection formula in "An Herbal Grimoire"). The rune sticks are held, the question or situation clearly visualized, and the sticks are cast to the ground.

Read the runes that are clearly visible. Or, with your eyes closed, pick out one rune stick at random. Divine its interpretation according to the above information, and then draw two more sticks at random, reading each as you take it from the pile on the floor.

Alternately, go to a riverbed, the beach, or a rock shop and collect twelve flat-sided stones. Draw or paint the runes on one side only of the stones. Visualize the question and cast the rune stones onto the floor. Interpret the runes on the stones that have landed face-up, reading them in a general order from right to left.

For example, the money rune next to "man" could signify that wealth will somehow come into your life connected with a man, or that money problems stem from a male influence. Interpretation of the stones relies heavily on your own intuitive and psychic powers, and the situation at hand.

Rune stones seem to have some built-in limitations. Most future readings cover a two-week period. Remember that as with all divinatory work, the runes show future *trends* only. If the picture they unfold for you is unappealing or dangerous, change your course to avoid such a future outcome.

The more you use rune stones, the more comfortable you will become with them. When not in use they can be placed in a basket, box or cloth bag.

Here are twelve runes often used for divinatory purposes. You can also design your own runes and use them.

 The Home: family relations, foundation and stability. Self-image.

 Possessions: tangible objects, the material world.

 Love: emotional states, romance, spouse difficulties or influences.

 Poison: gossip, slander, negativity, baneful habits, harmful attitudes.

Wealth: money, financial concerns, employment, employers.

 Disordered thoughts: emotional tension, irrationality, confusion, doubt.

 Woman: a female influence, or a woman.

 Man: a male influence, or a man.

 Gift: legacies, promotions, windfalls; also physical gifts, psychic and spiritual gifts, sacrifices, volunteering, giving of oneself.

 Comfort: ease, pleasure, security, happiness, joy, a turn for the better.

 Death: the end of a matter, a new beginning, initiation, change in all forms, purification.

 War: conflicts, quarrels, arguments, hostility, aggression, anger, confrontations.

SPELLS AND MAGIC

Protective Chant

Visualize a triple circle of purplish light around your body while chanting:

> *I am protected by your might,*
> *O gracious Goddess, day and night.*

Another of the same type: visualize a triple circle and chant:

> *Thrice around the circle's bound,*
> *Evil sink into the ground.*

A Mirror Spell of Protection for the Home

Compose an altar: place a censer in the center before an image of the Goddess. Have a twelve-inch (or so) round mirror there as well. Ring the altar with nine white candles. Burn a protective incense (such as sandalwood, frankincense, copal or rosemary) in the censer.

Beginning with the candle most directly before the Goddess image, say these or similar words:

> *Lunar light protect me!*

Repeat as you light each candle until all are glowing.

Now, holding the mirror, invoke the Goddess in Her lunar aspect with these or similar words:

> *Great Goddess of the Lunar Light*
> *and Mistress of the Seas;*
> *Great Goddess of the mystic night*

and of the mysteries;
Within this place of candles bright
And with your mirror nigh;
Protect me with your awesome might
While ill vibrations fly!

Standing before the altar, hold the mirror facing the candles so that it reflects their flames. Keeping the mirror toward the candles, move slowly, clockwise, around the altar, watching the reflected firelight bouncing off your surroundings.

Gradually increase your speed, mentally invoking the Goddess to protect you. Move faster and faster; watch the light shattering the air, cleansing it, burning away all negativity and all lines along which the ill energies have traveled into your home.

Charge your home with the protective light of the Goddess. Race around the candles until you've felt the atmosphere change, until you feel that your home has been cleansed and guarded by the Great Goddess.

When finished, stand once again before the image. Thank the Goddess in any words you wish. Pinch out the candles one by one, bind them together with white cord and store them in a safe place until (and if) you need to use them again for this same purpose.

A Spell to Break the Powers of a Spell

If you believe that a spell has been cast against you, place a large black candle in a cauldron (or a large black bowl). The candle must be tall enough to extend a few inches above the cauldron's rim. Affix the candle to the bottom of the cauldron with warmed beeswax or the drippings of another black candle so that it will not tip over.

Fill the cauldron to the rim with fresh water, without wetting the candle's wick. An inch or two of the candle should remain above the water. Deep breathe, meditate, clear your mind, and light the candle. Visualize the suspected spell's power as residing within the candle's flame. Sit in quiet contemplation of the candle and visualize the power flowing and growing with the candle's flame (yes, the power *against* you). As the candle burns down, its flame will eventually sputter and go out as it contacts the water. As soon as the flame has been extinguished by the water, the spell will be dispersed.

Break your visualization of the spell's power; see it explode into dust, becoming impotent.

Pour the water into a hole in the ground, a lake or stream. Bury the candle. It is done.

String Magic

Take cord, of the appropriate color, and shape it on the altar into a rune or the design of the object that you need: a car, a house, a pay check. While you do this, visualize the needed object; raise power and send it forth to bring it to manifestation. So shall it be.

To Protect an Object
(from Morgana)

With the first and middle fingers, trace a pentagram over the object to be protected. Visualize electric-blue or purple flame streaming from your fingers to form the pentagram. Say this as you trace:

> *With this pentagram I lay*
> *Protection here both night and day.*
> *And the one who should not touch*
> *Let his fingers burn and twitch.*
> *I now invoke the law of three:*
> *This is my will, so mote it be!*

Appendix 1

Occult Suppliers

This small listing includes mail-order suppliers of Wiccan books, tools, devotional materials, cassette tapes, herbs, candles and other items. Some catalogs are sent free; others require a small fee. Send a self-addressed, stamped envelope for information regarding catalogue price (if any).

Many small businesses continue to appear. It's a good idea to peruse the latest issue of *The Llewellyn New Times* or *Circle Network News* to find up-to-date mail-order listings.

CIRCLE
P.O. Box 219
Mt. Horeb, WI 53572

Circle publishes *Circle Network News*, a publication of interest to Wiccans and Pagans of all persuasions. Circle also offers Wiccan music tapes such as *Circle Magick Musick* by Selena Fox and Jim Alan, *Gwydion Sings Songs of the Old Religion* by the late, respected Gwydion Pendderwen, *The Mother Calls* by Angie Remedi and many others.

THE CRYSTAL CAVE
415 W. Foothill Blvd.
Claremont, CA 91711

Ritual jewelry, candles, censers, crystals, incense, herbs, oils, charcoal blocks, cauldrons and many other items.

EYE OF THE CAT
3314 E. Broadway
Long Beach, CA 90803

Ritual tools and jewelry, herbs and oils, charcoal blocks, books, candles, crystals, incenses, Goddess and God images.

ISIS
5701 E. Colfax
Denver, CO 80220

Ritual tools, candles, charcoal blocks, books, *Moon Magic* incenses and oils, crystals and stones, ritual jewelry.

MAGICKAL CHILDE
35 W. 19th Street
New York, NY 10011

Ritual tools, candles, charcoal blocks, books, incenses and oils, herbs, crystals and stones, Goddess and God images.

MAGICK BOOKSTORE
2306 Highland Avenue
National City, CA 92050

Athames and other ritual tools, herbs and oils, candles, incense, books, ritual jewelry.

MERMADE
P.O. Box 33-#402
Long Beach, CA 90801

Stones, scrying mirrors, incense and oils, amulets, Goddess images.

MOON MAGICK
P.O. Box 395
Littleton, CO 80160

High quality incense and oil blends.

Appendix 2

Wiccan, Pagan and
Shamanistic Publications

As stated before, solitary Wicca can be a lonely path, but it needn't be. Subscribing to such magazines and tabloids as the ones listed here is a way of connecting with others of like mind and of refreshing your spiritual experience. Additionally, many include contact ads or services to meet others of like mind.

Frequency of publication and subscription prices noted below were current as of this writing. Some changes may occur.

A great many Wiccan and Pagan publications are produced, so the list below is merely a sampling to get you started. The most complete guide to Wiccan publications, groups, networks and individuals is the *Circle Guide to Pagan Resources*. Updated yearly, the most recent issue is a bargain at $11. See their address below.

Happy reading and networking!

THE CAULDRON

A Welsh newsletter devoted to Wicca, Druidism, Odinism and Earth Mysteries. I don't know how many issues are published each year, but the subscription rate is $10/year in dollar bills only, no American checks. The editor asks that writers *do not* put "The Cauldron" on the envelope when addressing it to him. Simply use the address provided below.

Mike Howard Treforgan
Mansion Llangeodmor
Cardigan, Dyfed SA43 2LB
Wales, UK

CIRCLE NETWORK NEWS
P.O. Box 219
Mt. Horeb, WI 53572

A publication devoted to Wicca, Shamanism, Paganism and Earth Mysteries. Rituals, invocations and incantations, herbcraft, Pagan Progress (reports of efforts to broaden public understanding of Wicca), contacts and reviews. 4 issues yearly, $9 sent bulk mail; $13 first class mail. Sample copy, $3. Also publishes *The Circle Guide to Pagan Resources.*

CONVERGING PATHS
P.O. Box 63
Mt. Horeb, WI 53572

Traditional ways of Wicca. Articles, rituals, poetry, artwork. 4 times yearly, $13. Sample issue $4.

HARVEST
P.O. Box 228
Framingham, MA 01701

A Neo-Pagan journal. Articles, songs, news, poetry, rituals. 8 issues yearly, $10. Sample issue $2.

THESMORPHORIA
P.O. Box 11363
Oakland, CA 94611

A Dianic newsletter. Feminist Wicca, Women's mysteries, Goddess rituals, poems and contacts. 8 issues yearly, $13 a year. Sample issue free with self-addressed, stamped envelope.

THE UNICORN
P.O. Box 8814
Minneapolis, MN 55408

Wicca, herbalism, shamanism. Write for information regarding subscription price.

THE WAXING MOON
Box 4127
Sunland, CA 91040

The Waxing Moon was founded in 1965 as the first Wiccan publication in the United States. Since then it has undergone many changes in content and management. Today, *The Waxing Moon* has re-emerged as a journal of the Nature-oriented Shamanic experience with articles, rituals, crafts and reviews. 4 yearly issues. Free to members of the Temple of the Elder Gods; for nonmembers, a minimum donation of $10 yearly.

Glossary

I've included this glossary to provide easy access to definitions of some of the more obscure terms used in this book.

These are, of course, personal definitions, a reflection of my Wiccan involvement, and Wiccans may disagree with me on some small matters. This is to be expected, owing to our religion's individualistic structure. However, I've tried to make it as non-sectarian and universal as possible.

Italicized terms within the body of each discussion refer to other, related entries in the glossary.

Akasha: The fifth element, the omnipresent spiritual power that permeates the universe. It is the energy out of which the *Elements* formed.

Amulet: A magically *Charged* object which deflects specific, usually negative energies. Generally, a protective object. (Compare with *Talisman*.)

Asperger: A bundle of fresh herbs or a perforated object used to sprinkle water during or preceding *Ritual*, for purificatory purposes.

Athame: A Wiccan ritual knife. It usually has a double-edged blade and a black handle. The athame is used to direct *Personal Power* during *Ritual* workings. It is seldom (if ever) used for actual, physical cutting. The term is of obscure origin, has many variant spellings among Wiccans, and an even greater variety of pronunciations. American East-Coast Wiccans may pronounce it as "Ah-THAM-ee" (to rhyme with "whammy"); I was first taught to say "ATH-ah-may" and later "ah-THAW-may." For various purposes currently unknown to me I decided to substitute the term "magic knife" for athame in *The Standing Stones Book of Shadows*. Either term, or simply "knife," will do.

Balefire: A fire lit for magical purposes, usually outdoors. Balefires are traditional on *Yule, Beltane* and *Midsummer.*

Bane: That which destroys life, which is poisonous, destructive, evil, dangerous.

Beltane: A Wiccan festival celebrated on April 30th or May 1st (traditions vary). Beltane is also known as May Eve, Roodmas, Walpurgis Night, Cethsamhain. Beltane celebrates the symbolic union, mating or marriage of the Goddess and God, and links in with the approaching summer months.

Besom: Broom.

Bolline: The white-handled knife, used in magic and Wiccan ritual for practical purposes such as cutting herbs or piercing a pomegranate. Compare with *Athame.*

Book of Shadows: A Wiccan book of rituals, spells and magical lore. Once hand copied upon *Initiation,* the B.O.S. is now photocopied or typed in some *Covens.* No one "true" Book of Shadows exists; all are relevant to their respective users.

Censer: A heat-proof container in which incense is smouldered. An incense burner. It symbolizes the *Element* of Air.

Charge, To: To infuse an object with *Personal Power.* "Charging" is an act of *Magic.*

Circle, Magic. See *Magic Circle.*

Circle of Stones: See *Magic Circle.*

Conscious Mind: The analytical, materially-based, rational half of our consciousness. The mind at work when we compute our taxes, theorize or struggle with ideas. Compare with *Psychic Mind.*

Corn Dolly: A figure, often human-shaped, created by plaiting dried wheat or other grains. It represented the fertility of the Earth and the Goddess in early European agricultural rituals and is still used in Wicca. Corn dollies aren't made from cobs or husks; corn originally referred to any grain other than maize and still does in most English-speaking countries except the United States.

Coven: A group of Wiccans, usually initiatory and led by one or two leaders.

Craft, The: *Wicca. Witchcraft.* Folk magic.

Days of Power, The: See *Sabbat.*

Deosil: Clockwise, the direction of the Sun's apparent motion in the sky. In northern hemisphere magic and religion, deosil movement is symbolic of life, positive energies, good. It is much-used in spells and rituals; i.e. "walk deosil around the Circle of Stones." Some Wiccan groups below the equator, notably in Australia, have switched from deosil to *Widdershins* movements in their rituals, for the Sun "moves" in an apparent counter-clockwise motion from this vantage point. See also *Widdershins.*

Divination: The magical art of discovering the unknown by interpreting random patterns or symbols through the use of tools such as clouds, tarot cards, flames, smoke. Divination contacts the *Psychic Mind* by tricking or drowsing the *Conscious Mind* through *Ritual* and observation or of manipulation of tools. Divination isn't necessary for those who can easily attain communication with the psychic mind, though they may practice it.

Divine Power: The unmanifested, pure energy that exists within the Goddess and God. The life force, the ultimate source of all things. Compare with *Earth Power* and *Personal Power.*

Earth Power: That energy which exists within stones, herbs, flames, wind and other natural objects. It is manifested *Divine Power* and can be utilized during *Magic* to create needed change. Compare with *Personal Power.*

Elements, The: Earth, Air, Fire, Water. These four essences are the building blocks of the universe. Everything that exists (or that has potential to exist) contains one or more of these energies. The elements hum within ourselves and are also "at large" in the world. They can be utilized to cause change through *Magic.* The four elements formed from the primal essence or power—*Akasha.*

Esbat: A Wiccan ritual, usually occurring on the Full Moon.

Evocation: Calling up spirits or other non-physical entities, either to visible appearance or invisible attendance. Compare with *Invocation.*

Grimoire: A magical workbook containing ritual information, formulae, magical properties of natural objects and preparation of ritual equipment. Many of these works include "catalogues of spirits." The most famous of the old grimoires is probably *The Key of Solomon*.* Most first appeared in the 16th and 17th centuries, though they may be far older and contain traces of Roman, Greek, Babylonian, late Egyptian and Sumerian rites.

Handfasting: A Wiccan, Pagan or Gypsy wedding.

Imbolc: A Wiccan festival celebrated on February 2nd, also known as Candlemas, Lupercalia, Feast of Pan, Feast of Torches, Feast of the Waxing Light, Oimelc, Brigit's Day and many other names. Imbolc celebrates the first stirrings of spring and the recovery of the Goddess from giving birth to the Sun (the God) at *Yule*.

Initiation: A process whereby an individual is introduced or admitted into a group, interest, skill or religion. Initiations may be ritual occasions but can also occur spontaneously.

Invocation: An appeal or petition to a higher power (or powers), such as the Goddess and God. A prayer. Invocation is actually a method of establishing conscious ties with those aspects of the Goddess and God that dwell within us. In essence, then, we seemingly cause them to appear or make themselves known by becoming aware of them.

Kahuna: A practitioner of the old Hawaiian philosophical, scientific and magical system.

Labrys: A double-headed axe which symbolized the Goddess in ancient Crete, still used by some Wiccans for this same purpose. The labrys may be placed on or leaned against the left side of the altar.

Lughnasadh: A Wiccan festival celebrated on August 1st, also known as August Eve, Lammas, Feast of Bread. Lughnasadh marks the first harvest, when the fruits of the Earth are cut and stored for the dark winter months, and when the God also mysteriously weakens as the days grow shorter.

Mabon: On or around September 21, the autumn equinox, Wiccans

---

* See Mathers, S. L. MacGregor in the 'Magic' section of the Bibliography.

celebrate the second harvest. Nature is preparing for winter. Mabon is a vestige of ancient harvest festivals which, in some form or another, were once nearly universal among peoples of the Earth.

Magic: The movement of natural energies (such as *Personal Power*) to create needed change. Energy exists within all things—ourselves, plants, stones, colors, sounds, movements. Magic is the process of rousing or building up this energy, giving it purpose, and releasing it. Magic is a natural, not supernatural, practice, though it is little understood.

Magic Circle, The: A sphere constructed of *Personal Power* in which Wiccan rituals are usually enacted. The term refers to the cirle that marks the sphere's penetration of the ground, for it extends both above and below it. It is created through *Visualization* and *Magic.*

Magic Knife: See *Athame.*

Meditation: Reflection, contemplation, turning inward toward the self or outward toward Deity or nature. A quiet time in which the practitioner may dwell upon particular thoughts or symbols, or allow them to come unbidden.

Megalith: A huge stone monument or structure. Stonehenge is perhaps the best-known example of megalithic construction.

Menhir: A standing stone probably lifted by early peoples for religious, spiritual or magical reasons.

Midsummer: The summer solstice, usually on or near June 21st, one of the Wiccan festivals and an excellent night for *Magic.* Midsummer marks the point of the year when the Sun is symbolically at the height of its powers, and so too the God. The longest day of the year.

Mighty Ones, The: Beings, deities or presences often *Invoked* during Wiccan ceremony to witness or guard the rituals. The Mighty Ones are thought to be either spiritually evolved beings, once human, or spiritual entities created by or charged by the Goddess and God to protect the Earth and to watch over the four directions. They are sometimes linked with the Elements.

Neo-Pagan: Literally, new-Pagan. A member, follower or sympathizer of one of the newly formed Pagan religions now spreading throughout the world. All Wiccans are *Pagan*, but not all Pagans are Wiccan.

Old Ones, The: A Wiccan term often used to encompass all aspects of the Goddess and God. I've used it in this context in *The Standing Stones Book of Shadows*. Some Wiccans view it as an alternative of *The Mighty Ones*.

Ostara: Occurring at the spring equinox, around March 21st, Ostara marks the beginning of true, astronomical spring, when snow and ice make way for green. As such, it is a fire and fertility festival, celebrating the return of the Sun, the God and the fertility of the Earth (the Goddess).

Pagan: From the Latin *paganus*, country-dweller. Today used as a general term for followers of Wicca and other magical, shamanistic and polytheistic religions. Naturally, Christians have their own peculiar definition of this word. It can be interchanged with *Neo-Pagan*.

Pendulum: A divinatory device consisting of a string attached to a heavy object, such as a quartz crystal, root or ring. The free end of the string is held in the hand, the elbow steadied against a flat surface, and a question is asked. The movement of the heavy object's swings determines the answer. A rotation indicates yes or positive energy. A back and forth swing signals the opposite. (There are many methods of deciphering the pendulum's movements; use those that work best for you.) It is a tool which contacts the *Psychic Mind*.

Pentacle: A ritual object (usually a circular piece of wood, metal, clay, etc.) upon which a five-pointed star (*Pentagram*) is inscribed, painted or engraved. It represents the *Element* of Earth. The words "pentagram" and "pentacle" are not interchangeable, though they understandably cause some confusion.

Personal Power: That energy which sustains our bodies. It ultimately originates from the Goddess and God (or, rather, the power behind them). We first absorb it from our biological mothers within the womb and, later, from food, water, the Moon and Sun and other natural objects. We release personal power during stress, exercise, sex, conception and childbirth. *Magic* is often a movement of personal power for a specific goal.

Polarity: The concept of equal, opposite energies. The Eastern yin/ yang is a perfect example. Yin is cold; yang is hot. Other examples of polarity: Goddess/God, night/day, Moon/Sun, birth/death, dark/light, *Psychic Mind/Conscious Mind.* Universal balance.

Projective Hand, The: The hand that is normally used for manual activities such as writing, peeling apples and dialing telephones is symbolically thought to be the point at which *Personal Power* is sent from the body. In ritual, personal power is visualized as streaming out from the palm or fingers of the hand for various magical goals. This is also the hand in which tools such as the *Athame* and wand are held. Ambidextrous persons simply choose which hand to utilize for this purpose. Compare with *Receptive Hand.*

Psychic Mind: The subconscious or unconscious mind, in which we receive psychic impulses. The psychic mind is at work when we sleep, dream and meditate. It is our direct link with the Goddess and God and with the larger, non-physical world around us. Other related terms: *Divination* is a ritual process which utilizes the *Conscious Mind* to contact the psychic mind. Intuition is a term used to describe psychic information which unexpectedly reaches the conscious mind.

Psychism: The act of being consciously psychic, in which the *Psychic Mind* and *Conscious Mind* are linked and working in harmony. *Ritual Consciousness* is a form of psychism.

Receptive Hand: The left hand in right-handed persons, the reverse for left-handed persons. This is the hand through which energy is received into the body. Compare with *Projective Hand.*

Reincarnation: The doctrine of rebirth. The process of repeated incarnations in human form to allow evolution of the sexless, ageless soul.

Ritual: Ceremony. A specific form of movement, manipulation of objects or inner processes designed to produce desired effects. In religion, ritual is geared toward union with the divine. In *Magic* it produces a specific state of consciousness which allows the magician to move energy toward needed goals. A *Spell* is a magical ritual.

Ritual Consciousness: A specific, alternate state of awareness necessary to the successful practice of magic. The magician achieves this through the use of *Visualization* and *Ritual*. It denotes a state in which the *Conscious Mind* and *Psychic Mind* are attuned, in which the magician sense energies, gives them purpose and releases them toward the magical goal. It is a heightening of the senses, an awareness-expansion of the seemingly non-physical world, a linking with nature and with the forces behind all conceptions of Deity.

Runes: Stick-like figures, some of which are remnants of old Teutonic alphabets. Others are pictographs. These symbols are once again widely being used in *Magic* and *divination*.

Sabbat: A Wiccan festival. See *Beltane, Imbolc, Lughnasadh, Mabon, Midsummer, Ostara, Samhain* and *Yule* for specific descriptions.

Samhain: A Wiccan festival celebrated on October 31st, also known as November Eve, Hallowmas, Halloween, Feast of Souls, Feast of the Dead, Feast of apples. Samhain marks the symbolic death of the Sun God and His passing into the "land of the young," where He awaits rebirth of the Mother Goddess at Yule. This Celtic word is pronounced by Wiccans as: SOW-wen; SEW-wen; SAHM-hain; SAHM-ain; SAV-een and other ways. The first seems to be the one preferred among most Wiccans.

Scry, To: To gaze at or into an object (a quartz crystal sphere, pool of water, reflections, a candle flame) to still the *Conscious Mind* and to contact the *Psychic Mind*. This allows the scryer to become aware of possible events prior to their actual occurrence, as well as of previous or distant, simultaneous events through other than the normally accepted senses. A form of *Divination*.

Shaman: A man or woman who has obtained knowledge of the subtler dimensions of the Earth, usually through periods of alternate states of consciousness. Various types of *Ritual* allow the shaman to pierce the veil of the physical world and to experience the realm of energies. This knowledge lends the shaman the power to change her or his world through *Magic*.

Shamanism: The practice of shamans, usually ritualistic or magical in nature, sometimes religous.

Simple Feast, The: A *Ritual* meal shared with the Goddess and God.

Spell: A magical *Ritual*, usually non-religious in nature and often accompanied by spoken words.

Spirits of the Stones, The: The elemental energies naturally inherent at the four directions of the *Magic Circle*, personified within the *Standing Stones Tradition* as the "Spirits of the Stones." They are linked with the *Elements*.

Talisman: An object, such as an amethyst crystal, ritually *Charged* with power to attract a specific force or energy to its bearer. Compare with *Amulet*.

Tradition, Wiccan: An organized, structured, specific Wiccan subgroup, usually initiatory, with often unique ritual practices. Many traditions have their own *Books of Shadows* and may or may not recognize members of other traditions as Wiccan. Most traditions are composed of a number of *Covens* as well as solitary practitioners.

Trilithon: A stone arch made from two upright slabs with one lying atop these. Trilithons are featured in Stonehenge as well as the circle visualization in *The Standing Stones Book of Shadows*.

Visualization: The process of forming mental images. Magical visualization consists of forming images of needed goals during *Ritual*. Visualization is also used to direct *Personal Power* and natural energies during *Magic* for various purposes, including *Charging* and forming the *Magic Circle*. It is a function of the *Conscious Mind*.

White-Handled Knife: A normal cutting knife, with a sharp blade and white handle. It is used within Wicca to cut herbs and fruits, to slice bread during *The Simple Feast* and for other functions—but never for sacrifice. Sometimes called the bolline. Compare with *Athame*.

Wicca: A contemporary *Pagan* religion with spiritual roots in *Shamanism* and the earliest expressions of reverence of nature. Among its major motifs are: reverence for the Goddess and the God; reincarnation; magic; ritual observances of the Full Moon, astronomical and agricultural phenomena; spheroid temples, created with *Personal Power,* in which rituals occur.

Widdershins: Anti-clockwise motion, usually used in the Northern Hemisphere for negative magical purposes or for dispersing negative energies or conditions such as disease. Southern Hemisphere Wiccans may use widdershins motions for exactly the opposite purposes; namely for positive ends, for the reason stated in the entry under *Deosil.* In either case, widdershins and deosil motions are *symbolic;* only strict, close-minded traditionalists believe that accidentally walking around the altar backwards, for instance, will raise negativity. Their use in Wicca stems from ancient European rituals practiced by peoples who watched and reverenced the Sun and Moon in their daily revolutions. Widdershins motion, within ritual contexts, is still shunned by the vast majority of Wiccans, though others use it once in a while, for instance, to disperse the *Magic Circle* at the end of a rite.

Witch: Anciently, a European practitioner of the remnants of pre-Christian folk magic, particularly that relating to herbs, healing, wells, rivers and stones. One who practiced *Witchcraft.* Later, this term's meaning was deliberately altered to denote demented, dangerous, supernatural beings who practiced destructive magic and who threatened Christianity. This change was a political, monetary and sexist move on the part of organized religion, not a change in the practices of Witches. This later, erroneous meaning is still accepted by many non-Witches. It is also, somewhat surprisingly, used by some members of *Wicca* to describe themselves.

Witchcraft: The *craft* of the *Witch*—*Magic,* especially magic utilizing *Personal Power* in conjunction with the energies within stones, herbs, colors and other natural objects. While this may have spiritual overtones, Witchcraft, using this definition, isn't a religion. However, some followers of *Wicca* use this word to denote their religion.

Yule: A *Wiccan* festival celebrated on or about December 21st, marking the rebirth of the Sun God from the Earth Goddess. A time of joy and celebration during the miseries of winter. Yule occurs on the winter solstice.

Suggested Reading

This is a wide-ranging list of books related, in some way, to Wicca. A book's inclusion here doesn't necessarily indicate that I'm in perfect agreement with its contents. Many of these books were written from far different perspectives than the one you've been reading.

All, however, if read with intelligence and discrimination, will deepen your understanding of the Goddess and God, and of the myriad forms of Wicca, magic and shamanism.

Those asterisked (*) are highly recommended.

Where I felt it important, I have appended short comments concerning the book's contents, *not* my views on them.

Such a list as this cannot hope to be complete. Books on these subjects are being published every day. Still, this should serve as a starting point for those interested in reading further.

Shamanism

*Andrews, Lynn V., *Medicine Woman*. San Francisco: Harper & Row, 1981.

Bend, Cynthia and Tayja Wiger, *Birth of a Modern Shaman*. St. Paul: Llewellyn Publications, 1988.

Castaneda, Carlos, *The Teachings of Don Juan: A Yaqui Way of Knowledge*. New York: Ballantine, 1970.

Furst, Peter T., *Hallucinogens and Culture*. Corte Madera (California): Chandler & Sharp Publishers, 1976.

*Harner, Michael J., (editor), *Hallucinogens and Shamanism*. New York: Oxford University Press, 1978.

*Harner, Michael, *The Way of the Shaman*. San Francisco: Harper & Row, 1981. The first "how-to" book on this subject, *The Way of the Shaman* introduces simple techniques for acquiring alternate states of consciousness, on contacting your power animal, healing rituals and much else of interest.

*Howells, William, *The Heathens: Primitive Man and His Religions*. Garden City (New York): Doubleday, 1956. Covers the entire range of pre-Christian and pre-technological religion and magic, including totemism, ancestor worship, shamanism, divination, mana and tabu.

Kilpatrick, Jack Frederick and Anna Gritts, *Notebook of a Cherokee Shaman*. Washington D.C.: Smithsonian, 1970.

*Lame Deer, John (Fire) and Richard Erdoes, *Lame Deer: Seeker of Visions*. New York: Pocket Books, 1978. A portrait of a contemporary shaman, revealing the essential humanness of the subject. Much Sioux lore.

Lewis, I. M., *Ecstatic Religion: an Anthropological Study of Spirit Possession and Shamanism*. Baltimore: Penquin, 1976. This is a scholarly sociological investigation into shamanism and alternate states of consciousness.

Rogers, Spencer L., *The Shaman's Healing Way*. Ramona (California): Acoma Books, 1976.

*Sharon, Douglas, *Wizard of the Four Winds: A Shaman's Story*. New York: The Free Press, 1978. A portrait of Eduardo Calderon, a contemporary Peruvian shaman, detailing much of his rites and rituals.

*Torrey, E. Fuller, *The Mind Game: Witchdoctors and Psychiatrists*. New York: Bantam, 1973.

*Wellman, Alice, *Spirit Magic*. New York: Berkeley, 1973. This short paperback is a guide to shamanism as practiced in various parts of the world. One chapter, "The Tools of Wizardry," is of particular interest.

Goddess Studies

Briffault, Robert, *The Mothers*. (Abridged by Gordon Taylor.) New York: Atheneum, 1977.

Downing, Christine, *The Goddess: Mythological Images of the Feminine*. New York: Crossroad, 1984.

*Graves, Robert, *The White Goddess*. New York: Farrar, Straus and Giroux, 1973. Perhaps the book which has had the greatest effect on modern Wicca. A poetic investigation into the Goddess.

*Harding, Esther, *Women's Mysteries: Ancient and Modern*. New York: Pantheon, 1955.

James E. O., *The Cult of the Mother-Goddess*. New York: Barnes and Noble, 1959.

Leland, Charles G., *Aradia, or the Gospel of the Witches*. New York: Buckland Museum, 1968. This work presents a very different view of the Goddess than most others. The material was collected by Mr. Leland in the late 1800's and has had an affect on current Wicca.

*Newmann, Erich, *The Great Mother: an Analysis of the Archetype*. Princeton: Princeton University Press, 1974. A Jungian approach to the Goddess. This book concludes with 185 pages of photographs of Goddess images.

Stone, Merlin, *When God Was a Woman*. New York: Dial Press, 1976.

Walker, Barbara, *The Women's Encyclopedia of Myths and Mysteries*. San Francisco: Harper & Row, 1983.

Folklore, Mythology, Legend and History

*Bord, Janet and Colin Bord, *Earth Rites: Fertility Practices in Pre-Industrial Britain*. London: Granada, 1982. An account of Pagan rituals of Britain.

Busenbark, Ernest, *Symbols, Sex and the Stars in Popular Beliefs*. New York: Truth Seeker, 1949.

*Campbell, Joseph, *The Masks of God: Creative Mythology*. New York: Viking Press, 1971.

*Campbell, Joseph, *The Masks of God: Oriental Mythology*. New York: Viking Press, 1977.

*Campbell, Joseph, *The Masks of God: Primitive Mythology*. New York: Viking Press, 1977. These books cover the whole sweep of worldwide mythology.

Campbell, Joseph, *Myths to Live By*. New York: Bantam Books, 1973.

*Carpenter, Edward, *Pagan and Christian Creeds: Their Origin and Meaning*. New York: Harcourt, Brace and Company, 1920. An early work by a renegade scholar, it shows the origins of many Christian religious symbols from earlier Pagan religions. Along the way it covers food and vegetation magic, pagan initiations, ritual dancing, the sex-taboo and much else of interest.

*Dexter, T. F. G., *Fire Worship in Britain*. London: Watts and Co., 1931. A 43-page booklet, printed before World War II, detailing the survivals of ancient Pagan festivals in Britain before that conflict ended many of them forever.

*Ehrenreich, Barbara and Deirdre English, *Witches, Midwives and Nurses: a History of Women Healers.* Old Westbury (New York): 1973. An important investigation of the role of women as healers and witches in earlier times.

Frazer, Sir James, *The Golden Bough.* New York: Macmillan, 1956. (One volume abridged edition.)

Harley, Timothy, *Moon Lore.* Tokyo: Charles E. Tuttle Co., 1970.

Kenyon, Theda, *Witches Still Live.* New York: Washburn, 1929. An early collection of myths, legends and tales of Witches and folk magicians.

*Leach, Maria (editor) and Jerome Fried (associate editor), *Funk and Wagnalls Standard Dictionary of Folklore, Mythology and Legend.* New York: Funk and Wagnall's, 1972. This classic, one-volume collection nearly sums up the totality of mythic information. Of great interest to Wiccans.

Watts, Alan, *The Two Hands of God: the Myths of Polarity.* New York: Collier, 1978.

Wentz, W. Y. Evans, *The Fairy-Faith in Celtic Countries.* London: Oxford University Press, 1911. Gerrards Cross (Buckinghamshire, England): 1981.

Wicca

Bowness, Charles, *The Witch's Gospel.* London: Robert Hale, 1979.

Buckland, Raymond, *Witchcraft . . . The Religion.* Bay Shore (New York): The Buckland Museum of Witchcraft and Magick, 1966. An early explication of Gardnerian Wicca.

Buczynski, Edmund M., *The Witchcraft Fact Book.* New York: Magickal Childe, N.D.

Crowther, Patricia, *Witch Blood! The Diary of a Witch High Priestess.* New York: House of Collectibles, 1974.

Deutch, Richard, *The Ecstatic Mother: Portrait of Maxine Sanders—Witch Queen.* London: Bachman and Turner, 1977. One of the key figures of the Alexandrian Wiccan tradition is explored in this work.

*Gardner, Gerald, *The Meaning of Witchcraft.* London: 1959. London: Aquarian Press, 1971. An historical look at Wicca.

Gardner, Gerald, *Witchcraft Today.* New York: Citadel, 1955. The first book written about contemporary Wicca details what has come to be termed Gardnerian Wicca.

*Glass, Justine, *Witchcraft: the Sixth Sense and Us*. North Hollywood: Wilshire, 1965.

Johns, June, *King of the Witches: the World of Alex Sanders*. New York: Coward McCann, 1969. Another investigation of Alexandrian Wicca and a biography of its founder.

Lady Sara, *Questions and Answers on Wicca Craft*. Wolf Creek (Oregon): Stonehenge Farm, 1974.

*Leek, Sybil, *The Complete Art of Witchcraft*. New York: World Publishing, 1971. This influential work describes an eclectic Wiccan tradition.

Leek, Sybil, *Diary of a Witch*. New York: Prentice-Hall, 1968.

'Lugh', Old George Pickingill and the Roots of Modern Witchcraft. London: Wiccan Publications, 1982. Taray, 1984. This work purports to describe the historical background to the modern revival of Wicca by Gerald Gardner.

Martello, Leo L., *Witchcraft: the Old Religion*. Secaucus: University Books, 1974. An investigation into Sicilian Wicca.

Roberts, Susan, *Witches USA*. New York: Dell, 1971. Hollywood: Phoenix, 1974. This book, an investigation into Wicca by an outsider, created a storm of controversy when it was reprinted. It stands as an overview of part of the Wiccan scene *circa* 1970, and is no more flawed by inaccuracies than any other book included in this list.

Sanders, Alex, *The Alex Sanders Lectures*. New York: Magickal Childe, 1980. Another look at Alexandrian Wicca.

Sanders, Maxine, *Maxine the Witch Queen*. London: Star Books, 1976. Yet another look—this time autobiographical—at the founding and activities of Alexandrian Wicca.

*Valiente, Doreen, *An ABC of Witchcraft Past and Present*. New York: St. Martin's, 1973. A Gardnerian Wiccan's answer to earlier Witchcraft books, this is an encyclopedic look at British Wicca, folklore and legend.

*Valiente, Doreen, *Where Witchcraft Lives*. London: Aquarian Press, 1962. An early look at British Wicca and Sussex folklore.

Practical Instructions

*Alan, Jim and Selena Fox, *Circle Magic Songs*. Madison (Wisconsin): Circle Publications, 1977.

Budapest, Z., *The Feminist Book of Light and Shadows*. Venice (California): Luna Publications, 1976. An influential, first book of Feminist Wicca.

Budapest, Z., *The Holy Book of Women's Mysteries Part I*. Oakland: The Susan B. Anthony coven #1, 1979. An expanded version of the above book. A second volume was also published.

Buckland, Raymond, *The Tree: The Complete Book of Saxon Witchcraft*. New York: Weiser, 1974.

*Buckland, Raymond, *Buckland's Complete Book of Witchcraft*. St. Paul: Llewellyn Publications, 1985. A course in Wicca, drawn from several traditions. Includes a section on solitary practitioners.

Crowther, Patricia, *Lid Off the Cauldron: A Wicca Handbook*. London: Robert Hale, 1981. Another how-to book.

*Farrar, Janet and Stewart Farrar, *Eight Sabbats for Witches*. London: Robert Hale, 1981. These once-Alexandrian Wiccans have explored new territory, incorporating much Irish lore and deity-forms. This book also presents a unique look at the origins of the so-called Gardnerian Book of Shadows.

*Farrar, Janet and Stewart Farrar, *The Witches' Way: Principles, Rituals and Beliefs of Modern Witchcraft*. London: Robert Hale, 1984. Further revelations concerning Gardner's Book of Shadows and much practical information.

*Fitch, Ed, *Magical Rites From the Crystal Well*. St.Paul: Llewellyn Publications, 1984. A collection of Neo-Pagan rituals for every occasion.

K. Amber, *How to Organize a Coven or Magical Study Group*. Madison (Wisconsin): Circle Publications, 1983. Guidelines for doing just that.

*Slater, Herman (editor), *A Book of Pagan Rituals*. New York: Weiser, 1974. Another collection of rituals, this time drawn from the Pagan Way.

*Starhawk, *The Spiral Dance: a Rebirth of the Ancient Religion of the Great Goddess*. San Francisco: Harper and Row, 1979. It seems strange that it's been nearly ten years since this book was first published. It has had a tremendous impact on Wiccan groups and individuals. Definitely Goddess- and woman-oriented, it includes exercises for developing magical fluency and many rituals as well.

Valiente, Doreen, *Witchcraft for Tomorrow.* London: Robert Hale, 1978. Valiente's work, the first of the modern how-to-practice-Wicca books, contains a complete Book of Shadows—which she wrote just for publication—as well as several chapters covering various aspects of Wicca.

*Weinstein, Marion, *Earth Magic: A Diunic Book of Shadows.* New York: Earth Magic Productions, 1980. This is a Wiccan book like no other. It contains complete, explicit information on forming alignments with "all five aspects" of the Deities, working with familiars, the tools and much else of interest. An expanded version has been published.

Spell Books

Buckland, Raymond, *Practical Candleburning Rituals.* St. Paul, Llewellyn Publications, 1971.

*Chappel, Helen, *The Waxing Moon: A Gentle Guide to Magic.* New York: Links, 1974.

Dixon, Jo and James, *The Color Book: Rituals, Charms and Enchantments.* Denver: Castle Rising, 1978.

Grammary, Ann, *The Witch's Workbook.* New York: Pocket, 1973.

Huson, Paul, *Mastering Witchcraft.* New York: Berkeley, 1971. An early book responsible, in part, for the tremendous interest in occult matters during the early 1970's. Little of its information bears much resemblance to Wicca, or to the type of magic Wiccans practice.

Lorde, Simon and Clair Lorde, *The Wiccan Guide to Witches Ways.* New South Wales (Australia): K. J. Forrest, 1980.

Malbrough, Ray T., *Charms, Spells and Formulas for the Making and Use of Gris-Gris, Herb Candles, Doll Magick, Incenses, Oils and Powders to Gain Love, Protection, Prosperity, Luck and Prophetic Dreams.* St. Paul: Llewellyn, 1986. A collection of Cajun magic from Louisiana.

Paulsen, Kathryn, *Witches Potions and Spells.* Mount Vernon: Peter Pauper Press, 1971.

*Worth Valerie, *The Crone's Book of Words.* St. Paul: Llewellyn Publications, 1971, 1986.

Magic

Agrippa, Henry Cornelius, *The Philosophy of Natural Magic*. Antwerp, 1531. Secaucus: University Books, 1974. This is the first of the three books mentioned in the next entry.

*Agrippa, Henry Cornelius, *Three Books of Occult Philosophy*. London: 1651. London: Chthonios Books, 1986. This book constituted the bulk of magical information known in the 16th century. Stones, stars, herbs, incenses, sigils and all manner of delights are to be found in this book. Recently reprinted in its entirety for the first time in 300 years, it is expensive ($60.00) but well worth the price.

*Barrett, Francis, *The Magus, or Celestial Intelligencer, Being a Complete System of Occult Philosophy*. 1801. New Hyde Park (New York): University Books, 1967. Ceremonial (as opposed to natural) magic.

*Burland, C. A., *The Magical Arts: A Short History*. New York: Horizon Press, 1966. A history of folk magic.

Devine, M. V., *Brujeria: A Study of Mexican-American Folk-Magic*. St. Paul: Llewellyn Publications, 1982.

Fortune, Dion, *Psychic Self-Defence*. London: Aquarian, 1967.

*Howard, Michael, *The Magic of Runes*. New York: Weiser, 1980.

Howard, Michael, *The Runes and Other Magical Alphabets*. New York: Weiser, 1978.

Koch, Rudolph, *The Book of Signs*. New York: Dover, 1955. A book of signs, symbols and runes.

Leland, Charles Godfrey, *Etruscan Magic and Occult Remedies*. New Hyde Park (New York): University Books, 1963.

Leland, Charles Godfrey, *Gypsy Sorcery and Fortune-Telling*. New York: Dover, 1971.

Mathers, S. L. MacGregor (editor and translator), *The Key of Solomon the King*. New York: Weiser, 1972.

*Mickaharic, Draja, *Spiritual Cleansing: A Handbook of Psychic Protection*. York Beach (Maine): Weiser, 1982. Some of the magic in this work is shamanistic in tone and origin.

*Pepper, Elizabeth and John Wilcox, *Witches All*. New York: Grosset and Dunlap, 1977. A collection of folk magic drawn from the popular (now defunct) *Witches Almanac*.

Pliny the Elder, *Natural History*. Cambridge: Harvard University Press, 1956.

Shah, Sayed Idries, *Oriental Magic.* New York: Philosophical Library, 1957.

Shah, Sayed Idries, *The Secret Lore of Magic.* New York: Citadel, 1970. Extracts from several Renaissance books of ceremonial magic.

Shah, Sirdar Ikbal Ali, *Occultism: Its Theory and Practice.* Castle Books. N.D.

Valiente, Doreen, *Natural Magic.* New York: St. Martin's Press, 1975.

*Weinstein, Marion, *Positive Magic: Occult Self-Help.* New York: Pocket Books, 1978. An introduction to magic. An expanded edition of this popular book has also been published.

Periodicals Consulted

Some of these magazines and newspapers are still being published; others are not:

A Pagan Renaissance
Circle Network News
The Crystal Well
Earth Religions News
Georgian Newsletter
Gnostica
The Green Egg
Nemeton
The New Broom
New Dimensions
Pentagram
Revival
Seax-Wicca Voys
The Unicorn
The Waxing Moon
The Witch's Almanac

INDEX

LIVING WICCA

A FURTHER GUIDE
FOR THE SOLITARY PRACTIONER

THIS BOOK IS DEDICATED TO
SOLITARY WICCANS
EVERYWHERE

TABLE OF CONTENTS

A NOTE TO
'TRADITIONAL' WICCANS

This book, a further guide for Solitary practitioners of Wicca, isn't an attack on conventional Wicca, Wiccan traditions, covens or usual training procedures. It was written (as was its predecessor) for those without access to conventional Wicca, Wiccan traditions, covens or usual training procedures.

Some will see this book as an insult to their form of Wicca, so I repeat: this is a guide for Solitary practitioners who have no access to your form of Wicca. This in no way lessens it or any other Wiccan tradition.

Read with an open mind and remember the time when you, too, were seeking.

INTRODUCTION

This book consists of further instructions for the Solitary Wiccan Practitioner. It assumes that the reader has gained some experience in our religion and, thus, doesn't stop to define every specialized term and ritual reference. For a quick review, check the glossary.

Part I of this book contains essays on a variety of topic of importance or interest to Solitary Wiccans. Part II is a collection of daily prayers and rituals of offering and thanks, together with guides to effective prayer and magic. Part III is a recommended system for creating your own Wiccan tradition.

This book has been written with a single premise: that Wicca is an open religion. All can come before the altar and worship the Goddess and God, whether alone or in the company of others; initiated or not. Wicca is available to all interested people.

Living Wicca has been written for those who have become enchanted by the moon shining through trees; who have begun to investigate the sublime world that lies out beyond the fabric of daily life, and who stand in smoke-shrouded circles, raising aloft their hands to greet the Goddess and God as the candles flicker on the altar. It's written for those of us who, through choice or circumstance, meet with Silver Lady and the Horned God alone.

Readers of *Wicca: A Guide for the Solitary Practitioner* asked me to write another, similar work, because so little Wiccan writing is aimed at the solitary practitioner. I hope that this book fills at least part of this need.

Until next time, I'll say Blessed Be.

Scott Cunningham
La Mesa, CA
July 10, 1992

PART ONE:

LEARNING

1: TOOLS OF LEARNING

M EMBERS of covens have access to teachers, attend learning circles, and can enjoy the experience of other Wiccans in guiding and enriching their Wiccan knowledge. Solitary Wiccans lack all of these opportunities. What, then, are our tools of learning?

We must be creative. Self-teaching is a great challenge, but it can be accomplished through the use of four tools:

Study

Thought

Prayer

Experimentation

The use of these tools is the most effective method by which Solitary Wiccans can increase their knowledge and understanding of Wicca. This four-fold approach may answer nearly every question you have if you're willing to trust yourself; if you're willing to think; and if you're not caught up in worrying that you're doing something incorrectly.

There's no one correct method of casting a circle; of invoking the Goddess and God; of ritually observing the seasons or performing Wiccan magic. The fact that there are numerous methods of casting circles, invoking the Goddess and God and observing the seasons points to the unique opportunity that lies in wait for the Solitary Wiccan: to discover new forms of worship that others, conditioned to accept only certain avenues of Wiccan expression, may have missed.

How can you do this? By studying, thinking, praying and experimenting.

STUDY

Books have always been tools of magic. With the turn of a page, we can be transported to the bottom of the ocean; to the limitless desert; to the surface of the moon. Books can lift our spirits, heal our wounds, steel our courage and strengthen our religious resolve. They can also arouse our curiosity, sharpen our minds, teach us new skills and alter our opinions. Books are powerful tools of change.

Many people first learn of Wicca through reading books, and most use books to guide their first steps on the Wiccan path. Such books, if written in a clear manner by experienced Wiccans, can be valuable learning tools. Quality books of this kind become their readers' High Priestess and High Priest, coveners and friends.

Indeed, due to the scarcity of those willing to teach Wicca, and the small number of students that they can effectively instruct, we've thrown the mantle of experience and authority around books written by Wiccan authors. Such works have largely become the teachers of the new era of Wicca.

Sometimes, however, reading more than a few books may lead to confusion. Authors may make contradictory statements regarding Wiccan ritual practices and concepts. Some may deliberately obscure Wiccan knowledge with mystic prose. The Solitary Wiccan, grasping for answers, may only come up with more questions, as expert after expert states that her or his way is the best or most effective (this tendency is disappearing in Wiccan books today, but many older books that contain such statements are still in print).

One book may state, "the altar is always in the East"; in another, the North. An author might write that counterclockwise movement within the circle is forbidden; another will direct the reader to move in precisely this direction. Dates and names for the Sabbats and Esbats vary widely according to the author. Tools are given differing names, attributes and functions.

Eventually, the books that originally inspired the new Solitary Wiccan may become a source of confusion and despair, and she or he may pack them away, deciding that no real learning can be achieved with them. This is a shame, and can be avoided by keeping this concept in mind: Each book is a different teacher. Each teacher has distinct ideas concerning the subject being taught. Think of four experienced race-car drivers who are teaching beginners. Each instructs his or her student in the basics of this dangerous sport. The fastest engine designs; the best oil; the most effective strategy to use during the races themselves. Each driver teaches this subject in a different way, and expresses her or his biases, but they're all teaching racing.

Wiccan books, as teachers, are quite similar. Experience and training have created specific ideals concerning Wicca within each book's writer, and these ideals are clearly presented within her or his books. Divergences of opinion are natural in experts in any field and shouldn't dismay those who are confronted by them.

When you're challenged with seemingly contradictory information, examine this information and make a decision as to which to follow. Listen to your intuition. In other words, feel free to pick and choose among the published rituals and ritual textbooks to decide what *feels* right. It's this selectivity that will usually prove to be the most effective.

I can already hear some of you saying: "Wait! I could never do that! I—I wouldn't know if I was doing it right. I need someone to teach me!"

That's where you come in. You become your own teacher, and books provide some of the lessons. Learn to trust yourself. Settle questions in the best way that you can. Think. Pray. Experiment (see the next three sections of this chapter). And just do it.

Books aren't foolproof. Some books contain virtually no accurate information. Many readers are apt to believe anything in print. "After all," they say, "it's in this book right here. That proves it's true." Unfortunately, nearly anyone can write a book and even have it published. Does this ensure that its contents are true?

No. In fact, a few specialty publishers continue to publish lie-packed books describing the 'Satanic' nature of Wicca; that describe its rites as those of human sacrifice, orgies and prayers to the Devil. Such books, written by a few virulent self-styled Christians, are easily spotted among others on the shelves by the repeated use of Biblical quotations. These hateful tomes have nothing to teach and are best avoided.

Other books, while written by scholars or others interseted in accurately recording Wiccan beliefs and practices, may contain misinformation. Most surveys of Wiccan belief (such as by Tanya Luhrman's *Persuasions of the Witches' Craft*) are so slanted by the author's bias that little truth has managed to squeeze onto their pages. Again, it's best to avoid books of this nature and all books written by non-Wiccans about Wicca.

Another pitfall that may be encountered within books consists of glowing descriptions of negative magic. Such passages are usually found in spell books, not in Wiccan texts. Still, Solitary Wiccans are apt to peruse magical texts, and the majority of these describe the wonders of cursing and reveal numerous methods of hexing one's enemies. Such books may otherwise contain fine information, but passages like these can perpetuate the false idea that negative magic is acceptable. Material of this nature can be weeded out by a simple recitation of the Wiccan Law: *Harm none.*

Finally, some older books by Wiccans contain what seem to be absolute statements of fact that are absolutely false, such as "Wicca is a British religion"; "You must be naked in your rites"; "Sexual rites are necessary in Wicca", or our old friend, "Only a Witch can make a Witch" (i.e., initiation is necessary). These statements are framed within the context of these authors' Wiccan traditions, and may be quite correct within them. However, they have no validity to those outside their tradition. Such statements, where they appear in books, needn't concern us.

One of the most popular forms of misinformation concerning Wicca are found in books on the ancient history of Wicca. I won't add to this argument, but I will advise you to read tales of ancient Wicca with a great deal of discernment and a large grain of salt.

While books aren't infallible sources of information, they can be valuable allies on the Solitary Path if you keep these things in mind:

- Books are tools that are meant to be used. They provide lessons; we have to put the lessons to work.

- Books can't answer every question, but neither can any High Priestess or teacher.

- Be discriminating when reading books. If an author makes wild statements that you know to be untrue, consider the book as a *possible* source of incorrect information.

- Mark up your books. Underline (with pencils) important passages, or use bookmarks to indicate valuable sections. You may wish to add to the index (many Wiccans do this). (Purists may purchase a second copy of the same book and leave this one in pristine condition on the shelf.)

- Combine information from a number of books on a specific topic, such as magic, energy raising or circle construction. Write notes and study the combined teachings of several books. This may facilitate the process of assimilating (and using) this information, and will give you a greater chance of finding what's right for you. (This process of collecting information, combining it and utilizing it is one of the most important parts of learning any new skill, profession, hobby or religion.) (See Part III of this book.)

⊙ If books are too expensive for your budget, budget differently, or haunt used book stores in your area. Libraries are another possible source of Wiccan books, but don't expect to find them on the shelf: they're usually stolen if openly shelved. Most libraries keep occult books behind the counter or in storage. Some librarians may look with disgust at you for checking out books on Wicca. If this is a problem, say you're working on a paper, ask the person if she or he has a problem, or simply say nothing and stare down the librarian. (Actually, most librarians don't care what books are checked out.)

⊙ Finally, don't see reading as a passive activity. Make it an active process in which you play a vital role. Question everything, even this book and these instructions. Think about what you're learning (see next section). Never take an author at her or his word. Search for similar themes. Remember 'harm none'. Books are wonderful teachers, but we must allow ourselves to hear their messages and trust ourselves so that their lessons can begin to unfold.

THOUGHT

I've already mentioned the importance of independent thought during study. This thought process should continue after you've closed the book. Many Wiccan teachers state that the classes that they lead are just the beginning of the lesson; that they should be springboards to continual learning. This can take place only when we reflect upon what we're being taught.

This is in direct opposition to the 'think this way, believe this way' attitude of most educational systems in this country. Independent thought thrusts a stick into the spokes of conventional education, and is seen as a real threat to the old order. It's discourages at any but the highest levels of education and in the most obscure disciplines (Masters degree programs; medical research; physics and so on).

Thought is often combined with questioning. The question initiates (pardon the pun) the learning process. "How do I make a magic circle?" can be answered by reading, then reflecting on what's been learned. This thought process *must* follow the uncovering of new information if it is to be available for use as needed.

Thinking through new material (such as various methods of casting the circle) allows you to closely examine it to weed out unsatisfactory information. If a published athame consecration leaves you cold, or requires two people, you can easily place it in the inactive file of your mind. Thus, thinking about what you've learned is part of the process of elimination, and of finding your ideal Wiccan practice. It's an integral aspect of the learning process.

Everything stated above applies equally to questions regarding the nature of the Goddess and God, reincarnation, morality and every other aspect of Wiccan belief and practice.

Many new Solitary Wiccans have a great number of questions regarding the Goddess: "What does She look like?", "What's the best method of contacting Her?"; "Is She really real?"; "Can I touch Her?"; "Where did She come from?"; "Which myths should I use?" Many of these and similar questions can be answered through study and thought; others require prayer and experimentation.

Thought should also be combined with *feeling*. We've been taught to distrust our feelings. In Wicca, however, we can realize that our feelings are usually what attracted us to Wicca in the first place. Would it be wise to toss them aside. I don't think so.

Intuition (the unexplained knowledge or feeling that makes itself known in our conscious minds) is a form of psychic awareness. Use of this tool while learning Wicca is of the utmost importance, for it's the filter through which you can evaluate questionable information. Your reactions to this information may profoundly affect your final decisions.

Thought, then, is a necessary part of learning Solitary Wicca. It can be summed in the following manner:

○ Determine questions (if necessary).

○ Study to uncover knowledge.

○ Determine your feelings concerning this knowledge. Rely on your intuition.

○ Based on this, determine what information is applicable to your Solitary Wiccan practice.

Such processes are necessary for Solitary Wiccans. Reflect on what you've studied. Trust yourself, your intuition, your feelings. And learn.

PRAYER

Prayer is another tool open to the Wiccan. When you're absolutely stuck, when the information can't be found in books, or when found confuses you. When you have a real need for assistance, ask for it. Prayer of this nature needn't be accompanied by lengthy ritual (particularly if you haven't yet determined your best ritual forms). You might accompany your prayer with the lighting of a candle or a walk in the woods or park. You may pray while petting your cat, staring into a fire, standing in a shower or sinking into a tub. You might also use a popular tool of divination, such as tarot cards, a pendulum, rune stones, but use such tools *following* prayer – not before.

The structure of the prayer isn't as important as the emotion that you place within it, and the clarity of your request. You might direct it solely to the Goddess or to both the Goddess and the God. Express your need for this information or for guidance with the present situation, and thank Them in advance for Their assistance.

True prayer is more than spoken words, for the devotee releases energy through the prayer to the Goddess and God. Because nature abhors a vacuum, an answer will appear (see Chapter 8 for more information regarding Wiccan prayer).

This answer may take many forms. It can be something as simple as a voice suddenly saying, "I have much to teach you. Place two candles on the altar. Hold Sabbats at night after everyone else is asleep. You need not initiate yourself at this time. Wine is fine, but apple cider or grape juice can also be used." Such direct communication with the Goddess is possible because we each contain a spark of Her divine fire within us. However, such direct communication is rather rare.

More commonly, the messages may appear in symbolic form: a cloud may suggest a shape; the shape may suggest an answer. Cards or stones or the movement of a pendulum could give you answers. Prayers for information before going to sleep might be answered in dreams. Record all such important dreams, think about them and determine if they're relevant to your question. (During sleep, communication with the Goddess and God is much easier, for the doubting conscious mind has been unchained and we operate in the subconscious [psychic] mind.)

There are numerous other ways in which your prayer may be answered. You may suddenly find a book that contains the needed information, or come across an article in a Wiccan publication that's just arrived in the mail. Prayers are always answered, but not always in direct ways.

Keep in mind, however, that the answers you receive may not be relevant for anyone but yourself. If the Goddess has spoken to you, it is to you that She has spoken – not to all Wiccans. Her messages may have little or no meaning to others. If you've always been fascinated by semi-precious stones and She tells you to create a circle with them, this knowledge is correct for you but may be completely incorrect for others. Divine revelations are usually of a personal, not global, nature. Though knowledge received in this fashion certainly should be used, it doesn't invalidate the ways of other Wiccans. Though we may receive divine messages, no one can ever be *the* spokesperson for the Goddess.

Answers received in prayer deserve attention and thanks (rites of thanks to the Goddess and God can be found in Chapter 10).

Don't discount prayer as a tool of information gathering. It seems ethereal, but when we consider its source, is this so surprising?

EXPERIMENTATION

So, you've read many books, thought about what you've read and compiled information from a number of sources; you've filtered this knowledge through the sieve of your feelings (intuition) and have prayed to the deities for assistance. What's next? Putting the information into practice.

Wicca is, after all, a living religion. Religions don't exist within theories and ritual plans; they come to life only when they're being practiced and lived. The outer forms (rituals, uses of tools) are important because they symbolize non-physical processes, and remind us of what we're doing in Wicca in the first place.

Begin to experiment with various ritual forms. Piece them together in various ways, discarding unsuccessful combinations and holding onto those that you find fulfilling. Questions such as "Is this the right way? Am I doing it wrong?" should not be allowed to interfere with your creative process. Such questions will only delay your progress.

The process of experimentation is necessary for determining all aspects of Solitary Wicca: everything from seasonal festivals to Esbats, power raising and sending techniques, magical rituals, the use and meaning of tools, self-initiations and every other exterior aspect of Wicca.

❂ ❂ ❂

This four step self-learning plan can certainly be of value in sharpening your Wiccan beliefs and practices. How important is reincarnation in your Wiccan practice? How far can the law 'harm none' be taken? When's the best time to perform rituals? Do you have to hold a circle on every full moon and Sabbat? Can you do them at other times as well? Each of these questions can be answered through study, thought, prayer and experimentation.

A complete guide to creating your own Solitary Wiccan Tradition and writing your own *Book of Shadows* can be found in Part III of this book. The information in that chapter should be useful if you decide to take this step.

You may decide that none of this is necessary. You might find a set of rituals and follow them to the exclusion of any others. This, too, is fine. But when you have questions about these rituals you may wish to use the process outlined in this chapter to discover the answers.

The path of the Solitary Wiccan can be difficult, but the school of trial and error is an excellent one. As your experience increases, so will your knowledge, and so too will your questions, which will lead to *study, thought, prayer* and *experimentation.*

Having access to all the answers isn't the goal of the Solitary Wiccan – finding the most important of those answers is; and we can find them by practicing our religion and though the use of these tools of learning.

2 : SECRECY

Secrecy has been granted such importance in both Wicca and magic that a few words concerning it here seem appropriate. In this chapter, we'll separately discuss each topic.

KEEPING YOUR WICCAN ACTIVITIES SECRET

In the recent past, when there were far fewer members of our religion and public understanding of Pagan faiths was non-existent in this country, Wiccans were usually quiet about their religion. The threat of broken marriages, loss of home, job, and even children was quite real. Wiccans had learned to keep their religious activities wrapped in the shadows. Only the closest of relatives or friends knew what these people did on the nights of the full moon (and the reason why they always asked for the day off after the Sabbats).

These Wiccans were usually members of covens and had been sworn to secrecy during their initiations. Among the many things that they could not reveal were their magical names, the identities of other members of the coven, activities that occurred during a circle, and their group's specific religious and magical rituals. Even if some Wiccans were willing to speak of their religion, public opinion and oaths of secrecy were stacked against them. Most Wiccans lived double lives: one related to work, PTA, fighting with the neighbors, budgeting, washing the car and other mundane activities; the other immersed in religion and magic.

Today, the picture has somewhat changed. Every issue of *Circle Network News* (see the Appendix) lists a large number of positive articles that have appeared concerning Wicca in general-interest magazines and newspapers. Articles on Wiccans and Goddess-worshippers have appeared on the front page of the *Wall Street Journal*. Television talk shows revel in 'Witch' episodes, where invited Wiccans discuss their religion.

This coverage has tremendously expanded the awareness of the existence of our religion within non-Wiccans. They may have incorrect ideas concerning Wicca, but they've been exposed to its existence.

Recognized Wiccans are sometimes invited to speak to church congregations to explain their religion. Many work directly with prisoners, just as do the clergy of other religions. Some Wiccan groups are recognized by the I.R.S. as tax-exempt churches (though Wicca as a whole hasn't been granted this recognition). The U.S. Army instructs its chaplains to recognize Wicca as a legitimate alternative religion. Occasionally, articles about Wicca actually appear in the Religion section of newspapers.

Still, the prevailing climate is one of confusion, doubt and fear. Those raised to believe in one faith feel threatened when another makes its presence known; especially one as misunderstood as Wicca. Occasionally, this leads to violence and even murder.

Such reactions are the direct result of the misinformation continually being fed to an unsuspecting public. The major sources of these lies are television evangelists (who have had their day and who are now fading from existence), but many small-town preachers continue to speak of us as satanic, child-killing devils with one aim: to rule the world. Even the recent media-promulgated "New Age" has been widely discussed as a satanic threat to Christianity.

Though we know this is absurd, many non-Wiccans do not. In such a heady climate, is it best to reveal your religion to your parents, mate, children, friends, employers, landlords and neighbors? If only to some of these, which ones? Could such a revelation create anger, fear and misunderstanding to the point that you wished you'd never said a thing?

It's possible. The alternative is also possible. Telling your mate that you're practicing a different religion may actually strengthen your bond ("Well, at least you believe in *something*") or settle unresolved questions ("So *that's* what you've been doing at midnight once a month").

The alternative is true as well. Your mate may grow cold, your employer may let you go, your neighbors might shun you, your parents may become extremely distressed (if they subscribe to a more conventional religion), your landlord may give you 30 days notice, or up your rent.

An understanding employer might let you have days off for your religious practices. Your neighbors will know not to drop in on the nights of the full moon. Your landlord? Well, maybe it's best not to tell everyone. You must carefully weigh this decision, for such a revelation could quickly affect your place of residence.

The decision of if and when to break the news to others, and to whom, must be based upon your knowledge of Wicca, your involvement in the religion (after a while, it can become rather difficult to hide), your relationships with those you might tell, the prevailing religious climate of your area, and the ease with which you can discuss such a highly personal subject as religion.

It usually isn't necessary to make such a revelation, not even to your husband or wife. If she or he asks, you may wish to discuss it, but no one has the right to know what you do on October 31. Religious freedom is just that—freedom of religion, freedom from oppressive religions, and the freedom from discussing your faith.

For 13 years I lived in a second floor apartment in a rough neighborhood. The building was owned by a born-again Christian who ran a gun shop and vacuum cleaner repair business next door to the building. I saw this man on a daily basis; he was in my apartment many times, and I had met much of his family. While I lived there I had 10 magic and Wiccan books published, gave countless television, radio and newspaper interviews, taught hundreds of classes in the general area, performed many rituals and hosted dozens of coven meetings. I stared at the stars at night, recited incantations over the herbs and plants that I grew on my porch, meditated on thunderstorms and in every way acted as a Wiccan.

And yet, during all those years my landlord never spoke to me about my religion. Yes, he used to write rent receipts on the back of religious tracts, but the subject simply never came up. I held my tongue, he held his, and we had a satisfying business relationship.

If I'd marched into his store one day and announced that I was a Witch, he'd have certainly sent me packing. My decision not to discuss my religion allowed me to live in a large apartment, at low rent, for a great many years during my salad days as a writer.

The decision of whether to inform others of your Wiccanhood must be a personal one. However, I'll give you a warning: many people simply don't care what you believe or who you invoke. They have no interest in the subject.

Some Wiccans decide to tell the world that they're Wiccans (or 'Witches') purely for shock value, to attract attention, make money and to gratify their egos. This is the worst reason for revealing your religion to others.

MAGICAL SECRECY

Virtually everything said above also pertains to the practice of magic, but other factors are pertinent only to this subject. Magic, as the projection of natural energies to manifest needed changes, is a vital part of Wicca. Within the circle we send energy to our planet, assist in healing the sick, protect ourselves, draw love into our lives and plant the seeds for many changes.

Magic can be a daily activity. Many Wiccans practice folk magic, the creation of charms and enchanted herbal mixtures, the use of stones and other natural, energy-filled objects to create needed change. These changes may be minor or, at times, quite major. Folk magic usually isn't practiced inside the circle itself. This section will discuss secrecy for both ritual and folk magic.

It's commonly believed that secrecy is absolutely essential for successful magic. Don't speak of your magical workings, we're told. Don't tell your friends of your interest in magic, let alone discuss the candle ritual that you performed last night. Be still, we're told. Talk not. Let the power cook.

A few reasons are given for this magical secrecy. Some say that speaking of your magical operations disperses the energies that you've put into them. Others state that non-magicians who hear of your rituals will, by simply disbelieving in magic, unconsciously send energies that will block your spell's manifestation. A few Wiccans will state that secrecy about one's magical proclivities was once a necessity for saving one's neck. (This is certainly true.) For a very few, secrecy heightens the mysterious quality of magic. Others give no reason, but simply repeat the old code: "Be silent."

Is this superstition? Perhaps. Magic is still a somewhat uncertain practice. After all, we're using energies that even physicists haven't yet been able to locate or identify. We may have seen the effectiveness of our magical rituals. We may have even told a few close friends about these rituals prior to their manifestations, with no ill effects. But soon, the secrecy issue could creep back into our consciousness.

"Should I talk about these things?" some will ask. "After all, that book stated that loose lips sink spells. A Wiccan I know does rituals all the time, but she only tells me about them after they've taken effect. And I'm sure that there are lots of Wiccans who never breathe a word about their magical rites."

Doubt soon clouds the Solitary Wiccan's mind. Soon, she or he makes no mention of magic to others, even others of like mind. Secrecy has once again been conferred on the process.

This is unfortunate and unnecessary. True magic is limitless. Speaking of a ritual to others doesn't disperse its energies. On the contrary, it gives you another opportunity to quickly send more power toward your magical goal.

Disbelief also isn't a satisfactory reason for magical secrecy. The disbelief of others has as much effect on magic as does an unschooled person's doubt that a calculator can add 2 and 2 to equal 4. The calculator will work, regardless of the observer's doubt. So, too, will magic.

There are other possible reasons why the calculator won't perform this simple operation: faulty microchips; low battery power or a lack of batteries; an operator who pushes the incorrect buttons, or a button turned off. Still, observer's disbelief alone can't be the cause. The same is true of magic. Properly performed, magic will be effective. If energy is raised within the body, programmed with intent, and projected toward its goal with the proper force and visualization, it will be effective.

This manifestation may not occur overnight. Many repetitions of the magical ritual may be necessary, but they're usually effective if the Wiccan knows how to use this process.

Secrecy concerning magical rites is quite limiting and, indeed, can *reduce* their effectiveness. This is a bizarre statement, so I'd better explain.

If a person truly feels that secrecy is necessary to perform an effective rite of magic, she or he has accepted a limitation concerning magic's effectiveness. Acceptance of any form of limitation in magic reduces the Wiccan's ability to raise and send energy, for it breeds doubt within the

Wiccan's mind that magic isn't an all-powerful force that, correctly performed by properly experienced people, can truly manifest wondrous, positive changes.

Limitations (such as secrecy) are harmful to the effective practice of magic—both ritual and folk. If we accept one limitation, we may accept others that we either read in books or hear from others. (Examples include: You can't perform a positive ritual during the waning moon. You *must* check the lunar phase prior to performing any ritual. If you incorrectly time it, the ritual will flop. You have to have every single ingredient listed in a folk magic spell, for substitution of one item for another will render it void. There are many others – all are absurd.)

The third reason often proffered for magical secrecy, that it's a tradition handed down from earlier times when secrecy was necessary to save one's neck, is at least historically accurate. Fortunately, speaking of magical rituals to close friends today isn't likely to cause you to be hanged. The last rationale, that secrecy increases the mysterious nature of magic, may be necessary for some in the beginning of their magical experiences. They should soon lose the need for such mental stage settings.

Secrecy, then, isn't a necessary part of magic. It's no guarantee of magical success and may block your magic. This doesn't mean that you should walk around wearing a green button that states, "I did a money ritual last night!" It also doesn't mean that you *must* discuss your magical affairs with others, especially if you're working on intensely private matters.

It's perfectly fine to keep quiet concerning your magical activities – so long as your motivations aren't limiting. If you don't wish to discuss your magical activities with others, don't. Not because some Wiccan wrote that you shouldn't but because you don't want to.

Secrecy concerning magic is filled with superstition that has no place in the lives of Solitary Wiccans.

3: SHOULD I DO IT WHILE I'M SICK?

The question (do sickness and Wiccan ritual mix?) that entitles this chapter is an important one, yet is rarely mentioned in Wiccan books. Why? Information of this nature is usually provided by the High Priestess, High Priest or another experienced Wiccan. This is the type of question that usually doesn't pop up until the student is suffering through a cold or is taking a prescribed, powerful medication. The subject is so important (and so completely neglected in Wiccan literature) that it deserves a chapter within these pages.

When many Solitaries begin practicing Wicca, they hate to skip rituals for any reason, including sickness. Many coven members feel the same way. Is this wise?

Many types of illnesses create dramatic changes within humans. Some of these changes are physical; others are mental, emotional, spiritual or psychic. Are such temporary alterations beneficial or detrimental to the performance of Wiccan ritual?

These questions can be partially answered by an examination of illnesses and their effects. All information here pertains solely to religious Wiccan ritual and is generalized – you must use your own judgment.

Be attentive to your body. It usually knows what's best. Forcing yourself to perform Wiccan rituals while facing challenging illnesses and conditions can be dangerous. (For information on performing magic during sickness, see the end of this chapter.)

ILLNESS AND WICCAN RELIGIOUS RITUAL

PHYSICAL CHANGES

The physical aspects of sickness are usually the most obvious, so we'll begin here. Some illnesses create a pronounced lack of energy. It may be difficult to walk across the room, let alone cast a circle. In such a case, a ritual with limited physical activity is clearly indicated.

Casts on broken feet, hands, arms and other limbs may or may not restrict your ability to set up an altar and hold a Book of Shadows. At least in doing so you won't further endanger your health. Your movements in the circle, however, may have to be limited, so avoid slavishly following ritual directions. Adapt them to take into account your present physical condition.

If your health care practitioner has ordered bed rest, or told you to stay off your feet, follow her or his instructions. Either adapt ritual to a purely verbal and mental experience, or wait until you've recovered.

MENTAL CHANGES

During many types of sickness (including colds), a pronounced change of consciousness often occurs. Slight dizziness, sinus pressure, elevated temperature, pain and other symptoms can create the most remarkable shifts in consciousness—even in people who haven't attempted to mask the symptoms with drugs. This type of consciousness can lend the ill Wiccan a radically different perception of the world; one which usually hinders ritual work.

If you're staggering around and can't seem to concentrate, it's best to avoid working with magical knives, flames, incense and other potentially dangerous magical tools. If you're apt to 'space out' (that is, become mesmerized by objects, fall asleep or completely forget what you're doing), it's best to simply sit or lie comfortably and do little else. You might whisper a prayer to the Goddess and/or God, meditate upon an image, or perhaps draw a symbol and concentrate on it.

If you simply can't concentrate long enough to formulate any type of ritual, it's probably best to let it go for now and to resume ritual workings when you're once again able to do so.

EMOTIONAL AND SPIRITUAL CHANGES

Let's face it—most of us don't feel good when we're sick. We may be grumpy, irritable, impossible to be around, depressed, worried and stressed. Such emotional shifts often make us think, "Why bother doing ritual at all? I feel so bad I'll probably just blow it." Sometimes we're simply not in the mood. This is quite natural, and if you truly don't feel like doing ritual, don't. No one's keeping score.

On the other hand, if you're physically able to do so, performing ritual may actually make you feel better. Effective Wiccan ritual (which can be difficult to achieve during times of illness) gives us a spiritual boost, which in turn makes us feel better.

Finally, simple prayer to the Goddess and God may comfort you and if nothing else, give you a different focus than that of your illness.

PSYCHIC CHANGES

Illness can have great effects on our psychic awareness. Though this may not seem to be particularly important when doing rituals, our ability to tap into our psychic minds (psychic awareness) is necessary for effective ritual. Ritual is often empty and mechanical without this linking of the two minds (conscious and psychic).

You may possess the ability to physically, mentally and emotionally perform a Wiccan ritual, but if you seem to be psychically shut down (a difficult condition to describe that's immediately recognizable when it occurs), ritual probably wouldn't be a good idea.

NON-PRESCRIPTION AND PRESCRIPTION DRUGS

Drug reactions are perhaps the most important factor in determining whether to perform Wiccan rituals during illness. The vast number of such drugs now in use and their varying effects on their takers make it impossible to speak in any but the most general of terms.

Many drugs have no effect on consciousness, don't alter the emotions, have no noticeable physiological effect, and leave the psychic mind alone. However, some drugs (prescription and over-the-counter) can cause just these changes. Among these are, of course, narcotics. If you seem to be suffering from these or other negative side effects, limit ritual work while under their influence.

You must use your judgment and common sense in determining whether illness or prescription drugs will interfere with your Wiccan ritual. If your health care provider has told you to stay in bed, stay in bed and forget about setting up a circle. If you've just had stitches, don't do an ecstatic dance to the Goddess around the altar, no matter how much you may wish to do so. If you're suffering from lung complaints, don't burn incense. If you're taking a medication that prohibits alcohol use, don't drink wine after ritual. Solitary Wiccans can do ritual at any time and, if necessary, delay or miss ritual as well. Illness is a quite legitimate reason for skipping ritual.

Don't believe that you won't be a true Wiccan if you can't carry a candle around the circle on Imbolc because you're confined to your bed. Missing a ritual due to illness, infirmity or the influence of prescription drugs in no way makes you a lesser Wiccan. In fact, such a decision proves your intelligence and growing Wiccan experience: you've chosen to avoid performing what would most probably be a ritual lacking in energy and true contact with the Goddess and God. If this makes you a lesser Wiccan, I'll eat my cauldron.

MAGIC AND ILLNESS

Performing magic during periods of illness may or may not be a positive action. It's a natural time for self-healing spells, but spells for other reasons should be postponed, no matter how important the work may be. Waiting until you're well not only allows you to give the magical rite your full attention, it also assures that you'll be able to raise far greater amounts of energy.

When we're sick, our bodies have lowered reserves of energy (personal power). Not only aren't we producing as much as usual, we're also using more energy for healing ourselves. Less energy is available for any other physical task, including magic. This lowered reserve can make performing magic during serious illness quite dangerous, for you're drawing on the energy that would otherwise be working to heal you. This may extend the duration of your illness or slow the healing of wounds.

Willingly giving of this energy to solve someone else's problems is a good and noble deed—at any other time. When you're sick, you must be number one. Use this energy to heal yourself. Later, you'll be in shape to take care of the rest of the world.

The bottom line: no magic except self-healing during illness.

4: MAGICAL NAMES

M any Wiccan books discuss the taking of a Wiccan (magical) name. The ceremonial bestowing of such a name upon the initiate is a part of many initiation ceremonies. Afterward, the new Wiccan is usually exclusively called by this name within the circle.

Magical names are quite popular among Wiccans; so popular, in fact, that many Wiccans have two or even three such names: a public Craft name (used at Wiccan gatherings, when writing articles, and so on); a secret name (the one bestowed during initiation), and perhaps even a third name which is used only when addressing the Goddess and God, and is known only to Them and the Wiccan. Wiccans who are members of more than one tradition may have different names for each group.

For many Wiccans, taking a new name is an outward symbol of her or his devotion to Wicca. It's seen as a part of the process of rebirth into the religion.

Throughout history, names have been given considerable magical importance. A spirit's name had to be known before it could be exorcised from a sick person in ancient Sumer, Babylon and Assyria. In Hawaii, babies were given revolting names in infancy to guard them from molestation from evil during their early, vulnerable years. A more fitting name was given to the child when she or he reached a certain age and was less susceptible to the wiles of evil spirits. In some cultures, mothers will bestow a secret name on their children. This 'real' name, unknown to anybody but the mother, protects the child. The common name by which he or she is called has no power over them.

In our own country, numerology is used to discover the power of our names, and many people change their names to advance in their careers.

With all this importance attached to names, it's not difficult to understand why many Wiccans use Craft names. Though I didn't discuss this subject in *Wicca: A Guide for the Solitary Practitioner*, it deserves some comment here.

To cut to the heart of this matter: is it necessary for you to adopt a Wiccan name? If you wish your Wicca to correspond to conventional Wicca as far as is possible, yes. If you feel freer than these constraints, adoption of a special name isn't necessary. Once again, the decision is yours alone.

The major reason for utilizing a Craft name, as mentioned above, is that it represents the Wiccan you. For some, use of this name gives them a sense of power and mystery which they may otherwise not feel. We live in such a mundane world that it can indeed be difficult to "switch on" the magical side of our nature. Thus, use of a Wiccan name may assist in altering the conscious mind and preparing it for ritual.

Some people take an entirely different approach: they legally adopt their Wiccan name. Thus, Sally Thompson becomes Amber; Frank Jones, Greywolf. This name may even appear on driver's licenses, leases and other documents. This legal avenue is inadvisable unless you're completely open about your religion, since such a name will naturally draw attention to its bearer. Though many state that they've chosen to use their new name to the exclusion of the old one purely for spiritual reasons, most are also making a public statement regarding their religion—and not all of us are ready for such a step.

How do you find your magical name?

There are many approaches. Some Wiccans adopt the name of a Goddess or God, in honor of Them. Others look into their family's cultural history and choose a name from the associated folklore: a person with British ancestry may opt for a name culled from British folklore. Many contemporary American Wiccans incorporate an animal in their name, such as "Howling Wolf" or "Sweeping Eagle". Flower and plant names (such as Rose, Oak Keeper, Grove, Fir, Ash) are other possibilities.

You may also simply make up a name. Many Wiccan names consist of two words that have been put together. Such names are usually quite descriptive.

Some famous Wiccan names have been published. Gerald Gardner (one of the people who formed Wicca into the religion as we know it today) publicly used the name Scire. At least one of Doreen Valiente's magical names was Ameth. A well-known High Priest adopted the public Craft name of Phoenix.

Still other popular names include: Morgan, Morgana, Morgaine, Morgraine, Lugh and Arthur (all associated with Celtic mythology); Ariadne, Diana, Hermes, Poseidon, Cassandra and Triton (Greek and Roman mythology); Selket, Ma'at, Osiris, and other Egyptian names.

(Among the most commonly used names are Amber, Phoenix and Merlin. Calling out one of these names at a Pagan gathering will usually cause many heads to turn.)

So there are plenty of possibilities from which to choose. If you decide to use a Wiccan name in ritual, always use it. Use it in prayer. Use it in rituals. Write it, in runes or in English, on your tools. You may even wish to perform some sort of name-adoption ritual. This could consist of casting a circle and invoking the Goddess and God to be present and asking Them to recognize you by your new name.

Use of a Craft name may not give you any additional power, but it's a traditional practice, and many enjoy it.

5 : SELF-INITIATION

The most controversial subject matter in this book's predecessor was undoubtedly the chapter concerning initiation. Many Wiccan book reviewers were displeased with a simple idea presented within that chapter: that initiation isn't always a process that one human being performs on another. Some misinterpreted my words to the point that they believed I stated that initiation was to be avoided at all costs—a curious conclusion from my writing. (Not surprisingly, such comments were made by initiated coven members.) Some reviewers actually assumed that I'd never been initiated, and that this was the reason for my 'incorrect' views on the subject.

There are many types of initiations. Some are performed in a circle with others. Some are performed alone. Still others are never performed, but occur spontaneously within a Wiccan student's life.

An initiation into a coven (and thus into Wicca) is effective only if initiator and candidate are in perfect harmony, working within a mutually satisfactory Wiccan system or tradition. I've seen botched initiations and glorious initiations. *Any* initiation *isn't* better than no initiation, if it's performed for the wrong reasons (egotism, power over others) by the wrong person, or by the wrong coven. The rite itself isn't as important as its impact on the candidate and the spirit in which it's performed.

Though a physical initiation isn't necessary to practice Wicca, it is a ritual statement of one's allegiance to the Craft. The initiate can, from that day forward, clearly claim that they're Wiccan, for they have memories of a specific date that ceremonially began this kinship. This is important for some; for others, it's of little or no importance.

You have the right to perform a self-initiation. No one can take this right from you. If you've worked Wiccan ritual, met with the Goddess and God, have grown comfortable with Wicca, and have decided that it's your path, there's no reason on the Goddess' green Earth why you shouldn't undergo a self-initiation.

You may wish to perform a self-initiation found in a book; adapt a group initiation, or create your own. (The rite included in Chapter 12 of *Wicca* was a self-dedication—not an initiation. However, it could be incorporated into a full initiation.)

Before self-initiation, consider whether you've gained enough Wiccan experience to enter Wicca. Wiccan ritual experience is essential (reading doesn't count) before self-initiating yourself. A self-initiation rite performed by a person after, say, a year of study and ritual will be a rich and spiritually significant event, simply because the rite was preceded by the experience that makes it genuine. In other words, one can't become Wiccan (even a Solitary one) overnight.

This period of self-training and experience is absolutely vital. Yes, you'll learn the uses of the tools; the meanings of the Sabbats, the casting of the circle—but you'll also be meeting with the Goddess and the God. Becoming attuned to and establishing a relationship with Them is the heart of Wicca, and it takes time and dedication.

I'm hearing complaints.

"Sure, but during some initiations the initiator passes power to the candidate." *During a self-initiation, the Goddess and God pass power to the candidate.*

"But such initiations won't be recognized by covens." *Solitary Wiccans don't belong to covens.*

"Real initiations are designed to alter consciousness within the candidate." So, too, are properly designed self-initiations.

"Real initiations symbolize the death of the old (non-Wiccan) self and the rebirth of the Wiccan person." These can be incorporated into self-initiations.

Self-initiation is largely what you make it, but for the most satisfying results every such ritual should include the following steps. (What follows is the barest ritual outline. I've left out such things as lighting candles and charcoal.)

- Purification of some kind. (A shower or bath is fine.)

- The laying of the altar. (Use whatever tools you normally work with.)

- The circle casting. (Though this isn't absolutely necessary, it certainly heightens the atmosphere. It's best if you've already gained proficiency in circle casting before initiation. If you feel comfortable casting the circle, use it. If not, don't.)

- Opening invocations to the Goddess and the God. (These may be those that you use in your everyday Wiccan ritual work, or special ones composed for this rite

- A symbolic death of your old, non-Wiccan self. (Be creative. This may consist of wrapping yourself in black cloth; blindfolding yourself while sitting before the altar [not while walking]; even singing a dirge. Create a prayer appropriate for this moment. After a suitable time of meditation and reflection, cast off the trappings of death with a cry of joy.

○ Pray anew to the Goddess and God, dedicating yourself to them. State that you're now a Wiccan. If you've chosen a magical name (see Chapter 4), saying it aloud: "I, Dione, am now a Wiccan." would be a suitable formula for inclusion in your dedicatory prayer.

○ Relax in the circle for a few minutes. Watch the candle's flames. If you've brought cakes and wine into the circle, it's time to dedicate them and to share in the manifested love of the Goddess and God When you've finished your sacred meal, thank the Goddess and God for Their attendance and close the circle.

Conventional Wiccans may argue with this self-initiatory plan, but it's effective. I've presented it here as a pattern that others may use to create their own.

The Goddess and God, as the source of all life, health, food, the earth, the stars, the sun and moon and the universe, are also the true sources of initiation.

Self-initiation is an important ritual and isn't to be undergone lightly. The Wiccan should be ready for both spiritual and physical change following this rite. After all, once you've undergone a self-initiation, you're no longer just a student; you're a Wiccan: one of the few remaining humans who've decided to step past the veil of the materially-based world. You're now one of those who respects the Earth; who pours wine into sacred cups by candlelight surrounded by incense smoke; who communes with the Goddess and God in private meditation; who joyfully uses magic as a tool of positive change.

Self-initiation is a wonderful affirmation of our dedication to Wicca if it's performed for positive reasons, at the appropriate time, in the proper state of mind. If you haven't already ritually joined us, you'll know if—and when—it's time.

Initiation is no less than the beginning of a new life.

6: THE WICCAN MYSTERIES

Some readers and reviewers have complained that Wiccan books—mine included—don't contain "Wiccan mysteries." Such comments are quite true. Most books written about Wicca are either overviews of its practice or are instructions for the beginner. Wiccan writers can easily become caught up in describing circle castings, the proper use of tools, deity concepts and group dynamics. There's little room in such books for mysticism.

However, there's another reason. Mysteries are, by their very nature, difficult to frame in language. They can't truly be taught; they can only be experienced. Some manifest on other planes of existence. Many have profound emotional, psychic or spiritual effects. Some occur solely between a Wiccan and the Goddess; others between two or more Wiccans in circle.

Perhaps I'd better define my terms. First, the term 'Wiccan mysteries', as I use it here, doesn't refer to secret rituals, prayers or magical techniques, no matter how secret or effective they may be. Instead, it refers to extraordinary spiritual experiences and revelations of the highest order from the Goddess and God. The Wiccan mysteries can never be outwardly displayed. Wiccan Sabbats and Esbats celebrate them, but only in symbolic form.

If you're entirely confused at this point, it's okay. After all, these are the Wiccan *mysteries*, and this isn't the easiest topic about which to write or discuss.

One of the complaints of many Solitary Wiccans is that their rituals seem to lack depth of involvement and great spiritual meaning. There are many possible origins for this problem, but it could very well be a lack of knowledge of the Wiccan mysteries. This inner lore, when called upon in ritual, greatly enhances the proceedings.

Why? Because as previously stated, most Wiccan rituals are in some way celebrations of Wiccan mysteries. This may immediately give you a clue as to the nature of the mysteries: what are the Sabbats all about? The major, outward concept is the observation of the seasons. Once you begin to look at the seasons, you'll find a rich trove of possible Wiccan mystery material. In the mysteries, everything is both symbolic and quite real.

Most of the Wiccan mysteries relate to the Goddess and God and these have been placed within the context of sacred activities. Other mysteries are more Earth-based but, since the Goddess is the Earth, we're right back to Her.

It's possible for you to discover such mysteries. All the accumulated lore and mysteries of Wiccan traditions were discovered at some point. You can certainly continue this process to give body and depth to your Wiccan practice.

Wiccan mysteries may be discovered during meditation in ritual settings. They may be perceived while taking a walk, appear in our minds during sleep, even come in answer to fervent prayers to the Goddess and God. Such arcane secrets are usually only revealed to those who are truly involved with Wicca, for who else would have need of them?

On the other hand, some Wiccan mysteries are constantly occurring around us where we see the divine touch of the Goddess and God. However, such processes are only Wiccan mysteries once we become totally aware of them on every level of our beings.

If this is confusing, here's an example. A ripe apple falls onto the ground. It decomposes; fresh soil is blown over the fallen fruit. Rains fall. The sun heats the earth. A sprout struggles up from a seed contained within the apple. Within a few years, a new apple tree stands where the fruit had once fallen. A ripe apple falls onto the ground.

How is this a Wiccan mystery?

○ These processes (fall and rise; death and rebirth, etc.) are governed by and are created by the Goddess and God, the sole sources of fertility, life and death.

○ Such natural processes don't relate solely to apples; these cycles are evident in all the world.

○ A Wiccan becomes aware of this process by watching the apple fall and seeing it eventually sprout. By narrowing her or his focus to this one cycle, for at least a few minutes each day, the Wiccan aligns her or his consciousness with the processes of the Goddess and God. She or he may further meditate upon this process' meaning.

○ This realignment of consciousness creates a new awareness of the Goddess and God both within the world and within the self. This greater awareness creates deeper spiritual connections with Them. Additionally, the apple that served as the lesson-giver may become a powerful and profound ritual tool in this Wiccan's religious practice, symbolizing life, death and rebirth—three of the greatest mysteries that ever furrowed the human brow.

○ Finally, the apple's journey may become a potent spiritual memory that immediately unlocks the silver and gold avenues to the Goddess and to the God. In this Wiccan's mind, the apple becomes more than a memory of a fruit; more than a symbol: it becomes a direct link between Them and Us; a tangible reminder of intangible things; a symbol that's not only between the worlds, but that serves as a bridge. The apple then, in this Wiccan's mysteries, may be: the Celtic cauldron of regeneration; the womb of the Goddess; a symbol of birth and rebirth; representative of the underworld and the overworld; the Earth itself, upon which so many mysteries await our discovery.

The secret of the Wiccan mysteries is that there are no secrets. You need only alter your perceptions and sharpen your focus. Look beyond the material world to the timeless processes at work within it to discover Wiccan mysteries. Or spend time in ritual meditation specifically to deepen your understanding of the subtlest aspects of Wicca, the Goddess and the God.

Then, after you've discovered them, you can celebrate and sing and dance in circles created of light and love and re-experience these mysteries time and again. Rituals may be enlarged to include recognition of such experiences, or special rites may be performed in their honor.

The point here is that true Wiccan mysteries can't be found within Books of Shadows or in ancient secrets or within the words of others. They can only be found within our relationship with the Goddess and God, and in our understanding of nature as an illustration of Their energy.

Want some more hints?

Watch a birth.

Watch the sun melting ice.

Watch the unfurling of leaves on trees in the spring.

Watch the ocean.

Watch the clouds drifting far above.

Watch rain splattering onto pools of water.

Watch lightning crackling and sparking against the night sky.

Watch smoke rising from a sacred bonfire.

Watch an eclipse.

Watch a cat hunting in the backyard.

Watch a baby rediscovering our world.

✪　✪　✪

Don't only watch these things; experience them. Feel them. Then you'll have begun to draw the Wiccan mysteries closer to you. You'll have the rare opportunity to fleetingly draw back the veil that we've thrown over our world and see the face of the Goddess....

And the Wiccan mysteries will be yours.

7: EVERYDAY WICCA

I've already stated that, ideally, religion permeates all aspects of life. Even when we're not lighting candles and casting circles, it's best to live in a Wiccan manner. Life itself can be seen as a ritual to the Goddess and God. Many, however, have difficulty in finding the spiritual nature of their everyday lives. We can become mesmerized by the smoke and mirrors of society's trappings and diversions; equally, our home life, employment, bills and other mundane factors can weigh us down until we begin to question whether we ever spiritually felt a thing.

The solution isn't more ritual; it consists of subtly shifting our focus from solely physical forces and objects to the inherently spiritual nature of everything. Washing dishes can become an exploration of the powers of the element of Water. Working is an opportunity to feel the energy of other people. Cleaning up the yard teaches us important lessons regarding the seasons. Even attending school is an exercise in utilizing (and, hopefully, expanding) our consciousness, and viewing the lessons from a spiritual standpoint can be quite enlightening.

Indeed, a Wiccan viewpoint can get us through hard times, just as can adherence to any other religion. To be able to tap this source of peace, however, we must first realize that Wicca isn't limited to ritual, prayer and magic. Wicca is a way of life as much as it's a religion.

Applying Wicca's principles to our world is one of the simplest methods of bringing Wicca into our daily lives. The following discussions are suggestions. You may have different interpretations.

Harm none. Think about this when someone cuts you off on the road; steals 'your' parking space; is rude to you, or when you're facing all manner of trouble with mates, family, neighbors, friends or co-workers. Remembering this code allows us to rise above anger, jealousy and hatred, and may even transform such potentially destructive emotions into positive energies. It also presents the opportunity to care for ourselves by reducing stress. (I'll be the first to admit that this is far from easy.)

Reincarnation reminds us that we have more than one chance at life. This concept negates suicide as a solution to problems, or as an easy way out, since we'll be back sooner or later to confront those same issues that we believed were too difficult to face in this life. Additionally, thoughts of reincarnation can help us through periods of mourning. It can also free us of fear of death.

Karma. This concept states that right action is returned with positive energy, and negative action is returned with negativity. It's allied with 'harm none' and is again a quick reminder to act in a positive fashion. Additionally, we can see how good (positive; beneficial) actions are in themselves acts of spirituality.

Some Wiccans express a slightly different concept known as the law of three or the threefold law. This states that anything we do returns to us in triple strength. Thus, a small act of caring may be returned to us as a great act of caring by someone else. A petty act of revenge may result in great harm against us. The law of three is simply a different understanding of karma.

Magic reminds us that we do, indeed, have control over our lives. If we don't like them, we can change them through positive ritual. However, magic also teaches us patience: a cauldron placed on an open fire never immediately comes to a boil, and magic doesn't immediately manifest. We

may also be able to see little bits of magic at work in our everyday lives—
and this can be comforting.

Thought teaches us that thoughts are things; that is, thoughts generate
and release energy and, if repeated with intent, can be powerful sources of
energy. Thus, as we control negative thoughts, we improve our lives. Simply
refusing to recognize a negative thought and changing our focus from the
negative ("I have no money") to the positive ("I've got enough food to
eat") can produce dramatic effects. And so, because we can improve our
lives and harm none by positive thinking, even our throughts can be
expressions of spirituality.

Earth stewardship (caring for our planet) is another of Wicca's most
important concepts. There's nothing particularly spiritual about filling a
garbage can or chopping down a tree— two actions that are in violation of
Wiccan principles.

However, rinsing and reusing bottles; recycling paper, aluminum cans,
plastic and glass *is* an act of spirituality, for we're caring for our planet. Similarly, planting a tree; tending gardens; giving gifts of plants to others; refusing to use artificial pesticides; donating to ecological causes; writing letters
in support of preserving endangered animals and their environments
(forests, wetlands and other environmentally sensitive areas) are all further expressions of Wicca's concern and love for our planet. Even political
involvement, when it truly leads to better Earth stewardship, can have its
rewarding spiritual aspects.

The continuous presence of the Goddess and God is another important Wiccan teaching. If we're on the Earth, we're with the Goddess and
God. No part of us or our lives is divorced from Them, unless we deem that
this is true. In the heart of roaring cities; in the quiet of a country valley; in a
mobile home roasting in the desert, the Goddess and God are there. In our
office, school, neighborhood and favorite store, the Goddess and God are

there. In rush-hour traffic; in long lines at the bank; in the flowers and plants on our window sills, the Goddess and God are there.

The omnipresence of our deities isn't some exalted spiritual sentiment; it's true. The Earth isn't represented by the Goddess; it is a part of Her. She is everywhere. Similarly, She is also within us, as is the God. Thus, whatever we do, wherever we go, from a convenience store to a concert in the park, They are present. Remembering this fact may, once again, reveal the inherent spirituality in many situations.

OTHER METHODS OF ENHANCING EVERYDAY SPIRITUALITY

Make an offering to the Goddess and God each day (see Chapter 10: offerings, prayers, etc.).

Set aside at least five minutes a day as "sacred time". During this five minutes you can simply think about your place in life and Wicca's role, or you can perform other activities directly or indirectly related to Wicca. (Once again, reading can't be considered as sacred time.) Here are some examples of what you might do:

Morning and evening meditations

Working arts or crafts with a Wiccan theme

Listening to classical or contemporary Pagan music

Tending or planting plants

Volunteering

Recycling

Journalizing (writing) about your Wiccan involvement

Corresponding with other Wiccans

Meditating (or psychically attuning) with stones

Writing new rituals

Experimenting with new methods of divination

Collecting magical herbs

Visiting gardens or parks

Listening and communicating with animals

Reading Pagan fairy tales (there really isn't any other kind) to your children

This list can be greatly extended. Indeed, once we begin to think of how Wicca has influenced our lives, a wide range of activities can be performed during such sacred time.

This chapter has been a short introduction to some methods of strengthening the Wiccan nature of your life. In this pursuit, action is as important as thought.

Blessed Be.

PART TWO:

PRACTICE

PART TWO

8: EFFECTIVE PRAYER

Prayer is little-discussed in Wiccan books, probably because it is, by its very nature, a highly personal experience. Additionally, most Wiccan books seem to be more concerned with describing ritual motivations and mechanics than with delving into the truly spiritual aspects of our religion.

But behind the circles, the altars and the regalia, Wicca is designed to facilitate contact with the divine. We can certainly contact Them during our rites with memorized invocations, but what of non-ritual occasions? Will They hear us? Will they speak to us?

Of course. In Wicca, ritual is a framework in which prayer and magic take place. But prayer isn't solely a ritualistic act. We can pray at any time, and, utilizing our connections with the Goddess and God, contact Them for assistance and comfort.

Following are discussions of some aspects of Wiccan prayer.

PRAYER IS DIRECTED BOTH WITHIN AS WELL AS WITHOUT

Many religions preach that our bodies are filthy, disgusting things that even their deities dislike and hate. Such faiths deny the flesh and turn their eyes toward the skies when seeking the divine.

Most Wiccans, however, accept that the Goddess and God are within ourselves as well as outside us. If everything in nature is connected through subtle but real energies, so too are we linked with the Goddess and God.

We must become more intimately familiar with this connection. We can't accomplish this by searching our bodies and asking, "Where's the Goddess? Where's the God?" They don't reside in any one part of us; They're simply within. They exist within our DNA. They're present in our souls. The Goddess and God are infused into every aspect of our beings.

We gain familiarity with the divine spark within ourselves through ritual, meditation and prayer. It's during these moments, in which we expand our awareness beyond the physical world, that the divine energy within us rises and fills our consciousness. Though we may call the Goddess and God, we're actually becoming newly focused on Their presence inside us. Once this has occurred, we can become aware of Their greater presences beyond ourselves.

Prayer is the process of attuning and communicating with the Goddess and God. During prayer, we may call Them from the Moon, the Sun and the stars, from the seas, the deserts and caves, from the haunts of wild animals; from the Earth itself: but the call must first move us, must first renew our awareness of the Goddess and God within, before it can contact the universally manifested deities.

We might see a bunch of ripe peaches hanging from a tree and feel great desire to eat one. However, until we narrow our focus on just one peach, approach it and pluck it from the tree, we won't satisfy our craving. In prayer, we must narrow our focus, at first, upon the Goddess and God within, before we can contact the greater understanding of the Goddess and God.

This initial focus may be accomplished through words, visualizations, songs or by other means. There are no governing rules, though I present a few suggestions below. Experiment to discover the most effective technique.

To begin, a Wiccan adopts a prayerful attitude (see below). She may then begin each prayer with the following words:

O Goddess Within,

O God Within,

While saying these words, she shifts her consciousness to the warm, peaceful memories of her previous contacts with Them. This may put her into the proper mode of consciousness. She could then proceed to say:

O Goddess of the Moon, Waters and Earth;

O God of the Forests and Mountains;

This expands her conception of the Goddess and God, and contacts a greater part of Them. Once she's achieved a stronger connection, she then speaks to Them in specifics (i.e., states the reason for her prayer).

Wiccan prayer, then, isn't addressed to some distant deities who reside in alien cloud palaces. We needn't use a bullhorn to call to the Goddess and God. Rather, we need only become newly aware of Them within us. This is the secret.

PRAYERFUL ATTITUDES

Many people, of all religious persuasions, pray only in times of great need, terrific stress or spiritual crisis. This is a part of human nature: when all else fails, appeal to higher forces. Prayers at such times are certainly appropriate, and can often provide just what we need to get through such periods. However, they're not the ideal prayerful occasions, for we often don't take the time to truly contact the Goddess and God before we begin our communication. This may block the prayer's effectiveness.

Thus, it's quite important, even in moments of extreme desperation, to adopt a prayerful attitude before speaking to the Goddess and God. A prayerful attitude consists of peace and hope resting on an unshakable spiritual foundation.

It may be quite difficult to adopt such a state when a friend has just become ill, a child has run away from home, your cat is missing. However, attaining this peaceful, hopeful, spiritual state will lend greater power to your prayer, for it will allow you to more directly connect with the Goddess and God. Once you've linked with the Goddess and God, you can be as emotional as you wish.

Urgent, wild prayers ("Goddess, help me!") or demanding prayers ("You gotta help me out. Right now!") will lend you little or no spiritual support, and probably won't go farther than your lips or mind. A few of these prayers may indeed reach the Goddess and God, if their speaker is sufficiently aware of her or his connection with Them. However, they're far from the most effective form of prayer.

Such prayers are usually spontaneous. They may be the product of new information or fresh insight into a situation. Thus, they certainly can't be planned in advance. Or can they?

Indeed they can be. With a bit of practice and thought, you can transform ineffective prayers to quite effective prayers. How? Simply pray every day, in a prayerful attitude. Talk to the Goddess and God about positive events in your life. Thank Them for manifested prayers. Speak to Them about the moonrise, the sound of the birds in the morning, the new kittens. Speak to Them, too, of your needs and hopes and desires.

Make prayer a daily occurrence. Don't wait to pray solely during those rare occasions when crushing need forces you to turn to Them for assistance. Prayer – true prayer – on a daily basis sets up a regular line of communication. So long as you don't recite prayers without emotion or feeling, this prayer experience will come in handy when you're faced with a crisis. Your prayer may still be quick and to the point, but you'll have established a firm line of communication and have the capability to use it at any time.

Prayer should always be respectful. Wiccans don't bargain with the Goddess and God. We don't say, "Okay, Goddess. Give me that new car and I'll burn a candle for you for three full moons." That's not Wiccan. We never bargain with the Goddess and God. Prayer doesn't consist of deal-making.

We also never threaten or order around the Goddess and God in prayer. Doing so reveals that we've attempted to elevate ourselves to Goddess- and God-hood. Sorry; we're not deities.

Few people enjoy being commanded; no goddesses or gods enjoy it. Such 'prayers' have no place in Wicca. (This statement doesn't mean that it only has no place in my form of Wicca; it's universal. It isn't dependent upon your personal conception of the Goddess and God; it's dependent upon the nature of things: the Goddess and God are bigger than us. End of discussion.)

And so, having a prayerful attitude means being in a peaceful, hopeful, spiritual state. If you attain this prior to praying, your prayers will be that much more effective.

THE NATURE OF PRAYER

Many religious people will argue that prayer consists only of communication between humans and the divine. As Wiccans, however, we're aware of the non-physical energies contained within our bodies (the same energies used in creating the circle, in consecrating tools and in other works of magic). Effective prayer consists of more than words, for when prayers are made in the correct state, with pure, unadulterated emotion, we release energy with our words and direct it to the Goddess and God. Thus, certain forms of prayer (those in which we make requests, for example) are also acts of magic.

We needn't attempt to make true prayer into a magical act; (that is, we don't have to arouse, program and direct energy during prayer); this automatically occurs during emotional prayer. Fixing our minds upon a need, contacting the Goddess and God, and speaking to Them stirs up, programs and directs energy. It is an act of magic.

If we're not properly attuned with the Goddess and God – if we're not clearly focused – the energy raised by the prayer flies off into outer space in a willy-nilly fashion to no effect. Just as we must gather droplets of water into a tub to take a bath, so too must we gather our energies and direct them to the Goddess and God. To do otherwise is to perform ineffective prayer. Therefore, we must maintain our focus on Them and allow nothing to distract us.

Don't misunderstand this. Though some types of prayer can be considered to be spells, this certainly isn't true of all forms. Additionally, praying to the Goddess and God isn't spell casting; it's a religious act that happens to have a magical content.

Wiccan prayer is far more than a simple recitation of facts to the Goddess and God and more than form of communication. It's a flow of personal energy from a human to the deities.

TYPES OF PRAYERS

There are many types of prayers: prayers of thanks, of celebration, of need. Situations obviously frame the nature of most prayers. However, praying only when in need is using the least of prayer's potential. The following prayers are merely examples.

Prayers of thanks are just that:

O Goddess within;

O God within;

O Goddess of the Moon, Waters and Earth;

O God of the Forests and Mountains:

I give thanks for _____ (or, for my many blessings).

The prayer may then continue on to describe how this blessing has changed her or his life:

> Thank you for lending me spiritual strength in this time of need; it has refreshed and encouraged me.

Or:

> Thank you for assisting me in finding the perfect home; we're safe now.

Or:

> Thank you for touching my life and allowing me to find Mr. (or Ms.) Right; my world is filled with love and happiness.

Such prayers may be quite lengthy. In prayers of thanks, it's best to detail your specific reasons for thankfulness. This strengthens the fact that the Goddess and God have recently assisted you, and also strengthens the prayer's effectiveness.

If you need assistance in creating a ritual, you may pray for this:

> O Glorious Goddess;
>
> O Gracious God;
>
> You who created all that is;
>
> Help me create this ritual
>
> In Your honor
>
> At the time of the full moon (or Yule and so on).

Prayers of celebration may also be framed when the Wiccan has accomplished a tremendous feat, with or without the direct assistance of the Goddess and God:

> O Gracious Goddess,
>
> I passed the test.

Or:

O Mother Goddess
O Father God
I finished (the book, the song, the garden).

Prayers of need are just that:

O Goddess within;
O God within;
O Goddess of the Moon, the Waters, and the Earth,
O God of the Forests and Mountains;
O Shining Ones of Infinite Wisdom:
Teach me to understand my child (friend, lover, parents, boss).
Lend me the spiritual strength to overcome my anger and pain;
Quench my fires with love.

Certainly, there are many types of need. In our market economy, where we must work to earn money to buy things that others create, our needs are often physical: we need a new car, a home, a good job, more money. Prayers of need may also be involved with healing, compassion, love, protection and many other aspects of daily human life.

At times, our needs may seem insurmountable. We may temporarily lose our Goddess and God focus and descend into negative thinking, disillusionment and fear.

It's at such times that we may pray to them:

O Goddess within;
O God within;
O Goddess of the Moon, the Waters and the Earth;

O God of the Forests and Mountains:

I need to feel Your presence.

I need to be reminded of You.

Assist me to remember Your lessons;

Show me the key that will unlock my spirituality.

Blessed Be.

Or, we may pray regarding problems that we're having with our religion: After the introductory part of the prayer, you may say:

> *Goddess, I simply don't understand this. This book says that we never incarnate as the opposite sex of the one that we are in this life. Help.*

Or,

> *Goddess and God, I'm trying to find the perfect circle casting. Guide my mind, heart and hands as I try to figure this out.*

Keep in mind that, to be effective, all prayers of need must be stated with a prayerful attitude.

Wiccan prayer is a private, personal aspect of our religion. We all have our own methods of contacting the Goddess and God. However, the techniques outlined in this chapter may be of assistance in truly contacting Them, and of using prayer as a positive, supportive tool of everyday life.

Pray often – it's an essential part of Wicca.

9: DAILY PRAYER AND CHANTS

Our religion reveres the Goddess and God. As such, it's vital that we establish and maintain our relationships with Them. Everyday life presents many opportunities to strengthen this bond. Short prayers when we rise in the morning, before meals, before sleep and at other times of the day are highly appropriate.

This chapter includes a variety of both simple and formal prayers for many occasions. Feel free to use them as is or as a guide for creating your own. Though I've generically addressed these to the Goddess and God, you can use the names by which you've grown to know Them.

Daily prayer, both formal and spontaneous, is another method of truly making Wicca a part of your everyday life. The exact words don't matter much, for it's your involvement in the prayer that's most important.

EVERYDAY PRAYERS AND CHANTS

A Prayer Before Meals

Before eating, say these or similar words (if necessary, whisper or merely think these words):

From forest and stream;

From mountain and field;

From the fertile Earth's

Nourishing yield;

I now partake of
Divine energy;
May it lend health,
Strength and love to me.
Blessed Be.

Another Prayer Before Meals

Goddess of the verdant plain;
God of sun-ripe grain;
Goddess of the cooling rain;
God of fruit and cane;
Bless this meal I've prepared;
Nourish me with love;
Bless this meal I now share
With You both above.

A Third Prayer Before Meals

0 Goddess within,
0 God within,
I now partake of the
Fertility of the Earth.
Bless this food with Your love.

A Morning Prayer

Bless this day, sun of fiery light.
Bless this day; prepare me for the night.

Sunrise Chant

Fire growing,
Sun is glowing;
Glowing, flowing
Down on me.

Another Morning Prayer

0 Gracious Goddess,
0 Gracious God,
Lend me health, strength and love
During this coming day.
Assist me with the challenges ahead.
Share Your divine wisdom.
Teach me to respect all things.
Remind me that the greatest power of all is love.
Blessed Be.

An Evening Prayer

The moon illuminates the earth
With wondrous silver rays;
Illuminate me through the night
And through the sun-lit days.

A Prayer Before Sleep

0 Gracious Goddess;
0 Gracious God,
I now enter the realm of dreams.

Weave now, if You will, a web of protective light around me.
Guard both my sleeping form and my spirit.
Watch over me
Until the sun once again
Rules the Earth.
O Gracious Goddess,
O Gracious God,
Be with me through the night.

Invocation Before Sleep
Lady of the Moon;
Lord of the Sun;
Protect me and mine
Now day is done.

New Moon Chant
Silver flowing,
Diana's growing;
Growing, showing
Love for me.

A Short Chant For Help
Divine Mother,
Mother Divine,
Show me the way;
Give me a sign.

10: PRAYERS AND RITES OF THANKS AND OFFERINGS

OFFERING RITES

Many Wiccans follow ancient custom by making a small offering to the Goddess and God on a daily basis. This is usually done before images of deities, but may also be performed anywhere, including outside.

Making consistent offerings to the Goddess and God reinforces your involvement with both Them and our religion, so there's every reason to make periodic offerings.

The main tool of such rites is the offertory bowl, into which the offering is placed (if indoors). Though this may be of any natural material, a clay, wooden, ceramic or silver bowl is preferred.

What type of offerings are best? Generally, food in any form (save for meat) is fine, as are all small, precious objects. Even jewelry and expensive items are sometimes offered and buried in the Earth. If you have nothing else, and can spare no food, pure water (which is not only necessary to human life but is also filled with Goddess energy) can be used. Incense may also be smoldered in offering, but it should be a special type that you don't ordinarily burn. (I wish that it wasn't necessary for me to say so, but just in case some of you have missed an important lesson: we never sacrifice living things to the deities.)

Offerings must be consciously made, done with thanks, intent and focus. Empty offerings will have little effect. In past times, such offerings were considered vital to the worshipper's continuing existence. Today, we might see them as vital to our spiritual existence.

You may decide to make an offering once a day, once a week or once a month, every three weeks, every full moon. (Rhythms of this type are preferred rather than haphazard offerings) The time of day isn't really important, though most prefer the night. Again: find your own best plan.

Offerings certainly can also be made at any time in thanks for answered prayer.

The rites that follow are suggestions. Use your intuition and experiment to find the forms best suited to you.

After making the offering, reflect for a few moments on the meaning of your actions.

A Daily Offering

Place the offering in the bowl (or in the ground) while saying:

What I take I freely give.

Accept this offering, Goddess and God.

Another Daily Offering

Make the offering while saying;

I give you this symbol of my devotion.

May it strengthen my bonds with you.

An Offering for a Special Request

This should by no means be seen as a bribe. We don't bribe the Goddess and God, for They created and possess everything in existence. However, giving an offering before making a special request (during prayer) is again a symbol of our need. The actual energy that exists within the offering is sent by the power of our prayer to the Goddess and God, and so further emphasizes our need.

When you have a special request, choose a suitable offering: something quite important to you, either emotionally, mentally or monetarily. Bury it in the Earth while praying for the request.

It is done.

(Never dig up and retrieve offerings. Once you've given them to the Goddess and God, you've relinquished their physical forms. What's done is done.)

RITES OF THANKS

Thanks for An Answered Prayer

Goddess

What no human ear could hear, you heard.

What no human eye could see, you saw.

What no human heart could bear, you transformed.

What no human hand could do, you did.

What no human power could change, you changed.

Goddess of love; Goddess omnipotent;

You through Whom all power flows;

Source of all;

Queen of the Cosmos;

Creatrix of the Universe;

Accept this humble token of thanks

From a Solitary Wiccan

Who has spoken

And who has been heard.

(Place an offering, such as a flower, a coin, a jewel, a picture that you've drawn, or some other object precious to you on the earth. Or, bury it in the earth. If this can't be immediately done, place the object in the offering bowl and later give it directly to the Earth.)

A Solitary Ritual of Thanks

(You alone will know when to perform this ritual. It can be done at any phase of the moon, during the day or night, whenever needed.)

You'll need one large white or pink bowl; one white candle; water; small, fresh flowers (white blooms are best) and one piece of white cotton cloth.

Place the bowl on the altar (or on any table). If desired, cast a circle. Affix the white candle to the center of the bowl with warmed beeswax or with drippings from another white candle (so that the bowl acts as a candle holder).

Pour water into the bowl. Float the fresh flowers on the surface of the water. Light the candle.

Visualize your reason for the ritual; remember why you're thanking the Goddess and God. Touch the water on both sides of the candle with your fingertips, saying these or similar words:

Lady of the Moon, of the stars and the Earth;

Lord of the Sun, of the forests and the hills;

I perform a ritual of thanks.

My love shines like the flame;

My love floats like the petals

Upon You.

Lady of the Waters, of flowers and the sea;

Lord of the Air, of horns and of fire;

I perform a ritual of thanks.
My love shines like the flame;
My love floats like the petals
Upon You.

Lady of the Caves, of cats and snakes;
Lord of the Plains, of falcons and stags;
I perform a ritual of thanks.
My love shines like the flame;
My love floats like the petals
Upon You.

Look into the candle's flame, then down into the water. Blow gently upon the water's surface and watch the flower's movements. Meditate. Commune. Thank.

When it's time, remove the petals from the water. Place them in the center of the white cotton cloth. Wrap the cloth around the petals. If you've cast a circle, close it now. End your rite of thanks by quenching the candle's flame, pouring the water onto the ground and burying the flowers in the Earth. It is done.

11: SIMPLE WICCAN RITES

You're excited about an upcoming trip. Then you realize that your travel plans will interfere with the celebration of a Sabbat or Esbat. Since it wouldn't be practical (or advisable) to take along all your ritual tools, what can you do?

On other occasions, the desire or need for a ritual may suddenly occur. When this occurs there's little or no time for preparation. You may hear that a friend is in the hospital; that someone you love is in danger. Again, what are the options?

The answer lies in simplified Wiccan rites. In certain circumstances, a magical working (such as folk magic) may be more appropriate. For strictly spiritual occasions, even less complex rituals can produce powerful changes of consciousness and satisfying connection with the Goddess and God.

Ritual tools (athame, wand, cup, censer, incense, water and salt) are assistants to ritual. They aren't necessary, but when we're beginning to learn Wicca they're of invaluable help in creating ritual consciousness, defining and purifying sacred space, and invoking the Goddess and God. Once we've mastered the basics, such tools are always welcomed, but aren't necessary. Simplified ritual consists, as you might have guessed, of rites performed with a minimum of tools and ritual movements.

I've performed rituals with a paper packet of salt (such as is provided in some restaurants), a small paper cup of water, a birthday cake candle and a regular table knife. With the salt and water I consecrated the general area.

I used the knife to cast a small circle, and lit the candle to the Goddess and God. This was a satisfactory rite, though I'd had no ritual bath, few tools and little time to prepare.

Once, a few friends and I did an extremely simplified healing rite in a hospital room for a sick friend. I've chanted in the stillness of alien hotel rooms far from home and performed simple moon rites when I happened to see the moon peeking through the trees.

Then too, I've performed ritual with only the tools of nature, whether I was indoors or out. The earth beneath me; the water gushing before me; the air and the fiery force of the sun above. I've most often relied solely on my mind, emotions and magical visualization abilities to perform simplified Wiccan rituals.

I began practicing Wicca when I was still underage and living at home. This forced me to use simplified rituals: lighting candles and softly chanting; staring into the fire on the Sabbats; whispering full moon incantations while sitting on the window sill as I gazed up at the lunar globe.

Simply put, though the ritual tools and forms of Wicca are important because they, in part, define our religion, they're not necessary. Effective ritual isn't dependent upon the number of tools that you can pile onto the altar; it begins within you and continues from there. The tools and memorized chants are outward expressions of inward changes (such as the shift to ritual consciousness). They can assist us in creating these inner transformations, but they aren't prerequisite.

Below I present the suggested steps of all extemporaneous or greatly simplified Wiccan rites. Consider this as a pattern after which you can develop your own. The need for such rites may arise at any time, usually when you're away from home and books aren't available. To be prepared for such emergencies, think in advance of some ways in which you can perform simple yet effective Wiccan rituals at any time, and at any place, with few tools.

The following information is suitable for use during both emergency situations as well as when away from home (and tools) on the Sabbats and Esbats.

CASTING A CIRCLE

Stand, sit or lie, according to the situation. Raise energy by tightening your muscles. Visualize it glowing as a ball of purplish-blue flame within you. Using your protective hand, direct this energy out from you into a small magic circle. (The hand acts as the energy director). Alternately, send out the energy in a clockwise circle around you without moving your hand. Feel the circle shimmering and pulsing. (If desired and possible, sprinkle salt and/or water around you to bless the area before creating the circle.)

INVOKING THE GODDESS AND GOD

Prayers that you've memorized may feel right. Simply say what you feel. Remember to focus on your connections with Them while praying. If circumstances don't permit you to speak out loud, *think* your words. You might use something like this formula:

Mother Goddess, be here with me.

Father God, be here with me.

Then explain the situation or say words in celebration of the ritual occasion. These don't have to be lengthy. Here's a suggested format:

○ State the reason for the rite: recognition of a Sabbat (if so, which one), full moon, or a special need.

- State something about the occasion or ask for Their assistance, if appropriate.

- Thank the Goddess and God for their attentions. An example of this for, say, Yule might be something like this:

I come before you tonight (or today) to celebrate Yule. The sun is reborn of the Goddess.

Light is growing. The promise of spring has begun.

Meditate upon the meaning of the occasion for a few moments, then say:

Goddess and God, thank you for attending my simple circle. Hail and farewell.

You may also wish to recite memorized invocations, or say many more words. Follow your intuition.

CLOSING THE RITE

After thanking the Goddess and God, take up the energy with which you created the circle. If at all possible, eat something directly following the circle (if nothing else, taste a bit of salt). Your simplified rite has ended.

If you whisper and internalize your actions, such rituals can be performed in crowded rooms, in the presence of others, without their knowledge. You can truthfully state that you wish to pray for a few moments and in no way reveal to whom you're praying.

There's no reason to miss ritual just because you're physically distant from your tools, or have had no warning. This is one of the great advantages of Solitary Wicca: you don't have to call up the other members for ritual, nor do you have to feel that you simply can't do a ritual by yourself. You can – by using simplified Wiccan ritual.

12: MAGIC AND THE SOLITARY WICCAN

Magic is a tremendously powerful tool. With it, we can facilitate changes in both our spirituality and our physical lives. This natural (though little-understood) process of moving energy with purpose is certainly an important part of Wicca, for we (of course) create the circle in which we work our rites with magic. We may also use magic to purify and to consecrate ritual tools and jewelry.

This chapter is limited to discussions of Wiccan magic as opposed to folk magic (the non-religious use of tools such as candles, herbs, oils and colors, combined with personal power, to affect changes.)

THE CIRCLE

You should already know how to create a magic circle (or 'create sacred space') You raise energy, give it purpose and, using your mind and perhaps a tool, direct this energy outward from your body in the shape of a large sphere, in which you perform your rituals.

That much should be clear from your readings. Now, how *well* do you know this process? Do you take it for granted? Do you really know what's going on? Do you ever test the circle's strength? Have you ever felt the boundaries of the circle with an outstretched, sensitized hand? Is your circle (actually, a half-sphere) perfect? Lop-sided? Sunken? Oval-shaped? Too big?

Such questions can be answered by careful study of the next circle that you create. Using all your senses (especially your psychic abilities), examine your circle after finishing it. Give it a white glove test. Answer the questions mentioned above, then determine whether you feel different within the circle's boundaries. That's one of the clues. If you do find problems, close the circle and begin again with more attention to what you're doing. We must never become sloppy in our circle constructions. Creating the circle is similar to building a cathedral or raising the megaliths of Stonehenge: we're building a temple, *our* temple, in which we'll worship our deities. It deserves every bit of our time, energy and attention.

RAISING ENERGY IN THE CIRCLE

This form of magic should also be familiar. A need is visualized. While visualizing, the Wiccan raises energy from within her or his body and, through the visualization, imprints this need onto the energy. The power is then released.

Unfortunately, Solitary Wiccans have few energy-raising methods available to them. The first: you're sitting before the altar. You begin to slowly chant a statement of purpose, such as 'heal her' or 'protect me'. You slowly increase the speed of the chant, never wavering in your visualization. You begin tightening the muscles all over your body (this raises physical energy, even when you're still). The power builds within you and threatens to spill over. You release it.

Another method is far more physical. You begin a slow clockwise dance (or walk) around the altar while visualizing and/or chanting the need. The dance increases in speed. When you release the power, you may fall dramatically to the floor.

Yet a third method utilizes breathing techniques which tighten the muscles and raise energy.

And that, fellow Solitaries, is just about it. There are a few other methods, but they require the presence of several other persons and are, thus, limited to covens.

SENDING THE ENERGY

In coven magical workings, power is raised by any one of a number of methods. This continues for some time until the power that's been raised reaches its peak. At this point the participants let go of the power; they may drop to the floor, completely relaxing their muscles, while pushing out the power. Those present and participating in this process can, for our purposes, be termed Energy Raisers.

Usually, but not always, this power is then directed and released through the circle by a single person – often the High Priestess. (Sometimes the energy is sent into a physical object within the circle itself.) This person, whom I'll here call the Energy sender, has the ability to take all this energy within herself and direct it outward toward its goal. (Some covens work differently. Each member may send out her or his energy. Still, the Sender is there to direct any stray energies and to control the energy-raising process that proceeds this release.)

As Solitary Wiccans, we must always be both the Energy Raiser and the Energy Sender. This demands practice and control.

The method used by coven members to release energy mentioned above is the one that we use. When it's time, simply push it out. Relax your muscles – all at once. With visualization, direct the energy outward from your hand or athame.

Some find this difficult at first. The Wiccan may feel the energy, and attempt to send it out, but may question whether it reaches its goal. Many new Solitary Wiccans also wonder how the energy penetrates the circle and actually exits, when one of the circle's functions is to retain precisely this energy.

The perfect ability to raise and send energy is one of the challenges of solitary Wicca, and will come with time. When you've properly cast a circle, you've sent energy from your body for a specific purpose, and that purpose has been achieved. Thus, you've performed a magical working.

Once you've achieved this, the next step is to raise more energy (through one of the techniques mentioned above) and then to send it a bit further, through the circle and out toward its goal.

Don't worry about the circle somehow blocking the exit of the energy. It's somewhat akin to a door. You're inside the structure, and sending energy through it opens the door. Like doors, circles don't need their functions explained to them during magic. The circle 'knows' that one of its functions is to release energy. (The door automatically shuts once the energy has left.)

Okay, you might be saying, so the circle is like a room in which we stand, and we can send energy out from it. Fine. But why doesn't the energy leak out before we're ready to send it? Because we haven't sent enough energy to open the door. Simply grasping a door knob won't cause it to open. We must exert force and pressure in the correct combination to remove the obstacle. This is true of magic as well: only a concentrated, directed stream of energy is strong enough to punch a temporary hole in the circle and travel outside its boundaries.

A coven can raise energy over an extended period of time, certainly up to half an hour or longer, through ring dances, chanting and other techniques. During this time, the coveners will of necessity release some of their energy prior to the let-it-all-out moment which is determined by the High Priestess. The circle retains this energy until such time as the combined force of all the coveners, directed by the High Priestess, opens the door.

Solitary Wiccans also raise power within the circle. And yes, we may release a bit of energy too early. Still, it's important that we hold in the energy until the last possible moment. A single energy release is most effective.

Push the energy out of you. Feel it exploding away in a focused beam of energy, shooting from you, through the circle, and out to its goal. Visualize and feel any excess energy lying around the circle as joining the main stream of energy.

Since you don't have a second person directing the energy, you must do this yourself. Fortunately, with practice, it's really quite simple. Visualize!

After every Wiccan rite, especially those that have involved magic, some energy will naturally be retained within the circle. This energy can be subtly distracting so it's usual to earth it by consuming food after each ritual. Protein foods (such as beans and corn, dairy products, and so on) are ideal. Eating shifts the consciousness back to this reality, and also replenishes some of the energy lost during magic.

These, then, have been some specifics of Solitary Wiccan magical workings. At one time they were closely-held secrets. Today, all can share in this knowledge and utilize it to improve the quality of their lives.

A few further words are perhaps appropriate. Wiccan magic must, by its performance within a circle, be for positive change. Negative magic has no place in Wicca, and doing such a working within a magic circle may immediately backfire upon the perpetrator.

Energy raised within sacred space (the circle) is directly attuned to the Goddess and God. Send Them negative energy and you're likely to instantaneously receive it back – threefold.

Over the years, many well-meaning Wiccans have warned of the 'danger' of Solitary Wicca. They've argued that a coven can act as a safety valve, defusing a covener in a volatile state of mind who wants the coven to perform a negative magical working. (No covens would perform truly negative magic.)

This argument, which on the surface seems quite satisfactory, doesn't hold water. A moral person is a moral person. Anyone who accepts the primary tenet of Wicca (harm none) won't be tempted to perform a negative magical working, whether they're a coven member or a Solitary.

It can't be stated too often – harming none means harming *none*, in any way, including yourself. ('Harming' should be thought of as interference with or the manipulation of the lives of others, and includes hexing, cursing and person-specific love spells.) Once this tenet has been accepted, and it should be by all who profess to be Wiccans, the imaginary dangers of Solitary Wiccan magic vanish.

PART THREE:

YOUR OWN
TRADITION

13: CREATING A NEW PATH

Much of conventional Wicca is organized into traditions. Since traditions, by definition, are beliefs and practices that are passed from one generation or group to another, a Wiccan tradition is a specific form of Wiccan practice that is passed to other persons, usually following initiation.

Wiccan traditions are one of our religion's strongest survival mechanisms. Structure is necessary for every religion's survival. Without it, it will crumble in confusion and chaos.

If every Wiccan constantly reinvented every aspect of Wicca (tools, ritual forms, deity concepts), our religion as we know it would soon disappear. Lacking traditional forms and beliefs, it could hardly be passed on to others.

As Solitary Wiccans, we generally don't practice a specific Wiccan tradition (unless we've been so trained and have left a coven). This presents us with great freedom. Some Solitary Wiccans create new rituals for each Sabbat and Esbat and practice a rather loose form of Wicca.

However, many Solitaries feel the need to create their own traditions so that their religious practices and beliefs are supported by a solid foundation. Though such new traditions will evolve with time and experience, they do provide a valuable framework for the Solitary Wiccan's practices. If nothing else, it provides a firm rock to grasp in the often stormy sea of self-directed worship, and is a reassurance that the Wiccan is walking the right path. In a sense, a Wiccan tradition is a map pointing out a specific route to the Goddess.

Part III of this book consists of a guide to creating a new Wiccan tradition, one perfectly suited for you. In writing it yourself, you can focus it toward your personal needs, and the end result may well be far more spiritually satisfying than any other Wiccan tradition.

It's never necessary to take on this task. However, if you do decide to create your own tradition, this and the following chapters will present you with some ideas to help you get started.

WHY CREATE A TRADITION?

Why not? Few published Books of Shadows are complete, and virtually all are designed for group worship. Thus, none are ideally suited to the Solitary practitioner. This alone is reason enough to create your own Wiccan tradition.

Additionally, the published sets of rituals may seem distant, or foreign, or they may not move you to fully involve yourself in Wicca. You also may have far too many questions regarding a specific Wiccan tradition, even one that has been published, to adequately perform its rites.

Then again, a creative streak may be moving within you, searching for an outlet. Creating a Wiccan Tradition is a creative process, but it must be done with control.

HOW TO BEGIN

Right now, as you're reading this, grab a pen and several sheets of paper. On the top of the first page, write the following in large letters:

DEITY CONCEPTS

On the second, write TOOLS, ALTARS, DRESS, JEWELRY

On the third, RITUALS

On the fourth, BELIEFS

On the fifth, RULES

On the six, SYMBOLS AND RUNES

On the seventh, THE BOOK OF SHADOWS

Use these pages to make rough notes while reading the following chapters. Later, you'll probably need far more room for your thoughts and notes on each subject, but this is a fine start. (Utilizing a computer or a typewriter, at this early stage, might slow you down.)

The important part is to start actually putting thoughts into words on a page. These will eventually evolve into rituals, beliefs, rules and other things. A Wiccan tradition isn't misty or ethereal; it possesses specifics, and to create a Wiccan tradition you must first determine these specifics.

Wicca isn't a spiritual free-for-all. A true Wiccan tradition must be based upon Wiccan conventions. Though there's plenty of room for personal touches, some things are essentially Wiccan and can't be discarded. These will be clearly pointed out.

In the following chapters we'll be exploring one method of creating a Wiccan tradition. You're free to use it if it feels right; if it doesn't, don't. And if you don't wish to begin a new path, feel free not to.

Creating your own Wiccan tradition is exciting and challenging. It's a process of defining not only your means of spiritual expression, but also the nature of your spirituality itself. Thus, it's a journey of self-discovery.

14: DEITY CONCEPTS

Without deities, there would be no religions of any kind. How do you, personally, define the Deity concepts of your tradition? Every Wiccan possesses her or his own conceptions of the Goddess and God. We built these up through personal experience and interactions with Them as well as through research. Such images will, naturally, form the basis of your new tradition's Deity concepts. Research will also provide assistance. (See Suggested Reading at the end of this chapter.) The nature of your tradition's Deities is of great importance, as we'll see.

THE GODDESS AND THE GOD

Worship is at the heart of any religion, and it's important to firm your conceptions of the Goddess and God. If, up to this point, they've been like astral grandparents, or powerful but misty beings, it might be time to mentally bring them down to Earth.

The following notes can be used in sharpening your conceptions of the Goddess and God. These, combined with the readings listed at the end of this chapter and your own spiritual experiences, should allow you to gain a greater understanding of the Goddess and God.*

---

*Until recently, Wicca possessed few teachings concerning the Goddess and God. We gleaned what we could from the few myths (sacred stories) that were taught to us; from verbal teachings, personal experience and the hints provided by other Wiccans, but we had little upon which to base our conceptions save for personal experience. Today, however, renewed research and interest in Goddess worship and in pre-Christian religions in general has offered us much information, some of which we can utilize and frame within a Wiccan context. See the Bibliography.

THE GODDESS

The Goddess is, truly, all things. She's all power, all wisdom, all love, all fertility, all creativity; the nurturing as well as destructive force Who created our universe and Who shapes our lives.

This may be your concept of the Goddess: She Who Is All. Even so, you'll probably need to determine Her symbols and some of Her specific manifestations to adequately connect with Her. In other words, you'll have to discover Her private telephone number; Her personal portrait of power which, through ritual, will facilitate communication.

(The below list is merely a short catalog of a few of the Goddess' attributes. Please understand that these are aspects of the same being, The Goddess, and is far from a complete listing.)

Here are some clues to determining Her nature:

○ Goddess of outer space.
   Goddess of the stars.
   Goddess of galaxies.
   Goddess of the Universe.

○ Goddess of the Moon.
   Goddess of the Waxing Moon.
   Goddess of the Full Moon.
   Goddess of the Waning Moon.

○ Goddess of the Earth.
   Goddess of earth fertility and of plants.
   Goddess of the animals.
   Goddess of storms, earthquakes, volcanic activity.
   Goddess of gentle rain, wells, rivers, lakes, seas and oceans.

○ Goddess of freshness, renewal, beginnings, promise and potential.

- ❍ Goddess of childbirth, mothers and mothering.
- ❍ Goddess of love, beauty, compassion.
- ❍ Goddess of healing.
- ❍ Goddess of prophecy.
- ❍ Goddess of magic.
- ❍ Goddess of wisdom.
- ❍ Goddess of power.
- ❍ Goddess of destruction, retribution, war.*

A space goddess isn't a truly Wiccan concept. At least two more aspects must be added: Goddess of the Moon and the Earth. Indeed, most Wiccan conceptions of the Goddess are built upon the many combinations possible between these aspects. This signifies a Goddess related to everything, Whose closest symbols are the Moon and the Earth beneath our feet. Everything on the Earth and of the Earth is under Her domain.

Most Wiccans also acknowledge the Goddess' role in childbirth, healing, love; as the provider of wisdom and the sender of magical energy in times of need.

One conception of the Goddess has become quite popular. As the Triple Goddess (related to the phases of the moon), She's most closely linked with the New Moon and with freshness (in Her Maiden aspect); the Full Moon, mothers and childbirth (as The Mother); and the Waning Moon with wisdom, prophecy, magic, destruction and retribution (The Crone; source of all wisdom). What I might be forgiven for terming The Goddess of the Three Aspects is directly linked with women's lives and

---

*I'm aware that there are many other types of Goddesses. However, I'm limited here by those that have been either worshipped or acknowledged in contemporary Wicca. Pagan isn't necessarily Wiccan.

cycles and, thus, has become enormously popular both within and without Wicca proper. (See Suggested Readings.) (Some Wiccans seem to believe that this is the only conception of the Goddess that has ever existed. It certainly isn't, but is currently a quite popular Wiccan model.)

Most Wiccans acknowledge that the Goddess possesses a dark side. This is evident from nature itself: storms and earthquakes immediately come to mind. However, we've chosen not to focus on these aspects, and never invoke Her for such purposes. Let's face it: the last thing we need is to bring more destruction and violence into the world. If She sees fit to do so, fine; the same isn't true for humans.

In Wiccan workings, we look to the more uplifting aspects of the Goddess. To do otherwise would lead to misery and despair. If our religion is to provide us with spiritual refreshment, hope and love, we should focus on the Goddess as a being of love, compassion, nurturing and wonder. I'd rather worship Her in this guise than as a Warrior Queen, for I'm not a warrior, we've had far too many wars, and I have no wish to indirectly encourage any others.*

One of the aspects missing from my list is the Goddess of Fate. Wiccans rarely invoke Her in this way, simply because we don't believe in predestination. If we did, we wouldn't practice magic to alter our lives, for it wouldn't be effective. However, some Wiccans may argue that the Goddess does, indeed, have plans for us, and that She can set up situations that will gently remind us of our lessons, or that will sway us to make correct decisions in times of stress. In this way, perhaps, the Goddess can indeed be

---

*Many of you will disagree with me, especially those of you who work outside strict Wiccan practice. I'll admit that, yes, there may come a time when we must invoke The Lady of Justice, but such worship can become disheartening and even dangerous. Only she or he who is innocent of wrong-doing should dare to invoke this aspect of the Goddess, for She'll probably bring justice to the wrong-doer, even if it's Her worshipper. Think carefully concerning this.

seen as a Goddess of Fate, but not in the normally understood sense of the word. We don't do the Goddess' will; She always gives us options, and allows us to fall on our faces if (when) we take the wrong course.

As the Goddess of healing, love, beauty, compassion and prophecy, She's worshipped by nearly all Wiccans. Some emphasize these attributes, at least when in need of them. However, She's always a goddess of love and concern, and healing rituals directed to or through Her will receive Her blessing.

It's time to discuss the many forms that the Goddess may assume. You may have already seen Her in meditations, dreams, and during rituals. If so, think about how She appeared to you. She is the One with the Thousand Forms, and that which She revealed to you is a valuable tool in contacting her at later times.

If you haven't physically seen the Goddess yet (and many Wiccans have never seen Her), don't despair. It may occur. While waiting, build up your own image of the Goddess, using your feelings, intuitions and perceptions of Her. (Remember that she may secretly assist in this process.)

Some Wiccans see Her in quite specific ways:

"I see the Goddess as a rounded, earthy goddess-woman with hair the color of wheat, eyes as blue as the ocean, skin as dark as the rich black soil; naked, holding flowers in Her outstretched hands, standing beneath a tree and smiling."

"I see the Goddess as a celestial lunar being. Her skin is milky white (as it would appear by moonlight); She wears a white diaphanous robe that doesn't conceal Her body, which changes its shape with the Moon's phase; a necklace of pearls and moonstones encircles Her neck and an upturned crescent rests on Her forehead. Her hair is white (or silver or blonde) and She tosses the glowing Moon between Her hands."

"I see the Goddess as my late grandmother: dressed in old-fashioned clothes that She's made with Her hands, seated in a rocking chair by a fire of willow branches in a house without walls. She's slowly stitching a design of the universe on a dark blue cloth and tells me all the secrets as I sit near Her feet on a rag rug. She is the Crone."

These are highly personal visions of the Goddess. None are incorrect; these and many others are accepted by Wiccans.

Some Wiccan's conceptions may be closer to those formed in other cultures: "I see the Goddess as Athena, of the hunt." "I see the Goddess as Spider Grandmother." "As Diana." "Isis." "Hecate." (Photos of statues and other images of the goddess can be found in a number of books; see Suggested Reading at the end of this chapter.)

Again, it may be enough for you to feel Her presence. If you've already formed an image of the Goddess (or, putting it another way, if She has already revealed Her form to you), fine. If not, you may wish to discover Her form through ritual work, prayer and, perhaps, dreams.

One word of warning: if you've already developed a clear picture of the Goddess, and have already determined Her aspects, don't let the above information alter this. Hold fast to that which you discover; it's of the highest rarity and value.

Divine symbolism is another aspect of your personal conception of the Goddess. These include both those used in Her worship and those directly or indirectly related to Her.

This is in part determined by your understanding of the Goddess. If She's primarily linked with the Moon, symbols representing the Earth wouldn't speak of Her. Here are some suggested symbols of the types of Goddesses listed above, to be used in ritual design, poems, chants and invocations:

- Goddess of Outer Space. (Darkness; black cloth; stars; the night; the void; cauldron; nocturnal flowers and owls.)

- Goddess of the Moon. (Crescents; pearls; moonstones; mirror; silver; labrys.)

- Goddess of the Earth. (Fruits; plants, especially grains; fertilizing nature; corn dollies; Goddess animals such as cats, dolphins, lions, horses, dogs, bees; pure water; a shell collected on a beach; cups, chalices, cauldrons; emeralds.)

- Goddess of freshness, renewal, beginnings, promise and potential. (Unplowed fields; eggs; spring; New Moon.)

- Goddess of childbirth, mothers and mothering. (Full Moon; holed stones; round or oval-shaped objects; a baby.)

- Goddess of love, beauty, compassion. (Mirrors; hearts; flowers; honey.)

- Goddess of healing. (Purifying waters; power-streaming hands.)

- Goddess of prophecy. (Quartz crystal; psychic awareness; caves; nudity; pools of water.)

- Goddess of magic. (All magical tools; sword; athame; spindle; fire; cauldron.)

- Goddess of wisdom. (Fires; books; owls; Waning Moon.)

- Goddesses of destruction, retribution, war. (Not recommended.)

Keep in mind that such symbols may not be actually used in ritual, but can be utilized when writing ritual invocations. The mention of these tools immediately and directly connects your invocation with the Goddess.

Many other symbols and tools are connected with the Goddess in general and in Her particular aspects.

THE GOD

The God shares an equal place in the hearts of most Wiccans, for without Him, our world would be cold, desolate of fertility and all life. Though most Wiccans don't experience as emotional a response to the God as they do to the Goddess, he's certainly called upon in times of need (particularly for protection) Here are some attributes of the God in Wiccan thought:

- God of the Sun.
- God of human fertility (and, thus, sex).
- God of the Earth.
  God of wild animals.
  God of crops.
  God of deserts, plains, valleys.
- God of Summer.
- God of hunting.
- God of death and rebirth.
- God of retribution, war and conflicts.

This list pretty well sums the main aspects of the God in Wiccan thought. The God simply hasn't accumulated as many Wiccan-acknowledged aspects as has the Goddess. There are certainly many other aspects of the God (for example, as the inventor of tools; overseer of competitions, and so on) that haven't been adopted by Wiccans. This has resulted in a dearth of Wiccan mythic material involving the God.

Some recent authors (see readings) have tried to fill this void with rituals and myths concerning the Oak King and the Ivy King. This concept is now quite common, at least at public rituals and among some Solitary Wiccans. However, I know little of it, and direct the interested reader to the appropriate book by the Farrars (see readings).

Let's speak frankly here. The Goddess appears to be more loving, more understanding and caring than the God. The God, through no fault of His own, may appear to be unapproachable except in Wiccan ritual, and even then formalized prayers are necessary. This is a natural human reaction, even among Wiccans, and easily explains the lack of material regarding Him.

One of the underlying reasons for this problem isn't difficult to discover. Many new Wiccans have difficulty in approaching the God. For their entire lives, they've been taught that there's only one God. He's jealous, angry and promises we'll all end up in a place of darkness and suffering after death. Vivid portraits of His wrath were firmly imprinted in many children's minds at a quite impressionable age, and it can be difficult for some of these persons, now grown and entering Wicca, to remove such lingering conceptions of male Deity.

Then again, some feminists wish to direct their worship solely to the Goddess. Many of them have, quite frankly, had enough of male spiritual conceptions and have no desire to attune with them in Wicca. For them, worship of the Goddess is completely fulfilling and, except when trying to adapt Goddess-God rituals to strictly Goddess rites, they find few challenges in solely honoring the Goddess in Wiccan rites.

The God has been given a bad name by 2,000 years of patriarchal hyperbole that has strayed far off the path that Jesus allegedly once preached. Religious institutions have transformed the male conception of Deity into a wrathful being whose followers have wiped out entire civilizations and destroyed hundreds of cultures; a God in whose name millions of persons have been killed in holy wars; a God whose representatives have repeatedly stated that Deity is not female and that women cannot possibly achieve a rapport with the Divine to the extent that they should be allowed to be priests; a male Deity ruling over a male-oriented world in which men have long used religion as an excuse to dominate, subdue and abuse women.

In this long, bitter and inexcusably violent period of our species' short history, the male Deity has been given a negative, frightening image. We know him only as the god of vengeance and war. True, this god is nice to his worshippers, but any who don't worship Him, or who don't limit their worship to Him, are doomed to spend eternity in a pit of fire and torture, with no hope of another life or escape.

It isn't surprising, then, that many new Wiccans don't feel comfortable with the Wiccan concept of God, at least during their first ventures into Wiccan. Women may have a particularly difficult time. While they may be surprised and delighted to have found a religion that embraces women, that acknowledges their inner power and spiritual strength, that allows them to participate as leaders in ritual and that – incredibly – actually worships a Goddess, they may not quite be able to bring the God into their rites. It can be difficult to forget 20, 30 or 40 years of negative God Imagery.

Some Wiccans eventually adjust and have no difficulty in worshipping both the Goddess and the God in Wiccan ritual. Others decide to worship only the Goddess. (These are personal decisions but, once again, I'll state the party line: Wicca consists of the worship of the Goddess *and* the God.)

I've found in my own experience that those who come to Wicca having never truly believed in or practiced any other religion have no problems including the God in their rites. Additionally, even many who did emerge from conventional religious backgrounds experience no difficulty with the concept of the God.

To be old-fashioned, traditional Wicca, your rites should honor both. This may necessitate rediscovering the God by expanding your awareness of His presence and of His attributes. Below are some ideas.

Do you see the God as woman-hating? See Him instead as a being that the Goddess has brought into Her arms. Remember that thousands of priestesses worship Him every day. Invoke Him to assist in the furtherance of women's rights. Ask yourself how can any true conception of Deity can hate its children.

Do you see the God as bringer of death? Remember that death is necessary at some point, and that the Goddess brings us rebirth.

Do you see the God as the bringer of war? Recall that men have simply exploited His dark side for this purpose. Remember, however, that war is rarely religious in nature: it's main motivations are politics and money. Religion is often simply an excuse.

Do you see the God as a judge, as the caster-down of human souls into hell? Wiccans don't accept the existence of hell; no one casts us down anywhere, and the God unconditionally loves us.

Do you see God as a frightening, unknowable spirit hovering around the Earth? See Him, instead, in faces of your male friends and in the eyes of young boys. See Him in freshly-baked bread; in bunches of grapes; in towering, snow-capped mountains; in the Sun that warms the Earth and provides us our food and all of our tools for living.

I hope that these ideas provide some assistance to those who find it difficult to contact the God. This is a major problem and is one of the reasons why Goddess spirituality is so prevalent today: over the centuries, men have changed a gentle fertility god into a blood-thirsty monster. Erase such images and concentrate on the God's other aspects.

Again, you may have already seen the God in a vision, dream or meditation. He may have appeared in the incense smoke during ritual. If not, He may well yet make Himself visible to you.

Here are some Wiccan's visualizations of the God:

"He stands on a hill, naked, His skin reddish-brown from sunlight. His hair is long and black, and no razor has touched His chin or cheeks. He holds a shimmering golden knife; below Him are heaped piles of grain and vegetables."

"He's dressed in a brown, rustic tunic, holding a baby in one hand and the hand of an aged woman in the other. Dried flowers – symbolic of both fertility and its end – are entwined in His beard. He stands between light and darkness."

"The God is dressed in furs, but is bare foot. As I see Him among a forest of trees he wears horns on His head and a stag follows nearby. A bow is slung over one shoulder; a spear is in His hand. The aggressive expression on His face is softened by His caring eyes."

Again, some see the God in the terms of cultural concepts: "I see him as Pan." "The God appears to me as Grandfather." "As Belinus." "Osiris". "Apollo".

There are symbols that Wiccans use to represent the God in creating ritual and poetry. As you might imagine, there are fewer of these symbols than for the Goddess.

- God of the Sun. (Sun; gold; brass; bonfires; candles.)

- God of human fertility. (Acorns; pine cones; wands.)

- God of the Earth. (Grain; stones; valleys; seeds; forests; bull, snake, fish, wolf, eagle, lizard.)

- God of Summer. (Blazing fires; daylight; the South.)

- God of hunting. (Horns; spears; quiver; bow; arrows.)

- God of death and rebirth. (Sunset; winter; pomegranates; dried leaves; sickle; night; the West.)

○ God of retribution, war and conflicts. (Best not to invoke this attribute.)

Remember: the God is just as much a part of contemporary Paganism as is the Goddess. He isn't fearsome unless you decide to focus on his fearsome attributes. (This is also true of the Goddess.) He can be the epitome of compassion, caring, nurturing maleness, but only you can discover this.

AFTERWORD

I've got this nagging thought that my references to seeing the Goddess and God may make some of you feel left out. Don't worry about it. By the word 'see', I don't mean that, while completely awake, we look up and notice that the Goddess is physically standing in the room before us. Visitations of that magnitude are so rare that we needn't wait around for them. We have better opportunities for seeing the Goddess and God during alternate states of consciousness. In the circle, when we're in ritual consciousness, we're far more likely to see Them. We may also get glimpses, as I've already said, during dreams and meditations.

The first time I saw the Goddess was in a circle. I was seated before the altar and was meditating on Her. It can happen, but don't expect to use your eyes to see the forms of the Goddess and God. Realize, too, that the forms in which They come to you may be quite different from those that They present to others.

SUGGESTED READING

The Goddess:
There are simply too many books to list, and more are being released every day. Many of the new Goddess books aren't Wiccan in nature. I've largely tried to restrict myself here to Wiccan Goddess writings (or to those that have most profoundly affected Wiccan thought). For a wide variety of other titles, check the women's studies sections of virtually any new book store.

Farrar and Farrar, *The Witches' Goddess.* (The entire book.)

Graves, *The White Goddess.* (The entire book. Goddess speculations, poetry and mythic information that has had a tremendous impact on contemporary Wicca.)

Neumann, *The Great Mother: An Analysis of the Archetype.* (The entire book. A Jungian-based look at the Goddess. Zillions of photos of Goddess images.)

Walker, Barbara, *The Women's Encyclopedia of Myths and Secrets.* (Many of her research sources are highly questionable, but this remains a good encyclopedic look at women and goddesses.)

The God:
Farrar and Farrar, *Eight Sabbats for Witches.* (Information concerning the Oak King and the Holly King is scattered throughout this book.)

Farrar and Farrar, *The Witches' God.* (The entire book. Oak King and Holly King information can be found on pp. 35-38.)

Starhawk, *The Spiral Dance* (Pages 93-107 offer a somewhat feminist view of the God.)

Cunningham, *Wicca: A Guide for the Solitary Practitioner.* (Pages 12-14.)

15: TOOLS, ALTARS, DRESS AND RITUAL JEWELRY

TOOLS

Most Wiccan traditions use the same tools, with a few additions among certain groups. Since the tools are virtually mandatory in Wiccan ritual, you won't have to spend hours deciding on which to include in your new tradition. However, you can determine the exact forms of these tools, their symbolism and ritual uses.

For review, these are the main Wiccan tools:

⦿ *Images of the Goddess and God.* Many traditions place them on the altar. The nature of these images are of great variety. Some simply use candles; others natural objects representative of the Goddess and God. Still other Wiccans use hand-crafted sculptures or drawings. Genuine clay is available that, when dried in a normal oven, becomes quite hard. It can be used to create your own interpretations of the Goddess and God (good ideas for designs can be found in archaeological books).

⦿ *The Book of Shadows.* This hand-written book records the heart of any Wiccan tradition: rites, rules, magical techniques and other information. (See Chapter 21.)

- *The Athame* (black-handled knife). A director of energy used to create the magic circle.

- *The Censer.* In It, incense or herbs are burned to invite the presence of the Goddess and God, and to cleanse the ritual space. (A small box, bowl or bottle to contain the unburned incense is also used.)

- *The Cup (or Chalice).* This holds wine, water or other liquids for use during ritual.

- *The White-Handled Knife.* This is used for actual cutting purposes either within or within and without the circle.

- *Salt.* Generally used for circle casting, consecration of tools and for other purposes.

- *Water.* For purification of the circle.

- *The Pentacle.* This is a flat disk or plate bearing, at the least, the symbol of a five-pointed star.

- *The Wand.* A traditional tool, it's generally used in either power-raising or while inviting beings to attend the circle.

I've listed the tools here because they're an integral part of Wicca, and all Wiccan tradition should utilize most if not all of them. Why? Because the tools are among the outer aspects of Wicca by which we define our religion. If you created a tradition that never utilized any of these tools, it probably wouldn't be Wiccan. Hence, the tools should be used unless you decide to forge out on your own.

Other tools that aren't as widely used can be incorporated into your Wiccan tradition as you see fit.

○ *The Cauldron.* Some Wiccans utilize cauldrons as symbols of the Goddess, and they can be the center of religious rites. Fires are sometimes lit within them.

○ *The Bell.* Bells can be rung at specific points in rituals.

○ *The Broom.* My first teacher always cleansed the ritual area with her broom before ritual.

○ *The Cords.* Of importance in initiatory groups, in which cords often symbolize the bond of love and responsibility shared by the members, cords are also used in some initiation rites. Cords can certainly be used by the Solitary Wiccan, but needn't be constantly on the altar. The cords are truly tools of coven workings.

○ *Altar Cloth.* Some Wiccan traditions prescribe a specific color altar cloth for use on the altar. Certain designs (such as pentagrams) may be embroidered or painted onto these cloths. Many traditions, however, don't use them. (My first teacher usually used white cloths on the altar for Full Moons. I honestly can't remember [after all, this was 21 years ago] whether we used cloths for the Sabbats.)

Such tool lists can be extended: bottles of ritual oils, candle snuffers, incense spoons and swords immediately come to mind. Other objects may well be on the altar with the other tools from time to time: flowers or seasonal greens, sketches or runes or photographs for magical purposes.

In deciding which tools to use in your new tradition, always rely on your experience. You may read that the athame should be double-edged in one source; in another, single-edged. Some books state that the athame must be razor-sharp, while others say that it can be dull. You must decide what's right for you. Make a decision and keep it.

Put all such decisions in writing, first in rough notes and eventually in your Book of Shadows (see Chapter 21). You may well write in your Book of Shadows, "The athame – a double-edged, black-handled, hilted knife used for power-direction. It need not be sharp." This, then, will become part of your tradition.

ALTARS

As the physical center of your religious observances, the altar is of prime importance. Theories concerning the significance of and the proper arrangement of tools on altars vary. That altars are necessary, however, is rarely questioned. Once again, altars don't necessarily make the Wiccan, but the use of such altars is one of the defining yardsticks of Wiccan practices.

However much we may enjoy spontaneous rituals in a moonlit forest, while watching a desert sunset or lying on a grassy plain, structured rituals are an important part of long-standing Wiccan tradition, and structured rituals (more often than not) are performed with altars.

Many books contain altar designs and layouts that you can use to create your own. As most Wiccan traditions utilize a specific altar arrangement, so too can your tradition. Here are some basics:

○ The altar is always round. The altar is always square. The altar is always rectangular. The altar can be of any shape. This pretty much sums Wiccan thought regarding the appropriate shape of the altar. Many use round altars to symbolize, among other matters, the Goddess. Make your decision.

○ The Image or symbol of the Goddess can be placed to the left of the altar as you stand before it; the image of the God to the right.

○ Tools associated with the Goddess (the chalice, bells, sistrums, brooms, cauldrons) are often placed to the left. Tools associated with the God (swords, wands, the white-handled knife, bowl of salt, the censer) are often placed to the right on the altar. Other tools may be placed in the center: the pentacle, the censer, fresh flowers or greens.

○ A totally different method of arranging the altar takes the elements into account. Earthy tools (pentacle, salt) are placed to the North; the censer and incense to the East to represent Air; a red candle to the South and the bowl of water, chalice, cauldron, bell and other tools to the West. (This and the above system can't be used simultaneously, and neither is more correct.)

○ Candles are usually placed where they can't easily be knocked over, such as to the rear of the altar.

○ Leave space on your altar for your opened Book of Shadows. If not, create or find a small stand on which to place the Book during rituals. Though our rituals should be memorized, we can all have lapses of memory and it's nice to have a reminder close at hand.

○ The altar is sacred. Not that the Goddess and God live within it, but because we utilize it and the tools that it bears for spiritual purposes. Thus, only objects directly connected with Wicca and/or magical rites performed in the circle should be placed on the altar.

○ If, after ritual, the altar is used for other purposes (as, perhaps, a coffee table), at such times it ceases to be an altar. Only when it's covered with the tools of our religion and used as a focal point for ritual does it become an altar.

From these generalities, and by studying the sample altar designs included in other Wiccan books, you should be able to come up with a suitable design for your tradition. Include a sketch or a diagram of your altar design in the Book of Shadows.

Be certain that you know the *whys* of your arrangement. If you decide to place the athame directly in front of a goddess image, with its point directed at Her symbol, know why you've decided to do this.

ROBES

Many Wiccans dress in special robes for worship. Such garments are usually worn solely for ritual observances, and may be plain or decorated with symbols or embroidery.

Some Wiccans worship naked. This is a personal decision. Though a robe might seem to be useless to a Solitary Wiccan that practices ritual nudity, it's still good to have a robe around somewhere, in case you ever change your mind, or are invited to a robed ritual. It does happen.

Patterns for robes can be found in most yardage shops. If you make your own, use natural cloth. Polyester and other synthetic fabrics will leave you hot and uncomfortable in circle, and will hardly connect you with the Deities of nature.

Robes are also available at many occult shops and from mail-order businesses.

RITUAL JEWELRY

By ritual jewelry I'm not referring to rings and necklaces worn on a daily basis, even if they're symbolic of the Goddess and/or God. This term refers to jewelry worn only in the circle for ritual purposes.

In many Wiccan traditions, a necklace is considered the ideal piece of ritual jewelry for women, for it symbolizes reincarnation as well as the Goddess. Some traditions virtually demand that women wear a necklace of some type in the circle. Other traditions may use bracelets (usually flat and inscribed with runes or symbols) or rings in ritual. The famous garter is usually worn only by High Priestesses of certain traditions.

You can simply wear whatever you wish in the circle. Alternately, you may wear a special piece of jewelry that you specifically dedicate to your tradition, or may even state in the Book of Shadows that a certain piece of jewelry (such as a moonstone ring) should be worn in the circle at all times.

If you're expert at jewelry making you may create a unique piece: a beaded necklace, a ring or pendant created by the lost-wax method.

Remember: ritual jewelry isn't worn outside the circle. When it is, it loses its specialness and its direct links with ritual. Other pieces can be worn around the clock, but if you choose to use ritual jewelry, save it for the circle.

16: RITUAL DESIGN PART 1

Rituals will certainly be an important part of your new tradition. Thus, we'll be spending some time discussing their creation. Save in rare cases (emergencies), or during spontaneous rites, all Wiccan rituals should include the following:

- ○ Purification of Self

- ○ Purification of Space

- ○ Creation of Sacred Space (including the altar)

- ○ Invocation

- ○ Ritual Observance (and/or)Raising of Energy

- ○ Earthing the Power

- ○ Thanking the Goddess and God

- ○ Breaking the Circle

As you well know, ritual observances certainly aren't necessary during every single Wiccan ritual, and neither is energy raising (magic). They're done when appropriate. However, the remaining ritual aspects are vitally necessary if your tradition's rituals are to be Wiccan.

The exact ways in which you observe these ritual necessities are, of course, up to you. Following is the way one Solitary Wiccan might construct her or his basic rituals (allowing for changes depending on the occasion):

- Purification of Self (bathe and/or anoint with oil)

- Purification of Space (sprinkle fresh water or sweep area)

- Creation of Sacred Space (set up altar; cast circle with athame; carry around salt, censer, candle and water)

- Invocation (pray to the Goddess and God, either with memorized invocations or with spontaneous words)

- Ritual Observance (perform rituals recorded in the Book of Shadows, if a Sabbat or Esbat)

- Raising of Energy (this Wiccan has chosen not to do so on the Sabbats, but performs magic on the Full Moons)

- Earthing the Power (eating crackers and drinking wine, milk or water)

- Thanking the Goddess and God (in spontaneous words or written words)

- Breaking the Circle (cut circle with athame, draw energy back into the knife; dissemble the altar)

This is one method of fulfilling the basic requirements for a Wiccan ritual. Once you've found your own, discover precisely how these elements can be fit together in order to create a flowing ritual.

ESBATS

Generally speaking, any Wiccan ritual held at any time other than a Sabbat is an Esbat. Full Moon rituals are Esbats, but they aren't the only Esbats. Some traditions hold circles on the New Moons as well. These, too, are Esbats.

There are many reasons to observe Esbats. You may wish to talk to the Goddess, and there's no better place to do so than safely within a circle. You may have an urgent magical need (such as a friend's sickness) that demands a circle be held and power raised within it.

And, like most Wiccans, you simply may wish to re-experience the serene, otherworldly atmosphere of the circle. That's okay too.

Many Esbats aren't pre-planned. Still, virtually all follow the basic ritual format outlined above, with one exception: ritual observances aren't held, and magic may or may not be made. Other than that, it's the same.

Full Moon rituals are a bit different. As you well know, most Full Moon rituals observed in Wicca today are held, naturally enough, on the Full Moon. If this isn't possible, two days prior to or two days after the actual phase is considered to be close enough to the time. Here's one suggested plan for a Full Moon Esbat:

- Have a purification bath.

- Fumigate the room in which the Esbat is to be held with a mixture of sandalwood and frankincense burning on incense charcoal.

- Create the altar with the usual tools. (Some Wiccans use a slightly different altar arrangement for the Esbats; others use the same plan for all rites. Additional tools, connecting this occasion with the Moon, may include white altar cloths, silver objects, crescent moons, moonstone, white flowers and other lunar objects.)

- Circle casting. (This usually isn't different from that used in Sabbat rituals.)

- The Goddess (and usually, the God) are asked to be present at the circle.

○ The Goddess is invoked in a fairly long, flowery chant that acknowledges Her and connects Her with the Moon (though we don't specifically pray to the Moon). This period of invocation may, alternately, consist of a song either sung or played on an instrument; a dance; even a series of properly lunar gestures.

○ Following this invocation, some Wiccans then meditate upon the Moon itself or upon a Goddess image (but such meditation may come later).

○ Then, after the meditation, or in its place, a work of magic may be performed, to take advantage of the Moon's more powerful force. (We don't necessarily take lunar energy directly from the Moon. But just as the Moon rules the tides, so too does it rule the tides of our bodily energy. At its full, the Moon subtly increases the amount of energy available from our bodies, thus making magic performed during this phase that much more powerful. Women whose menstruation coincides with the Full Moon may be doubly or triply empowered.)

○ After the energy has been raised and sent toward its destination, many Wiccans will sit, meditate, pray or simply relax.

○ Next, the Wiccan grounds herself or himself by eating the traditional crescent-shaped cakes* and by sipping wine, apple cider, lemonade or juice.

---

*For a tasty recipe, see Wicca: A Guide for the Solitary Practitioner, p. 152.

⊙ Finally, the Goddess and God are thanked for attending the rites, the circle is broken, and the altar tools are safely put away.

This general Full-Moon ritual structure can be personalized in many ways, according to your desires and spiritual needs. You may wish to jot down some ideas for your own Full Moon rituals.

Invocations can be obtained from a number of books (see the reading list at the end of this chapter), and you can use any that appeal to you. For the Full Moon, however, use only those that invoke the Goddess in Her lunar aspect.

You may also wish to create your own invocations. The best are in rhyme, or in carefully-constructed, soothing, flowing language.

SABBATS

Sabbats are quite different. As you've probably seen from reading published Sabbat rituals, there's little agreement as to each holiday's meanings and appropriate ritual actions. Some Sabbat rites have been heavily influenced by a specific culture; others are more generic. Certain Sabbat ritual cycles are directly related to a tradition's sacred stories concerning the Goddess and God; in other traditions, little mythic information is evident in the Sabbat scripts.

In any case, most published Sabbat rituals are designed for groups. Since you can't be at two places at once in the circle, it's difficult to act out seasonal plays, or to respond to your own statements, without feeling quite silly. What to do? Write your own.

Keep these things in mind:

Wicca's vaguely British/Middle Eastern cultural framework can be used to determine Sabbat themes (and often is). These include: birth of the God (sun) at Yule; the Goddess' recovery at Imbolc; the coming of

Spring (Ostara); the mating or wedding of the Goddess and God (Beltane); the coming of Summer (Litha); the first harvest (Lughnasadh); the final harvest (Mabon); the death of the God (Samhain).

There are few other options. You may create your own mythic story of the Goddess and the God (intertwined with the seasons, the Sun and the Moon) based on the below list of basic, seasonal symbolism of the Sabbats:

○ *Yule*: renewal and rebirth during winter

○ *Imbolc*: the festival of lights (to encourage the sun's return)

○ *Ostara*: The start of Spring

○ *Beltane*: The return of full-blown fertility

○ *Litha*: Great, magical power

○ *Lughnasadh*: Harvest and thanksgiving

○ *Mabon*: Second harvest and mysteries

○ *Samhain*: the end of Summer; the dead are honored

In your new myth, each Sabbat should, in light of Wiccan tradition, have something to do with the actual agricultural and/or astronomical phenomena that are then occurring. To ignore this would be to deny the night's (or day's) special power. This would invalidate any reason for a ritual's observance. In other words: don't stray too far from the path. Frankly, it's best to utilize traditional Sabbat symbolism and to write new rituals that celebrate this heritage.

The basic structure of Sabbat rites can be divided into two parts: spoken words and ritual actions. The spoken words are nearly always directly related to the Sabbat. The Goddess is invoked on Imbolc as the Lady of Fertility; farewells are said to the God at Samhain. Additionally, words may be spoken by the Wiccan of the internal changes that occur at the Sabbats.

In creating your own tradition, you may choose to use appropriate passages from published Sabbat rituals. Alternately, you may write your own words. The second method is certainly best, but many beautiful Sabbat prayers and words have been printed, and I see no reason why you shouldn't incorporate them in your new tradition If you're comfortable in doing so, and if the words move you. That's what's important.

Ritual actions are just as important a part of Sabbats as are words. Here are some familiar ones for each holiday*:

○ *Yule:* Fires are lit within cauldrons; candles may be carried around the circle; trees or potted evergreens may be honored as symbols of continuing fertility of the Earth; a Yule log may be lit if a fire is physically within the circle.

○ *Imbolc:* candles or torches are lit and held in circle, and are usually carried around the altar at some point; symbol of the wheel is placed on the altar; ritual blessing and planting of seeds in pots in the circle with requests to the Goddess and God.

○ *Ostara:* A fire is lit in the circle with appropriate words during the rite itself – not before.

○ *Beltane:* weaving ribbons (not traditional, but a solitary version of creating and dancing the May pole); bonfire leaping; the blowing of horns.

---

*These basic ritual actions have been culled from many books of shadows.

○ *Midsummer:* cauldron, ringed with flowers (or filled with fresh water and flowers); sword plunged into cauldron; bonfire leaping; drying herbs over the balefire.

○ *Lughnasadh:* bread is eaten, tossed into flames, or otherwise used in ritual; wheat may be woven into Goddess images or symbols.

○ *Mabon:* fruit is praised as proof of the Goddess' and God's love; a ritual sprinkling of leaves.

○ *Samhain:* scrying in smoke, candle flame or fire; calling the departed ones; leaving food outside after ritual for the dead.

There are symbols, specialized tools and colors associated with each Sabbat that can also be used to create the Sabbat rites of your new tradition. Here's a list of some of these:

○ *Yule:* The colors are green and red. A wheel symbol (which can easily be made from a wreath or a wreath form; use your imagination); evergreens; Yule log; small tree (potted).

○ *Imbolc:* The colors are white, or green and white, or blue. A dish of snow; evergreens; candles.

○ *Ostara:* The color is white. A potted plant; cauldron or bonfire.

○ Beltane: The color is white. Fresh flowers; cauldron filled with flowers. Mirrors are also appropriate.

○ *Litha:* The color is white. Mugwort. Mirrors to capture the sun (or the flames of the fire).

○ *Lughnasadh:* The colors are red and orange. Corn dollies; special loaves of bread; grain.

○ *Maybon:* The colors are red and brown. Pine cones; acorns; wheat; dried leaves.

○ *Samhain:* The colors are red or black. Pomegranates; pumpkins; apples.

You may wish to follow the below plan in creating your tradition's Sabbat rituals.

○ Write the name of each Sabbat on a separate piece of paper.

○ Jot down notes regarding each Sabbat's significance (see reading list at the end of this chapter)

○ Decide which of these influences is of special importance; the ones that seem to flow from one Sabbat to another.

○ Begin with Yule. Read every ritual that you can find for this Sabbat. Afterward, leave the books open to the correct pages and study the rituals together. What are their common themes? Which structures or ritual actions do you enjoy the most? Next, read the lists of ritual actions and ritual symbols I've given above. On the page entitled 'Yule', write down your choices of Yule actions, symbols, and ritual structure that most appeal to you.

○ Continue this process for each of the remaining seven Sabbats. Realize that you probably won't be able to do this in one night.

○ Find, borrow, or write your own words for each Sabbat. Don't be hesitant to borrow or adapt printed invocations – it's an old Wiccan habit. Use extra pages if necessary. Work through the Sabbats in the same order, recording the words that you've chosen for each ritual occasion. Don't rush this; these words may very well become the heart of your Wiccan rites.

- Finally, 'marry' the elements that you've assembled for Yule into a presentable ritual. Write out your ritual. Include the symbols, the colors (if appropriate, for altar cloths, candles and etc.), the words and ritual actions. Repeat this process for the rest of the Sabbats.

- Fine-tune the rituals. Add 'Cast the circle' and any other ritual instructions that you've left out.

- Copy the rituals into your Book of Shadows – and be prepared to make further corrections or changes as you feel fit.

- Finally, during the next year, try your rituals on the appropriate dates.

Creating the Sabbat rituals is a challenging process that requires thought, research and time. The ultimate result, a set of workable Sabbat rituals specifically designed to meet your needs, is clearly worth the effort. Creating your own Sabbat rituals is a wonderful way to demonstrate your devotion to Wicca.

SABBAT	SYMBOLISM	RITUAL ACTIONS	SYMBOLS
Yule	Renewal and rebirth during Winter	Fires lit, candles carried around the circle, Yule log	Colors are green and red; wheel symbol, evergreens, Yule log, small potted tree
Imbolc	Festival of Lights	Candles lit and held in Circle, Blessing of seeds, wheel symbol placed on altar	Colors are white, green and white, or blue. Dish of snow; evergreens; candles
Ostara	The start of Spring	Fire is lit in Circle during (not before) rite itself	Color is white. Potted plant; cauldron or balefire
Beltane	The return of Fertility	Weaving ribbons, bonfire leaping, horn blowing	Color is white. Fresh flowers; cauldron filled with flowers; mirrors
Litha	Great, magical power	Flower-ringed cauldron, sword plunged into cauldron, bonfire leaping, herb-drying	Color is white. Mugwort; mirrors to capture the sun (or the flames of the fire)
Lughnasadh	Harvest and thanksgiving	Bread eaten and thrown into fire, grains woven into Goddess and God symbols	Colors are red and orange. Corn dollies; special loaves of bread; grain
Mabon	Second harvest and Mysteries	Fruit is honored; ritual sprinkling of leaves	Colors are red and brown. Pine cones; acorns; wheat; dried leaves
Samhain	The end of Summer; the Dead are honored	Scrying in smoke, candle flame, fire or mirror; calling departed ones; leave food outside after ritual	Colors are red or black. Pomegranates; pumpkins; apples

AFTERWORD

Following these guidelines to fashion your Esbat and Sabbat rituals will create basically Wiccan rituals. Breaking with such traditional patterns could, however, lead you into decidedly non-Wiccan territory.

Just as one bolt of cloth can be cut and stitched into a huge variety of objects, from pillow cases to teddy bears to clothing, so too can Wiccan ritual be fashioned in many ways. However, if you wish to make a shirt from that cloth but decide not to include sleeves, you won't end up with a shirt.

A new Wiccan tradition's rituals must also be carefully crafted, following established forms, to avoid sewing a shirt that can't be worn. Though Wiccan ritual structure is a bit loose, those aspects of it that are set must be followed if you're to continue practicing Wicca.

These words aren't meant to frighten you. Creating a new Wiccan tradition can be difficult. It requires attention to detail and a bit of imagination or creativity – but this creative thought must be placed within a Wiccan context.

If not, you'll simply be creating a new religion.

SUGGESTED READING

For background information regarding Esbats, see:

Valiente's *An ABC of Witchcraft*, pages 135-137.

Guiley's *The Encyclopedia of Witches and Witchcraft*, pages 113-114.

For actual Esbat and Full Moon ritual texts, see:

Valiente's *Witchcraft For Tomorrow*. (See pages 168-170)

Buckland's *The Complete Book of Witchcraft*. (Page 61-62)

Buckland's *The Tree*. (Pages 50-53)

Slater's *A Book of Pagan Rituals*. (The rite termed 'Pagan Ritual For General Use' on p. 8-10 is essentially an Esbat; pages 55-57 contain a Pagan solitary full moon rite. Please note: these aren't strictly Wiccan rituals.)

Cunningham, *Wicca: A Guide for the Solitary Practitioner*. (Pages 124-126)

For background information concerning the Sabbats, see:

Valiente's *An ABC of Witchcraft*. (Article headed "Yule", pp.406-408)

Farrar's *What Witches Do*. (Pages 95-107)

Farrar and Farrar's *Eight Sabbats for Witches* (Pages 61-150)

Guiley's *The Encyclopedia of Witches and Witchcraft*. (Pages 288-290).

Frazer's *The Golden Bough*. (Pages 705-763. Bear in mind that much of what Frazer discusses isn't performed by Wiccans. However, these words preserve proof of the ancient existence of the Pagan fire festivals that eventually evolved into what we know today as the Sabbats. This section of the book is virtually required reading for all Wiccans.)

Burland, *Echoes of Magic*. (The entire book is of great interest. Unfortunately, it's now impossible to find and was never printed in the U.S. Check libraries – that's where I found a copy.)

For actual Sabbat ritual scripts, see:

Starhawk, *The Spiral Dance*. (Pages 169-183 contain a full set of 8 Sabbat rites.)

Z Budapest, *The Holy Book of Women's Mysteries*. (The God isn't included.)

Farrar and Farrar, *Eight Sabbats for Witches*. (Pages 61-150)

Buckland, *The Tree: The Complete Book of Saxon Witchcraft*. (Pages 57-77 includes 8 complete Sabbat rites.)

Slater (editor), *A Book of Pagan Rituals*. (Written for non-initiates. Pages 23-42 nominally describe Wiccan group Sabbat rituals; here termed "The Eight Grove Festivals". Pages 58-79 include complete Solitary rituals, which is one of the reasons for this book's popularity. This isn't strictly Wiccan, but it's pretty close.)

Cunningham, Wicca: A Guide for the Solitary Practitioner. (This book's complement includes 8 Solitary Sabbat rites on pages 127-143.)

17: RITUAL DESIGN PART 2

Yes, there's more, but relax. This part's much easier than writing your Esbat and Sabbat rites. It consists of determining the shape of a few other, far less complicated rites.

THE CIRCLE

By this time you've probably found a suitable circle casting. If not, now's the time to decide. You should know which tools are used and how they're used. The readings offer many examples.

So much has been written about the circle casting itself that I feel that to rephrase it here would be meaningless. Therefore, I'll discuss other aspects below.

In actually determining the circle casting to use, you may adopt one that's appeared in a book, or utilize it as the basis to your own. In any case, the circle casting is an important ritual.

To be as brief as possible, here's a breakdown on the outer ritual steps that usually compose a circle casting:

- Purifying the area.

- Setting up the altar.

- Lighting the candles and incense.

- Consecrating the water.

- Blessing the salt.

- Actual magical creation of the circle.

- Sprinkling of salt around circle. Carrying of smoking censer around circle. Carrying of flaming candle around circle. Sprinkling of water around circle. (I stress that, while such a form is used by many Wiccans, it's hardly the only method of casting the circle.)

Besides knowing the outer mechanics of circle casting, you should also be well aware of the internal processes that occur within you during circle casting (including energy raising and releasing, visualizations and changes in consciousness). Once you've decided on one specific circle casting, become completely familiar with and comfortable with it. It's best if it can be memorized in its entirety.

It's also time to determine your tradition's basic concept of the circle. How strong is it? Can you walk through it, or do you have to cut a doorway to leave the circle? If so, how do you make a doorway? What about pets and children who roam into your circle? Will they harm it? Will it have to be recast when this occurs?

What's the circle's function? To keep energy in? To keep something else out? Both? Or it is simply a place that you create to meet with the Goddess and God? Is the circle necessary for every ritual, even those that occur outdoors? What about emergencies?

Determining this information will allow you to make stronger, more effective circles. Why? Because you'll know your circle forward and backward. You'll have no uncertainties regarding its purpose or function. (You'll also have to create your circle releasing rite. See the readings.)

TOOL CONSECRATION

Many traditions utilize a specific ritual for the consecration of tools. Some use the four elements (Earth, Air, Fire and Water) in such rituals. Others, a sprinkling of blessed salt and consecrated water. Some type of incantation should be created, borrowed or adapted which aptly sums up the ritual action. Such rites are usually quite short and rely far more on the consecrator's energy than on the ritual form itself.

CAKES AND WINE

Cakes and Wine (also known as Cakes and Ale and, in this book's successor, as The Simple Feast) is the rite-within-a-rite that both grounds energy and directly links us with the Goddess and God, since we're consuming food created on Their planet.

The ritual is quite simple: the cakes (cookies) and wine (juice) are blessed by a short prayer dedicated to the Goddess and God. A small portion may be left on the altar or in an offering bowl to be given later to the earth, and the food is eaten in ritual. Again, this is a short rite.

Many Wiccans use cookies that they've specially baked for the 'cakes'. Others use crackers or even store-brought cookies. Many Wiccans don't drink wine. If you do, which type is most appropriate for Cakes and Wine? If you don't drink wine, what's a good substitute? Grape juice? Apple juice?

Writing these rituals isn't as difficult as it may appear, especially if you adapt and borrow from other traditions. They're necessary in every Wiccan tradition and should be finalized for your new tradition.

There are other rites that you can write or adapt as you see fit. These aren't strictly necessary in what will probably be a Solitary Wiccan tradition, but you might wish to have them on hand and copy them into your

Book of Shadows – just in case. (For examples, see the readings listed at the end of this chapter.)

HANDFASTING
(A WICCAN MARRIAGE CEREMONY)

You may not need one, but then again, you just might. Such ceremonies, of course, aren't legally binding unless they're performed by a person so empowered by the state in which the people reside. This may or may not be of concern.

BIRTH CEREMONY

Some call these 'Wiccanings' but I dislike the term. You may have questions concerning this rite as well: is the baby being dedicated to the Goddess and God? If so, shouldn't she or he have a say in the matter? And, thus, should this be done at a later age? If the rite is purely protective and celebratory, in which the child is shown to the Goddess and God, such questions need not arise. It depends on the way you write the ritual.

DEATH CEREMONY

Wiccans as a group don't ritualize mourning. Death is a doorway through which souls pass to re-enter the realm of the Goddess. Bodies are simply suits that we wear and use until they wear out, or until we have no need for further lessons and opportunities in this lifetime. Bodies should be taken care of, but their deaths (the soul never dies) aren't, traditionally speaking, times for *ritualized* sorrow. How can it be in a religion that embraces reincarnation; that sees bodily death as but one of many such transitions that the human soul will experience?

Naturally, Wiccans grieve, and many have small rites to mark the transition of a loved one. Few of these rites have been printed. You may write your own if you feel the need.

SELF-INITIATION AND INITIATION RITUALS

Finally, you may wish to record your own self-initiation ceremony. You may even write or adapt an initiation ceremony, if you have any plans to ever teach others your Wiccan tradition. It's never too early to start planning.

SUGGESTED READING:

Circle Castings:
(Most of the below include both creating and releasing the circle.)

Farrar, *What Witches Do*. (Pages 56-60)

Valiente, *Witchcraft For Tomorrow*. (Pages 155-159)

Starhawk, *The Spiral Dance*. (Pages 55-57)

Cunningham, *Wicca: A Guide for the Solitary Practitioner*. (Pages 115-122)

Buckland, *The Tree*. (Pages 38-41; here entitled 'Erecting the Temple' and 'Clearing the Temple')

Consecration of Tools:
Farrar and Farrar, *The Witches' Way*. (Pages 44-48)

Cunningham, *Wicca: A Guide for the Solitary Practitioner*.

Slater, *Pagan Rituals III*. (Page 59)

Valiente's *Witchcraft For Tomorrow*. (Pages 164-166)

Cakes and Wine:
Farrar and Farrar, *Eight Sabbats for Witches*. (Page 46)

Slater, *Pagan Rituals III*. (Pages 69 and 70 contain blessings for the cakes and the wine.)

Buckland's *The Tree*. (Pages 54-56; here termed 'Cakes and Ale')

Buckland, *Buckland's Complete Book of Witchcraft*. (Page 63)

Cunningham's *Wicca: A Guide for the Solitary Practitioner*. (page 123; here termed the 'Simple Feast')

Handfastings:

Buckland, *Buckland's Complete Book of Witchcraft*. (Pages 97- 99; includes, wisely, a Handparting as well.)

Buckland's *The Tree*. (Pages 78-81; a 'Hand-Parting' ceremony can be found on pp. 82-84.)

Farrar and Farrar, *Eight Sabbats for Witches*. (Pages 160- 165)

Birth Celebrations:

Farrar and Farrar, *Eight Sabbats for Witches*. (Pages 153- 159)

Buckland, *Buckland's Complete Book of Witchcraft*. (Pages 99- 100)

Buckland's *The Tree: A Book of Saxon Witchcraft*. (Pages 85-87)

Death Ceremonies:

Farrar and Farrar, *Eight Sabbats for Witches*. (Pages 166-173; here termed 'Requiem'.)

Buckland, *The Tree*. (Pages 88-90; here termed 'Crossing the Bridge [At Death]'.)

Buckland, *Buckland's Complete Book of Witchcraft*. (Pages 100-101; termed as in the above entry.)

Self-Initiation:

Valiente's *Witchcraft For Tomorrow*. (Pages 159-164)

Farrar and Farrar, *The Witches' Way*. (Pages 244-250)

Initiations:

Farrar and Farrar, *The Witches' Way*. (Pages 9-20)

Buckland's Complete Book of Witchcraft. (Pages 46-49)

> I've listed the above two sources because they're among the most complete treatments of initiation in print, but many, many other Wiccan books discuss initiation and/or provide ritual scripts. These are all for coven use, of course.

18: BELIEFS

'Beliefs' isn't the best word, but the only other ones that I could come up with were 'tenets' and 'concepts', neither of which is satisfactory. Since religion is usually conceived of as being built on beliefs, this word will have to serve.

GENERAL TRADITIONAL WICCAN BELIEFS

Aside from strictly deity-oriented beliefs, Wiccans share a few others, including:

- The Goddess and God are revered. This is central to Wiccan thought.

- Human souls enjoy a series of incarnations in human form. Reincarnation is one of the most wide-spread of Wiccan beliefs. Precisely how and why we incarnate several times is open to mystical speculation. Few Wiccan traditions have specific teachings regarding this doctrine. Some simply state that we reincarnate and meet others we've known in past lives. Others are more specific, some less specific. Some traditions say that we never switch sexes from one life to another; still others state that we choose whichever gender is appropriate for our evolutionary lessons. There's little agreement.

○ Power can be sent in non-physical form to affect the world in positive ways. Thus, we accept both the practice of magic and its effectiveness.

○ What is done will be returned to the doer. Precisely how this energy is returned has been a matter of great speculation. Some Wiccans state that the Goddess performs this function; others that it's a law of the universe, like gravity, and that no one being is in charge of seeing that this occurs. It's an automatic response, like a ricochet.

○ The Earth is our home, our Goddess. It's not a tool that we can ruthlessly abuse. Ecological concerns are rather new in Wicca, but now play an important role. Many rituals are performed to give healing strength to the Earth. The ecological movement has had a tremendous impact on Wicca.

○ Wiccans aren't evangelical. We have no need to go out and spread the word. Answering questions about our religion is far different from knocking on doors and asking strangers, "Have you heard the word of the Goddess today?" Such practices are certainly understandable (though irritating) in religions whose members believe that they've really found the only way, but are absurdly out of place in Wicca.

○ Wicca accepts that every religion is correct to its adherents. This doesn't mean that we like every representative of every religion, but ecumenicism must be the way of life. Not only must we all tolerate each other, Wiccans will, in the future, share more dialogue with representatives of other religions to increase their knowledge of our ways. This is already occurring to a limited degree.

○ Wicca accepts members from both sexes, from every race, national origin and, usually, of every sexual preference. Unfortunately, racism and prejudice does exist in Wicca: many covens simply won't let non-Caucasians receive training and initiation. Such racism is usually covert and is rarely openly stated, but it does exist. Though Wiccans are human, and we've been taught from birth to like certain groups and to dislike others, we must overcome such idiotic concepts and realize that we're all people. Racism and prejudice in any form is anti-Wiccan. (Besides, who ever said that the Goddess is Caucasian?)

○ Wicca is a religion, not a political organization. Groups of Wiccan can and sometimes do work toward a common cause, and individual Wiccans may indeed become personally involved in the political system, but Wicca as a whole isn't a religion that preaches issues or supports specific political candidates. Some issues in which individual Wiccans have become involved include women's rights; reproductive freedom; land conservation; animal rights; restrictive religious legislation and other issues.* However, Wicca isn't a political religion. Some covens, in fact, ban discussion of politics before, during and after circle.

○ Wicca doesn't charge for private lessons or for initiation. Physical objects created by Wiccans (pentacles, knives, wands, incenses, oils, books) and services (such as public classes and Wiccan-based

---

*A good summary of a national example of individual Wiccan involvement in politics can be found in the article concerning the Helms Amendment (which would have removed tax-exempt status for religious Witchcraft and Neo-Pagan groups) in Rosemary Guiley's The Encyclopedia of Witches and Witchcraft, p. 156.

counseling) can and should be paid for, but not personal, private Wiccan instruction or initiation. In some groups, coven funds are kept to pay for ritual supplies; this is the only exception.

Virtually all Wiccans subscribe to the above list of beliefs. Certainly most traditions do. It's impossible to discover precisely how every individual Wiccan interprets these beliefs, but we can be assured that most of them do in one form or another.

It could be valuable for you to make a list of your personal Wiccan beliefs. Not just the raw beliefs themselves, but your interpretations of them. For example, you may write the following:

REINCARNATION

- We incarnate many times to learn our lessons.

- We may incarnate with people we've known in other lives.

- Cats reincarnate too.

What's important is to bring your beliefs to paper. This crystallizes them; firms them. Beliefs can become rather hazy. Such an exercise can define them.

Your interpretations of the general Wiccan beliefs may and probably will change as you grow in experience and understanding. This is natural. The list that you've made may become out of date. This, too is fine.

Wicca is a religion that teaches specific beliefs. We should be fully familiar with them if we're to practice this religion. It may take time for you to completely accept some of these beliefs. Study, think, pray and experiment.

Wiccan beliefs are the heart of Wicca.

19: RULES

Virtually all religious organizations give their adherents a set of guidelines or rules of conduct. In such laws we often find the true nature of the faith, which can be difficult to determine from the actual behavior of most of its representatives.

Wicca possesses not one but several sets of such rules. The most famous of these, which has been published in several different forms, originally stemmed from what is now known as Gardnerian Wicca.*

Many other versions exist, and some covens create their own set of laws for use by its members. Underlying all such Wiccan rules is one basic concept: Harm none.

Traditional Wiccan laws can be grouped into specific categories for study. Looking at these, and reading a few sample sets (included at the end of this chapter), should readily provide all that you need to write or adapt a set of laws for your tradition.

Here's a basic breakdown of traditional Wiccan laws. The first section details laws specifically concerned with coven working, which are of less importance to Solitary Wiccans. The second section is devoted to laws of great potential use to the Solitary practitioner.

---

*For a fascinating look at the possible origins of these laws, see Witchcraft For Tomorrow by Doreen Valiente.

TRADITIONAL WICCAN LAWS — COVEN ORIENTED

COVEN HEIRARCHY/ORGANIZATION

Usually lists duties of High Priestess and High Priest. The average length of time that the 'offices' are held is also often discussed. Many delineate initiatory levels and define the nature of the 'council of elders' (usually made of those who have received the highest elevation, and who are called upon for guidance and counsel by coven members), or other such groups within the group. Many also describe other coven officers.

SECRECY

Traditional warnings to keep secret those things which are only for the eyes and ears of other initiates of the same tradition. Some laws threaten the oath-breaker with divine retribution if the oaths are broken. (Solitary Wiccans can certainly create a 'secret' tradition. Whether you care to discuss your religion and your religious practices with others must be a personal decision. Only you can decide precisely what to reveal.)

COVEN PROBLEMS

Dictates the proper method of settling problems. Some covens utilize their 'council of elders' in the decision-making process, or to provide guidance to those with grievances. In most traditions, the highest-elevated Wiccans are free to leave and form their own covens, if they can no longer work with their parent coven. Many laws also concern High Priestesses and High Priests who break the laws or who lose interest in the coven.

PERSECUTION TALES AND ADVICE

These supposedly ancient laws allow for confession during extreme torture, but thoughtfully permits denial of all information given to the 'magistrates'. It also contains the promise that drugs will reach those who have been condemned as Witches so that their certain deaths by execution will be less painful. (This is obviously of little help today.)

RITUAL ATTENDANCE

Many traditions possess laws regarding attendance at rituals. Great latitude exists, and not all traditions even have such laws. In most, Wiccans are expected to show up for all rituals unless previously excused by the coven leader(s). In some sets of rules, missing six consecutive meetings is grounds for 'banishment' from the coven, if only because the Wiccan is showing little or no interest. (This is of little concern to Solitaries. However, a few words of encouragement concerning the regular observance of our rituals would be a nice touch to include in your set of laws.)

TRADITIONAL LAWS OF INTEREST TO SOLITARY WICCANS

WORSHIP

Sometimes lists times and dates of ritual observances; more generally, the laws state that the Goddess and God are deserving of worship, and remind the Wiccans to be worshipful. (This makes sense. Why else would we be Wiccans? Such words might appear in the beginning of the law.)

BLOODSHED

Many laws state that blood is not to be shed within the circle; no ritual animal sacrifices may be made. (This is a universal Wiccan tradition, whether or not it's explicitly stated in the laws.)

AVOIDANCE OF HARM

The central, unifying theme of most laws: Wiccans simply don't cause harm to others. (This law, in some form or another, should be in your set.)

USE OF MAGIC

Generally states that magic is not to be worked for pay, as it could lead to performing destructive rites. Magic is also never to be used to boost one's pride or to cause harm in any way. However, some sets of laws do allow Wiccans to use 'the power' (i.e., magic) to 'prevent or restrain' others from causing harm (this is generally known as binding). (See "'The Law of the Power' below.)

CONDUCT

Such laws warn Wiccans not to boast or to threaten others, and to treat others – Wiccans and non-Wiccans – with kindness and compassion. Additionally, some laws state that Wiccans must not use drugs within or without the circle; must not gossip about other members, and mustn't interfere with the teachings of other Wiccans .(It never hurts to include such messages in your laws. Though you may be the only one to read these reminders of the importance of kindness, the message may, at times, be necessary.)

TEACHING

Some laws state that all who express interest in Wicca should be taught, unless they begin to misuse their instructions. Such laws have largely been either dropped or reinterpreted. Truly following them today could lead to each Wiccan teaching 100 or more students, which would result in poor lessons and, thus, poorly-instructed students. Such laws simply aren't practical in today's world when so many clamor for teachings.

KEEPING THE LAW

Wiccans are reminded to keep the law and not to allow it to be broken. (Sound advice. This usually appears near the end of the laws.)

THE LOVE OF THE GODDESS AND THE GOD

A gentle reminder that we're not alone. (Generally, it's best to begin and to end the law with confirmations of divine concern.)

○ ○ ○

After reading all this, you might be thinking, "Why do I even need a Law if I'm just doing my rituals alone?" A fair question, even if we set aside those laws concerning covens.

The answer is simple; most of the laws appropriate to Solitary Wiccans form part of the general Wiccan tradition. Without them, we are left without guidance. Forming them into set sentences and including them in your tradition's Book of Shadows ensures that you can study them at your leisure, and refer to them for guidance.

It's all very well to state, "I won't do this, and I'll remember to do that." Having a set of laws concerning these things is a great memory assistant.

SAMPLE LAWS

Using the above outlines of laws, we can come up with our own. Their precise form, and their method of presentation, is completely up to you. Some sets of laws are numbered; others aren't. Some are written in rhyming couplets, but most are in prose.

Here are three versions, that I've written. The first is partially based on the above analyses; the second is reprinted from *Wicca: A Guide for the Solitary Practitioner*, as is the third, which deals exclusively with magic.

THE LAW

○ We are of the Old Ways, among those who walk with the Goddess and God and receive Their love.

○ Keep the Sabbats and Esbats to the best of your abilities, for to do otherwise is to lessen your connections with the Goddess and God.

○ Harm none. This, the oldest law, is not open to interpretation or change.

○ Shed not blood in ritual; the Goddess and God need not blood to be duly worshipped.

○ Those of our way are kind to all creatures, for hurtful thoughts are quite draining and aren't worth the loss of energy. Misery is self-created; so, too, is joy, so create joy and disdain misery and unhappiness. And this is within your power. So harm not.

○ Teach only what you know, to the best of your ability, to those students whom you choose, but teach not to those who would use your instructions for destruction or control. Also, teach not to boost pride, for ever remember: she who teaches for vain-glory shall take little pride in her handiwork; she who teaches out of love shall be enfolded in the arms of the Goddess and God.

○ Ever remember that if you would be of our way, keep the Law close to your heart, for it is the nature of the Wicca to keep the Law.

○ If ever the need arises, any law may be changed or discarded, and new laws written to replace them, so long as the new laws don't break the oldest law of all: harm none.

○ Blessings of the God and Goddess on us all.

THE NATURE OF OUR WAY

○ As often as possible, hold the rites in forests, by the seashore, on deserted mountain tops or near tranquil lakes. If this is impossible a garden or some chamber shall suffice, if it is readied with fumes or flowers.

○ Seek out wisdom in books, rare manuscripts and cryptic poems if you will, but seek it out also in simple stones and fragile herbs and in the cries of wild birds. Listen to the whisperings of the wind and the roar of water if you would discover magic, for it is here that the old secrets are preserved.

○ Books contain words; trees contain energies and wisdom books ne'er dreamt of.

○ Ever remember that the Old Ways are constantly revealing themselves. Therefore be as the river willow that bends and sways with the wind. That which remains changeless shall outlive its spirit, but that which evolves and grows will shine for centuries.

○ Mock not the rituals or spells of another, for who can say yours are greater in power or wisdom?

○ Ensure that your actions are honorable, for all that you do shall return to you three-fold, good or bane.

○ Be wary of one who would dominate you, who would control and manipulate your workings and reverences. True reverence for the Goddess and God occurs within. Look with suspicion on any who would twist worship from you for their own gain and glory, but welcome those priestesses and priests who are suffused with love.

○ Honor all living things, for we are of the bird, the fish, the bee Destroy not life save it be to preserve your own.

○ And this is the nature of our way.

THE LAW OF THE POWER

○ The Power shall not be used to bring harm, to injure or control others. But if the need arises, the Power shall be used to protect your life or the lives of others.

○ The Power is used only as need dictates.

○ The Power can be used for your own gain, as long as by doing so you harm none.

○ It is unwise to accept money for use of the Power, for it quickly controls its taker. Be not as those of other religions.

○ Use not the Power for prideful gain, for such cheapens the mysteries of Wicca and magic.

⊙ Ever remember that the Power is the sacred gift of the Goddess and God, and should never be misused or abused.

⊙ And this is the Law of the Power.

Most Craft laws are secret, and can't be published in any form. However, the above examples included in this chapter, and in the suggested readings, should provide you with enough information to create your own laws.

May you do so with wisdom and love.

SUGGESTED READINGS

Published laws

Few sets of Wiccan laws have been published. Even most of the standard Wiccan guidebooks fall to include laws.

However, a few books do include discussions of and/or complete texts of laws. Here are most of them. Studying these laws in concert with this chapter will greatly assist in the creation of your own set. (For additional publication information regarding these books, see this book's Bibliography.)

Kelly, Aidan A., *Crafting the Art of Magic, Book 1*. Contains one version of the 'Gardnerian' laws on pp. 145-161. Also includes an intriguing 'Proposed Rules for the Craft' on pp. 103-105.

See also Doreen Valiente's *The Rebirth of Witchcraft*, pp. 69-71 for background information concerning both the "Proposed Rules" as well as the Gardnerian laws. The whole inside story concerning the most famous set of Wiccan laws is quite fascinating.

Additional information concerning these laws – without the text itself – can be discovered on pp. 303-304 of Janet and Stewart Farrar's *The Witches Way*.

Johns, June, *King of The Witches*. Contains another version of the Gardnerian laws in Appendix A, where they're mislabeled as 'The Book of Shadows'.

Slater, Heron (editor), *Pagan Rituals III, Outer Court Book of Shadows*. Originally written by the late Ed Buczynski for students of his Welsh tradition, this book contains a rather forceful section entitled 'The Laws' on pp.113-115. Though short, it's a good guide to some tradition's secret (non-Gardnerian) laws, though many are far gentler.

(Keep in mind that this was written for students, not for experienced Wiccans.)

Various other sets of Wiccan laws have been published in old pagan periodicals, most notably in the earlier format of *Green Egg*. The issues that contain these laws are now out of print and are, thus, avidly sought by collectors. (Some of these laws, by the way, have been added to 'traditional' Books of Shadows with no hint as to their origination.)

20: WICCAN SYMBOLS

Symbols are an important part of many Wiccan traditions. They're used as magical shorthand in the Book of Shadows; as a graphic representation of Wicca or a specific Wiccan tradition (on correspondence, perhaps) and to empower magical tools and jewelry.

The first ritual symbols used in Wicca stemmed largely from ceremonial magic (particularly those found in *The Key of Solomon*; see Bibliography) and alchemy. Their number soon increased and became more specifically Wiccan, such as symbols for levels of initiation, the circle, the Goddess and the God. Traditions shared symbols among their adherents. They began to be published, further widening their usage.

Your tradition should probably utilize some symbols. Symbols (which are, in a sense, a compact alphabet) trigger powerful psychological responses, if their observer is aware of their meanings, because they speak to the subconscious mind.

You can create your own symbols or choose ones from those lists given below. I have only one warning: never use an unfamiliar symbol. If you don't know a symbol's meaning, it's best not to utilize it in any way.

Here are some specific types of symbols:

SYMBOLS OF OUR RELIGION

The most famous of these is the pentagram, an interlaced five-pointed star. With one point upward, it represents Wicca. The pentagram's connection with our religion seems to be fairly modern (though the symbol itself has been in use since at least 2,400 B.C.E., when it appeared on Middle Eastern pottery).

Other symbols include small representations (usually in jewelry form) of goddesses, particularly the so-called 'Venus' statuettes such as the famous Venus of Willendorf.

(One recent symbol of Wicca was a plain green button, without lettering or signs, that was worn by Wiccans in public places so that they could greet each other. The practice has, as far as I know, died out on a national basis.)

TRADITION SYMBOLS

Many Wiccan Traditions use a specific symbol. Though it may be of any design, most include one or more of the following parts, which can be arranged in a number of unusual and striking ways:

Pentagram

Ankh

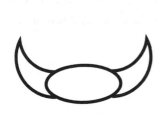

Crescent Moon

Horns

Eight-pointed Star

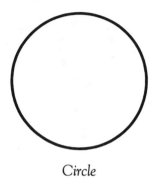

Circle

Yonic Symbols
(particularly popular with some
feminist Wiccans)

As can be seen from the illustrations, there are many potential combinations of these elements.

Such a symbol need not be created for your tradition. However, if you do design one, it can be copied into the Book of Shadows; stitched onto robes; painted onto tools and otherwise used in ritual ways.

BOOK OF SHADOWS SYMBOLS AND SHORTHAND

Following are some symbols used in various Wiccan traditions, with a few variations and quite a few of my own. Once you're comfortable with them, using them in writing rituals or in the Book of Shadows is quite convenient. For example, it's much easier to write "Cast O" than it is to write "Cast the magic circle."

Here are some traditional (and new) symbols:

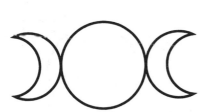

Goddess

God

Magic Circle

Goddess Position

(a body posture sometimes used in Wiccan ritual the Wiccan stands with legs spread and holds her arms out to her sides to represent the Goddess)

God Position

(sometimes used in Wiccan ritual; the Wiccan stands with legs firmly together and wrists crossed on his chest, usually right over left, to represent the God)

Female

Male

Broom

Wand

Cauldron

Pentacle

Athame

Sword

Cord

Balefire

Altar

Cup

Cakes and Wine

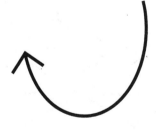

Deosil

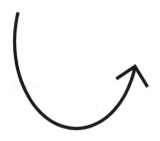

Widdershins

Maiden

Mother

Crone

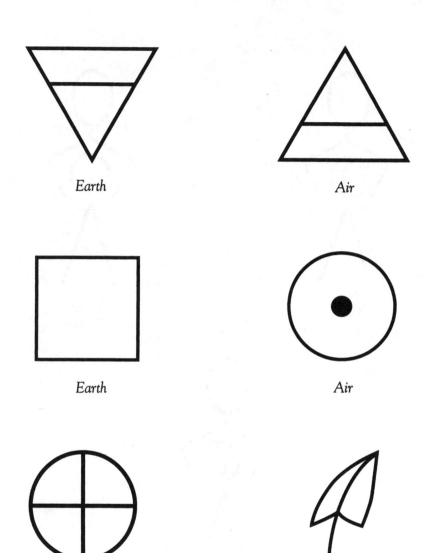

Earth

Air

Earth

Air

Earth

Air

Fire

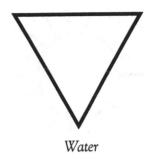

Water

Fire

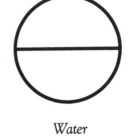

Water

Fire

Water

Sun

Moon

Earth

Mercury

Venus

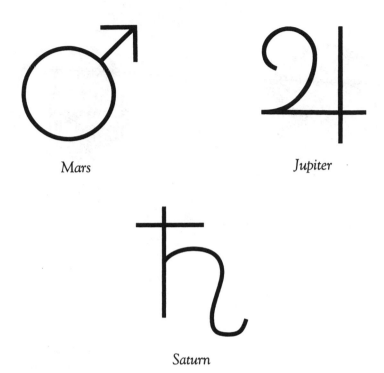

Mars

Jupiter

Saturn

Uranus

Neptune

New Moon

Waxing Moon

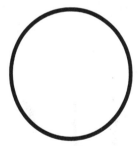

Full Moon

Waning Moon

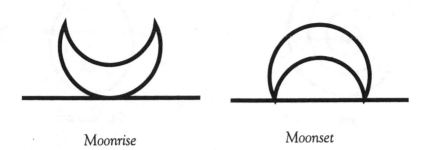

Moonrise   Moonset

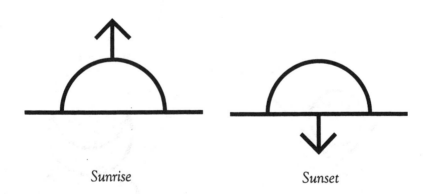

Sunrise   Sunset

Rebirth

Purification

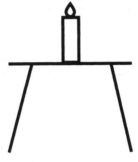

Spell

Bane; Deadly

Blessings

Spirituality

Spirituality

Peace

Protection

Protection

Healing & Health

Courage

Magical Energy

Physical & Magical Strength

Beauty

Love

Love

Marriage

Friendship

Love

Psychic Awareness

Psychic Awareness

Conscious Mind

Money

Money

Rain

Storm

Sex

Fertility

Essential Oil

Plant
(herbs, flowers, leaves)

Water

Salt

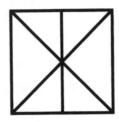

Witch Sign

*(used to mark tools, places
where rituals are held, altars;
it's the Roman numeral for the
number 13, slightly rearranged)*

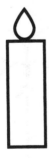

Candle

Wine

Spring

Summer

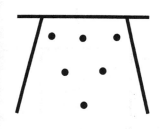

Winter

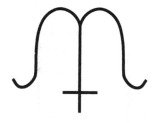

Autumn

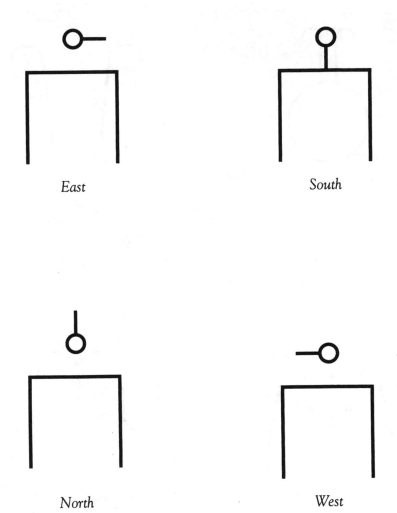

East

South

North

West

Use the above symbols to create your own rituals. You can tailor your spells to your specific need. The following are a few of my own. Refer to Chapter 19 of *Earth, Air, Fire & Water* (Llewellyn Publications) for more information on creating your own rituals.

To Cause Sleep

To Have Psychic Dreams

To Remember Dreams

To Prevent Drowsiness

For Studying

To Release Jealousy

To Release Guilt

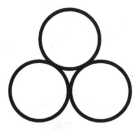

To Reduce Stress

To Quit Smoking

To Lose Weight

To Succeed in Business

To Excel in Interviews

To Gain Employment

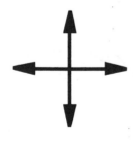

Travel

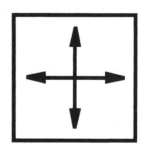

Protection During Traveling

To Protect 1 Child

To Protect 2 Children

To Protect 3 Children

To Strengthen Marriage

PERSONAL WICCAN SYMBOLS

Many Wiccans place a special symbol next to their signature as a sign of their religion and also, sometimes, for protective reasons. In some traditions, the symbol signifies the initiatory degree that she or he has reached. I usually place a pentagram near my signature. You may use this or create your own symbol. It might be connected with the Goddess or God; it may be something entirely personal and unique. Call upon your imagination and creativity.

RUNIC ALPHABETS

Some Wiccans write their rituals in runes. Many don't, for complete familiarity with runes is necessary before they can be read at will, and few persons today are willing to learn a new alphabet. Still, most Wiccan traditions include a runic alphabet in their Books of Shadows.

Why? Runes may be used in specific magical rites for their symbolism and their inherent power. Additionally, runes are often painted or carved onto tools to enhance their effectiveness. Besides, it's traditional for Wiccans to use runes in one way or another.

Many runic alphabets have been published. (At one time, while these were still considered to be secret, entire runic alphabets could be found in many dictionaries). Today, the wide range of books available on this subject allows us to choose the system best-suited to our purposes.

There's so much disagreement concerning the precise form of runic alphabets (let alone their meanings) that I won't add to it here by including yet another variation. I suggest, if you're interested, to read the books listed below.

SUGGESTED READING

Howard, Michael, *The Magic of Runes*. (The entire book)

Koch, Rudolf, *The Book of Signs*. (The entire book)

Tyson, Donald, *Rune Magic*. (The entire book)

21: THE BOOK OF SHADOWS

Most Wiccan traditions treasure a Book of Shadows. Such books are rarely published or even shown to non-initiates. In them, the tradition's specific beliefs and modes of worship are thoroughly or sketchily outlined.

Though contents and organization of these ritual manners vary, most Books of Shadows include instructions for the circle casting and banishing; religious rituals; the consecration of tools; laws; coven organizational notes; magical rites; prayers and perhaps herbal lore. Some contain lists of the tradition's pantheon, training exercises for new students and, finally, initiation ceremonies.

Such books are vitally important to the establishment and maintenance of all Wiccan traditions, for without them, the tradition's specific rites and other lore must be carefully memorized and passed down by word of mouth. This always leaves room for error, misinterpretation, and even loss of the material.

Don't misunderstand this: no Wiccan tradition that I know of has recorded every single bit of information. Much is verbally passed from teacher to student. Still, a tradition's Book of Shadows provides an unchanging guide and memory-trigger for the practitioner.

There are many different Books of Shadows today. Some are used by hundreds or thousands of Wiccans. Others are created by Solitary Wiccans and are never shown to others.

This chapter is a guide to writing your own Book of Shadows. In a sense, it's the culmination of Part III of this book – for it's in this book that you'll record your new tradition.

The book itself can be of any type. Bound blank books are widely available today and can certainly be used – but only if you're sure that your tradition has stopped evolving. (It's difficult to make changes in a bound book.) If you have any doubt whatsoever, a loose-leaf notebook might be the answer. This allows you to add or delete new materials if and when the need arises.

Many traditional Wiccan Books of Shadows begin with initiation rituals, and contain other information that isn't directly applicable to Solitary Wiccans. If we set aside these sections, we can view the general (very general) outline of a typical Book of Shadows. This can be used when creating your own.

The process is simple; fill in the blanks with all the information, rituals, rules and other information that you've determined are a part of your tradition. Add your own touches – a bit of poetry here, maybe a section of songs or chants. Most Solitary Books of Shadows are highly personal creations.

(If you feel uncomfortable thinking about creating your own Book of Shadows, don't. Every Book of Shadows was written at sometime or another.)

○ *Title Page*. This may say 'Book of Shadows', 'The Book of Shadows', or something more specific to your tradition, such as 'The Night Moon Tradition Book of Shadows' (if you've come up with a name for it). Alternately, the title page may bear only a pentagram, your name in runes, or other symbols. It can also be blank.

○ *Laws.* These could also be termed 'Rules', 'codes' or 'Codes of conduct'.

○ *Invocations of the Goddess and God* may appear next, or before the laws. One or two invocations often appear early in the book to 'bless' it.

○ *An altar diagram.*

○ *Circle casting and dispersing instructions.* Be as specific as possible.

○ *Rituals:* Sabbats, Full Moon rite, tool consecrations, Cakes and Wine.

○ *Prayers, chants and invocations* (for use as you see fit).

○ *The Tools of the Craft.* (This can be placed in other locations. In some traditions, this information forms part of the initiation rites.)

○ *Self-Initiation ritual.* And, if you desire, a coven initiation ritual. All other rituals of all kinds.

○ *Magical rites and information,* including herbal lore and recipes as well as specifically Wiccan spells (i.e., those that directly involve the Goddess and God). Also, symbols and signs used in magical shorthand (in the Book of Shadows) as well as for magical purposes. Runes.

This sketchy outline can be altered to your liking.

Do you have to hand-write your Book of Shadows? Traditional Wiccans might say yes, but today many are typed or stored on disk and photocopied. still, there's no doubt that hand-writing every single word does enhance the effectiveness of the Book of Shadows, for a part of your energy then physically exists within the words and the book itself.

If you have terrible handwriting, or simply don't like to write, you can either type it or key it into a computer and print it out.

Though computing your Book of Shadows may seem to be quite convenient, nothing is more evocative than turning to a hand-written book during ritual. It's part of the romantic legacy of Wicca, and one we shouldn't be without. (I would agree, however, due to recent personal experience, that a typed copy of everything hand-written can come in handy. In other words, the Book of Shadows in both forms may well be the ideal.)

SUGGESTED READING

Many alleged Books of Shadows have seen print, in varying formats. They're in more or less complete versions, but many have been highly altered for publication by their presenters. Here are a few of them, with notes regarding each:

Valiente, 'The Liber Umbrarum' in *Witchcraft For Tomorrow*. (Written specifically for the Solitary Wiccan, this work unfortunately lacks Sabbat rituals.)

Buckland, *The Tree: A Book of Saxon Witchcraft*. (A new Wiccan tradition based on a Saxon cultural framework, but clearly Wiccan through and through.)

Farrar and Farrar, *The Witches' Way*. (Bits and pieces of the Gardnerian Book of Shadows and rituals; nothing complete. Chapters IV and V are of especial interest.)

Slater (editor), *A Book of Pagan Rituals* (Pagan-Way public materials, not quite Wiccan.)

Slater (editor), *Pagan Rituals III: Outer Court Training Coven*. (The second half of this work, 'Book of Mysteries' is a fairly complete coven-based Book of Shadows written for students of a Welsh tradition.)

Weinstein, *Earth Magic: A Dianic Book of Shadows*. (Perhaps the most singular of these works; an unusual guide to some aspects of Wiccan religious workings. No Sabbat rituals are included.)

Starhawk, *The Spiral Dance*. (A Book of Shadows is scattered throughout this book.)

Reading just three or four of these published Books of Shadows may cause some confusion, but you'll quickly grasp the concept of Wicca's great variety. Remember: just because one Book of Shadows says that Wiccans do such-and-such is no reason why you must do so as well.

If you wish to create your own Wiccan tradition, it should possess a Book of Shadows. Though it can (and probably will) evolve over time, your Book of Shadows will stand as a symbol of your personal involvement with our religion; as a reaffirmation of your Wiccanhood.

And please, no matter how much you may dislike it, consider hand-copying your Book of Shadows. Think of it as an act of dedication to your religion.

22: TEACHING
(WIDENING THE CIRCLE)

You already know more about Wicca than many others. You may not be an expert, and you probably have many questions, but others who've never read a book or performed a Wiccan ritual have even more questions. As you continue to practice, read and reflect on your Wiccan activities, your knowledge and experience will grow. If you mention your religion to even a few other persons, chances are that, eventually, someone will ask you to teach her or him because, after all, you're an expert.

This may not occur, but if it does you have an important decision before you: to teach or not to teach. Answering the below questions may assist you in making this decision.

Do I have the necessary knowledge and experience?

In other words, are you proficient at basic Wiccan ritual skills; familiar with the tools; have a good understanding of the Sabbats, and enjoy a deep relationship with the Goddess and God? Even if you aren't an expert at coven-oriented Wicca, are you an expert in your own form?

Do I have the skills to teach others?

Can you explain complex theories in simple language? Are you skilled at actually demonstrating Wiccan techniques to a student? You needn't have chalkboard and ruler to be a teacher. There are many forms of teaching. The best of these, when teaching Solitary Wicca, is a mixture of honest talk and ritual demonstration (nothing heavy).

Do I have unlimited patience?

Can you repeat an answer to a question many times? Are you easily frustrated, especially with other humans? Do you believe that there are 'dumb questions'? Do you mind an occasional phone call at 2 AM?

Do I know how to pick a student?

This is an important question. Potential students are of every kind of human. If someone studies for a few months and then never calls again, you haven't wasted much time, and you may indeed have had a positive impact upon that person's life. If you teach someone who's unable to accept 'harm none' and goes on to utilize Wiccan magical techniques in harmful ways, you may feel guilty at your choice of students. If you teach a man or woman simply because you're involved with her or him, you may well be wasting your breath. Friends are another iffy proposition, for an established friendship doesn't guarantee a suitable student.

Do I really want to teach?

Are you pleased with the idea of revealing a very personal aspect of your life to others? Do you wish to assume the responsibility of teaching?

If so, why?

What are your true motivations? Glory? Worship from your student? Ego-strokes? Or the need to assist other humans with their spiritual development and happiness? Do you have an unconscious desire to 'spread the word' of Wicca (a taboo), or do you simply wish to fulfill a need that has expressed itself?

How much time are you willing to invest in classes?

Even if you have only one student, you may wish to prepare notes for upcoming classes; read up on different aspects so that you'll be fresh; find ways of communicating difficult Wiccan subjects in a way that they're comprehensible to your student; block out time for classes and/or rituals, and other time-consuming projects. The number of classes that you teach is up to you – once a week seems to be about right.

How much can your student afford to spend?
Though there's no fee for private Wiccan instruction, there are supplies that have to be purchased: tools, books, candles, incense. If your student has a tight budget, are you willing to loan books and tools to your student, or purchase duplicate supplies for their use? (Warning: most loaned Wiccan books are never returned.)

Your answers to these questions may well assist you in making the decision. If you decide that you're simply not ready, or don't want to begin teaching, explain this to the person who asked for instruction. If you do decide to teach others, it's time to begin planning your classes.

The format of such lessons, as well as their length and frequency, are entirely in your hands. Classes on a specific day of the week (or month) are a good idea, since this helps the student to remember the date.

Generally, it's best to teach in your own home. This way, when a question arises, you'll be able to show the student precisely what you've been talking about (in a book, with an illustration or using a tool that you may not have with you at the student's house).

Classes are best held in private, though not necessarily in secret. Trying to explain the casting of a circle while three small children run underfoot, turn on the television, and let the dogs and cats into the living room will result in a wasted lesson. Ensure that you and your student will be alone together.

Here are some more suggested guidelines for teaching:

Teach what you know.

This may seem obvious, but many persons try to pass on knowledge that they've barely grasped themselves. If you're no expert in certain subjects, don't pretend to teach them. If these topics come up in class, make a short explanation and continue; don't make them the focus of the class. *Teach with honesty.* When you don't know the answer to a question, simply say so, and perhaps you and your student can discover the answer together.

Don't let teaching rule your life.

It can be one aspect of it, and an important, fulfilling aspect, but it shouldn't become the sole purpose of your existence.

Teach with humor.

Forget the method in which you may have been taught the religion of your childhood. Wicca is far from a stern, forbidding religion. It's a religion of joy and love and pleasure, and your classes should reflect the nature of our way. If you're no stand-up comic, at least teach Wicca in a light-hearted way. No solemn warnings; no stern lectures.

Teach with humility.

Pomposity may temporarily impress the wide-eyed student, but extravagant claims concerning your power and wisdom can be quickly disproved even by the newest of students. Additionally, don't make your version of Wicca seem carved in stone. Remind your student that this is simply the way that you do things, and that there are many other ways. Don't constantly warn the student of the 'dangers' that may befall her or him after a skipped word in ritual. Such superstitious teachings have no place in Wicca.

Don't teach the ancient history of Wicca unless you're sure that it really exists.

Most books on this subject can't be trusted – even those written by Wiccans. If you wish, teach the modern history of Wicca, beginning with Gerald Gardner. We can at least be sure of the last 40 or so years.

Teach with common sense.

Don't have your student jump into the deep end the first few times out. Start small and increase the scope and complexity of your lessons. Ask your students if they've understood particularly important points, and be certain that they have before continuing on to more challenging topics. (You can always test them.)

Don't think of these classes as something to be endured.

Don't continue to teach a person who shows little interest in the subject, or who hints that she or he is practicing destructive magic.

Don't teach folk magic (see Glossary) as Wicca.

We all know that Wicca doesn't consist of spell casting and candle magic. Keep such distinctly non-religious, non-Wiccan practices limited to separate classes if you decide to teach them.

Don't teach to gain control over others.

This may seem to be another obvious warning, but some truly feel the need to dominate other persons. Since religion has been a dominant force in cultures throughout history, some begin teaching Wicca in order to become an authority figure. This, along with financial gain, are two of the worst reason for teaching.

Teach with love.

You may not love your student, but you should certainly love your religion. Let your feelings for Wicca show in your classes, but beware becoming a proselytizing, frothing, ranting fanatic in front of your students. Balance is recommended.

Never forget that you've made this decision to teach.

No one can truly force you to do anything. You've widened your circle and invited another to join it. Celebrate this fact.

Some sticky situations can arise when teaching, but all can be handled. After some training, or perhaps even before, your student may begin hinting around about initiation. This hinting may become more direct and open as time passes.

Never let such requests pass by without comment. Never give students false hope. If you don't wish to perform an initiation ritual upon another human being, tell your student this on the first day of class. Suggest self-initiation and, if you wish, describe your own rite. Make this perfectly clear. Some students will still harbor a faint hope, but at least you've set the record straight from the onset.

If you don't mind initiating others but don't yet know if the student is worthy, say that they'll have to pass a test after completing instruction before the possibility would even arise. And if you're already sure of the student's sincerity, simply say, "When the time is right." (Such initiation ceremonies aren't necessarily the culmination of private Wiccan teachings. In fact, they're rather rare. Still, every student wants an initiation. As a teacher, you'll have to deal with this.)

Another situation may arise. You'll most probably demonstrate a few rituals to your student. And eventually, your student will do ritual with you. This may lead to the false notion that you've formed a coven.

Once again, explain from the beginning that you're not forming a coven; you're not looking for other members, and the rituals will last only as long as the classes. (Students who have completely accepted the coven organization of Wicca often find it hard to let it go. This will come up in their attitudes.)

There's much more to be said regarding teaching, but you'll discover it as you go along. Since we're Solitary Wiccans, it certainly isn't necessary to teach others. However, it can be an especially rewarding activity on many levels.

Widening the circle is both a commitment to your religion and a celebration of your faith. It's also an endless learning experience. As I've always said, if you want to learn something, teach it.

23: LIVING WICCA

I titled this book *Living Wicca* for two reasons. First, Wicca is indeed living. It's thrived and grown in both popularity as well as in stature. The name of our religion is more frequently met with in the outside world, and sometimes in the most unexpected of places. Public awareness – and even a bit more understanding – is also growing. (The trend against public use of the terms 'Witchcraft' and 'Witch' has been a tremendous help to this process.)

This book's title also refers to its practitioners. We strive to live Wiccan lives, just as members of other religions attempt to fit their religious beliefs into their existences. Naturally, none of us is SuperWiccan; we all have to make difficult choices as the outside world intrudes into our lives. Some of these choices may well fly in the face of Wiccan teachings. Still, making the attempt to live a Wiccan life is certainly worth the effort, and is a reminder that Wiccan practice isn't limited to candles, athames and cauldrons.

When we've made a conscious decision to bring our spirituality into our everyday lives, our entire existences considerably brighten. Wicca, after all, consists of reverence of the sources of everything that exists. I hardly think that the Goddess' and God's teachings are relevant solely on the Sabbats and Esbats.

We needn't change our entire lives to live within Wicca's framework. We don't have to abandon our families and move to Tibet, or spend all day, every day, in ritual. Often, the greatest changes that need to be made are mental, not physical. A truly positive outlook ruled by 'harm none' is an excellent first step in Wiccan living. It can also be quite challenging (especially when driving in rush-hour traffic or vying for a parking space).

There are no failures. When we get angry, we can remember that the deities have such emotions within them as well (though we don't spend time invoking these particular divine aspects). If a temporary lapse of consciousness allows us to litter, we needn't ask forgiveness of anyone but ourselves as we bend to retrieve that candy wrapper.

There are two things to remember when attempting to live a Wiccan life: there's nothing that we can do that, mythologically speaking, the deities haven't done. (They're unshockable.) The Goddess and God understand everything; nothing is beyond their ken.

Second, we're not here on this planet to ask forgiveness of our deities. This would be similar to apologizing to our stylist or barber because our hair just keeps on growing. The Earth is a classroom. We're the students. Karma, life, ourselves, others and the Goddess and God are the teachers, and we can't always know the answers. Mistakes are a part of human life. Apologize all you want, if you wish, but learn from your mistakes and, if possible or necessary, correct them. Forgive yourself and move on.

Once we've learned the basics of Wiccan beliefs and practices, living our religion is, logically, the next step. How we allow it to affect our lives is completely up to us.

I've written this book as a guide not only to Wiccan practice, but to Wiccan life. Still, its contents are merely ideas and suggestions. Each of us has to find the perfect path. May the Goddess and God assist you in this quest.

Blessed Be.

GLOSSARY

This is both a glossary and a review of general Wiccan ritual techniques and beliefs. I've tried to make the glossary as non-sectarian and universal as possible. Many Wiccan traditions possess specific concepts concerning some of these terms and will disagree with me. That's fine. Italicized terms within the body of each entry refer to other, related entries in the glossary.

Athame: A Wiccan *Ritual* knife. It may possess a double-edged blade and a black handle. The athame is used to direct *Personal Power* during ritual workings. It is seldom used for actual, physical cutting. The term is of obscure origin; has many variant spellings among Wiccans, and an even greater variety of pronunciations. British and American East Coast Wiccans may pronounce it as "Ah-THAM-ee" (to rhyme with "whammy"); I was first taught to say "ATH-ah-may" and, later, "Ah-THAW-may."

Balefire: A fire laid and lit for magical or religious purposes, usually outdoors. Balefires are tradition adjuncts to Wiccan *Ritual* on *Yule*, *Beltane* and *Midsummer*.

Bane: That which destroys life; is not useful, is poisonous, destructive or evil.

Baneful: See *Bane:*

B.C.E.: Before Common Era; the non-religious equivalent of B.C.

Beltane: A Wiccan religious festival, observed on April 30th, that celebrates the burgeoning fertility of the Earth (and, for some Wiccans, the wedding of the *Goddess* and the *God*). Synonyms include May Eve, Roodmas, Walpurgis Night and Cethsamhain

Besom: Broom.

Boline: The white-handled knife, used in Wiccan and magic Ritual, for practical purposes such as cutting herbs or piercing pomegranates Compare with *Athame*.

Blessing: The act of conferring positive *Energy* upon a person, place or thing. It's a spiritual or religious practice.

Book of Shadows, The: A collection of Wiccan *Ritual* information that usually includes religious rituals, magic and advice. There are many Books of Shadows; there is no one correct Book of Shadows.

Cakes and Wine: Also known as Cakes and Ale, this is a simple ritual meal shared with the *Goddess* and *God*, usually within the *Circle*, near the completion of a religious ritual. Such ritual meals predate Christianity.

C.E.: Common Era; the non-religious equivalent of A.D.

Censer: A heat-proof container in which incense is smoldered during ritual. An incense burner. Usually associated, in Wicca, with the *Element* of Air.

Charging: See *Empowering*.

Circle, Magic: A sphere constructed to *Personal Power* in which Wiccan rituals are usually enacted. The area inside the circle is seen as being common ground on which Wiccans and their Deities can meet. The term refers to the circle that marks the sphere's penetration of the ground, for it extends both above and below it. The magic circle is created through *Magic*.

Circle Casting: The process of moving positive energy from the body and forming it into a large, non-physical sphere of power in which Wiccan rituals usually occur. Circle castings usually begin each Wiccan ritual. The process is also known as 'laying the circle' and 'creating sacred space', among other terms.

Clockwise: The traditional form of movement in positive magic and in Wiccan ritual. (If you're standing facing a tree, move to your left and walk in a circle around it. That's clockwise motion.) Also known as Deosil movement.

Conscious Mind: The analytical, materially-based, rational half of our consciousness. Compare with *Psychic Mind*.

Consecration: The act of conferring sanctity. In Wicca, tools used in religious and magical rites are consecrated with Energy during specific rituals.

Coven: A group of Wiccans, usually initiatory and led by one or two leaders, that gathers together for religious and magical workings. Most covens operate within a specific Wiccan *Tradition*.

Craft, The: Wicca.

Deosil: See *Clockwise*.

Divine Power: The unmanifested, pure energy that exists within the *Goddess* and God. The life force; the ultimate source of all things. It is this energy that Wiccans contact during *Ritual*. Compare with *Earth Power* and *Personal Power*.

Divination: The magical art of discovering the unknown by interpreting random patterns or symbols. Sometimes incorrectly referred to as 'fortune-telling'.

Earth Power: That energy which exists within stones, herbs, flames, wind, water and other natural objects. It is manifested *Divine Power* and can be utilized during *magic* to create needed change. Compare with *Personal Power*.

Elements, The: Earth, Air, Fire and Water. These four essences are the building blocks of the universe, and ancient magical sources of *Energy*.

Empowering: The act of moving Energy into an object.

Energy: A general term for the currently unmeasurable (but real) power that exists within all natural objects and beings— including our own bodies. It is used in *Folk Magic*. See also *Personal Power*.

Esbat: A Wiccan ritual occurring on any day other than the eight *Sabbats* Esbats are often held on full moons, which are dedicated to the *Goddess*

Folk Magic: The practice of magic utilizing *Personal Power*, in conjunction with natural *Tools*, in a non-religious framework, to cause positive change.

Goal, The: See *Intent*.

God, The: Generally, in Wicca, the God is the male principle; the perfect complement to the Goddess. He's often identified with the sun; with deserts and forests, and with wild animals. Some see Him as the Lord of Death and Resurrection. In the eight *Sabbats* the Wiccans celebrate His birth, maturity, union with the Goddess and His death. The God is not to be confused with common Christian conception of 'God'.

Goddess, The: There are as many definitions of the Goddess as there are Wiccans. Generally, She's seen as the creatress of the universe; the unfaltering, ultimate source of fertility, wisdom, love, compassion, healing and power. Often associated with the Moon, the seas and the Earth in Wiccan thought, the Goddess has been worshipped in many religions across the globe and throughout time.

Handfasting: Within Wicca, a ritual joining of two human beings in a bond of love, and before the Goddess and God.

Herb: Virtually any plant used in magic.

High Priest: In group Wicca, either one of two visible leaders of a *Coven*; a man who co-leads the rituals, or a man who has reached a certain level of proficiency, achievement and wisdom. The term usually denotes a man who has received not one but several initiations.

High Priestess: A highly experienced leader of a *Coven*; the woman who leads or co-leads the rituals, or a woman who has reached a certain level of Wiccan proficiency, achievement and wisdom. The term usually denotes a woman who has received not one but several initiations.

Imbolc: A Wiccan religious festival celebrated on February 1st or 2nd that marks the first stirring of Spring.

Intent: In magic, the goal of the working.

Initiation: A process whereby an individual is introduced or admitted into a group, interest, skill or religion. Initiations may be *Ritual* occasions, or may spontaneously occur.

Invocation: An appeal or petition to a higher power (or powers). Invocation is a method of establishing conscious ties with those aspects of the Goddess and God that dwell within us. Invocation seemingly invites Them to appear. In actuality, invocation simply makes us newly aware of Their presence.

Law of Three, The: A Wiccan belief that our actions, both positive and negative, will be returned to us three-fold.

Litha: The Summer Solstice, a Wiccan religious festival and a traditional time for magic. Also known as Midsummer.

'Luck, Good': An individual's ability to make timely, correct decisions, to perform correct actions and to place herself or himself in positive situations. 'Bad luck' stems from ignorance and an unwillingness to accept self-responsibility.

Lughnasadh: A Wiccan religious festival celebrated on August 1st that marks the first harvest.

Magic: The movement of natural (yet subtle) *Energies* to manifest positive, needed change. Magic is the process of rousing energy, giving it purpose (through *Visualization*), and releasing it to create a change. This is a natural (not supernatural) practice.

Magic Circle: See *Circle*.

Mabon: A Wiccan religious festival celebrated on the Autumn Equinox that marks the second harvest.

Meditation: Reflection, contemplation, turning inward toward the self or outward toward Deity or nature.

Ostara: A Wiccan festival celebrated on the Spring Solstice that marks the beginning of the return of evident fertility to the Earth.

Pagan: From the Latin *paganus*, a 'country dweller' or 'villager' Today it's used as a general term for followers of Wicca and other polytheistic, magic-embracing religions. Pagans aren't Satanists, dangerous, or evil.

Pentacle: A ritual object (usually a circular piece of wood, clay or metal) upon which a five-pointed star *(Pentagram)* is inscribed, painted or engraved. It represents the *Element* of Earth. The words 'pentagram' and 'pentacle' are not interchangeable in Wiccan use.

Pentagram: An interlaced five-pointed star (one point at its top) that has long been used as a protective device. Today the pentagram is also associated with the *Element* of Earth and with Wicca. It has no evil associations.

Personal Power: That energy which sustains our bodies. We first absorb it from our biological mothers within the womb and, later, from food, water, the moon and sun and other natural objects. We release personal power during stress, exercise, sex, conception and childbirth. *Magic* is usually a movement of personal power for a specific goal.

Power: See *Energy; Personal Power; Earth Power; Divine Power.*

Prayer: The act of focusing one's attention on Deity and engaging in communication. In Wicca, prayer is directed to the *Goddess* and *God* (or sometimes, to one or the other).

Psychic Awareness: The act of being consciously psychic, in which the *Psychic Mind* and the *Conscious Mind* are linked and working in harmony.

Psychic Mind: The subconscious or unconscious mind, in which we receive psychic impulses. The psychic mind is at work when we sleep, dream and meditate.

Reincarnation: The doctrine of rebirth. The process of repeated incarnations in human form to allow evolution of the sexless, ageless human soul. One of the tenets of Wicca.

Rite: See *Ritual.*

Ritual: Ceremony. A specific form of movement, manipulation of objects or inner processes designed to produce desired effects. In religion, ritual is geared toward union with the divine. In *Magic* it allows the magician to move energy toward needed goals. A *Spell* is a magical rite.

Ritual Consciousness:

Runes: Stick-like figures, some of which are remnants of old Teutonic alphabets; others are pictographs. These symbols are once again being widely used in all forms of *Magic.*

Sabbat: A Wiccan religious festival.

Samhain: A Wiccan religious festival celebrated on October 31st, which marks the last harvest and the preparations for Winter.

Scrying: The process of gazing at or into a shiny object, flame or water for the purposes of contacting the *Psychic Mind.*

Solitary Wicca: Wicca practiced, due to either choice or circumstance, by individuals without group support. Compare with *Group Wicca.*

Spell: The mainstay of *Folk Magic,* spells are simply magical rites. They're usually non-religious and often include spoken words.

Tools: A word much-used in Wicca, this term includes both physical objects used to facilitate Wiccan *Ritual* (censers, wands, candles, salt, water and incense) as well as internal process (visualization and concentration, among others). In some forms of *Magic,* this term also refers to stones, herbs, colors and other sources of power utilized in *Spells.*

Tradition, Wiccan: An organized, structured, specific Wiccan subgroup, usually initiatory, often with unique ritual practices. The basis of any tradition is its *Book of Shadows* and specific oral instructions revealed only to initiates. Most traditions are comprised of a number of covens. Most recognize members of other traditions as Wiccans. There are many Wiccan traditions; perhaps the most famous of these is the Gardnerian.

Visualization: The process of forming mental images. Magical visualization consists of forming images of needed goals during *Magic.* It is a function of the *Conscious Mind.*

Wand: One of the ritual *Tools* used in Wicca, the wand is an instrument of *Invocation,* usually utilized to call upon the *Goddess* and the *God.*

Widdershins: Counter-clockwise ritual motion. Compare with *Clockwise.*

Wicca: A contemporary *Pagan* religion with spiritual roots in the earliest expressions of reverence of nature as a manifestation of the divine. Wicca views Deity as *Goddess* and *God;* thus it is polytheistic. It also embraces the practice of *Magic* and accepts reincarnation. Religious festivals are held in observance of the Full Moon and other astronomical (and agricultural) phenomena. It has no associations with Satanism.

Wiccan: Of or relating to *Wicca.*

Witch: Anciently, a European practitioner of pre-Christian *Folk Magic,* particularly that relating to herbs, healing, wells, rivers and stones. One who practiced *Witchcraft.* Later, this term's meaning was altered to denote demented, dangerous beings who practiced destructive magic and who threatened Christianity. This latter definition is false. (Some *Wiccans* also use the word to describe themselves.)

Witchcraft: The Craft of the *Witch. Magic,* especially magic utilizing *Personal Power* in conjunction with the energies within stones, herbs, colors and other natural objects. While this does have spiritual overtones, witchcraft, according to this definition, isn't a religion. However, many followers of *Wicca* use this word to denote their religion. (When it is used in this manner, the first 'w' should be uppercase).

Yule: A Wiccan religious festival celebrated on the Winter Solstice that marks the rebirth of the Sun.

ANNOTATED BIBLIOGRAPHY

M any new books have been published in the last few years. Many others are once again in print. Though all of these works will prove to be of value, I certainly don't agree with every single statement contained within them. Read, as always, with discretion.

WICCA

Anderson, Victor H., *Thorns of the Blood Rose*. Edited and introduced by Gwyddion Pendderwen. Nemeton, 1980. (An intriguing collection of Goddess-inspired poetry.)

Bourne, Lois, *Conversations With a Witch*. London: Robert Hale, 1989. (An English Wiccan's life.)

Cabot, Laurie and Tom Cowan, *Power of the Witch: The Earth, The Moon, and The Magical Path to Enlightenment*. New York: Delta, 1989. (An introduction to Wicca and a guide to folk magic.)

Crowley, Vivianne, *Wicca: The Old Religion in the New Age*. Wellingborough (Northamptonshire, England): Aquarian, 1989. (This is one of the few books published to date that include the word 'Wicca' in its title.)

Crowther, Patricia, *Witch Blood! The Diary of a Witch High Priestess*. New York: House of Collectibles, 1974.

Farrar, Stewart, *What Witches Do: The Modern Coven Revealed*. New York : Coward, McCann, and Geoghehan, 1971 (A look at a coven's activities.)

Farrar, Janet and Stewart Farrar, *The Life and Times of a Modern Witch*. Custer (Washington): Phoenix, 1988. (A fine introduction to Wicca.)

Gardner, Gerald, *The Meaning of Witchcraft*. London: 1959. Reprint. London, Aquarian Press, 1971. Reprint. New York: Magickal Childe Publishing, 1984.

Gardner, Gerald, *Witchcraft Today*. New York: Citadel, 1955. Reprint. New York: Magickal Childe Publishing, 1988. (The first book ever published concerning contemporary Wicca.)

Glass, Justine, *Witchcraft, the Sixth Sense and Us*. North Hollywood: Wilshire, 1965. (Photographs.)

Martello, Leo Louis, *Witchcraft: The Old Religion*. Secaucus (New Jersey): University Books, ND.

Valiente, Doreen, *Where Witchcraft Lives*. London: Aquarian Press, 1962. (An early look at British Wicca and Sussex folklore. Charming and enjoyable reading.)

PRACTICAL INSTRUCTIONS

Budapest, Z., *The Holy Book of Women's Mysteries, Part I*. Oakland: The Susan B. Anthony Coven #1, 1979.

Buckland, Raymond, *The Tree: The Complete Book of Saxon Witchcraft*. New York: Weiser, 1974. (Complete guide to a Wiccan tradition.)

Buckland, Raymond, *Buckland's Complete Book of Witchcraft*. St. Paul: Llewellyn Publications, 1986.

Campanelli, Pauline and Dan Campanelli, *Wheel of the Year: Living the Magical Life*. St. Paul: Llewellyn Publications, 1989. (These two Wiccans have created a charming and eminently usable collection of Wiccan, Pagan and magical information and activities for every month of the year. A true delight.)

Crowther, Patricia, *Lid Off The Cauldron: A Handbook for Witches*. London: Robert Hale, 1981. (Another practical guide.)

Farrar, Janet and Stewart Farrar, *Eight Sabbats for Witches*. London: Robert Hale, 1981. (The Sabbat rituals, plus a unique look at the origins of the first Book of Shadows, courtesy of Doreen Valiente.)

Farrar, Janet and Stewart Farrar, *The Witches' Way*: Principles, Rituals and Beliefs of Modern Witchcraft. London: Robert Hale, 1984. (Further revelations concerning Gardner's Book of Shadows and much practical information. Note: This book has been reprinted and bound with the Farrars' Eight Sabbats For Witches by Magickal Childe Publishing; the combined volume is entitled A Witches' Bible Compleat.)

Fitch, Ed, *Magical Rites From the Crystal Well*. St. Paul: Llewellyn Publications, 1984. (Neo-Pagan rituals for every occasion.)

Green, Marian, *A Witch Alone: Thirteen Moons to Master Natural Magic*. London: Aquarian Press, 1991. (An unusual book; each chapter guides the reader through lessons designed to increase her or his magical and Wiccan proficiency. Not entirely Wiccan in focus, but well-crafted, with an obvious British audience in mind.)

K., Amber, *How To Organize a Coven or Magickal Study Group*. Madison (Wisconsin): Circle Publications, 1983. (Explicit guidelines for doing just that.)

Slater, Herman (editor) *A Book of Pagan Rituals* New York Weiser, 1974. (Another collection of rituals drawn from the Pagan Way.)

Slater, Herman (editor) *Pagan Rituals III: Outer Court Training Coven*. New York: Magical Childe Publishing, 1989. (The first part of this book reprints The Witchcraft Fact Book, written by the late Ed Buczynski. The second half contains a complete "outer court" (i.e., non-initiatory) Book of Shadows originally written for students of a Welsh tradition.)

Starhawk, *The Spiral Dance*. San Francisco: Harper and Row, 1979. (The classic guide to Goddess worship.)

Valiente, Doreen, *Witchcraft For Tomorrow*. London: Robert Hale, 1978. (Contains a partial Book of Shadows as well as several chapters covering various aspects of Wicca.)

Valiente, Doreen and Evan Jones, *Witchcraft: A Tradition Renewed*. Custer (Washington): Phoenix. (A curious reconstruction of the rituals and beliefs of Robert Cochrane that, in part, inspired the Regency and 1734 traditions of Witchcraft. Far different from anything else that has ever been published.)

Weinstein, Marion, *Earth Magic: A Dianic Book of Shadows*. New York: Earth Magic Productions, 1980. Reprint. Custer (Washington): Phoenix, 1986. (A unique guide like no others. Not a complete Book of Shadows, perhaps, but certainly fascinating and useful.)

THE GODDESS

Downing, Christine, *The Goddess: Mythological Images of the Feminine*. New York: Crossroad, 1984.

Gimbutas, Marija, *The Goddesses and Gods of Old Europe*. Berkeley: The University of California Press, 1982.

Gimbutas, Marija, *The Language of the Goddess*. San Francisco: Harper & Row, 1989. (A monumental, overwhelming work. Many photographs and illustrations.)

Graves, Robert, *The White Goddess*. New York: Farrar, Straus and Giroux, 1973.

Neumann, Erich, *The Great Mother: An Analysis of the Archetype*. Princeton: Princeton University Press, 1974. (A Jungian approach to the Goddess. This work concludes with 185 pages of photographs of Goddess images.)

Stone, Merlin, *When God Was a Woman*. New York: Dial Press, 1976.

Walker, Barbara, *The Woman's Dictionary of Symbols and Sacred Objects*. San Francisco: Harper & Row, 1988.

Walker, Barbara, *The Woman's Encyclopedia of Myth and Secrets*. San Francisco: Harper & Row, 1983.

WICCAN REFERENCE WORKS

Adler, Margot, *Drawing Down the Moon: Witches, Druids, Goddess-Worshippers, and Other Pagans in America Today*. Revised and Expanded Edition. Boston: Beacon Press, 1986. (This book is must reading, for it provides an overview of contemporary Wicca and Paganism. Photographs.)

Burland, C. A., *Echoes of Magic: A Study of Seasonal Festivals Through the Ages* London : Peter Davies, ND. (An engrossing study of the symbolism of the seasonal festivals [Sabbats] by an expert folklorist. The entire volume is somewhat peculiarly given over to the author's great joy in writing of sexual matters. Still a wonderful source.)

Farrar, Janet and Stewart Farrar, *The Witches' God: Lord of the Dance.* Custer (Washington): Phoenix, 1989. (A book-length look at the God in Wicca. Photographs.)

Farrar, Janet and Stewart Farrar, *The Witches' Goddess.* Custer (Washington): Phoenix, 19??. (Photographs.)

Guiley, Rosemary, *The Encyclopedia of Witches and Witchcraft.* New York: Facts on File, 1989. (A well-researched, sympathetic, encyclopedic work.)

Kelly, Aidan A., *Crafting the Art of Magic: A History of Modern Witchcraft, 1939-1964.* St. Paul: Llewellyn Publications, 1991. (A speculative reconstruction of the creation of modern Wicca.)

Mathers, S. L. MacGregor, (editor and translator), *The Key of Solomon the King.* New York: Weiser, 1972 (Some modern Wiccan rites were partially based on this work. Wicca has also borrowed some symbolism from the Key.)

Valiente, Doreen, *The Rebirth of Witchcraft.* London: Robert Hale, 1989. Reprint. Custer (Washington): Phoenix, 1989. (An important addition to Wicca's recent history; informative and enthralling.)

MAGIC

K., Amber, *True Magick: A Beginner's Guide*. St. Paul: Llewellyn, 1990. (An extremely Wiccan-based introduction to folk magic.)

Howard, Michael, *The Magic of Runes*. New York: Weiser, 1980.

Howard, Michael, *The Runes and Other Magical Alphabets*. New York: Weiser, 1978.

Koch, Rudolph, *The Book of Signs*. New York: Dover, 1955.

Mathers, S. L. MacGregor (editor and translator), *The Key of Solomon The King*. New York: Weiser, 1972.

Pepper, Elizabeth and John Wilcox, *Witches All*. New York: Grosset and Dunlap, 1977. (A collection of folk magic drawn from the popular *Witches' Almanac*, which is once again in annual production.

Tyson, Donald, *Rune Magic*. St. Paul: Llewellyn Publications, 1988.

Valiente, Doreen, *Natural Magic*. New York: St. Martin's Press, 1975.

Weinstein, Marion, *Positive Magic: Occult Self-Help*. New York: Pocket Books, 1978. (A wonderful introduction to magic. An expanded edition has also been published.)

INDEX

THE COMPLETE BOOK OF INCENSE, OILS & BREWS

Illustrated by
Victoria Poyser-Lisi

For Morgana, *kahuna la'au lapa'au* of Hawaii

Acknowledgements

My thanks go to Marilee and Ed for once again giving me access to their comprehensive herb library, as well as to Marilee for sharing her expertise in incense composition and allowing some of her formulas to be published here.

My especial thanks to fellow author M.V. Devine for allowing me to reprint some oil and incense recipes from her entrancing book *Brujeria: A Study of Mexican-American Folk-Magic*.

I'm also indebted to Ron Garst for his gracious help and willingness to discuss oils and incenses.

Thanks are in order to the many friends, readers and reviewers who gave me ideas toward this revised edition and who compelled me to complete it, and to Carl Weschcke of Llewellyn for presenting the opportunity.

To Annella of The Crystal Cave (Claremont, California), Judy of Eye of the Cat (Long Beach, California) and Karen of Moon Magic (Littleton, Colorado) for assistance in obtaining unusual herbs and oils.

I certainly must express my gratitude to the authors who, in the past, committed some of these secrets to paper so that later generations could reap the rich rewards of working in harmony with the Earth's fragrant treasures.

Finally, I must express my thanks to Morgan (Dorothy), my first teacher, who instructed me in the mysteries of the brews, incenses and oils long before I understood what it was all about.

Contents

Preface to the New Edition

Several years ago I began work on a collection of magical perfumery—incenses, oils, sachets and other occult herb products. I decided to include such obscure subjects as inks and ointments in an attempt to broaden public interest in all phases of magical herbalism. I completed the book in 1985; Llewellyn published *The Magic of Incenses, Oils and Brews* the following year.

Even as I sent the book off I realized that much remained to be said on this subject. I continued practicing the arcane arts of herbalism. As my knowledge grew, I knew that a greatly expanded edition of this book was necessary.

Hence, this volume. Most of the original information remains, but in more complete form. Well over 100 new formulas have been included, and most now contain proportions that many readers of the first edition of this book seemed to want.

Every page, every chapter, has been clarified and rewritten. Several new chapters and sections have also been added:

Chapter Four: Ingredients is a look at common and rare botanical substances and oils used in creating herbal compounds, together with some recommended substitutions.

Chapter Five: Creating Your Own Recipes is a guide to just that—an in-depth discussion with step-by-step instructions.

Tinctures—examines the art of capturing plant fragrances with alcohol, a simple and easy alternative to oil extraction.

Ritual Soaps details an easy method of creating spell soaps for various magical purposes—without the use of lye or fat.

Powders discusses the compounding and unique uses of finely ground herbal blends.

Part III: Substitutions replaces Chapter 13 of the last edition. The introduction consists of a lengthy example of proper magical substitution, and the tables have been vastly enlarged. One new feature is a list of specific substitutions: tobacco for nightshade, cedar for sandalwood, for example.

Additionally, a *Glossary* has been added to define various terms; a list of *Sources* of herbs and oils has been included; a *Botanical Index* lists all plants and their Latin names for clarity and a *General Index* completes the major additions to this book.

In manuscript form this edition is nearly twice the size of the last. Though I'm still learning, naturally, I feel that *The Complete Book of Incense, Oils and Brews* can now stand as a comprehensive introduction to the subject.

Though it is meant to be read and used in conjunction with *Magical Herbalism* and *Cunningham's Encyclopedia of Magical Herbs*, it can certainly be used alone.

After all, the greatest teachers are the herbs themselves—words merely echo their lessons. It is to the plants, flowers and trees that we must turn if we would know the secrets of the Earth. Books such as this are signposts to guide the way.

So meet the plants. Bring them into your life and discover their energies. As incense smolders, brews bubble and oils release their fragrances, invite their energies within.

Ritual herbalism is a gift from our long-gone predecessors—an ancient art of touching nature. The secrets await those who wish to discover them.

Scott Cunningham
San Diego, California
October 31, 1987

Introduction

For millenia our ancestors have used herbs to create a vast array of magical substances. Precious ointments secreted within horn containers or crystal jars were rubbed onto the body to effect magical transformations. Brews were sipped or sprinkled to ward off evil and negativity. Fragrant barks and woods were thrown onto hot coals to release their scents and powers.

The actual formulas for such sachets, ointments, brews, incenses and oils were often kept secret, locked within the Witches' spellbooks and magicians' grimoires, or even deeper in the farthest recesses of the human mind. Upon entrance ineo the starlit circles of the "wise ones," these secret recipes were revealed, enabling the student to use them in rite, spell and everyday life.

Today, when the twilight curtains of secrecy are being drawn back so that all may share in the old ways of magic, there is a growing need for a comprehensive, responsible book of magical formulas that will satisfy the needs of those who would mix up the old brews and incenses—not only for magical purposes but also for the sheer joy in so doing.

The composition of incenses, blending of oils, mixing of herbs—such is the work necessary to keep a well-stocked magical pantry. Many delight in putting herbs to work, aligning their powers, mingling energies as they mix leaves and oils; but many more seem to be in the dark about such things.

Hence, this book. Few seem to know how to compound incense—once far more important in magic and religion than oils. And despite public stereotypes of the Witch with cauldron and brew, the art of brew-making seems to be dying out as rapidly as that of ointment composition.

Therefore, this is a guide to little-known methods of magical cookery. The results don't fill our stomachs, but do enrich and better our lives and the lives of those we love.

It should hardly be necessary to say that no cursing or "evil" recipes appear here, as they do in other books.

Also, these recipes are primarily from European magical and Wiccan sources. I have purposely deleted the so-called Voodoo formulas, since they have been covered well in other works (see Bibliography). I have also resisted including recipes that have constantly appeared in print during the last 50 years or so.

Some of the formulas appearing in this volume were passed to me by teachers; others came from old manuscripts, were shared by friends, or evolved themselves as the need arose. Some are indeed ancient, but all will work with proper preparation, empowerment and use.

The best way to become truly intimate with herbs and their magic is to work with them. Let them teach. Compounding incense, oils and brews is one of the easiest and most productive means to learn herb magic.

I have said before that magic must be practical. If you need protection incense at three A.M., you should be able to prepare it yourself. With this book the way is open to you.

Some may find it amusing that, in this day of incredible technology, many are turning to Mother Earth, to herbs and magic. Folks are programming computers to cast spells, etching runes on glowing cathode ray tubes, and waiting for *magic* to dazzle their eyes.

But the keepers of the old ways—the Witches, magis, wizards and wise women—pour scented oils into tubs of warm water, set incense alight and drink brews. They weave spells with herb, gesture and word, utilizing the simple but potent powers resident within the products of nature, directing them with their intent. Power flashes forth; magic is made.

Because herb magic is natural, it requires only those tools of nature. The most potent are the ones included in this book: protection incense, love oil, healing bath. These are the tools with which we can transform our lives and, therefore, ourselves.

May all your transformations be joyous.

Part I

Basics

Warning

Some of these recipes contain dangerous ingredients. Such formulas are marked with the word caution, and an asterisk (*) appears beside each hazardous substance. These herbs (henbane, hellebore, yew, etc.) can be poisonous or fatal if eaten, drunk, rubbed onto broken skin, or inhaled when burned as incense. Caution must be observed in any attempts to use such ingredients.

In fact, it's safer not to utilize them at all. The sale and use of these baneful herbs are mostly restricted by law, so mere possession of many of them can be hazardous.

Recipes containing such herbs have been included here because they are traditional, but sufficient warnings are present so that anyone foolish enough to try a toxic mixture cannot do so unaware of the attendant dangers.

In addition, within the botanical index beginning on page 255, plants have been marked according to their safety. Plants labeled (x) should never be ingested. Plants labeled (~) should be used with caution, since they may adversely affect some people due to their specific health problems (i.e. diabetes, using MAO inhibitors, kidney disease, etc.) Plants labeled (P) should not be used when pregnant or nursing.

Other important cautions:

Oils, incense, bath salts, soaps, tinctures, sachets and powders should never be swallowed. Always dilute essential oils. Keep essential oils out of reach of children. In the event of an overdose, call your poison control center.

Many plants and essential oils are poisonous. All that is knowable about herbs is not yet known, so use herbs and oils with caution and respect. Plants are drugs. Check everything you put into your body with up-to-date herbal reference books.

The information contained within this book is for informational purposes only and is not intended as legal, medical or psychological advice. For help in these matters, consult a lawyer, doctor or psychiatrist.

1
On Magic

MAGIC IS A BYPRODUCT of the oldest science—far older than astronomy, chemistry or biology. This "science" constituted the earliest investigations into nature. What caused the seasons to turn, the sea to rise and fall, the birth and death of all living things?

Magic—the use of natural energies to bring about needed change— arose when those early humans discovered invisible forces around them. Humans were aware of the effects of gravity, electricity and magnetism long before such terms were coined. Nuts fell to the ground. Lightning blasted trees. Animal fur created sparks when stroked on dry days. Metallic rocks strangely attracted bits of iron.

But these early humans discovered more than has been accepted into scientific doctrine. They sensed connections between humans and specific places, between them and the Earth. They intuited forces residing within plants, animals and stones. They felt energies within their own bodies that could be moved according to will and need.

Through centuries of experimentation, error and inspiration, magic was born. It evolved into a tool of personal power, one with a fantastic potential to both help and harm.

The power of magic springs from the Earth itself, as well as from stars and celestial bodies. It resides within winds, rocks and trees; in flames and water and our bodies. Rousing and directing such forces sums up the practice of magic.

Herb magic is a specialized form that utilizes the power of plants. This is the realm of incense, oils, baths, brews and tinctures. An act of herb magic may be as simple as rubbing a scented oil onto a colored candle, setting it in a holder, lighting it and visualizing your magical need.

A more complex ritual may involve several candles, many oils, incense, chants, ritual clothing—all in harmony with your goal. Herb magic can be simple or complex. You're the only one calling the shots.

This is a personal art. It is certainly one in which the practitioner must actually participate. Armchair magicians do not produce results. Those who are willing to dirty their hands and to actually *practice* herb magic are soon improving their lives and themselves.

This book is a compendium of ritual herbal processes and recipes. Though these mixtures contain energies in and of themselves, they are far more effective when used in conjunction with simple rituals.

If you are new to magic you may find yourself asking, "Terrific. So how do I use these things?"

Though directions for use are given in Part II for each type of mixture, a few pages devoted to the basics of magic are perhaps warranted here.

Harm None

How's that for an opener? This is the basic, unrelenting rule of all magic: *harm no one.* Not yourself, not your enemies, no one.

To me, magic is an act of love, a method of bringing light and order into my life. It is to most other practitioners as well. But not to some.

Many become involved in magic because they see it as a great weapon to use against their nagging bosses, unfaithful friends and mates, and a host of imaginary enemies.

They soon learn the truth.

If you want to control or manipulate people, to bend others to your will, magic isn't for you. If you wish to harm, hurt or even kill others, magic isn't for you. If you want to force a man or a woman to fall in love or jump into the sack with you, magic isn't for you.

Not that there aren't people who attempt such things with magic. They certainly exist . . . for a time. Then, for some reason or another, they quietly fade into the sunset.

Some amateur evil magicians (there really isn't any other kind) think, "Hey! I can hex that guy and nothing will happen to me. I'm too well protected! Ha!"

Perhaps they do have magical protections that will fend off any outside negative forces. However, these magical guards are power-less against the attack that will ultimately kick them off their feet. Where does this "curse" come from? From within.

Practicing harmful magic arouses the darkest, most dangerous aspects of the inner being. No superhero has to throw a curse at the evil magician to right their wrongs. No faery princess need zap him or her with her wand. *Misusers of magic curse themselves.* They do this by unlocking a forceful stream of negative energies from inside themselves. This is one hex that—sooner or later—never fails to hit home.

So if you're thinking about using magic in this way, think again! You've been warned.

There are subtler misuses of magic. Threatening to curse some-one, or intimating that you're able to perform such an action, violates the "harm none" rule even if you don't intend to perform the action. Harming someone psychologically is as negative as doing so psychi-cally or physically, and will eventually lead the boaster to curse themselves.

Promising a man or a woman to teach them the secrets of magic as a way of getting into their pants is another sure-fire way to lead yourself to ruin.

These are facts, not personal opinions.

The choice is yours.

Working for Others

A friend of yours is sick. You want to help. Before performing any healing ritual for that friend, it's best to ask them if they want you to. Abide by their wishes.

The same is true for any ritual you may wish to do for some other person. Obtain their permission in advance, even if it's a laughing one. Working positive magic for another person who doesn't want it—or who isn't ready for the results—is manipulative.

So, to make sure that you are truly harming none, ask them before mixing up those herbs.

The Goal

House protection. Good health. Love. Money. These are magical goals or intents.

The goal is at the heart of all magic. Without a goal, no rituals need be performed. Goals aren't always earthly. Some rites are formed to help the magician tune into spirituality—to Deity, if you will. Others are designed to strengthen psychic awareness (the unconscious mind) or mental alertness (the conscious mind).

When a goal presents itself to a magician, she or he will usually take physical steps to attain it. If these fail, rituals are performed.

Some goals, obviously, can't be accomplished through normal means. When this is the case, magic is immediately used.

The Power

The power at work in magic is within our bodies as well as within herbs, stones and other natural products of the Earth. It is not satanic, dangerous or evil; nor is it supernatural. Magical power is the power of life itself.

After you exercise for an extended period you're tired. Why? Your body has released a large amount of energy.

A flower dies prematurely after being cut from the ground. It is no longer receiving energy (in the form of nutrients) from the Earth.

This is the energy used in herb magic: personal power and that which resides in plants. By combining these two forces, by moving them from within to without and by giving them purpose and direction, herb magicians create needed changes.

In herb magic—or any form of magic—we must raise and release this energy. There are many methods used to accomplish this. One of the most effective ways is through your emotions.

Why do a magical ritual? Usually, it's because of a need. If you *need* and *want* something badly enough, your personal power is focused toward that purpose. In mixing up an incense, you *mix in* that power. In lighting a candle, you light it *with that power*.

Many rituals are ineffective precisely because the magician wasn't concentrating on the work at hand. Or, she or he simply *needed* something but didn't *want* it. In either case, personal power wasn't properly transferred to the incense, oil or brew, so it was ineffective.

This doesn't mean that herbs and scents aren't powerful on their own. They are. But just as a car refuses to budge without a start, so too do herbal mixtures have to be "started" with personal power to get them moving.

A few pointers here: *Concentrate* on the work you're doing. If

you're grinding rosemary to be used in a healing incense for a friend, *see* that friend in a healthy state. While mixing oils to bring money into your life, concentrate on the oil doing just that.

If you're able to form clear mental pictures, practice *magical visualization* during preparations as well as during the rite itself. See in your mind's eye that the mixture is effective. See it as having already done its work. This moves your personal power into the herbs. In ritual, the energies released by the herbs combine with your own to bring about your magical need.

Magical visualization is the best way to "jump-start" herbal mixtures, but don't worry if you're unable to adequately visualize. Simply concentrate on your needed goal. The herbs will do their work.

The Altar

The altar is the center of magical practice. It isn't necessarily a religious shrine, though the powers used in magic are at the heart of every religion (a key to unlocking magic, religion and the nature of Deity). The altar is simply any flat area at which you can work with herbs and perform magical rites.

Though magic can, and should be, practiced anywhere as needed (preferably outdoors), indoor magic is best done in one specific place—hence the advisability of creating a permanent altar or working space. This need be nothing more than a coffee table, a cleared dresser top, or a small table placed in an inconspicuous corner. Ideally, it will be in a spot where objects can be left for several days, for some spells must be worked for that length of time.

Though many herb magicians drape their altars with colored cloth, this is unnecessary. So too are fancy altar tools such as expensive censers and gleaming silver candlesticks. A flat, plain space (preferably wooden) is all that is necessary.

If you wish to burn candles on the altar in recognition of higher powers, do so. Ditto for placing flowers as offerings to the gods (or however you view Deity). For best results, magic should be personally satisfying, so create an altar that moves you.

Timing

In the past, when humans lived in tune with the cycles of nature, much emphasis was placed on magical timing. Love spells (and all constructive rituals) were performed while the Moon was waxing (i.e., from New Moon to Full Moon). Spells involving the destruction of disease, pests and problems were best cast during the waning of the Moon (from Full to New).

Then, too, the hours of the day, days of the week, and even the months and seasons of the year were sometimes taken into account when deciding the most advantageous moment for magical ritual. If the magician was knowledgeable about astrology, the positions of the planets were also perused.

Such complex magical timing was beyond the means of the vast majority of illiterate farming families and common folk who practiced the bulk of natural magic a few centuries ago. If the baby was sick its mother didn't wait two weeks for the correct lunar phase. She cast a spell when it was needed, with the firm knowledge (not belief) that it would help.

Timing is still important to some herb magicians, but I feel that, save for rare situations, its day is past. In magic we work with universal energies that are channelled through our bodies, through herbs and colors. Because they are universal energies, they are universal in origin, scope and influence.

If someone tells me that they can't do a prosperity ritual because the Moon is waning, I tell them that another moon circling another planet is waxing, and that the two balance each other out.

This is the way I see magical timing. But those who feel that it is prerequisite are free to follow the old ways.*

Tools

The tools of magic can be found around the house, purchased through the mail (see Appendix 2) or easily made. For most herb magic and processing, these few tools should suffice:

- a mortar and pestle (for grinding herbs)
- a large nonmetallic bowl (for mixing)
- a small spoon (for incense)
- a censer (for burning incense)
- eyedroppers (for mixing oils)
- a nonmetallic pan (for brewing)

---

* For more information regarding magical timing, see Scott Cunningham's *Magical Herbalism* (Llewellyn, 1982).

- small funnels (for use with oils)
- self-igniting charcoal blocks (see Appendix 2 or Incense in Part II of this book)
- cheesecloth (for straining brews and tinctures)
- colored cotton cloth and wool yarn (for sachets)
- candles and candle holders
- a large quantity of jars (to store herb products)

A Basic Spell

We'll use a healing ritual as an example of how magic works. If this spell is for a friend, you've already asked for and received permission from the person to perform the spell.

Take a healing incense, a healing oil, and a purple or blue candle to your altar. Before it, with your mind composed and calm (and the room quiet), light a charcoal block, set it in your censer, and sprinkle a bit of the incense onto the block. As it rises in fragrant, powerful clouds, *will* your mind to focus on your magical goal of healing.

Visualize yourself (or your sick friend) clearly in your mind. Do not see the sickness—visualize perfect health. If thoughts of the sickness enter your mind, banish them immediately; they will only hinder your magic.

Open the oil, and while concentrating on you or your friend, wet two fingers of your right hand with the oil. Holding the candle in your left hand (or right, if you're left-handed), rub the oil onto the candle from the top or wick-end to its center, and then from the base to the center, until the entire candle is covered with a thin, shiny coating of oil.

As you rub it you're sending power into the candle—personal power as well as that resident within the oil. *Feel* the oil's power and your personal power becoming one with the candle. Sense them fusing together with your magically empowered imagination. Visualize!

Now hold the candle, calling upon any powers or deities with which you feel comfortable, asking that they aid in healing the person.

Firmly place the candle in the holder. Add more incense to the censer. Strike a match and light the candle. Watch its flame for a few seconds, still holding your image of perfect health, then leave the area. As you do so, push all thoughts of the ritual completely out of your mind.

Let the candle burn as long as you wish. If you have to leave home, snuff its flame out with your fingers or a snuffer (blowing out candles is seen as an affront to the element of Fire).* Relight the candle upon your return.

This deceptively simple ritual can be repeated for several days in a row or performed once and never again. As you use herb magic you'll discover the number of repetitions necessary for the successful accomplishment of a magical goal.

If you wish, you can greatly complicate this spell. You may stitch a robe of the color corresponding to the spell (purple or blue for healing, green for money; see Appendix 1) and wear this while you perform the rite.

You may involve planetary magic in your ritual. This may mean performing the spell on a Sunday (a great day for healing). Or, you could wear a stone such as amber, which has legendary healing properties. The spell might be preceded with a bath in which a sachet of healing herbs has been steeped.

Since spells often utilize spoken words, invocations or prayers to specific deities can be added, as can chants or magical "words of power," which can be used to direct your energies into the candle.

Then, too, some magicians add music or dance to their spells, or the use of intoxicants (which I don't recommend), strange props, and on and on, with an infinite number of possible alterations to this basic candleburning rite.

How does it work? From the moment you select the incense and oil to be used† to the time you light the candle, you are setting powers into motion. Through your concentration on the goal (in this case, healing) you are sending power, for *concentration is power!*

As you anoint the candle with the energy-packed oil, still visualizing the person (or you) in a healed state, you are sending energy into it from the oil but also from yourself, from the store of personal power that sustains our lives.

The incense smoke sets the atmosphere, sending out showers of healing vibrations, which are absorbed into the candle just as your concentration is absorbed.

Any spoken invocations or prayers to higher beings will also

---

* See Part III of *Earth Power* for more information regarding elemental magic.

† Or, when selecting the ingredients for the incense and oil if you have no appropriate mixtures in stock.

help align your spell with your magical need, and should add energy as well.

As the candle burns, the power you've concentrated within it is slowly released through the agency of flame. Wax is transformed from a solid into a liquid and a gas, a miraculous process in and of itself. At the same time, the energy and power you've poured into the candle is released and speeds on its way.

A spell of this type need not take much more than ten to fifteen minutes once you're comfortable with it. It certainly doesn't require a huge investment in tools and regalia. You'll need a comprehensive stock of herbs, incenses and oils, but that's what this book is all about.

This same basic spell can be used for any magical need. If bills have to be paid, use a green candle, a money oil and incense, and visualize yourself paying the bills: writing checks for them or stamping them "paid in full."

If love is your quest, see yourself with the perfect mate (remember: no one person in particular) as you light the love-type incense.

Magic is not instantaneous, or "snap-crackle-pop," as a friend calls it. You can't snap your fingers or wiggle your nose and expect your life to fall into place overnight. You must back up your magical work with physical exertion.

Certainly all the spells in all the grimoires in the world won't help you find employment if you sit at home all day, never checking the want ads or hitting the streets. The same is true of any type of magic.

Magic is truly an all-involving art. If you're willing to expend psychic energy, you must also be prepared to exert physical energy as well. In doing so, your magical needs will be transformed into solid reality.

2
On Proportions

THE BULK OF the recipes included in the first edition of this book lacked proportions. I explained that herb magic is a personal art and encouraged readers to determine each ingredient's amount.

Many readers who have written to me since the first edition (as well as a few reviewers) have said that they wanted specific proportions in the recipes. So most of the recipes in this revision contain *guidelines* on proportions. Again, these aren't holy writ; they are suggestions.

Many belong to the "cookbook" school of herb magic, in which recipes are strictly followed to produce the finest results, but this isn't necessarily desirable or even possible. While most cooks will have a large stock of such staples as flour, salt, spices, eggs and vegetable oils, many of the ingredients used in magical herb compounds are difficult to obtain, and when available, almost prohibitively expensive.

So the herb magician who insists on using the exact amounts of ingredients for, say, Spirit Incense #6 may end up spending $40 or more to create it. For example, wood aloe currently sells for around $30 a pound—when you can find it. A few years ago it was being sold for around $5.00 *a gram.*

An intuitive (rather than by-the-book) herbalist with just a pinch of wood aloe would add that amount to the product, thereby avoiding a costly purchase for the sole purpose of "accurately" mixing up the incense. Or, she or he may simply substitute another ingredient. (See Part III: Substitutions.)

Feel free to follow these recipes as they are written, but remember that these are suggested proportions. As I said in the first edition:

Keep in mind that even if every recipe contained exact proportions, you'd often have to adjust them to compensate for the cup of sandalwood you don't have, the empty rosemary jar in your magical pantry, and the missing phials of tonka and patchouly oil.

If you decide to alter the quantities of recipe ingredients, it is advisable to record your proportions in a small notebook or on three-by-five-inch index cards, to save for future reference.

Don't hesitate to do this, for if you come up with a wonderful oil formula but haven't recorded the proportions, it might take you weeks of testing to duplicate it again—if you ever do succeed.

For instance, when I began practicing herb magic, I mixed up a sachet (which I still have) that smelled indescribably delicious. Being a new student, I ignored my teacher's warnings to record recipes and proportions. (I had invented the mixture on the spot.) After letting it sit for six months, forgotten behind a shelf of herbs, I found it again and attempted to reproduce it—but failed. To this day (19 years later) I still haven't found the secret.

If you decide to create your own formulas (see Chapter 5) or change quantities, take a few seconds to scribble down ingredients and proportions. Don't wait until after you've made the product to do this. It's easy to forget just how many drops of oil or ounces of herb you used. Write down each amount *as you add it* to the mixture.

Another factor that faces us concerns the amount of herb product to make. One ounce, or one pound? Here are some suggestions:

Generally, on your first try with a recipe, keep the amounts small until you've used it and have determined its effectiveness. This avoids making costly mistakes.

Incense is usually made up in quantities of one cup or so, since only a small amount is needed for smoldering during rituals. It also keeps well in tightly capped or corked jars. If you wish, once you have perfected the recipes, make up a pound or more so that you have a ready stock on hand.

For cone, stick or block incense, follow the same guidelines— small at first. Once you've perfected the dipping and molding process, it's better to make up large quantities of these items, since they can be messy and time-consuming.

Paper incense is easily made in any amount.

Oils are created by mixing true essential oils in a base of ⅛ cup of some vegetable oil. This is a suitable amount for making the first batch.

Once you're satisfied with the blend, make a larger quantity, using the same proportions that you originally used. See why you have to keep records?

Ointments, brews and tinctures are usually compounded in one-cup quantities; at least that's how I make them. Only a minute amount of ointment is necessary for anointing purposes, so mixing up much more is needlessly wasteful.

Brews won't last for more than a few days before losing their powers (and possibly molding), so they should be prepared in small quantities.

Tinctures have lasting properties, but again, only a small amount is needed at any time.

Ritual soaps should be in the amounts given in the recipes in that section.

Make up *inks, bath salts, herb baths and powders* in the amounts that you feel you can use. This depends entirely on their frequency of use.

Herbal charms (sachets) are simply created when needed. They don't have to be kept in stock.

Keep in mind that in the event of an emergency you can throw together an incense or oil, empower it (see Chapter 3) and use it immediately without recording the amounts. In fact, sometimes I've made up no more than a few teaspoons of incense for a particular use. That's fine—but when time allows, record everything.

When mixing, if it feels comfortable, do it. If you decide to adjust the amounts of ingredients in these recipes, trust yourself. Learn from your mistakes, too, but trust your intuition when compounding mixtures. How much frankincense should be added to the Ritual Full Moon incense, if you decide that my suggested amount is incorrect? Add it until it seems to smell right.

So much for ancient magical rules!

3
Empowering Rites

IN MAGICAL HERBALISM we use the powers within plants to manifest needed changes. Herbs do indeed contain energies that we can use to improve our lives. But these powers aren't enough. We must add *personal power* to the herbs and the mixtures we produce with them. Only by combining plant and human energies will herb magic be truly effective. Herbs have long been known to possess energies useful for specific needs. Lavender purifies, rosemary draws love, sandalwood heightens spirituality, yarrow increases psychic awareness. Many herbs, such as rosemary, have several traditional magical uses. A healing incense containing rosemary as its main ingredient should be programmed with strictly healing energies. In effect, this redirects rosemary's love-inducing, purificatory and protective powers toward healing, creating a mixture aligned with your needs. This is done by sending personal power, infused with your magical goal, into the mixture.

This process is known as empowering, charging or enchanting. For this purpose you can use the enchanting procedure described in *Cunningham's Encyclopedia of Magical Herbs* or the following ritual. Neither is more correct. If they don't speak to you, compose your own rite.

No ritual is necessary to infuse herbal mixtures with your power. If you can visualize well, simply touch the herbs (or hold the mixture in a bottle) and send your energy into it. However, ritual is a remarkably effective tool. It allow us to:

• Focus on the magical operation (in this case, empowering)

- Build energy within our bodies
- Move energy into the mixture
- Impress upon the conscious mind that the operation has been done, thereby soothing our societally conditioned doubts.

So experiment with various empowering rituals until you find or create the one that produces the most satisfactory results.

Preparations

Have the completed herb mixture in a jar, bowl or bottle. This empowering ritual is performed with the finished product, not the raw ingredients.

Empower mixtures when you are alone. If others are present in the house, go outside to a quiet spot or shut yourself in a room. Ensure that you won't be interrupted for a few minutes.

Just before the ritual, close your eyes for ten seconds or so and breathe slowly, to relax your conscious mind and to prepare for the coming transference of power.

Open your eyes and begin.

The Ritual

Light a candle of the color appropriate to the mixture's nature— blue for healing, white for purification, red for love. See Appendix 1 for a list of colors and their magical effects.

Hold the jar, bottle or bowl of mixture in your hands. Sense the nonaligned (i.e., nonspecific) energies it contains.

Visualize yourself with the type of power desired for the mixture. For example, see yourself bursting with health and vitality, or happily in love.

This can be difficult. If you aren't adept at visualization, simply *feel* your magical need. Build up your emotions regarding the mixture's purpose. If you're sick, *feel* the depth of your desire and need to be well.

Now begin to build up your personal power. You might do this by slowly tensing your muscles, working from your feet up. When your whole body is tense, *visualize* (or feel) the power concentrating in your hands.

Next, with the energy tingling in your hands, visualize it streaming into the mixture, perhaps as shimmering strands of purplish white light that pour from your palms and enter the herbs. You may wish to visualize this energy in accordance with the candle's color— blue for healing, for instance.

If you have difficulty imagining this, state in a firm voice your magical intention. For a healing bath mixture you might say something along the lines of:

I charge you by the Sun and Moon
To consume disease,
To wash away its causes and to heal.
So mote it be!

A protective incense may be empowered with such words as these:

I charge you by the Sun and Moon
To drive off negativity and evil
Wherever you are consumed by fire.
So mote it be!

An oil might be empowered to "destroy disease where you are rubbed" or to "spread peace and calm." Again, feel free to compose your own words, suiting them to the mixture and the magical need.

When you feel drained of energy, when you know that it has left your body and entered the mixture, set it down and shake your hands vigorously for a few moments. This cuts off the flow of energy.

Relax your body. Pinch out the candle flame (or snuff it out) and save for use with another empowering ritual of the same type.
The empowerment is done.

This ritual takes little time and can be incredibly powerful. It doesn't require memorizing pages of archaic language or purchasing expensive tools. Once you've become accustomed to the ritual it becomes second nature.

Using herb mixtures that haven't been empowered is one mark of a lazy herbalist. After all, why go to the trouble of creating your own incenses, oils and brews and then omit the final step that energizes and prepares the mixture for ritual use?

Such a ritual, by the way, can be used to charge herb products purchased from occult supply stores.

4
Ingredients

PLANTS, GUMS, RESINS and oils are the tools of the herb magician. These are manifested energies that are available for use in magic.

It is to the benefit of all who use herbs to learn them as intimately as they can. It's important that herb magicians know not only which herbs to use in compounding mixtures but also how to obtain them, as well as something of their natures.

On a purely physical level, it's vital to be able to identify the best quality ingredients—the freshest herbs and the finest gums and resins.

A chapter of this type may not seem necessary to many herb magicians. "Give us the recipes and forget all this junk," some might say.

To those I answer, "Fine. Skip this chapter and jump right into Part II."

Serious herb magicians can continue reading, and in doing so, learn some of the finer aspects of magical herbalism.

Obtaining Herbs
There are three main methods of obtaining herbs for use in compounding magical mixtures: collection, growing and purchasing.

Collection
Walking in the woods, striding through deserts, climbing mountains or strolling along beaches are refreshing activities in and of themselves. When combined with a quest for magical herbs they can be exciting adventures.

There are some basic ideas to follow here:

* Collect only what you need. Do you really need five paper sacks full of mugwort?

* Attune with the plant before collecting from it. You may do this by placing your hands around it and feeling its energies, chanting a simple rhyme or a few words that describe why you're taking part of its energy (leaves and flowers), and/or by placing an object of worth in the soil at the base of the plant. If you have nothing else with you, put a coin or dollar bill beneath the plant before harvesting. This represents your willingness to give of yourself in exchange for the plant's sacrifice.

* Never collect more than 25 percent of the plant's growth. If you're collecting roots you must, of course, take the whole plant, so be sure to leave other nearby plants of the same type untouched.

* Don't collect after rain or heavy dew. At least, not until the Sun has dried the plants. Otherwise they might mold while drying.

* Choose your collection site carefully. Never collect plants near highways, roads, stagnant or polluted waters, near factories or military installations.

To dry herbs you've harvested, strip off the leaves or flowers and lay on ceramic, wooden or steel racks in a warm, dry place out of direct sunlight. Or place them in baskets and shake the herbs daily until dry. Store in airtight, labelled jars.*

Growing

Growing your own herbs is an intriguing art. Herbs can be difficult to successfully grow, but when they do, you're rewarded with a plentiful supply of flowers, leaves, seeds, barks and roots.

Any bookstore or library will have good books outlining the basic steps in growing herbs. Find one and utilize the information in it, taking into account local growing conditions. Most nurseries and department stores stock herb seeds and starter plants.

Magically guard herbs when growing them by placing small quartz crystals in the soil. To ensure that they flourish, wear jade

---

* See *Magical Herbalism* for more information on harvesting and drying herbs.

when watering or tending them, or put a piece of moss-agate in the earth. When the plant has matured or is large enough, begin harvesting by using the basic system mentioned above. Thank the plant and the Earth for its treasures.

Purchasing

Many of the ingredients used in herb magic come from far-flung parts of the globe. While I'd love to grow a sandalwood tree on my front porch, it's just not possible.

So, many herbs have to be purchased. This doesn't lessen them in any way; in fact, the herb trade ensures that plant materials which would otherwise be unavailable can be obtained and used in magic.

Mail-order herb and essential oil suppliers are listed in Appendix 2. Send away for their catalogs, and you'll be able to buy magical botanicals from around the world while sipping herb tea in your living room.

Then again, most larger cities and towns have at least one herb shop or health food store which stocks herbs. Check your phone book.

Take care when buying essential oils. If the salesperson says, "Yes, it's *real* jasmine oil!" and it carries a $3.00 price tag, it's real *synthetic* jasmine oil. Even those oils labelled "essential" are usually the products of the laboratory rather than of the fields.

One good yardstick is price. Most true essential oils sell for between $10 and $40 per 1/3 or 1/2 ounce. Some, such as camomile, yarrow, cardamom, neroli, jasmine and rose can be far costlier. Buy carefully!

Synthetics have long been used in magical herbalism, but I urge you to use only true essential oils. (See the Oils section in Part II for more information.)

Regarding herbs: Many stores can't be relied upon to lay in fresh stock at regular intervals, so the rosemary you buy may be several years old. In general, choose dried herbs with bright colors, with few stem pieces and with fresh smells.

Avoid all herbs that are mostly stem, that have varying discoloration, are insect-damaged or moldy. Also avoid any with little scent if the herb is usually heavily fragranced.

Buying by mail complicates this process—it's tough to determine whether the frankincense you've ordered is top quality. Simply avoid ordering more herbs from suppliers who send you lesser-quality botanicals.

And remember—suppliers are at the mercy of the growers. Obtaining a year-round supply of first-grade herbs is often difficult. So use what you can find and hunt for better supplies in the future.

A Dictionary of Plant Materials Used in Magic

This is an alphabetical listing of some of the herbs, gums and oils found in this book's recipes. A few other substances—such as sulfur—are also included. Additionally, this section discusses plant materials that haven't been mentioned in my previous herb books.

It is designed to introduce you to exotic herbs and oils, with hints on their magical effects. Specific guidelines on selecting the best quality gums and resins are also included. For some of the difficult-to-obtain oils, gums and woods, I've suggested substitutes that can be used in preparing the formulas in this book. (More substitution information can be found in Part III.)

ACACIA, GUM
(Acacia senegal)

Also known as acacia, gum senegal and gum arabic, this is produced by a tree that grows in Northern Africa. The species of acacia which produce gum arabic and gum acacia are so closely related that one product can be substituted for the other. (See Appendix 2 for mail-order sources.) Gum acacia is used in protective and psychic-awareness formulas.

ALOE, WOOD
(Aquilaria agallocha)

Wood aloe, also known as lignaloes, oriental lignaloes, wood aloes and lignum aloes, is a tree native to India. The odor of the wood is described as a combination of ambergris and sandalwood. If this wood is unavailable, try substituting it with the same amount of sandalwood sprinkled with a few drops of synthetic ambergris for incense use.

The last I purchased in San Diego cost, as mentioned previously, about $30 a pound.

Wood aloe is usually used in incenses of protection, consecration, success and prosperity.

Victoria
© 89

AMBER OIL

True amber oil is created from lesser-quality amber, which is fossilized pine resin millions of years old. It has a camphor-like odor with touches of pine scents, and is rarely available.

Most amber oils on the market today seem to be artificial ambergris mixtures.

It is used in love and healing mixtures.

AMBERGRIS

This scent, the product of sperm whales, was originally (and rarely) found washed up on beaches. It was heavily used in magical and cosmetic perfumery. Early Arabs used it in cooking. Once the origins of ambergris were discovered, countless whales were killed to collect this precious substance.

It has long been used in aphrodisiac-type oils and perfumes. Its odor is usually described as musty, musky and earthy.

True ambergris is best avoided in these ecologically minded times. Many whale species are nearly extinct. Its exorbitant price is another reason for leaving it to the top perfumery companies to use in compounding perfumes (if it is used at all).

Artificial ambergris or ambergris compounds are widely available, and are usually sold simply as "ambergris."

If you can't find even artificial ambergris oil, try substituting the following bouquet, or compound, which approximates true ambergris:

AMBERGRIS BOUQUET

Cypress Oil
Patchouly Oil (a few drops)

ASAFOETIDA
(*Ferula asafoetida*)

This native of Afghanistan and Eastern Iran has a nauseating odor to which the frequent user eventually becomes accustomed, some claim. Even so, I don't keep asafoetida in my home, let alone add it to protective or exorcistic incenses.

If you wish, substitute tobacco, valerian root or any of the herbs listed under these headings (protection, exorcism) in Part III of this book. Rather unbelievably, asafoetida is used in Indian cooking.

BDELLIUM, GUM
Please see introduction to Part III.

BERGAMOT MINT OIL
(*Mentha citrata*)
Bergamot is a small plant with a minty-lemony fragrance. It is commonly used in money and prosperity oils. Synthesized versions of this oil abound but should not be used. Instead, make up the bouquet suggested below:

BERGAMOT MINT BOUQUET
Lemon Oil
Lemongrass Oil
Peppermint Oil

CAMPHOR
(*Cinnamomum camphora*)
This white, intensely scented crystalline substance is distilled from a tree native to China and Japan.

For many years true camphor wasn't sold in the United States. All "camphor blocks" and mothballs were made of synthetic camphor, which is extremely poisonous.

Quite recently, through the help of a friend, I discovered a commercial source for camphor in San Diego. Camphor currently sells for around $8.00 a pound.

It is added in small amounts to Lunar and chastity-type mixtures.

CIVET
Real civet is the product of the civet cat, which lives in Sri Lanka, India and Africa. Unlike other animal oils, the animal wasn't usually killed to obtain civet but was painfully scraped.

True civet has an overpowering gamey odor, which is highly offensive to the nose. In tiny amounts it smells sweet, so it has been used in nearly every high-priced perfume.

Today, artificial civet is widely available, and is fine for use in magical oils designed to attract love and passion.

Again, as with all animal products, I don't recommend using the actual substance. The synthetics and compounds that duplicate their aromas are preferred to the genuine and expensive substances. Avoid using all animal products in herb magic!

COPAL
(Bursera spp.)

Copal is a white, pale yellow or yellowish orange gum resin. When smoldered on charcoal it produces a rich, delicious, piney-lemony fragrance. Copal is the North American equivalent of frankincense. While it lacks some of the latter's bittersweet odor, it is a fine substitute for the famous gum resin. When frankincense is left smoldering on charcoal for some time, it eventually emits a very bitter scent. Copal's odor, however, never varies as it burns.

It is native to Mexico and Central America, and has been used as incense in religious and magical ceremonies for untold hundreds of years, beginning perhaps with the Mayans or even prior to the days of that fabled people.

Copal is my favorite gum resin. Frequent trips to Tijuana (I live about 20 miles from the border) have yielded a wide range of copal, varying greatly in price, appearance, scent and quality. The finest copal is a pale to dark yellow color with an intense resinous-citrus odor. It is usually sold in large chunks and may contain leaf fragments.

It is excellent used in all protection, purification and exorcism incenses. It is also effective when burned to promote spirituality.

Copal makes a fine if rather sticky tincture (see Part II: Tinctures). Most of the copal sold in the United States is grown on plantations in the Phillipines.

EUPHORBIUM
Please see the introduction to Part III.

LOTUS OIL
There are no genuine lotus oils, though such are frequently sold. Perfumers simply haven't found a way to capture the scent of this aquatic plant. All lotus oils are blends of natural essential oils or synthetic substances that strive to duplicate the delicious scent of the lotus.

Lotus oil is used in spirituality, healing and meditation formulas.

Commercial lotus oil can certainly be used where called for. However, if you wish to create your own, try the following recipe:

LOTUS BOUQUET

Rose
Jasmine
White (or light) Musk
Ylang-Ylang

Mix until the scent is heavy, floral and "warm."

MAGNOLIA OIL
(*Magnolia spp.*)
Just as with lotus, no genuine magnolia oil exists. Use a compound magnolia oil or compose your own. If possible, have a fresh magnolia flower nearby while mixing the below recipe. Try to capture its haunting fragrance by combining the following oils:

MAGNOLIA BOUQUET

Neroli Oil
Jasmine Oil
Rose Oil
Sandalwood Oil

Magnolia oil is often used in recipes designed to promote harmony, psychic awareness and peace.

MASTIC, GUM
(*Pistachia lentiscus*)
This resin can be quite difficult to find (but see Appendix 2 for possible sources). If it is unavailable, try substituting a combination, equal parts, of gum arabic and frankincense.

MUSK
A famous perfumery substance, musk was extracted from the scent glands of the musk deer, a native of China and the Far East. Though the extraction could be made without killing the deer, the wild animals were usually slaughtered. Thus, high-priced perfumes

were made at the expense of life.

Currently, synthetic musks are readily available and have virtually overtaken the major perfumers, who seldom use genuine musk. As with ambergris, civet and all animal products anciently used in magic, genuine musk isn't necessary or even recommended for use.

When selecting a musk, choose one that smells warm, woodsy, gamey and rich.

Musk is generally used in formulas involving courage, sexual attraction and purification.

Herbal musk substitutes include ambrette seeds, spikenard roots, sumbul roots, musk thistle flowers and mimulus flowers.

NEW-MOWN HAY OIL
This is another perfumer's fantasy. To capture the honey-fresh scent of a just-mowed field of hay, try the below recipe:

NEW-MOWN HAY BOUQUET

Woodruff Oil
Tonka Oil
Lavender Oil
Bergamot Oil
Oakmoss Oil

New-mown hay oil is used to "turn over a new leaf," to attain a fresh perspective on a difficult problem, and especially to break negative habits (such as addictions) and thought patterns.

OAKMOSS
(*Evernia prunastri; E. fururacea*)
Oakmoss is any of several lichens growing on oak and spruce trees in central and southern Europe.

Oakmoss has a warm, slightly spicy odor and is used in money-drawing mixtures. It is most often encountered in recipes in its oil form. It can be imitated with the following compound:

OAKMOSS BOUQUET

Vetivert Oil
Cinnamon Oil

SANDALWOOD
(*Santalum album*)
Sandalwood is one of the most valuable woods in the world. It has a rich, mysterious scent and is widely used in magical and religious incenses. Heartwood produces the best quality sandalwood. It is a light brown to reddish color with a deep scent. Lower grades, which are white with little scent, aren't recommended for use in magic. Sandalwood is used in protection, exorcism, healing and spirituality formulas. Cedar can be substituted for sandalwood if the true wood can't be found.

STORAX (Also known as "styrax.")
(*Liquidambar orientalis*)
This resin, which originates in a tree growing in southwest Asia Minor, has a resinous floral scent. It has long been used in magical and religious perfumes and incenses.
It is difficult to obtain. Low-priced storax oil, when found, is usually an imitation of the genuine product. Substitute benzoin essential oil for storax. This doesn't duplicate the fragrance, but it can be used in magical formulas. Or, use any of the oil forms of the herbs mentioned under the appropriate heading in Part III: Substitutions.

SULFUR
This is a light yellow mineral that is fairly odorless until burned, upon which it sends up clouds of the familiar rotten-egg scent.
It is used in exorcistic and protective incenses but isn't recommended because of its persistent, nauseating scent.
Substitute any of the exorcistic or protective herbs listed in Part III of this book, or simply use tobacco.

SWEET PEA OIL
(*Lathrys odoratus*)
No genuine sweet pea oil is available. Try creating your own along the lines of the following formula:

SWEET PEA BOUQUET
Neroli
Ylang-Ylang Oil
Jasmine Oil
Benzoin Oil

It is used in love and friendship recipes.

TONKA
(*Dipteryx odorada; D. spp.*)
    Tonka beans are obtained from Eastern Venezuela and Brazil.
They have long been used in creating artificial vanilla, which was
widely sold in the United States until it was determined that this
product was a health hazard.
    Tonka beans are used in love and money-attraction sachets. The
synthesized oil is also used. Try this substitute instead:

TONKA BOUQUET
Benzoin Oil
a few drops Vanilla tincture (extract)

TRAGACANTH, GUM
(*Astragalus gummifer; A. spp.*)
    Gum tragacanth is used as a binding agent in creating incense
cones, blocks, and sticks. It is a white, slightly bitter-smelling powder
which originates in Asia Minor. Some herb shops stock gum tragacanth, as do a few mail-order suppliers. It (or gum arabic) is a necessity
in the manufacture of all combustible incenses.

TUBEROSE
(*Polianthes tuberosa*)
    A richly scented, intensely sweet white flower native to Mexico.
The synthesized oil is used in love-attracting mixtures, but true
tuberose essential oil (actually an absolute) is rarely available. Create
a useful substitute:

TUBEROSE BOUQUET
Ylang-Ylang Oil
Rose Oil
Jasmine Oil
Neroli Oil (just a hint)

YLANG-YLANG
(*Cananga odorata*)
This strange, beautifully scented flower is native to the Phillipines. Ylang-ylang essential oil is used in love formulas. It is available from virtually every mail-order supplier of essential oils and has a delicious scent.

5
Creating Your Own Recipes

THIS CHAPTER JUMPS into the future just a bit, but stay with me.

Say you've been working with herb magic, mixing up some of the recipes contained in this book. Once you've made up several mixtures you might grow restless. Though your magical pantry is stocked with incenses, oils, ointments and bath salts, that may not be enough. You want to make your own recipes.

This is to be expected. Experienced cooks usually create new dishes as situations demand. They may also whip up a new culinary creation for the pure enjoyment of so doing. The magical herbalist is often of the same temperament.

If after trying some of these formulas you'd like to make up your own recipes, you might wonder how to do it. In this chapter we'll discuss this process with full examples to make each step in the creation process clear. Though I recommend it, don't feel that you have to utilize this information. You can make one recipe from this book every week and not run out of projects for several years.

However, this chapter explains the basics for those who wish to create their own formulas.

Why bother doing this? Why not! Such mixtures will be yours alone, intimately connected with your personal beliefs and energies. In short, they may be more powerful simply because they're from you. Old recipes and those created by others certainly work, but it's exciting to create your own unique blends and see their results.

Here's one method to do this. Remember, though, to rely on your intuition when determining which ingredients to add, as well as their exact proportions. And have fun.

THE GOAL

The first step toward creating a new herb mixture is to determine the future product's *magical goal* or intent. You may have a definite need and are creating this substance to address that need. Or, you may simply be making a mixture to use in the future when some problem arises. If so, decide what you want it to do: bring money into your life, ease depression, create new love interests, draw health or power, protection or peace. For demonstration purposes here, let's say you need to make up a new magical protectant.

THE FORM

Once you've determined its purpose, decide on its *form*—incense, oil, bath salt, bath herbs, tincture, amulet, ointment and so on. Decide this by answering a few questions:

Which form is best suited to this type of goal? Obviously, some forms are more suitable to certain magical interests than others. You wouldn't make up a protection incense, for example, if you need to use it at the office or on your way to work. A protective amulet or oil would be more easily utilized.

Which procedures do I know the best? It's wise to use those processes that you have worked with in the past when creating your own blends. Better products are almost guaranteed. (I realize this may be premature if you're just starting to work with herbs.)

Which procedures produce the best results for me? For instance, if you're partial to incense, and find the combustible types (cones, blocks, sticks) to be less spectacular in creating your needed magical goal, mix a noncombustible incense. If you've found that burning oil-anointed candles produces the most satisfying results, blend an oil. Remember: Though such products do contain energies, it is their ability to put us into the state of *ritual consciousness* (see Glossary) that determines their effectiveness.

Which forms do I enjoy the most? If you abhor the thought of carrying a sachet, there's no reason to create one. However, if slipping into an herb-scented tub of warm water gets your powers flowing, you may decide to create a protective bath sachet or bath salt.

THE HERBS

Next, decide which herbs to use. Check the Magical Goals tables in Part III: Substitutions to find which type of herbs are magically related to your particular magical goal. For our purposes here, say you'll create a preliminary list of *protective herbs.*

Now check your herb stock. Though time-consuming, it's a good idea to maintain lists of your herb magic supplies. Keep a small notebook near your herbs. On one page (or more if necessary) write down all herbs and botanicals. On another page note the oils you have. On still a third, list all processing supplies: cheesecloth, bottles, eyedroppers, cloth, cord and thread, potassium nitrate, alcohol. On a fourth, keep a list of herbs and oils you wish to obtain.

Each time you run out of an herb or oil, make a notation on the fourth page to remind yourself. And remember to update all lists as you lay in new stock.

This may seem to be unnecessary work, but such a book will save you from rummaging through your assorted bottles just to discover what you have.

The most experienced magical herbalist usually has a cluttered herb cabinet, with dozens or hundreds of jars of varying sizes crowded onto shelves and stuffed into corners. Even if they're kept in roughly alphabetical order or divided by type (such as gums, barks, flowers), checking each bottle can be a monumental job.

Back to our plan. Compare your preliminary list against your stock list. If you have several of the herbs mentioned, fine. If not, buy or harvest more.

Or, determine other herbs that could be used in a protection formula. There are a number of ways to do this. Use your intuition. Look in other books. Or consult the planetary and elemental lists in Part III of this work, cross-referencing the various lists.

For example, since protection is a magical act closely related to the Sun and Mars and often utilizes herbs of the element of Fire, check these tables in Part III as well. Below is a list of various types of magical intentions, together with planets and elements that govern these goals:

BANISHING: Saturn, Fire
BEAUTY: Venus, Water
COURAGE: Mars, Fire
DIVINATION: Mercury, Air
EMPLOYMENT: Sun, Jupiter, Earth
ENERGY: Sun, Mars, Fire
EXORCISM: Sun, Fire

FERTILITY: Moon, Earth
FRIENDSHIPS: Venus, Water
HAPPINESS: Venus, Moon, Water
HEALING, HEALTH: Moon, Mars (to burn away disease),
    Fire (ditto), Water
THE HOME: Saturn, Earth, Water
JOY, HAPPINESS: Venus, Water
LOVE: Venus, Water
MONEY, WEALTH: Jupiter, Earth
PEACE: Moon, Venus
POWER: Sun, Mars, Fire
PROTECTION: Sun, Mars, Fire
PSYCHISM: Moon, Water
PURIFICATION: Saturn, Fire, Water
SEX: Mars, Venus, Fire
SLEEP: Moon, Water
SPIRITUALITY: Sun, Moon, Water
SUCCESS: Sun, Fire
TRAVEL: Mercury, Air
WISDOM, INTELLIGENCE: Mercury, Air

Find the planet(s) and element that governs your particular magical need and consult the tables in Part III to enlarge your preliminary list of herbs.

Once again compare this list with your stock list. Cross out any you don't have at the present time. Let's say the following is the corrected and enlarged list of protective herbs that you have in stock:

Rosemary	Frankincense
Dill	Fennel
Rose Geranium	Rue
Tarragon	Fern
Basil	Cinnamon
Orange peel	Garlic
Mint	Allspice
Pine	Cedar
Juniper	

Now determine which herbs are most favorable to the type of product you've decided to make. Some of these are immediately inappropriate for incense use. Though garlic is a fine protective herb, it's best not to use it in incense formulas. So cross this one off. If necessary, and if you haven't already done so, light a charcoal block (see Incense in Part II), place it in an incense burner, and burn a bit of each of these herbs. Once again, remove those which don't appeal to you from your enlarged preliminary list. Your smaller list of herbs may now now look something like this:

Rosemary	Frankincense
Basil	Cinnamon
Orange peel	Pine
Cedar	Juniper

Eight herbs are left. In a sense, the recipe has formulated itself. After determining the relative amounts of each ingredient, you could mix the above herbs, empower them, and burn as a protective incense.

Or you could create a recipe using only a few of these. Some possible combinations include:

#1	#2	#3	#4
Frankincense	Frankincense	Frankincense	Frankincense
Cinnamon	Juniper	Pine	Orange peel
Juniper	Cedar	Basil	Cinnamon
	Pine		Juniper

Many others are possible. You'll notice that I've included frankincense in each combination. In general, use at least one gum resin in every recipe. Resins include frankincense, myrrh, benzoin, arabic, mastic, copal and dragon's blood. Even if one of these gums doesn't show up on the substitution lists in Part III, include one for best results in your new incense.

Once you've decided on a formula, copy it down on a three-by-five-inch index card or in your herbal notebook. Even if you think you'll change it later, *copy it down!* Give the blend a name as well.

Now compound the incense, grinding herbs if necessary in your mortar and pestle, mixing and aligning their energies. Then empower and use, or store in a labelled bottle until needed. You've just created a new incense.

This same basic system can be used to formulate nearly any personal recipe for any type of magical product. Those which are dedicated to specific deities, however, are created in a somewhat different manner.

If you wish to invent a formula in honor of a goddess or god, check into mythology to discover which plants (if any) were used in their worship.* These are ritually appropriate.

Or, use the herbs and plants which relate to the deity's basic influences. For example, in the Pele Incense recipe included in this new edition, fiery herbs are used to honor the Hawaiian goddess of volcanoes. Though fiery Hawaiian plants would be ideal, they aren't easily obtainable on the mainland. Therefore, the ones listed are acceptable substitutes.

With these simple steps you can create magical products for an endless variety of uses. Rely on your inner wisdom. Research. Experiment.

And most of all, enjoy the powers of herbs.

---

* A list of such plants can be found in *Wicca: A Guide for the Solitary Practitioner* (Scott Cunningham, Llewellyn, 1988).

Part II

Processing and Recipes

Incense

INCENSE HAS SMOLDERED on magicians' altars for at least 5,000 years. It was burned in antiquity to mask the odors of sacrificial animals, to carry prayers to the Gods, and to create a pleasing environment for humans to meet with Deity.

Today, when the age of animal sacrifices among most Western magicians is long past, the reasons for incense use are varied. It is burned during magic to promote ritual consciousness, the state of mind necessary to rouse and direct personal energy. This is also achieved through the use of magical tools, by standing before the candle-bewitched altar, and by intoning chants and symbolic words.

When burned prior to magical workings, fragrant smoke also purifies the altar and the surrounding area of negative, disturbing vibrations. Though such a purification isn't usually necessary, it, once again, helps create the appropriate mental state necessary for the successful practice of magic.

Specially formulated incenses are burned to attract specific energies to the magician and to aid her or him in charging personal power with the ritual's goal, eventually creating the necessary change.

Incense, in common with all things, possesses specific vibrations. The magician chooses the incense for magical use with these vibrations in mind. If performing a healing ritual, she or he burns a mixture composed of herbs that promote healing.

When the incense is smoldered in a ritual setting it undergoes a transformation. The vibrations, no longer trapped in their physical form, are released into the environment. Their energies, mixing with those of the magician, speed out to effect the changes necessary to the manifestation of the magical goal.

Not all incense formulas included in this book are strictly for magical use. Some are smoldered in thanks or offering to various aspects of Deity, just as juniper was burned to Inanna 5,000 years ago in Sumer. Other blends are designed to enhance Wiccan rituals. You needn't limit incense use to ritual, but avoid burning healing incense just for the smell, or to freshen up your stale house. Burning magically constructed and empowered incenses when they're not needed is a waste of energy. If you wish to burn a pleasant-smelling incense, compound a household mixture for this purpose.

The Materials

Incenses are composed of a variety of leaves, flowers, roots, barks, woods, resins, gums and oils. Semiprecious stones may also be added to incenses to lend their energies to the mixture, much as emeralds were once burned in fires by ancient Meso-American peoples.

Out of the literally hundreds of potential incense ingredients, perhaps 14 are most frequently used. Keep a stock of these herbs on hand if you plan to make several incenses. These might include:

Frankincense	Pine needles or resin (pitch)
Myrrh	Juniper
Benzoin	Sandalwood
Copal	Cedar
Rose petals	Thyme
Bay	Basil
Cinnamon	Rosemary

Be aware that many plants (if not all!) smell quite different when being smoldered. Sweet scents turn sour fast.

If you wish, take a large number of dried and finely ground plant substances (flowers, leaves, bark, roots) and drop a small portion of each herb onto a hot charcoal block; then decide whether the scent is pleasing or not. You might make a notation of each botanical and its scent in a special notebook reserved for this purpose or on three-by-five-inch cards. Also note any psychic or other sensations you notice with each burning herb. In this way you'll eventually build up a thorough knowledge of incense materials, which will aid you in your herbal magic.

Do remember that, as surprising at it sounds, scent isn't a factor in magical incense, except very generally: sweet odors are usually used for positive magical goals, while foul scents are used for banishing rituals.

Scent is power. It allows us to slip into ritual consciousness, thereby allowing us to raise power, infuse it with the proper energies, and send it forth toward the magical goal. However, not all magical incenses smell sweet. Some have strong, resinous odors; others, intensely bitter scents. Incenses intended for ritual use are blended to provide the proper energies during magical operations—not to smell pleasing to the human nose.

Don't let this scare you away from incense, however. Most of our associations with "pleasant" and "foul" odors are learned, and our noses aren't as capable of determining various scents as they should be. Retrain your nose to accept exotic scents, and the art of incense burning will become a joy, not something to be tolerated for the sake of magic.

Occult supply stores stock incense intended for use in magic. Many rare blends can be purchased for a few dollars. While these are magically effective, you may wish to make some of your own.

The Two Forms of Incense

Incense is virtually a necessity in magical practice, but there seems to be a great mystery surrounding its composition. Fortunately with practice, it's surprisingly easy to make incense.

Two types of incense are used in magic: the *combustible* and the *noncombustible*. The former contains potassium nitrate (saltpeter) to aid in burning, while the latter does not. Therefore combustible incense can be burned in the form of bricks, cones, sticks and other shapes, whereas noncombustible incense must be sprinkled onto glowing charcoal blocks to release its fragrance.

Ninety-five percent of the incense used in magic is the noncombustible, raw or granular type. Why? Perhaps because it's easier to make. Herbal magicians are notoriously practical people.

Also, some spells (particularly divinatory or evocational rites; see the Glossary for unfamiliar words) call for billowing clouds of smoke. Since cone, stick and block incense burn at steady rates, such effects are impossible with their use.

The advantages of combustible incense can outweigh its

drawbacks, depending on circumstance. Need to burn some money-drawing incense for an unexpected ritual? You could take out the censer, a charcoal block and the incense, light the charcoal, place it in the censer and sprinkle incense onto it. Or you could pull out a cone of money-drawing incense, light it, set it in the censer and get on with your ritual.

Different magicians prefer different types of incense. I'm partial to raw or noncombustible incenses, but the wise magical herbalist stocks both types. Hence, instructions for the preparation of both forms appear here.

Noncombustible Incense

Be sure you have all necessary ingredients. If you lack any, decide on substitutions (see Chapter 5 or Part III for ideas).

Each ingredient must be finely ground, preferably to a powder, using either a mortar and pestle or an electric grinder. Some resins won't powder easily, but with practice you'll find the right touch. When I first worked with herbs I couldn't powder frankincense. It kept on gumming to the sides of the mortar and to the tip of the pestle. After a while I stopped fighting it (and cursing it, I'll admit—not a good thing to do with herbs used in incenses) and got into the flow of the work. The frankincense came out just fine.

When all is ready, fix your mind on the incense's goal—protection, love, health. In a large wooden or ceramic bowl, mix the resins and gums together with your hands. While mingling these fragrant substances, also mix their energies. Visualize your personal power—vibrating with your magical goal—exiting your hands and entering the incense. It is this that makes homemade incense more effective than its commercial counterparts.

Next, mix in all the powdered leaves, barks, flowers and roots. As you mix, continue to visualize or concentrate on the incense's goal.

Now add any oils or liquids (wine, honey, etc.) that are included in the recipe. Just a few drops are usually sufficient. On the subject of oils: If there's a sufficient amount of dry ingredients in the recipe, you can substitute an oil for an herb you lack. Simply ensure that the oil is an essential oil, for synthetics smell like burning plastic when smoldered.

Once all has been thoroughly mixed, add any powdered gemstones or other power boosters. A few—not many—of the recipes in this book call for a pinch of powdered stone.

To produce this, simply take a small stone of the required type and pound it in a metal mortar and pestle (or simply smash it with a hammer against a hard surface). Grind the resulting pieces into a powder and add no more than the scantest pinch to the incense. One general power-boosting "stone" is amber. A pinch of this fossilized resin added to any mixture will increase its effectiveness, but this can be rather expensive.

The incense is now fully compounded. Empower the incense (see Chapter 2) and it is done. Store in a tightly capped jar. Label carefully, including the name of the incense and date of composition. It is ready for use when needed.

Combustible Incense

Combustible incense (in the form of cones, blocks and sticks) is fairly complex in its composition, but many feel the results are worth the extra work.

To be blunt, this aspect of incense composition isn't easy. Some of the ingredients are difficult to obtain, the procedure tends to be messy and frustrating, and some even question whether combustible incense is as magically effective as its noncombustible counterpart. For years I hesitated making or using sticks, cones or blocks because they contain potassium nitrate. This substance is magically related to Mars, and I felt this might add unneeded aggressive energies to the incense.

But when I considered that the charcoal blocks I use to burn noncombustible incense also contain saltpeter, I relented and experimented. However, to this day I prefer the raw form. To each their own.

At first, making combustible incense may seem impossible to accomplish. But persevere and you'll be rewarded with the satisfaction of lighting incense cones you've made yourself.

Gum tragacanth glue or mucilage is the basic ingredient of all molded incenses. Gum tragacanth is available at some herb stores; at one time in the past every drugstore carried it. It is rather expensive ($3.00 an ounce as of this writing), but a little will last for months.

To make tragacanth glue, place a teaspoon of the ground herb in a glass of warm water. Mix thoroughly until all particles are dispersed. To facilitate this, place in a bowl and whisk or beat with an egg beater. This will cause foam to rise, but it can be easily skimmed off or allowed to disperse. The gum tragacanth has enormous absorption qualities; an ounce will absorb up to one gallon of water in a week.

Let the tragacanth absorb the water until it becomes a thick, bitter-smelling paste. The consistency of the mixture depends on the form of incense desired. For sticks (the most difficult kind to make) the mixture should be relatively thin. For blocks and cones a thicker mucilage should be made. This is where practice comes in handy; after a session or two you will automatically know when the mucilage is at the correct consistency.

If you can't find tragacanth, try using gum arabic in its place. This, too, absorbs water. I haven't tried using it for incense yet, but all reports say it works as well as tragacanth.

When you have made the trag glue, cover with a wet cloth and set aside. It will continue to thicken as it sits, so if it becomes too thick add a bit of water and stir thoroughly.

Next, make up the incense base. Not all formulas in this book can be used for combustible incense; in fact, most of them were designed to be used as noncombustible incenses. Fortunately, by adding the incense to a base it should work well. Here's one standard formula for an incense base:

CONE INCENSE BASE

6 parts ground Charcoal (*not* self-igniting)
1 part ground Benzoin
2 parts ground Sandalwood
1 part ground Orris root (this "fixes" the scent)
6 drops essential oil (use the oil form of one of the ingredients in the incense)
2 to 4 parts mixed, *empowered* incense

Mix the first four ingredients until all are well blended. Add the drops of essential oil and mix again with your hands. The goal is to create a powdered mixture with a fine texture. If you wish, run the mixture through a grinder or the mortar again until it is satisfactory.

Add two to four parts of the completed and empowered incense mixture (created according to the instructions for Noncombustible

Incense above). Combine this well with your hands.

Then using a small kitchen scale, weigh the completed incense and add ten percent potassium nitrate. If you've made ten ounces of incense, add one ounce potassium nitrate. Mix this until the white powder is thoroughly blended.

Saltpeter should constitute no more than ten percent of the completed bulk of the incense. If any more is added, it will burn too fast; less, and it might not burn at all.

Potassium nitrate isn't difficult to obtain. I buy mine at drug stores, so check these (it isn't usually on the shelf; ask for it at the pharmacy). If you have no luck, try chemical supply stores.

Next, add the tragacanth glue. Do this a teaspoon at a time, mixing with your hands in a large bowl until all ingredients are wetted. For cone incense you'll need a very stiff, dough-like texture. If it is too thick it won't properly form into cones and will take forever to dry. The mixture should mold easily and hold its shape.

On a piece of waxed paper, shape the mixture into basic cone shapes, exactly like the ones you've probably bought. If this form isn't used, the incense might not properly burn.

When you've made up your cone incense, let it dry for two to seven days in a warm place. Your incense is finished.

For *block incense* make a 1/3 inch-thick square of the stiff dough on waxed paper. Cut with a knife into one-inch cubes as if you were cutting small brownies. Separately slightly and let dry.

Stick incense can be attempted as well. Add more tragacanth glue to the mixed incense and base until the mixture is wet but still rather thick. The trick here is in determining the proper thickness of the incense/tragacanth mixture and in finding appropriate materials to use. Professional incense manufacturers use thin bamboo splints, which aren't available. So try homemade wooden or bamboo splints, broom straws, very thin twigs, or those long wooden cocktail skewers that are available at some grocery and oriental food stores.

Dip the sticks into the mixture, let them sit upright and then dip again. Several dippings are usually necessary; this is a most difficult process.

When the sticks have accumulated a sufficient amount of the incense, poke them into a slab of clay or some other substance so that they stand upright. Allow them to dry.

One variation on stick incense making uses a stiffer incense dough. Pat down the dough on waxed paper until it is very thin. Place the stick on the dough. Roll a thin coating of dough around the stick. The incense shouldn't be more than twice the thickness of the stick. Squeeze or press it onto the stick so that it will stay put, and let dry.

Personally, I find the inclusion of charcoal in this recipe to be distasteful and unnecessary. It makes it imperative that you wash your hands numerous times throughout this process. Although traditional, charcoal also lends a peculiar odor to the incense. So here's another recipe I've used with good results:

CONE INCENSE BASE #2

6 parts powdered Sandalwood (or Cedar, Pine, Juniper)
2 parts powdered Benzoin (or Frankincense, Myrrh, etc.)
1 part ground Orris root
6 drops essential oil (use the oil form of one of the incense ingredients)
3 to 5 parts *empowered* incense mixture

In this recipe, powdered wood is used in place of the charcoal. Use sandalwood if it's included in the incense recipe. If not, use cedar, pine or juniper, depending on the type of incense to be made. Try to match the wood base of this incense to the incense's recipe. If you can't, simply use sandalwood.

Mix the first three ingredients until combined. Add the oil and mix again. Then add three to five parts of the completed incense to this. Again, this should be a powder. Weigh and add ten percent potassium nitrate.

Mix, add the gum tragacanth glue, combine again and mold in the methods described above.

Rules of Combustible Incense Composition

Here are some guidelines to follow when compounding combustible incense. These are for use with the Cone Incense Base #2 recipe above. If they aren't followed, the incense won't properly burn. There's less room for experimentation here than with noncombustible incenses.

First off, *never* use more than ten percent saltpeter. Ever!

Also, keep woods (such as sandalwood, wood aloe, cedar, juniper and pine) and gum resins (frankincense, myrrh, benzoin, copal) in the proper proportions: *at least twice as much powdered wood as resins*. If there's more resinous matter, the mixture won't burn. Naturally, depending on the type of incense you're adding to the base, you may have to juggle some proportions accordingly. Simply ensure that frankincense and its kin never constitute more than one-third of the final mixture, and all should be well.

Though this hasn't covered all aspects of combustible incense making (that could be a book in itself), it should provide you with enough guidelines to make your own. Experiment, but keep these rules in mind.

Incense Papers

Incense papers are a delightful variation of combustible incense. Here, rather than using charcoal and gum tragacanth, tinctures and paper are the basic ingredients. When finished you'll have produced several strips of richly scented paper that can be smoldered with a minimum of fuss.

To make incense papers, take a piece of white blotter paper and cut it into six-inch strips about an inch wide.

Next, add one and one-half teaspoons potassium nitrate to one-half cup very warm water. Stir until the saltpeter is completely dissolved.

Soak the paper strips in the saltpeter solution until thoroughly saturated. Hang them up to dry.

You now have paper versions of the charcoal blocks used to burn incense. The obstacle in scenting them is to overcome the normal smell of burning paper. For this reason, heavy fragrances should be used, such as tinctures. (See Tinctures section in this book.)

Tinctures compounded from gums and resins seem to produce the best results. I've tried using true essential oils with incense papers but without much success.

Empower the tincture(s) with your magical need, then pour a few drops of the tincture onto one strip of paper. Smear this over the paper and add more drops until it is completely coated on one side.

Hang the strip up to dry and store in labelled, airtight containers until needed.

To speed drying, turn on the oven to a low temperature, leave the door open, and place the soaked incense papers on the rack. Remove them when dry.

Generally speaking, incense papers should be made with one tincture rather than mixtures. But, once again, try various formulas until you come up with positive results.

To use incense papers, simply remove one paper and hold it above your censer. Light one tip with a match, and after it is completely involved in flame, quickly blow it out. Place the glowing paper in your censer and let it smolder, visualizing or working your magical ritual.

Incense papers should burn slowly and emit a pleasant scent, but again your results will vary according to the strength of the tincture and the type of paper used.

Plain unscented incense papers can be used in place of charcoal blocks. For this purpose soak the papers in the potassium nitrate solution and let dry, then set one alight in the censer. Sprinkle a thin layer of the incense over the paper. As it burns the paper will also smolder your incense.

You may have difficulty in keeping incense paper lit. The secret here is to allow air to circulate below the papers. You can ensure this by either placing the paper on some heat-proof object in the censer, or by filling the censer with salt or sand and thrusting one end of the paper into this, much as you might with incense sticks. The paper should burn all the way to its end.

Incense papers are a simple and enjoyable alternative to normal combustible incense. Try them!

The Censer

Whether you use raw incense, blocks or incense papers, you'll need an incense burner. The censer can be anything from a gilt, chain-equipped, church-type affair to a bowl of sand or salt. It truly doesn't matter. I know occultists who've used the bowl-and-salt method for years, long after they could have afforded to purchase other censers.

Although I have several, perhaps my favorite censer is actually a mortar from Mexico. It is carved from lava, stands on three legs and is perfect for use as a censer.

Your own taste should determine which censer is right for you. If nothing else is available, use a bowl half-filled with sand or salt and get on with it. The sand protects the bowl and the surface on which it sits against heat. It also provides a handy place on which to prop up stick incense.

Using Combustible Incense

Simply light it, blow out the flame after the tip is glowing, and set it in the censer. As it burns visualize your magical goal manifesting in your life. It's that simple. You may wish to also burn candles of the appropriate color, perhaps anointed with a scented oil that is also aligned with your goal.

Naturally, incense may also be smoldered as a part of a larger ritual.

Using Noncombustible Incense

Light a self-igniting charcoal block (see below) and place it in a censer. Once the block is glowing and saltpeter within it has stopped sparkling, sprinkle a half-teaspoon or so of the incense on the block. Use a small spoon if you wish. It will immediately begin to burn, and in doing so, release fragrant smoke.*

Remember: Use just a small amount of incense at first. When the smoke begins to thin out, add more. If you dump on a spoonful of incense it will probably extinguish the charcoal block, so use small amounts. Incenses containing large amounts of resins and gums (frankincense, myrrh and so on) burn longer than those mainly composed of woods and leaves.

Don't knock off the ash that forms on top of the charcoal unless the incense starts to smell foul. In such a case, scrape off the burning incense and the ash with a spoon and add a fresh batch. Frankincense does tend to smell odd after smoldering for some time.

Incense can be burned as part of a magical ritual, to honor higher forces, or as a direct act of magic, such as to clear a house of negativity and to smooth peaceful vibrations throughout it.

---

* There's a difference between burning and smoldering; though I use such terms as "burn this incense" several times in this book, I really mean "smolder."

Charcoal Blocks

These are necessities for burning noncombustible incense. They're available in a wide range of sizes, from over an inch in diameter (they're usually round) to about a half-inch size. Most religious and occult supply stores stock them, and they can be obtained from mail-order suppliers (see Appendix 2).

Potassium nitrate is added to these charcoal blocks during their manufacture to help them ignite. When touched with a lit match, fresh charcoal blocks erupt into a sparkling fire which quickly spreads across the block. If you wish, hold the block. It may light easily. If so, quickly place it in the censer to avoid burning your fingers. Or, light the block in the censer itself, thereby preventing burns. This is somewhat harder to do.

Unfortunately, some charcoal blocks aren't fresh, have been exposed to moisture, or haven't been properly saturated with the potassium nitrate solution and so don't light well. If this is the case, relight the block until it is evenly glowing and red. Then pour on the incense.

Simple Incenses

These are one-herb incenses that can be burned on charcoal when needed. Since they aren't mixtures, I didn't include them in the following alphabetical listing of recipes but placed them here.

In effect they're instant incenses, needing no mixing or measuring. Simply grind and empower them before use.

Allspice

Burn to attract money and luck and to provide extra physical energy.

Arabic, Gum

Use for purification and protection of the home.

Bay

Use a small amount for purification, healing, protection and to sharpen psychic powers.

Benzoin

For purification, prosperity and increasing mental powers.

Cedar
Smolder for purification, protection, to speed healing and promote spirituality, and to obtain money.

Cinnamon
Burn to sharpen psychic powers, to draw money, speed healing, confer protection and to strengthen love.

Clove
Protection, exorcism, money, love and purification.

Copal
Burn for protection, cleansing, purification, to promote spirituality, and to purify quartz crystals and other stones before use in magic.

Dragon's Blood
Use for love, protection, exorcism and sexual potency.

Fern
Burn the dried fronds indoors to exorcise evil, and outdoors to bring rain.

Frankincense
Protection, exorcism, spirituality, love and consecration.

Juniper
Exorcism, protection, healing and love.

Myrrh
Healing, protection, exorcism, peace, consecration, meditation.

Pine
Smolder for money, purification, healing and exorcism.

Rosemary
Burn for protection, exorcism, purification, healing and to cause sleep; to restore or maintain youth, to bring love and to increase intellectual powers.

Sage
Smolder to promote healing and spirituality.

Sandalwood
For protection, healing, exorcism, spirituality.

Thyme
Health, healing, purification.

Incense Recipes

These recipes, unlike those that appeared in the previous edition of this book, now contain *suggested* proportions. Several new recipes have also been included, and others have in some instances been improved.

Those ingredients which are poisonous, restricted or illegal under current laws in the United States have been marked with an asterisk (*). These herbs aren't recommended! For best results substitute other, less dangerous ingredients for these herbs. Tobacco is always appropriate (see the introduction to Part III).

ABRAMELIN INCENSE

2 parts Myrrh
1 part Wood Aloe
a few drops Cinnamon oil

Burn to contact spirits during rituals or as a simple consecration incense to sanctify the altar or magical tools.

AIR INCENSE (*caution!*)

4 parts Benzoin
2 parts Gum Mastic
1 part Lavender
1 pinch Wormwood*
1 pinch Mistletoe*

Burn to invoke the powers of the element of Air, or to increase intellectual powers; to obtain travel; for communication, study and concentration, or to end drug addiction. Smolder during divinatory rituals.

ALTAR INCENSE

3 parts Frankincense
2 parts Myrrh
1 part Cinnamon

Burn as a general incense on the altar to purify the area.

APHRODITE INCENSE

1 part Cinnamon
1 part Cedar
a few drops Cypress oil

Burn during rituals designed to attract love.

APOLLO INCENSE

4 parts Frankincense
2 parts Myrrh
2 parts Cinnamon
1 part Bay

Burn during divination and healing rituals.

APPARITION INCENSE (*caution!*)

3 parts Wood Aloe
2 parts Coriander
1 part Camphor
1 part Mugwort
1 part Flax
1 part Anise
1 part Cardamom
1 part Chicory
1 part Hemp*

Burn to cause apparitions to appear, if you really want this to happen.

ARIES INCENSE

2 parts Frankincense
1 part Juniper
3 drops Cedarwood oil

Burn as a personal altar or household incense to increase your own powers.

ASTRAL TRAVEL INCENSE

3 parts Sandalwood
3 parts Benzoin
1 part Mugwort
1 part Dittany of Crete

Burn a small amount in the room to aid in projecting the astral body.

AQUARIUS INCENSE

1 part Sandalwood
1 part Cypress
1 part Pine resin

Burn as a personal altar or household incense to increase your own powers.

BABYLONIAN RITUAL INCENSE

3 parts Cedar
2 parts Juniper
1 part Cypress
1 part Tamarisk

Burn during Babylonian and Sumerian magical rituals, or when attuning with such deities as Inanna, Marduk, Enlil, Tiamat and others.

BELTANE INCENSE

3 parts Frankincense
2 parts Sandalwood
1 part Woodruff
1 part Rose petals
a few drops Jasmine oil
a few drops Neroli oil

Burn during Wiccan rituals on Beltane (April 30th) or on May Day for fortune and favors and to attune with the changing of the seasons.

BINDING INCENSE (*caution!*)

4 parts Nettle
4 parts Thistle
4 parts Knotgrass
1/4 part Nightshade*
1/4 part Aconite (Wolfsbane)*

Burn with caution during outdoor rituals to destroy baneful habits and thoughts. Small amounts only. *Do not inhale fumes!*

BORN AGAIN INCENSE

3 parts Frankincense
1 part Mullein
1 part Mums (Chrysanthemums)

Burn when distraught over the passing of a friend or loved one.

BUSINESS INCENSE

2 parts Benzoin
1 part Cinnamon
1 part Basil

Burn to attract customers.

CANCER INCENSE (MOONCHILDREN)

2 parts Myrrh
1 part Sandalwood
1 part Eucalyptus
1 part Lemon peel (or a few drops Lemon oil)

Use as a personal altar or household incense to increase your own powers.

CAPRICORN INCENSE

2 parts Sandalwood
1 part Benzoin
a few drops Patchouly oil

Use as a personal altar or household incense to increase your own powers.

CEREMONIAL MAGIC INCENSE

3 parts Frankincense
2 parts Gum Mastic
1 part Wood Aloe

This formula, from the *Key of Solomon* (see Bibliography), is typical of grimoire-type recipes. It can be used in general magical workings to raise power and to purify the area. Other recipes include such ingredients as mace, brandy and vervain.

CEREMONIAL MAGIC INCENSE #2

2 parts Frankincense
1 part Wood Aloe
a few drops Musk oil
a few drops Ambergris oil

Another like the above.

CIRCLE INCENSE

4 parts Frankincense
2 parts Myrrh
2 parts Benzoin
1 part Sandalwood
1/2 part Cinnamon
1/2 part Rose petals
1/4 part Vervain
1/4 part Rosemary
1/4 part Bay

Use for general workings in the Circle,* the ritual working space of Wiccans and magicians, and as a general ritual incense.

---

* The Circle is created by directing personal power to form a sphere of energy surrounding the ritual area. See Raymond Buckland's *The Complete Book of Witchcraft* or Scott Cunningham's *Wicca—A Guide for the Solitary Practitioner* for details.

CLEARING INCENSE

3 parts Frankincense
3 parts Copal
2 parts Myrrh
1 part Sandalwood

Burn this incense to clear your home of negative vibrations, especially when household members are arguing or when the house seems heavy and thick with anger, jealousy, depression, fear and other negative emotions. Leave the windows open while burning this mixture.

CONSECRATION INCENSE

2 parts Wood Aloe
1 part Mace
1 part Storax (or Gum Arabic)
1 part Benzoin

When purifying or consecrating magical tools, jewelry, quartz crystals and other stones, smolder this incense and pass the tool through its smoke several times. Do this while visualizing the fumes purifying the tool.

COURAGE INCENSE

2 parts Dragon's Blood
1 part Frankincense
1 part Rose Geranium leaves (or a few drops Rose Geranium oil)
a few drops Tonka bouquet
a few drops Musk oil

Smolder this incense when you lack courage. If you are in a situation where you cannot burn it, recall its scent and be strong. If tonka bouquet is unavailable, use tonka tincture or vanilla tincture (or extract).

CRYSTAL PURIFICATION INCENSE

2 parts Frankincense
2 parts Copal
1 part Sandalwood
1 part Rosemary
1 pinch finely powdered Salt
1 small, purified Quartz Crystal point

To use, pour a bit of the incense (leaving the crystal in the jar) onto charcoal. Smolder, and pass the crystals to be purified through the smoke, visualizing the smoke wafting away the stone's impurities. Naturally, this incense can be used in conjunction with the other recommended purifying rituals, or in place of them.*

CURSE-BREAKER INCENSE

2 parts Sandalwood
1 part Bay

Burn at night near an open window if you feel "cursed." Though curses are rare, if we believe we are cursed, we are! Therefore, smolder this incense and visualize it banishing all negativity from you. Repeat this ritual for seven nights during the Waning Moon, if possible or desirable.

CURSE-BREAKER INCENSE #2

2 parts Sandalwood
1 part Bay
1 part Rosemary

Another like the above.

CURSE-BREAKER INCENSE # 3

2 parts Frankincense
1 part Rosemary
1 part Dragon's Blood

Smolder to remove negativity in general.

---

* To cleanse the small quartz crystal, leave it in sunlight for a few days, place it in running water overnight, or bury it in the Earth for a week.

DIVINATION INCENSE (*caution!*)

1 part Clove*
1 part Chicory
1 part Cinquefoil

Smolder during or directly before using tarot cards, magic mirrors, quartz crystal spheres, rune stones and so on. But be aware: this incense doesn't smell great!

DIVINATION INCENSE # 2

2 parts Sandalwood
1 part Orange peel
1 part Mace
1 part Cinnamon

Another like the above, and this one smells better.

DREAM INCENSE

2 parts Sandalwood
1 part Rose petals
1 part Camphor
a few drops Tuberose bouquet
a few drops Jasmine oil

Burn a bit in the bedroom prior to sleep to produce psychic dreams. Remove the censer from the room before retiring. Use only genuine camphor (see Chapter 4). If this is unavailable, add a few drops spirits of camphor, which is available in most drug stores.

EARTH INCENSE (ELEMENTAL)

2 parts Pine resin (pitch) or needles
1 part Patchouly
1 pinch finely powdered Salt
a few drops Cypress oil

Burn for invoking the powers of the element of Earth for money, stability and so on. (See Part III for more information relating to the element of Earth.)

EARTH INCENSE (PLANETARY)

1 part Pine needles
1 part Thyme
a few drops Patchouly oil

Burn to honor the Earth, and for all Earth-reverencing rituals (see Part III for details.)

EGYPTIAN INCENSE

4 parts Frankincense
3 parts Gum Arabic
2 parts Myrrh
1 part Cedar
1 part Juniper
1 part Calamus
1 part Cinnamon

Burn during Egyptian rituals, or to honor any ancient Egyptian deity such as Isis, Osiris, Thoth, Anubis, Selket, Heket and so on.

EIGHTFOLD HEARTH INCENSE

2 parts Dragon's Blood
2 parts Myrrh
1 part Juniper
1/2 part Sassafras
1/2 part Orange flowers
1/2 part Rose petals

Burn for a safe, warm, loving home. Also give as a gift to others.

ESBAT INCENSE

4 parts Frankincense
3 parts Myrrh
2 parts Benzoin
1 part Sandalwood
1 part Gardenia petals
1/2 part Orris
1/2 part Thyme
1/2 part Poppy seed
1/2 part Rose petals

Burn during rituals and spells on the Full Moon, or at any Wiccan gathering other than the Sabbats (see Glossary).

EXORCISM INCENSE

3 parts Frankincense
1 part Rosemary
1 part Bay
1 part Avens
1 part Mugwort
1 part St. John's Wort
1 part Angelica
1 part Basil

Burn with open windows in disturbed places as a heavy purificatory incense, and breathe through your mouth while smoldering this.

FIRE INCENSE (ELEMENTAL)

3 parts Frankincense
2 parts Dragon's Blood
1 part Red Sandalwood
1 pinch Saffron
a few drops Musk oil

Smolder for summoning the powers and beings of Fire, and also for success, strength, protection, health, passion and other similar goals. Genuine saffron is prohibitively expensive; hence, the smallest pinch will suffice. If you have none in stock, substitute orange peel.

FIRE OF AZRAEL

1 part Sandalwood
1 part Cedar
1 part Juniper

Burn while scrying, or throw onto the coals of a fire once the flames have been quenched and gaze into them to see images form within them. The latter rite is best performed on a beach at night. Fire of Azrael incense is also used as a general psychism-inducing incense.

"FOR EMERGENCIES" INCENSE (*caution!*)
(inspired by Jim Alan's song "Talkin' Wicca Blues"*)

3 parts Frankincense
2 parts Dragon's Blood
2 parts Myrrh
1 part Rosemary
1 part Asafoetida*
1 part Cayenne*
1 part Grains of Paradise
1 part Rue*
1 part Garlic*

Burn to be rid of foul demons, wrathful spirits, tax collectors, drunks, and other noisome creatures. Stand back and hold your nose—or better still, leave the room while this incense is smoldering. Those herbs marked with an asterisk above aren't necessarily dangerous or baneful, but they emit powerful smoke that is irritating to the eyes, nose and lungs.

FULL MOON RITUAL INCENSE

3 parts Frankincense
1 part Sandalwood

Burn during Full Moon rituals, or simply to attune with the Moon.

---

* Write to Circle (you'll find their address in Appendix 2) for information on obtaining the tape *Circle Magick Music*, which includes this funny, clever song.

FULL MOON RITUAL INCENSE # 2

2 parts Sandalwood
2 parts Frankincense
1/2 part Gardenia petals
1/4 part Rose petals
a few drops Ambergris oil

Another like the above.

FULL MOON RITUAL INCENSE # 3

3 parts Gardenia petals
2 parts Frankincense
1 part Rose petals
1/2 part Orris
a few drops Sandalwood oil

A third like the above.

GAMES OF CHANCE INCENSE

2 parts Gum Mastic
2 parts Frankincense

Burn before gambling.

GEMINI INCENSE

2 parts Gum Mastic
1 part Citron (or 1 part mixed Orange and Lemon peel)
1/2 part Mace

Use as a personal altar or household incense to increase your powers.

GREEK GOD AND GODDESS INCENSE

4 parts Frankincense (sacred to Apollo)
2 parts Myrrh (Demeter)
1 part Pine (Poseidon)
1 part Rose petals (Aphrodite)
1 part Sage (Zeus)
1 part White Willow bark (Persephone)

a few drops Olive oil (Athena)
a few drops Cypress oil (Artemis/Hecate)

Burn to honor Them.

HEALING INCENSE

1 part Rosemary
1 part Juniper berries

Burn to speed healing while visualizing.

HEALING INCENSE # 2

2 parts Myrrh
1 part Cinnamon
1 pinch Saffron

Another like the above.

HEALING INCENSE # 3 (*caution!*)

3 parts Myrrh
2 parts Nutmeg
1 part Cedar
1 part Clove *
1/2 part Lemon Balm
1/2 part Poppy seeds
a few drops Pine oil
a few drops Almond oil

A third like the above.

HEALING INCENSE # 4

3 parts Myrrh
1 part Rose Petals
1 part Eucalyptus
1 pinch Saffron
a few drops Cedarwood oil

HEALING INCENSE # 5

2 parts Juniper berries
1 part Rosemary

HECATE INCENSE

3 parts Sandalwood
2 parts Cypress
1 part Spearmint or Peppermint

To honor Her, burn at a crossroads or during ritual at the waning of the Moon.

HONORS INCENSE

2 parts Benzoin
1 part Wood Aloe
1/2 part Pepperwort (or Rue)

Burn for honors and favors.

HORNED GOD INCENSE

2 parts Benzoin
1 part Cedar
1 part Pine
1 part Juniper berries
a few drops Patchouly oil

Burn to honor Him in His many guises, especially during Wiccan rituals.

HOUSE PURIFICATION INCENSE

3 parts Frankincense
2 parts Dragon's Blood
1 part Myrrh
1 part Sandalwood
1 part Wood Betony
1/2 part Dill seed
a few drops Rose Geranium oil

Burn in your home to cleanse it at least once a month, perhaps on the Full Moon. Additionally, burn this mixture in a new home before moving in.

IMBOLC INCENSE

3 parts Frankincense
2 parts Dragon's Blood
1/2 part Red Sandalwood
1 part Cinnamon
a few drops Red Wine

To this mixture add a pinch of the first flower (dry it first) that is available in your area at the time of Imbolc (February 1st). Burn during Wiccan ceremonies on Imbolc, or simply to attune with the symbolic rebirth of the Sun—the fading of winter and the promise of spring.

INCUBUS, INCENSE AGAINST THE (*caution!*)

2 parts Sandalwood
2 parts Benzoin
2 parts Wood Aloe
2 parts Cardamom
1/2 part Calamus
1/2 part Birthwort
1/2 part Ginger
1/2 part Pepper

1/2 part Cinnamon
1/2 part Clove*
1/2 part Carnation
1/2 part Nutmeg*
1/2 part Mace
1/2 part Cubeb seed
a few drops Brandy

This ancient mixture is burned to ward off the incubus (see Glossary).

ISIS INCENSE

3 parts Myrrh
2 parts Sandalwood
1 part Frankincense
1 part Rose petals
a few drops Lotus bouquet (see Chapter 4)

Burn while reverencing Isis. Or, burn during any type of magical operation, since Isis is the Goddess of All Things.

JUPITER INCENSE (PLANETARY)

2 parts Wood Aloe
1 part Benzoin
1 part Storax (or Gum Arabic)
1/4 part Ash seed
1 pinch powdered Lapis Lazuli
a few drops Olive oil

Mix and burn. This unusual formula includes a stone (lapis lazuli), and could also be mixed together and carried as a Jupiterian talisman charm. Burn for spells involving riches, expansion, the law and luck.

JUPITER INCENSE # 2

3 parts Frankincense
1 part Mace
1 part Cardamom
1/2 part Balm of Gilead
1/4 part pulverized Oak leaves
1/8 part pulverized Pomegranate rind
1 pinch Saffron
a few drops Ambergris oil

Another like the above.

JUPITER INCENSE # 3 (*caution!*)

1 part Clove*
1 part Nutmeg*
1 part Cinnamon
1/2 part Lemon Balm
1/2 part Citron peel (or equal parts dried Lemon and
    Orange peel)

A third like the above.

KYPHI

4 parts Frankincense	1/2 part Cinnamon
2 parts Benzoin	1/2 part Cassia
2 parts Gum Mastic	1/2 part Juniper berries
2 parts Myrrh	1/2 part Orris
1 part Cedar	1/2 part Cypress
1 part Galangal (or Ginger)	a few drops Lotus bouquet
1/2 part Calamus (or Vetivert)	a few drops Wine
1/2 part Cardamom	a few drops Honey
	7 raisins

Mix the ground dry ingredients thoroughly. Let sit in an airtight container two weeks. In a separate bowl, mix together the oil, wine, honey and raisins. Add to the dry ingredients and blend with the hands. Let sit another two weeks. Then, if desired, grind to a fine powder. Kyphi is used in night rituals, to invoke Egyptian Goddesses and Gods, and as a general magical incense. (This recipe is a more refined version of the one that appeared in *Magical Herbalism*.)

KYPHI # 2 (simplified)

3 parts Frankincense	1/2 part Cedar
2 parts Benzoin	2 drops Lotus bouquet
2 parts Myrrh	2 drops Wine
1 part Juniper berries	2 drops Honey
1/2 part Galangal	a few raisins
1/2 part Cinnamon	

Mix, burn, use as the above.

LEO INCENSE

2 parts Gum Mastic
1 part Sandalwood
1 part Juniper berries

Use as a personal altar or household incense to increase your powers.

LIBRA INCENSE

2 parts Sandalwood
1 part Thyme
a few drops Rose oil

Use as a personal altar or household incense to increase your powers.

"LOCK" INCENSE

3 parts Frankincense
2 parts Juniper berries
1 part Vetivert
1/2 part Cumin

To guard your home from thieves: During the day smolder this mixture in a censer before the front door, then move it to each opening in the house (doors, windows, cellars, etc.) through which thieves may enter. Visualize its smoke forming an invisible but impenetrable barrier. Move in a clockwise circle throughout your home, replenishing the incense as necessary. Repeat monthly at the time of the Full Moon, if possible; or, use as needed. This incense is designed to "lock" your home against unwanted intruders—but don't forget to bolt your doors as well.

LOVE INCENSE

2 parts Sandalwood
1/2 part Basil
1/2 part Bergamot
a few drops Rose oil
a few drops Lavender oil

Burn to attract love, to strengthen the love you have, and to expand your ability to give and to receive love.

LOVE INCENSE # 2

2 parts Dragon's Blood
1 part Orris
1/2 part Cinnamon
1/2 part Rose petals
a few drops Musk oil
a few drops Patchouly oil

Another like the above.

LUGHNASADH INCENSE

2 parts Frankincense
1 part Heather
1 part Apple blossoms
1 pinch Blackberry leaves
a few drops Ambergris oil

Burn Lughnasadh Incense during Wiccan rituals on August 1st or 2nd, or at that time to attune with the coming harvest.

MABON INCENSE

2 parts Frankincense
1 part Sandalwood
1 part Cypress
1 part Juniper
1 part Pine
1/2 part Oakmoss (or a few drops Oakmoss bouquet)
1 pinch pulverized Oak leaf

Burn during Wiccan ceremonies on Mabon (the Autumnal Equinox, circa September 21st), or at that time to attune with the change of the seasons.

MARS INCENSE (PLANETARY)

4 parts Benzoin
1 part Pine needles (or resin)
a scant pinch Black Pepper

Burn to attract its influences, or during spells involving lust, physical strength, competitions, rituals concerning men and so on.

MARS INCENSE # 2 (caution!)

2 parts Galangal
1 part Coriander
1 part Clove*
1/2 part Basil
a scant pinch Black Pepper

Another like the above.

MARS INCENSE # 3 (caution!)

2 parts Dragon's Blood
1 part Cardamom
1 part Clove.*
1 part Grains of Paradise

A third like the above.

MEDICINE WHEEL INCENSE

2 parts Sage
1 part Sweetgrass (see Appendix 2 for possible sources)
1 part Pine resin or needles
1 part Osha root (or Angelica root)
a scant pinch Tobacco

Burn during rites revering American Indian deities and spirits, and to attune with the energies of this land.

MEDITATION INCENSE

1 part Gum Acacia (or Gum Arabic)
1 part Sandalwood

Burn a small amount prior to meditation to relax the conscious mind.

MERCURY INCENSE (PLANETARY)

2 parts Benzoin
1 part Mace
1/2 part Marjoram
a few drops Lavender oil

Burn to invoke its powers, or during spells involving intelligence, travel, divination and so on. (See Part III for more information regarding the magical powers of Mercury.)

MERCURY INCENSE # 2

2 parts Benzoin
1 part Frankincense
1 part Mace

Another like the above.

MERCURY INCENSE # 3

2 parts Sandalwood
1 part Gum Mastic
1/2 part Lavender (or a few drops Lavender oil)

A third like the above.

MEXICAN MAGIC INCENSE

2 parts Copal
1 part Frankincense
1 part Rosemary

Smolder during Mexican-American folk magic rituals and spells.

MIDSUMMER INCENSE

2 parts Sandalwood
1 part Mugwort
1 part Camomile
1 part Gardenia petals
a few drops Rose oil
a few drops Lavender oil
a few drops Yarrow oil

Burn at Wiccan rituals at the Summer Solstice (circa June 21st) or at that time to attune with the seasons and the Sun.

MIDSUMMER INCENSE # 2

3 parts Frankincense
2 parts Benzoin
1 part Dragon's Blood
1 part Thyme
1 part Rosemary
1 pinch Vervain
a few drops Red Wine

Another like the above.

MOON INCENSE

2 parts Frankincense
1 part Sandalwood
a few drops Eucalyptus oil
a few drops Jasmine oil
a few drops Camphor oil

Burn to attract its influences, and also during psychic workings, love magic, healing, rituals involving the home and dream magic.

MOON INCENSE # 2

4 parts Sandalwood
2 parts Wood Aloe
1 part Eucalyptus
1 part pulverized Cucumber seed
1 part Mugwort
1/2 part Ranunculus blossoms
1 part Selenetrope
a few drops Ambergris oil

I still don't know what selenetrope is; substitute gardenia or jasmine.

MOON INCENSE # 3

2 parts Juniper berries
1 part Orris
1 part Calamus
a few drops Spirits of Camphor (or Camphor tincture; or
    1/4 part genuine Camphor)
a few drops Lotus bouquet

A third like the above.

MOON INCENSE # 4

2 parts Myrrh
2 parts Gardenia petals
1 part Rose petals
1 part Lemon peel
1/2 part Camphor
a few drops Jasmine oil

MOONFIRE INCENSE

1 part Rose
1 part Orris
1 part Bay
1 part Juniper
1 part Dragon's Blood
1/2 part Potassium Nitrate

Burn for divination, love and harmony. The potassium nitrate is included in this incense to make it sparkle and glow. If you add too much it will explode!

NINE WOODS INCENSE

1 part Rowan wood (or Sandalwood)
1 part Apple wood
1 part Dogwood
1 part Poplar wood
1 part Juniper wood
1 part Cedar wood
1 part Pine wood
1 part Holly branches
1 part Elder (or Oak) wood

Take sawdust of each, mix together, and burn indoors on charcoal when a ritual fire is necessary or desired but not practical. The incense emits the aroma of an open campfire.

OFFERTORY INCENSE

2 parts Frankincense
1 part Myrrh
1 part Cinnamon
1/2 part Rose petals
1/2 part Vervain

Burn while honoring the Goddesses and Gods, and as an offering.

OSTARA INCENSE

2 parts Frankincense
1 part Benzoin
1 part Dragon's Blood
1/2 part Nutmeg
1/2 part Violet flowers (or a few drops Violet oil)
1/2 part Orange peel
1/2 part Rose petals

Burn during Wiccan rituals on Ostara (the Spring Equinox, which varies from March 20th to the 24th each year), or to welcome the spring and to refresh your life.

PELE INCENSE

2 parts Frankincense
1 part Dragon's Blood
1 part Red Sandalwood
1 part Orange peel
1 part Cinnamon
a few drops Clove oil

Burn while honoring Pele,* the Hawaiian goddess of volcanoes; when needing additional strength for any ritual; when you feel manipulated by others, or for Fire spells in general. Burn when you wish to be filled with the power of Pele.

PISCES INCENSE

2 parts Frankincense
1 part Eucalyptus
1 part Lemon peel
a few drops Sandalwood oil

Use as a personal altar or household incense to increase your powers.

---

* Pele isn't just a goddess of destruction. She's also a goddess of creation, a true Mother Goddess, since she creates new land every time one of Her lava flows reaches the sea. She is a powerful deity still respected in present-day Hawaii.

A GENERAL PLANETARY INCENSE (*caution!*)

1 part Myrrh	1 part Frankincense
1 part Gum Mastic	1 part Camphor
1 part Costus	1 part Red Sandalwood
1 part Opoponax	1 part Wood Aloe
1 part Storax	1 part Euphorbium*
1 part Thyme	

For general magical workings. The baneful substance in this recipe, euphorbium, can be replaced with tobacco. Gum arabic can be used in place of the storax, as mentioned previously. Gum opoponax is virtually unobtainable; use an opoponax oil or substitute with gum arabic.

PROPHECY INCENSE (*caution!*)

1 part Fleawort seed
1 part Violet root
1 part Parsley
1 part Hempseed*

Burn for divination and psychic work.

PROPHETIC DREAM INCENSE

2 parts Frankincense
1 part Buchu

Burn before bedtime to stimulate the psychic mind to produce future-revealing dreams, and to ensure that the conscious mind remembers them in the morning.

PROSPERITY INCENSE

2 parts Frankincense
1 part Cinnamon
1 part Nutmeg
1 part Lemon Balm
1 part Citron

Burn to attract wealth.

PROTECTION INCENSE

2 parts Frankincense
1 part Dragon's Blood
1/2 part Wood Betony

Burn for both physical and psychic protection while visualizing.

PROTECTION INCENSE # 2

2 parts Frankincense
1 part Sandalwood
1/2 part Rosemary

Another like the above.

PROTECTION INCENSE # 3 (*caution!*)

1 part Frankincense
1 part Myrrh
1/2 part Clove*

A third like the above.

PROTECTION INCENSE # 4

2 parts Frankincense
1/2 part Cumin

PROTECTION INCENSE # 5

4 parts Frankincense	1/2 part Mugwort
3 parts Myrrh	1/2 part Yarrow
2 parts Juniper berries	1/2 part St. John's Wort
1 part Rosemary	1/2 part Angelica
1/2 part Avens	1/2 part Basil

PROTECTION INCENSE #6

2 parts Frankincense
1 part Copal
1 part Dragon's Blood

PSYCHIC INCENSE

3 parts Frankincense
1 part Bistort

Smolder to sharpen psychic powers.

PSYCHIC INCENSE # 2

2 parts Sandalwood
1 part Gum Acacia (or Gum Arabic)

Another like the above.

PSYCHIC INCENSE # 3 (*caution!*)

1 part Frankincense
1 part Sandalwood
1 part Cinnamon
1 part Nutmeg*
a few drops Orange oil
a few drops Clove oil

PURIFICATION INCENSE (*caution!*)

4 parts Frankincense
2 parts Bay
1 part Camphor
1 pinch finely powdered Salt
1 pinch Sulfur*

Burn to purify the atmosphere of a disturbed home. Leave the windows open and do not inhale the sulphurous fumes!

PURIFICATION INCENSE # 2

2 parts Sandalwood
1 part Cinnamon

Another like the above. Though no sulfur is included in this formula, it's best to leave the windows open during all types of purification rites.

PURIFICATION INCENSE # 3

3 parts Frankincense
1 part Vervain

A third like the above.

RAIN INCENSE (*caution!*)

4 parts Heather
1 part Fern
1/2 part Henbane*

Burn out of doors on a deserted hill to attract rain. Do not inhale fumes!

"RAISE THE DEAD" INCENSE

1 part Pepperwort
1 part Red Storax
1 pinch Saffron
a few drops Musk oil

Compound and fumigate about the tombs and graves of the dead. This will cause spirits and ghosts to gather, at least according to ancient writings.

RICHES AND FAVORS INCENSE (*caution!*)

2 parts Benzoin
1 part Wood Aloe
1/2 part Pepperwort
1/2 part Clove *

Burn when you need favors and wealth.

SABBAT INCENSE (*caution!*)

4 parts Frankincense	1/2 part Solomon's Seal
2 parts Myrrh	1/4 part Rue*
2 parts Benzoin	1/4 part Wormwood*
1/2 part Bay	1/4 part Camomile
1/2 part Fennel	1/4 part Rose petals
1/2 part Thyme	
1/2 part Pennyroyal	

Burn at Wiccan Sabbats.

SAGITTARIUS INCENSE (*caution!*)

2 parts Frankincense
1 part Myrrh
1 part Clove*

Use as a personal altar or household incense to increase your own powers.

SAHUMERIA AZTECA INCENSE

3 parts Copal
2 parts Frankincense
1 part Rosemary
1 part Sage
1 part Lemongrass
1 part Bay
1/2 part Marigold
1/2 part Yerba Santa

For ancient Aztecan rituals and all Mexican-American folk magic. Also, use as a general purification incense. I first learned of this mixture a decade ago from a Latina who owned an herb shop not far from my home. Later I found it for sale in *botanicas* (herb and occult supply shops) in Tijuana. It's a famous incense in contemporary Mexican folk magic.

SATURN INCENSE (PLANETARY) (*caution!*)

2 parts Frankincense
2 parts Poppy seed
1 part Gum Arabic
1 part Myrrh
1/4 part Henbane seed*
1/4 part Mandrake*
a few drops Olive Oil

Burn for Saturnian influences; also for spells dealing with buildings, studying past lives, banishing illnesses, pests and negative habits. This incense can be hazardous to your health; for a recommended Saturnian incense see formula #3 below *or* substitute 1/2 part tobacco for the henbane and mandrake listed above.

SATURN INCENSE # 2 (*caution!*)

2 parts Cypress
2 parts Ash leaves
1 part Alum
1 part Gum Scammony
1 part Asafoetida*
1 part Sulphur*
1/4 part Black Nightshade*

Another like the above, but not recommended. By omitting the black nightshade, the incense is fairly innocuous but still smells incredibly foul!

SATURN INCENSE # 3

2 parts Sandalwood
2 parts Myrrh
1 part Dittany of Crete
a few drops Cypress oil
a few drops Patchouly oil

This is the recommended Saturn incense formula. If you're going to use one of these four, this should be it!

SATURN INCENSE # 4 (*caution!*)

1 part Pepperwort
1 part Mandrake*
1 part Myrrh
a few drops Musk oil

SCORPIO INCENSE

2 parts Frankincense
1 part Galangal
1 part Pine resin (pitch)

Use as a personal altar or household incense to increase your powers.

SCRYING INCENSE (*caution!*)

1 part Mugwort
1 part Wormwood*

Burn a small amount prior to scrying in a quartz crystal sphere, in flames, water and so on. Be warned—this one doesn't smell so good.

SIGHT INCENSE

2 parts Gum Mastic
2 parts Juniper
1 part Sandalwood
1 part Cinnamon
1 part Calamus
a few drops Ambergris oil
a few drops Patchouly oil

Mix, empower and burn to promote psychic awareness. This is another version of the recipe that appeared in *Magical Herbalism*. Other variants include hemp.

SPIRIT INCENSE (*caution!*)

4 parts Coriander
1 part Smallage (Parsley)
1/4 part Henbane*
1/4 part Hemlock*

Burn outdoors to draw spirits together. As usual, do not inhale fumes!

SPIRIT INCENSE # 2 (*caution!*)

root of the weedy herb Sagapen (?)
juice of Hemlock*
juice of Henbane*
Tapsus barbatus (?)
Red Sandalwood
Black Poppy seed

Fume to make spirits and strange shapes appear. To make them flee, add parsley to this mixture, as this chases away all spirits and destroys all visions (which seems to contradict Spirit Incense #1 above!) This 500-year-old formula is virtually impossible to compound. I included this recipe as an example of an authentic, ancient herbal incense. Most of these are as difficult to make as this one. What is the "weedy herb Sagapen"? I haven't the slightest idea!

SPIRIT INCENSE # 3

1 part Anise
1 part Coriander
1 part Cardamom

Smolder to cause spirits to gather.

SPIRIT INCENSE #4

1 part Sandalwood
1 part Lavender

Burn on the altar to invite good energies (or spirits) to be present during magical rituals.

SPIRIT INCENSE #5

2 parts Sandalwood
1 part Willow bark

Burn out of doors at night during the Waxing Moon.

SPIRIT INCENSE # 6

3 parts Wood Aloe
1 part Costus
1 part Crocus
a few drops Ambergris oil
a few drops Musk oil

SPIRIT INCENSE #7 (*caution!*)

3 parts Frankincense
2 parts Coriander
1 part Fennel root
1 part Cassia
1/2 part Henbane*

Take all ingredients to a dark, haunted, enchanted forest. Sprinkle dried mullein or patchouly on an old tree stump. On this set black candles, a censer and the incense. Light the tapers, burn the incense and wait until the candles are suddenly extinguished. There in the darkness around you will be the spirits. To be rid of them, burn asafoetida or frankincense.

So you're wondering why I included seven spirit incenses in this book? Well, they're traditional. I'm not recommending anyone to actually use these recipes; again, they're a part of the colorful heritage of the magical herbalist and of magicians in general. To reiterate Chapter 1, magic isn't performed through the use of spirits. Magic is a direction of personal power (the energy within), as well as of Earth power (that resident in plants and stones) to effect needed goals. Besides, what would you do with all those spirits if they did indeed appear?

SPIRITS DEPART INCENSE (*caution!*)

1 part Calamint
1 part Peony
1 part Mint (Spearmint)
1/4 part Castor Beans*

Burn out of doors to drive away all evil spirits and vain imaginings. If you wish to use this formula, substitute a few drops castor oil for the beans, as these are poisonous.

SPIRITS DEPART INCENSE #2

2 parts Fennel seed
2 parts Dill seed
1/2 part Rue

Another like the above.

STUDY INCENSE

2 parts Gum Mastic
1 part Rosemary

Smolder to strengthen the conscious mind for study, to develop concentration and to improve the memory.

SUCCESS INCENSE (*caution!*)

3 parts Wood Aloe
2 parts Red Storax
1 part Nutmeg*

Burn for success in all undertakings. Since red storax (indeed, all storax) is unavailable, substitute frankincense or gum arabic.

SUN INCENSE

3 parts Frankincense
2 parts Myrrh
1 part Wood Aloe
1/2 part Balm of Gilead
1/2 part Bay

1/2 part Carnation
a few drops Ambergris oil
a few drops Musk oil
a few drops Olive oil

Burn to draw the influences of the Sun and for spells involving promotions, friendship, healing, energy and magical power.

SUN INCENSE #2

3 parts Frankincense
2 parts Sandalwood
1 part Bay
1 pinch Saffron
a few drops Orange oil

Another like the above.

SUN INCENSE #3 (*caution!*)

3 parts Frankincense
2 parts Galangal
2 parts Bay
1/4 part Mistletoe*
a few drops Red Wine
a few drops Honey

A third like the above.

TALISMAN CONSECRATION INCENSE (*caution!*)

Alum
Gum Scammony
Asafoetida*
Sulphur*
Cypress
Black Hellebore*
Ash leaves

Burn in an earthen dish and hold the talismans in the smoke. I've refrained from including proportions in this recipe because I don't recommend its use. Try the following nonpoisonous version or the Consecration Incense to consecrate all forms of amulets and talismans.

TALISMAN CONSECRATION INCENSE (nontoxic version)

2 parts Frankincense
1 part Cypress
1 part Ash leaves
1 part Tobacco
1 pinch Valerian
1 pinch Alum
1 pinch Asafoetida*

Though this one won't kill you, like the above version it still stinks. I heartily recommend the Consecration Incense.

TAURUS INCENSE

2 parts Sandalwood
2 parts Benzoin
a few drops Rose oil

Use as a personal altar or household incense to increase your powers.

TEMPLE INCENSE

3 parts Frankincense
2 parts Myrrh
a few drops Lavender oil
a few drops Sandalwood oil

Smolder in the temple or "magic room," or as a general magical incense. This incense increases spirituality.

THIEF INCENSE (to see a thief)

1 part Crocus
1 pinch Alum

In ancient Egypt this mixture was placed on a brazier and the seer stared into the coals.

THOUSAND-NAMED SOLAR INCENSE (*caution!*)

3 parts Frankincense
1 part Clove*
1/2 part Red Sandalwood
1/2 part Sandalwood
1/4 part Orange flowers
3 pinches Orris

Burn for Solar influences (see Part III).

TRUE LOVE INCENSE

1 part Cinnamon
1 part Orris
a few drops Patchouly oil

Burn for love.

UNIVERSAL INCENSE

3 parts Frankincense
2 parts Benzoin
1 part Myrrh
1 part Sandalwood
1 part Rosemary

Burn for all positive magical purposes. If this formula is used for negative magical goals, the incense will cancel out the spell or ritual.

VENUS INCENSE (PLANETARY)

3 parts Wood Aloe
1 part Red Rose petals
1 pinch crushed Red Coral (optional)
a few drops Olive oil
a few drops Musk oil
a few drops Ambergris oil

Mix well and burn for Venusian influences, such as love, healing, partnerships and rituals involving women. The inclusion of coral in this recipe dates it to about the 16th century, when coral was considered to be a powerful love stimulant. Now that we know that coral is the skeleton of a living creature, it's best to omit it entirely.

VENUS INCENSE #2

1 part Violets
1 part Rose petals
1/2 part Olive leaves

Another like the above.

VENUS INCENSE #3

2 parts Sandalwood
2 parts Benzoin
1 part Rosebuds
a few drops Patchouly oil
a few drops Rose oil

A third like the above.

VIRGO INCENSE

1 part Mace
1 part Cypress
a few drops Patchouly oil

Use as a personal altar or household incense to increase your powers.

VISION INCENSE

3 parts Frankincense
1 part Bay
1/2 part Damiana

Burn a small amount prior to psychic workings.

VISION INCENSE #2 (*caution!*)

1 part Calamus
1 part Fennel root
1 part Pomegranate skin
1 part Red Sandalwood
1 part Black Poppy seeds
1/2 part Henbane*

Another like the above, but not recommended.

WATER INCENSE (ELEMENTAL)

2 parts Benzoin
1 part Myrrh
1 part Sandalwood
a few drops Lotus bouquet
a few drops Ambergris oil

Burn to attract the influences of this element, as well as to develop psychism, to promote love, fertility, beauty and so on.

WEALTH INCENSE

1 part Nutmeg
1 part Pepperwort
1 pinch Saffron

Burn to attract wealth.

WEALTH INCENSE #2

2 parts Pine needles or resin
1 part Cinnamon
1 part Galangal
a few drops Patchouly oil

Another like the above.

WEALTH INCENSE #3 *(caution!)*

2 parts Frankincense
1 part Cinnamon
1 part Nutmeg
1/2 part Clove*
1/2 part Ginger
1/2 part Mace

A third like the above.

YULE INCENSE

2 parts Frankincense
2 parts Pine needles or resin
1 part Cedar
1 part Juniper berries

Mix and smolder at Wiccan rites on Yule (on or around December 21st), or during the winter months to cleanse the home and to attune with the forces of nature amid the cold days and nights.

Oils

IT HAS BECOME quite popular to use essential oils for magical purposes. Blends such as Controlling Oil and Come to Me Essence are in daily use by many practitioners of Voodoo-flavored folk magic.

Such practices, often thought of as being ancient, do indeed date back thousands of years in one form or another; but not until recently were the array of true and synthetic botanical oils available for ritual purposes.

Scented oils were used in antiquity. These were created by heating fragrant plant materials in oil or fat. The plant's scent was transferred to the oil and thus was fragranced.

Many people tell me that they want to make their own oils. Unfortunately, this is a difficult process. Why? Here are a few reasons:

It requires a large investment in equipment. Much of this must be specially adapted for this purpose. Condensers, fractionating columns and other exotica are necessary and expensive.

It requires a large amount of fresh plant materials. Do you have a couple hundred pounds of, say, fresh tuberose petals? Additionally, the petals, leaves or roots must be of the appropriate species. For example, the best rose oils are created from the "old world" varieties, which are rarely available in large quantities.

The process must be carefully carried out to exacting standards. If just one step is missed or overlooked—if, perhaps, the temperature reaches an inappropriate high or low—the oil will be of lesser quality.

Often the results aren't worth the investment of time and money. Homemade carnation oil certainly won't smell like carnations.

There are few plant oils that can be extracted at home without much difficulty. For the rest, simply buy and blend high quality oils for ritual use.

Buying Oils

Numerous companies offer oils for purchase. Some of these sell only genuine, authentic *essential* oils—i.e., those extracted from the natural botanical material after which they're named (lavender oil made from lavender, for example). Many others sell *blends*, compounds or bouquets, which reproduce a specific scent by mixing various true essential oils (see Chapter 4 for examples of bouquets). Most companies offer either partially or totally *synthetic* oils, though they're never labelled as such.

It's best to use only genuine, authentic essential oils in magic. These contain the sum of the plant's magical energies and so are the most effective. True, they aren't cheap, but they last longer because only small amounts are necessary. It is expensive to build up a good stock of genuine essential oils, but this is necessary to create quality magical oils.

I have worked with synthetics for years. Some of them are effective but pale in comparison with the aromas and power of true essential oils. Remember not to be fooled by the "essential oil" tags which manufacturers often attach to synthetic scents. Buying from the mail-order sources that sell essential oils listed in Appendix 2, or from retail stores that stock these oils, is virtually your only assurance of getting the real thing.

I know that some of you will continue to use synthetic oils. However, if my words here convince a few of you to make the great leap into the world of truly *natural* magic I'll be happy.

For those fragrances unavailable in essential oil form (such as tuberose, sweet pea and others) see Chapter 4 for recipes of bouquets that can be blended from true essential oils and used in place of, say, lotus.

Blending Oils

There's no magic secret for blending and mixing magical oils. Here's the basic method:

• Assemble the essential oils (and bouquets) called for in the recipe.

• In a clean, sterilized glass jar, add 1/8 cup of one of the following vegetable oils:

Safflower	Almond
Sunflower	Hazelnut
Coconut	Grapeseed
Apricot Kernel	
Jojoba	

I've found jojoba is the best to use. Because it isn't truly an oil but a liquid form of wax, it never becomes rancid and can be kept for longer periods of time.

• Using an eye dropper or the convenient single-drop dispensers which are included in virtually every bottle of true essential oil, add the essential oils in the proportions recommended in the recipes that follow.

• Swirl the essential oils into the base oil, don't stir. Gently rotate the oil clockwise.

• Finally, store all oils away from heat, light and moisture (not in the bathroom) in airtight, opaque or dark-colored glass bottles. Label and keep for use.

AN EXAMPLE
We'll make Fast Money Oil. Here's the recipe:

FAST MONEY OIL

7 drops Patchouly
5 drops Cedarwood
4 drops Vetivert
2 drops Ginger

While visualizing my magical goal—money—I add 1/8 cup jojoba oil to a sterilized glass jar. In front of me on the table I've placed jars of patchouly, cedarwood, vetivert and ginger essential oils—not synthetics.

I visualize money. I add seven drops patchouly to the jojoba and swirl to mix it in with the base oil. I sniff. The fragrance has overpowered the light odor of the pure jojoba oil.

Visualize. Add five drops cedarwood. Swirl. Sniff. The scent is building.

Four drops of vetivert essential oil follow. While visualizing, swirl. Sniff. The aroma of the magical oil in the making deepens as the three fragrances and their energies mingle.

Finally, the ginger essential oil. This is such a strong, heady scent that only two drops are required. I mix again, smell again, visualize again. After a short empowering rite the magical Fast Money Oil is ready for use.

It is a rich, evocative scent. Used with visualization it will be effective in manifesting an increased cash flow.

Could I make this with synthetics? Of course. Would it be as effective? No.

Using Oils

Oils are used in innumerable ways in magic. Remember: Always use oils with visualization and with power.

Most often, they're rubbed onto candles which are then burned in ritual. The magical goal determines the type of oil and the color of the candle used. The oil's powers mix with that of the color and the candle flame. All these energies are further boosted by the magician's personal power and are sped toward the magical goal through visualization.

Oils are also simply used to anoint the body to bring their energies within. Thus, rubbing a Love Oil onto the wrists, the neck, and over the heart infuses the magician with love-attracting energies. Courage Oil similarly imbues her or him with the strength to forge ahead in the face of adversity.

A simple bath can be transformed into a ritual by adding several drops of oil to the water. Slipping into it and inhaling the fragrance, the magician once again brings the oil's energies inside.

Talismans and amulets (often termed "charms" or "sachets") may be anointed with a few drops of the appropriate mixed oil. This is done, of course, with the specific magical goal in mind.

Quartz crystals and other stones are also rubbed with oils to boost their energies during spells and rituals. The stones are then worn, carried or placed in mystic patterns to bring about specific magical goals.

Other ritual uses of oils will become apparent once you start using them.

A Guide to True Essential Oils and Bouquets

This is an alphabetical listing of the magical properties of the most commonly used essential oils and bouquets. No synthetics have been included here. They can be used by themselves for any of the purposes mentioned directly above, but truc cssential oils should be diluted before applying them to the skin.

Diluting True Essential Oils

As a general guideline, add 5 to 7 drops to 1/8 cup of base oil, such as jojoba. This dilutes the essential oil so that it won't irritate the skin, but you will still be able to smell it.

Some true essential oils are such severe skin irritants that I've rarely included them in any of the recipes in this section, and have noted this property below.

For more in-depth magical information concerning true essential oils, see *Magical Aromatherapy: The Power of Scent* (Cunningham, Llewellyn Publications, 1989).

APRICOT OIL: This oil, pressed from apricot kernels, is aphrodisiac in nature. It is used as a base for mixing true essential oils but does not have an apricot-like scent.

BASIL: The scent of basil causes sympathy between two persons and so is worn to avoid major clashes. Basil essential oil is useful in blends for encouraging happiness and peace and for stimulating the conscious mind. It is fine in money-attracting magical oils, which might be why prostitutes once wore it in Spain to attract customers.

BENZOIN: This is a rich, thick essential oil with a natural vanilla-like scent. Dilute and rub onto the body to increase your personal power. It awakens the conscious mind as well.

BERGAMOT MINT BOUQUET: Use for money and protective rituals. Add the diluted bouquet to your bath water for these purposes.

BLACK PEPPER: Use the essential oil for protection and to promote courage. It has a sharp, sweet scent and is best added to blends rather than worn alone, even if diluted.

CAMOMILE: A fruity, incredibly full scent. Sparingly use camomile essential oil for meditation and inducing peace. Expensive but worth it!

CAMPHOR: The cooly scented essential oil is fine for purification and promoting celibacy.

CARDAMOM: Deliciously spicy, cardamom essential oil brings a nice jolt of energy to love and sexually oriented formulas.

CEDARWOOD: This essential oil has a woodsy scent. Its energies are useful in enhancing spirituality.

CINNAMON: True cinnamon oil is irritating to the skin. Use sparingly in money and psychic awareness blends—no more than one drop!

CLOVE OIL: Another irritant. Add one drop to 1/8 cup of base oil. Useful in courage and protection blends.

CORIANDER: Coriander essential oil works well in love and healing mixtures.

CYPRESS: Cypress is an essential oil of blessing, consecration and protection. This unique scent stimulates healing and eases the pain of losses of all kinds.

EUCALYPTUS: Perhaps the ultimate healing oil. Add to all healing blends. Apply (undiluted, in this case) to the body to relieve colds. Also used in purification mixtures.

FRANKINCENSE: An incredibly rich scent, frankincense essential oil is useful in promoting spirituality and meditative states. Dilute before applying to the skin; it may be irritating.

GERANIUM, ROSE: This essential oil (usually sold simply as "Geranium") is a powerful protectant. Wear diluted, or add to happiness blends.

GINGER: Powerfully spicy. Ginger essential oil is useful in sexuality, love, courage and money-attracting blends.

GRAPEFRUIT: The essential oil is a powerful purifier and is added to purification fragrances.

JASMINE: Symbolic of the Moon and of the mysteries of the night. Jasmine essential oil (or absolute) is a wonderfully evocative aroma. Though incredibly expensive, one precious drop can be added to love, psychic awareness, peace and spirituality blends. It is also useful for sexuality. Do, however, avoid synthetic jasmines!

JUNIPER: The resinous essential oil is useful in protection, purification and healing blends.

LAVENDER: This clean, refreshing essential oil is included in health, love, peace and conscious mind-oriented formulas.

LEMON: Use in Lunar oils. Wear diluted lemon oil during the Full Moon to attune with its energies. Use in purification and healing oils.

LEMONGRASS: This essential oil strengthens psychic awareness and is also useful in purification mixtures.

LEMON VERBENA: Often sold simply as "Verbena," this full, lemon-scented essential oil is wonderful in love blends.

LIME: A refreshing scent, useful in purification and protection.

LOTUS BOUQUET: Add the diluted bouquet to formulas designed to promote spirituality, healing or meditation.

MAGNOLIA BOUQUET: An excellent addition to meditation and psychic awareness oils, as well as love mixtures.

MYRRH: The essential oil can be added to blends designed to enhance spirituality and meditation. It is also often used in healing mixtures.

NEROLI: Also known as Orange Flower essential oil. A fabulously rich, citrous scent, neroli essential oil is quite expensive. However, a drop added to happiness and purification blends works wonders.

NEW-MOWN HAY BOUQUET: Add a few drops of the bouquet to transformative oils, especially those designed to break negative habits and addictions. Also, anoint the body in the spring with this bouquet (diluted, of course) to welcome the turning of the seasons.

NIAOULI: The remarkably exotic scent of niaouli essential oil is excellent when used in protection formulas.

OAKMOSS BOUQUET: Use to attract money. Dilute and wear or rub onto cash before spending.

ORANGE: A highly Solar scent, orange essential oil is added to purification blends.

PALMAROSA: A unique essential oil, palmarosa smells like a combination of citrus and rose. Useful for love and healing.

PATCHOULY: Useful in money, sex and physical energy blends. Or, dilute and wear for these purposes.

PEPPERMINT: This familiar scent is excellent when used for purification.

PETITGRAIN: A protective, bitter orange scent. This essential oil is useful in protective blends.

PINE: The resinous scent of pine is commonly added to purification, protection, money and healing formulas.

ROSE: The accepted love scent. True rose essential oil (known as *otto*) and rose absolute (a different form) are expensive but, as with jasmine, one drop has powerful scenting properties. Rose essential oil is used in formulas designed to attract love, confer peace, stimulate sexual desires and enhance beauty. Do not use synthetics!

ROSEMARY: The familiar aroma of the culinary herb is captured in its essential oil form. Add to love and healing magical blends.

SANDALWOOD: This ancient, sacred scent is used in spirituality, meditation, sex and healing formulas. Or, dilute and wear to bring these influences inside you.

SWEET PEA BOUQUET: Diluted with a base oil, sweet pea bouquet is worn to attract new friends and to draw love, and so it is also used in such blends.

TANGERINE: An energy scent drenched with the powers of the Sun. Add tangerine essential oil to power and strength mixtures.

TONKA BOUQUET: This warm, vanilla-like scent can be included in money recipes.

TUBEROSE BOUQUET: This bouquet is a wonderful relaxer, and so is used in peace blends. The scent also induces love.

VETIVERT: A money scent. Add to such mixtures or dilute and wear. Anoint cash before spending.

YARROW: One of the true treasures of the Earth, yarrow essential oil is naturally blue, possesses an incredible scent, and can be added in small amounts (due to its price) to love, courage and psychic-awareness blends.

YLANG-YLANG: The rich, tropical aroma of this essential oil is useful in promoting love, peace and sex. It can be worn on the body or included in such mixtures.

The Recipes

Once again, the proportions listed here are the *suggested* ones. If you wish to deviate from these, simply keep in mind that the first ingredient listed should generally constitute the main scent. Each succeeding ingredient should be added in consecutively smaller amounts.

Remember:
- add these essential oils to 1/8 cup of a base oil
- visualize as you mix and smell
- for best results, don't use synthetics

AIR OIL (ELEMENTAL)

5 drops Lavender
3 drops Sandalwood
1 drop Neroli

Wear to invoke the powers of Air and to promote clear thinking, for travel spells, and to overcome addictions. (See Part III for more information regarding the elements.)

ALTAR OIL

4 drops Frankincense
2 drops Myrrh
1 drop Cedar

Anoint the altar with this oil at regular intervals, calling your Deity (Deities) to watch over it.

ANOINTING OIL

5 drops Sandalwood
3 drops Cedarwood
1 drop Orange
1 drop Lemon

Use for general ritual anointing purposes.

ANOINTING OIL #2

5 drops Myrrh
2 drops Cinnamon

Another like the last.

APHRODITE OIL

5 drops Cypress
2 drops Cinnamon
a small piece of dried Orris root

Add the true essential oils and the orris root to an *olive-oil* base. Anoint your body to bring a love into your life.

AQUARIUS OIL

5 drops Lavender
1 drop Cypress
1 drop Patchouly

Wear as a personal oil to increase your own powers.

ARIES OIL

3 drops Frankincense
1 drop Ginger
1 drop Black Pepper
1 drop Petitgrain

Wear as a personal oil to increase your own powers.

ASTRAL TRAVEL OIL

5 drops Sandalwood
1 drop Ylang-Ylang
1 drop Cinnamon

Add these to the base oil as usual and mix. Anoint the stomach, wrists, back of the neck and forehead (but remember—these essential oils are added to a base). Lie down and visualize yourself astrally projecting.*

BUSINESS SUCCESS OIL

3 parts Bergamot Mint Bouquet
1 part Basil
1 part Patchouly
1 pinch of ground Cinnamon

Mix the oils and add the pinch of ground cinnamon to the base oil. Anoint the hands, cash register, business card or the front door of the place of business to increase cash flow.

CANCER OIL (MOONCHILDREN)

4 drops Palmarosa
1 drop Camomile
1 drop Yarrow

Wear as a personal oil to increase your own powers.

---

* Denning and Phillip's *Astral Projection* (Llewellyn Publications, 1979) is an excellent guide.

CAPRICORN OIL

3 drops Vetivert
2 drops Cypress
1 drop Patchouly

Wear as a personal oil to increase your own powers.

CITRUS PURIFICATION OIL

3 drops Orange
2 drops Lemongrass
2 drops Lemon
1 drop Lime

Anoint white candles and burn in the home to purify it.

COME AND SEE ME OIL

5 drops Patchouly
1 drop Cinnamon

To attract the ideal mate, mix these true essential oils in an olive-oil base, smear on a white image candle of the appropriate sex, and burn with visualization.

COURAGE OIL

3 drops Ginger
1 drop Black Pepper
1 drop Clove

Wear to increase your courage, especially before being introduced to people, prior to public speaking, and other nerve-wracking situations.

DEMETER OIL

3 drops Myrrh
2 drops Vetivert
1 drop Oakmoss Bouquet

Anoint to attract money and for the successful completion of your protections and dreams. Also wear when planting, tending, harvesting or working with herbs and plants to ensure a fruitful yield. Helps us tune in with the energies of the Earth.

EARTH OIL (ELEMENTAL)

4 drops Patchouly
4 drops Cypress

Wear to invoke the powers of the Earth to bring money, prosperity, abundance, stability and foundation. (See Part III for more elemental information.)

ENERGY OIL

4 drops Orange
2 drops Lime
1 drop Cardamom

Wear when feeling depleted, when ill, or just to strengthen your own energy reserves. Especially useful after heavy magical ritual to recharge your bodily batteries.

FAST MONEY OIL

7 drops Patchouly
5 drops Cedarwood
4 drops Vetivert
2 drops Ginger

Wear, rub on the hands, or anoint green candles to bring money. Also anoint money before spending to ensure its return.

FAST MONEY OIL # 2

4 drops Basil
2 drops Ginger
1 drop Tonka Bouquet

Another like the last.

FIRE OIL (ELEMENTAL)

3 drops Ginger
2 drops Rosemary
1 drop Clove
1 drop Petitgrain

Wear to invoke the powers of Fire, such as energy, courage, strength, love, passion and so on.

GEMINI OIL

4 drops Lavender
1 drop Peppermint
1 drop Lemongrass
1 drop Sweet Pea Bouquet

Wear as a personal oil to increase your own powers.

HEALING OIL

4 drops Rosemary
2 drops Juniper
1 drop Sandalwood

Wear to speed healing.

HEALING OIL #2

3 drops Eucalyptus
1 drop Niaouli
1 drop Palmarosa
1 drop Spearmint

Another like the above.

HECATE OIL

3 drops Myrrh
2 drops Cypress
1 drop Patchouly
1 dried Mint leaf

Mix the essential oils in a base of sesame oil. Add the dried mint leaf to the blend. Wear during rituals of defensive magic. Also wear during the Waning Moon in honor of Hecate, Goddess of the Fading Crescent.

INITIATION OIL

3 drops Frankincense
3 drops Myrrh
1 drop Sandalwood

Use for mystic initiation ceremonies and also to increase your awareness of the spiritual realm.

INTERVIEW OIL

4 drops Ylang-Ylang
3 drops Lavender
1 drop Rose

Wear to interviews of all kinds to calm you. Helps make a favorable impression.

JUPITER OIL (PLANETARY)

3 drops Oakmoss Bouquet
1 drop Clove
1 drop Tonka Bouquet

Wear for wealth, prosperity, help in legal matters and all other Jupiterian influences.

LEO OIL

3 drops Petitgrain
1 drop Orange
1 drop Lime

Wear as a personal oil to increase your own powers.

LIBRA OIL

4 drops Rose Geranium
2 drops Ylang-Ylang
2 drops Palmarosa
          or
1 drop Rose absolute or otto
1 drop Cardamom

Wear as a personal oil to increase your own powers.

LOVE OIL

7 drops Palmarosa
5 drops Ylang-Ylang
1 drop Ginger
2 drops Rosemary
1 drop Cardamom

Wear to draw love. Anoint pink candles and burn while visualizing.

LUNAR OIL

4 parts Sandalwood
2 parts Camphor
1 part Lemon

Wear to invoke the Goddess within.

MARS OIL (PLANETARY)

2 drops Ginger
2 drops Basil
1 drop Black Pepper

Wear for physical power, lust, magical energy and all Martian influences.

MERCURY OIL (PLANETARY)

4 drops Lavender
2 drops Eucalyptus
1 drop Peppermint

Wear to draw Mercurial influences, such as communication, intelligence, travel and so on.

MOON OIL

1 drop Jasmine
1 drop Sandalwood

Wear to induce psychic dreams, to speed healing, to facilitate sleep, to increase fertility and for all other Lunar influences. Also wear at the time of the Full Moon to attune with its vibrations.

PAN OIL

3 drops Patchouly
2 drops Juniper
1 drop Pine
1 drop Oakmoss Bouquet
1 drop Cedarwood

Wear to be infused with the spirit of Pan. Ideal for magical or ritual dancing, music-making, singing and so on. Also for attuning with the Earth.

PEACE OIL

3 drops Ylang-Ylang
3 drops Lavender
2 drops Camomile
1 drop Rose absolute or otto

Wear when nervous or upset to calm you down. Stand before a mirror, and while looking into your eyes, anoint your body.

PISCES OIL

3 drops Ylang-Ylang
3 drops Sandalwood
1 drop Jasmine

Wear as a personal oil to increase your own powers.

POWER OIL

4 drops Orange
1 drop Ginger
1 drop Pine

To infuse yourself with additional power during potent rituals, anoint with Power Oil.

PROTECTION OIL

5 drops Petitgrain
5 drops Black Pepper

Wear for protection against all kinds of attacks. Also anoint windows, doors and other parts of the house to guard it.

PROTECTION OIL #2

4 drops Basil
3 drops Geranium
2 drops Pine
1 drop Vetivert

Another like the last.

PSYCHIC OIL

5 drops Lemongrass
1 drop Yarrow

Wear to increase psychic powers, especially when working with rune stones, quartz crystal spheres and other such tools.

PURIFICATION OIL

4 drops Frankincense
3 drops Myrrh
1 drop Sandalwood

Add to the bath or wear to be rid of negativity.

PURIFICATION OIL # 2

4 drops Eucalyptus
2 drops Camphor
1 drop Lemon

Another like the last.

SABBAT OIL

3 drops Frankincense
2 drops Myrrh
2 drops Sandalwood
1 drop Orange
1 drop Lemon

Add to an olive-oil base and wear to Wiccan Sabbats.

SABBAT OIL #2

2 drops Pine
1 drop Ginger
1 drop Cinnamon
1 drop Sandalwood

Add to any base oil. Another like the above.

SABBAT OIL #3

1 tsp. Frankincense, powdered
1 tsp. Myrrh, powdered
1 tsp. Benzoin, powdered

Add to 1/4 cup olive oil. Heat slowly over low flame until the gums have melted into the oil. Cool and apply sparingly as you would any oil for the Wiccan Sabbats.

SACRED OIL

3 drops Frankincense
2 drops Sandalwood
1 drop Cinnamon

Anoint your body prior to religious rituals to stimulate spirituality. Also, anoint others during mystical and religious group rites.

SAGITTARIUS OIL

4 drops Rosemary
2 drops Oakmoss Bouquet
1 drop Clove

Wear as a personal oil to increase your powers.

SATURN OIL (PLANETARY)

4 drops Cypress
2 drops Patchouly
1 drop Myrrh

Wear to break negative habits, when looking for a house, to create an aura of mystery around you, when going antiquing to find bargains, or for any Saturnian-type rituals.

SCORPIO OIL

3 drops Pine
2 drops Cardamom
1 drop Black Pepper

Wear as a personal oil to increase your powers.

SEXUAL ENERGY OIL

2 drops Ginger
2 drops Patchouly
1 drop Cardamom
1 drop Sandalwood

Wear to attract sexual partners. And please, safe sex!

SLEEP OIL

2 drops Rose
1 drop Mace

Anoint the temples, neck, pulses of both wrists, soles of the feet. It brings on natural sleep.

SLEEP OIL (DELUXE)

2 drops Rose
1 drop Jasmine
1 drop Camomile

Use as the above.

SUN OIL

4 drops Frankincense
2 drops Cinnamon
1 drop Petitgrain
1 drop Rosemary

For healing, vitality, strength, promotions and all Solar influences.

SUN OIL #2

1 tsp. Cinnamon, ground
1 tsp. Juniper berries, mashed
1 Bay leaf, crumpled
a scant pinch genuine Saffron

Gently heat over low flame in 1/4 cup base oil. Strain and use for the above purposes.

TAURUS OIL

4 drops Oakmoss Bouquet
2 drops Cardamom
1 drop Ylang-Ylang

Wear as a personal oil to increase your powers.

TEMPLE OIL

4 drops Frankincense
2 drops Rosemary
1 drop Bay
1 drop Sandalwood

Wear during religious rites, those designed to promote spirituality, "temple workings" and so on.

VENUS OIL (PLANETARY)

3 drops Ylang-Ylang
2 drops Geranium
1 drop Cardamom
1 drop Camomile

Wear to attract love and friendships, to promote beauty, and for other Venusian influences.

VIRGO OIL

4 drops Oakmoss Bouquet
2 drops Patchouly
1 drop Cypress

Wear as a personal oil to increase your powers.

VISIONS OIL

4 drops Lemongrass
2 drops Bay
1 drop Nutmeg

Anoint the forehead to produce psychic awareness.

WATER OIL (ELEMENTAL)

3 drops Palmarosa
2 drops Ylang-Ylang
1 drop Jasmine

Wear to promote love, healing, psychic awareness, purification and so on.

WEALTH OIL
———————
4 drops Tonka Bouquet
1 drop Vetivert

Wear to attract wealth in all forms. Also anoint candles and burn while visualizing.

End Note:

Those who have read the earlier edition of this book will note many changes in these oil recipes. In fact, I've changed virtually all of them for this new edition to include only true essential oils and a few bouquets.

Folk magicians have always had to invest in tools. Crystals, candles and herbs are three examples. True essential oils, despite their higher prices, are also an investment, but a necessary one for the satisfactory practice of folk magic.

Ointments

WHEN THE SUBJECT of Witches' ointments is mentioned, the infamous "flying ointments" immediately come to mind, at least to those with some interest in the history of Witchcraft and magic. These salves, consisting of psychoactive plants steeped in a fatty base, were rubbed onto the skin to aid in what is known today as astral projection.

These are not the only types of ointments known to Witches and magicians, however. Many others have more earthly uses that correlate to those of oils. In fact, any of the oils mentioned in the preceding section can be converted to ointments simply by adding them to melted beeswax, lard or (in today's world) vegetable shortening.

However made, ointments should ideally be kept in crystal or porcelain containers. Realistically, any jars with tight-fitting lids will do fine. Keep ointments away from heat and light.

Be warned—though most of the ointments discussed in this section are fairly innocuous, some of them are poisonous and may be lethal. By including them in this work, I'm in no way advocating the use of such hazardous mixtures. These ointments form a part of the herb magic of long-gone days, and so are included here solely for their historical interest.

After the first edition of this book was published, I received many letters from readers who were searching for henbane, hemlock and other baneful herbs. They had obviously ignored my warnings and were intending to make a flying ointment. Needless to say, I didn't help them out—or into an early grave.

Some folks, it seems, won't listen.

Making Ointments

Ointments are easily made. They consist simply of herbs or oils and a base. In the past, hog's lard was the preferred base because it was readily available, but vegetable shortening or beeswax produces the best results. The base must be a greasy substance that melts over heat but is solid at room temperature. Some herbalists actually use dinosaur fat (i.e., Vaseline, which is prepared from petroleum)!

There are two basic ways to create magical ointments.

The Shortening Method

Gently heat four parts shortening over low heat until liquified. Watch that it doesn't burn. Add one part dried herbal mixture, blend with a wooden spoon until thoroughly mixed, and continue heating until the shortening has extracted the scent. You should be able to smell it in the air.

Strain through cheesecloth into a heat-proof container, such as a canning jar. Add one-half teaspoon tincture of benzoin (see Tinctures in this book or buy at a drugstore) to each pint of ointment as a natural preservative. Store in a cool, dark place, such as the refrigerator. Ointments should last for weeks or months. Discard any that turn moldy, and lay in a fresh batch.

The Beeswax Method

This process creates a more cosmetic ointment without a heavy, greasy feeling. It is best to prepare it with oils rather than herbs, as it is difficult to strain.

If possible, use unbleached beeswax. If not, use what you can find. Chip it with a large, sharp knife so that you can pack it into a measuring cup. Place one-fourth cup or so of beeswax in the top of a double boiler (such as a coffee can set into a larger pot of water). Add about one-fourth cup olive, hazelnut, sesame or some other vegetable oil. Stir with a wooden spoon until the wax has melted into the oil.

Remove from the heat and let cool very slightly, until it has just begun to thicken. (This step is taken so that the hot wax won't evaporate the oils.) Now add the mixed oils to the wax. Stir thoroughly with a wooden spoon and pour into a heat proof container. Label and store in the usual way.

In the recipes that follow, the recommended method of preparation will be mentioned.

Empowering Ointments

Once the ointment is made and has cooled in its jar, empower it with its particular magical need. This vital step, remember, directs the energy within the ointment, readying it for your ritual use.

Using Ointments

Ointments are usually rubbed onto the body to effect various magical changes. As with oils, this is done with visualization and with the knowledge that the ointment will do its work.

The Recipes

EXORCISM OINTMENT

3 drops Frankincense
2 drops Peppermint
1 drop Clove
1 drop Pine

Add the oils to the beeswax/oil base. Anoint the body when you feel the need for a strong purification.

FLYING OINTMENT, NONTOXIC

1 part Dittany of Crete
1 part Cinquefoil
1 part Mugwort
1 part Parsley

Add the herbs to shortening and prepare in the usual way. Anoint the body prior to attempting astral projection.

FLYING OINTMENT, NONTOXIC #2

2 drops Sandalwood oil
1 drop Jasmine oil
1 drop Benzoin oil
1 drop Mace oil

Add the oils to the beeswax/oil base. Use as the above formula.

FLYING OINTMENT #1 (*don't even consider using this!*)

Cinquefoil
Parsley
Aconite*
Belladonna*
Hemlock*
Cowbane*

FLYING OINTMENT #2 (*ditto!*)

Hog's lard
Hashish*
Hemp flowers*
Poppy flowers
Hellebore*

I ain't kidding!

HEALING OINTMENT

4 drops Cedarwood
2 drops Sandalwood
1 drop Eucalyptus
1 drop Cinnamon

Add to the melted beeswax/oil base, cool, and anoint the body to speed healing as needed. Do not apply to wounds, burns or broken skin!

HEX-BREAKER OINTMENT

3 parts Galangal
2 parts Ginger root, dried
2 parts Vetivert
1 part Thistle

Steep the herbs in shortening, strain, cool, and anoint the body at night.

LOVE OINTMENT

4 drops Ylang-Ylang
2 drops Lavender
1 drop Cardamom
1 drop Vanilla extract

Add the oils to the beeswax/oil base. Make in the usual way and anoint the body when looking for love.

LUST OINTMENT

3 parts Galangal
2 parts Dill
1 part Ginger
1 part Peppermint
1 whole Vanilla bean

Prepare with shortening in the usual way. Anoint the body (but not *too* tender areas).

MOON GODDESS OINTMENT

5 drops Sandalwood
3 drops Lemon
1 drop Rose

Prepare with the beeswax/oil base. Anoint yourself to attune with the Goddess of the Moon and during Full Moon rituals.

PROTECTION OINTMENT

2 parts Mallow
2 parts Rosemary
1 part Vervain

Make in the usual way with shortening. Rub onto the body to drive out negative influences and to keep them far from you.

PSYCHIC POWERS OINTMENT

3 parts Bay
3 parts Star Anise
2 parts Mugwort
1 part Yerba Santa

Make in the usual way with shortening. Anoint the temples, middle of the forehead and back of the neck to improve psychic powers.

PSYCHIC POWERS OINTMENT #2

3 drops Lemongrass
2 drops Bay
1 Yarrow

Mix with the beeswax/oil base and anoint as with the above formula.

RICHES OINTMENT

4 drops Patchouly
3 drops Oakmoss Bouquet
1 drop Clove oil
1 drop Basil oil

Make according to the beeswax/oil method and anoint the body and hands daily to attract riches.

SUN GOD OINTMENT

4 drops Frankincense
3 drops Orange
1 drop Cinnamon

Make according to the beeswax/oil method. Anoint the body to attune with the Solar God, especially on Wiccan Sabbats.

VISIONS OINTMENT (*caution!*)

Hemp*
Angelica
Kava Kava

Make with shortening. Anoint to produce visions. Substitute star anise for the hemp to have *legal* visions.

WITCHES' OINTMENT, NONTOXIC

3 parts Vervain
3 parts Sandalwood
2 parts Cinnamon
1 part Carnation petals

Make in the usual way with shortening. Store in a container marked with a pentagram (five-pointed star, one point facing up). Anoint the body prior to Wiccan rituals to become one with the Goddess and God and that which lies beyond them.

WITCHES' OINTMENT, NONTOXIC #2

3 drops Frankincense
2 drops Myrrh
1 drop Sandalwood
1 drop Orange
1 drop Lemon

Make according to the beeswax/oil method. Use as with the above ointment.

WITCHES' OINTMENT (*caution!*)

Hemlock*
Poplar
Aconite*
Soot

YOUTH OINTMENT

4 parts Rosemary
2 parts Rose petals
1 part Anise
1 part Fern
1 part Myrtle

Make with shortening. For preserving or re-attaining youth, stand nude before a full-length mirror at sunrise and lightly anoint your body, visualizing yourself as you would like to be.

Inks

OIL LAMPS FLICKERED in the crudely constructed hut. An aged woman gently took her client's hand. The seer lifted a crystal bottle, and muttering an incantation, spilled a pool of ink into the young man's outstretched palm. As the black spot reflected the dancing flames, she divined his future.

Ink has long been used in magic. Perhaps its most useful application lies in its ability to transform symbols or images of our magical goals into visible form. These pictures are then used as focal points during magical ritual to stir up, program and send forth personal energy. Ink, then, is a tool of magic.

Many secret magical textbooks were carefully culled or transcribed during the Middle Ages and Renaissance. Some of these (a few of which have been published in recent times—see the Bibliography) contained sections devoted to the purification and "exorcism" of inks. The inks were used to draw symbols and signs thought to invoke or banish a horde of potentially dangerous beings. Therefore, it was deemed necessary to properly purify inks prior to their use.

Today the magical uses of ink have mostly been forgotten, though some still cast spells with the likes of pseudo "Bat's Blood Ink." When instructed to "inscribe two hearts and the symbol of Venus in green ink" or to "draw an image of your home," many magicians will grab a ball-point pen and scribble away on lined paper. In so doing they're cheating themselves of total involvement in the ritual. Many of us create incenses and oils—why shouldn't we make inks as well?

The first "ink" was probably charcoal; the first pen, a charred stick. Some proto-human who casually scraped a blackened stick on a rock must have been startled to see a dark line trailing after its point.

This can still be done today, of course. Simply burn a stick or branch until its end is reduced to charcoal—not ash. When cool, use the stick as a natural charcoal pencil to trace an image of your goal. A new char-pen should be created for each ritual. As it burns, and as you draw, visualize your magical need.

Such primeval rites may be sufficient to spark your ability to move and direct personal power. If not, try creating your own magical inks.

All magical inks require the use of sharpened quills or dip pens, the latter usually available at stationery and office supply shops. Practice using the dip pen to gain sufficient proficiency before using it for magic.

Two recipes have been preserved from ancient times for magical inks. Unfortunately, they're difficult to make and may not produce satisfactory results. Purely for curiosity's sake, here they are:

MAGICAL INK #1

10 oz. Gall nuts
3 oz. Green Copperas
3 oz. Rock Alum or Gum Arabic

Reduce all ingredients to a powder and place in a newly glazed earthen pot with river water. Make a fire of sprigs of fern gathered on St. John's Eve (Midsummer) and vine twigs cut on the Full Moon in March. Add virgin paper to this fire and set the pot over it. When the water boils, the ink will be made.

MAGICAL INK #2

Frankincense "smoke"
Myrrh "smoke"
Rose Water
Sweet Wine
Gum Arabic

Take the smoke of frankincense and myrrh (presumably obtained by holding a spoon over the smoldering gums—see the section on lampblack below). Mix this in a basin with a little rose water and sweet-smelling wine. Add enough gum arabic to make the mixture thick enough to write with.

Such recipes, which date from the 1600s or even earlier, are perfect examples of why magical ink-making has died out. A more simplified version of the second recipe actually does produce a useable ink for those willing to invest time and work in the project. It is printed below.

Lampblack

Lampblack is used in both the previous and following formulas. It is obtained through the use of a candle. If you're making ink for general magical needs, use a white candle. Inks created for specific goals call for colored candles. For instance, if you're creating an ink for money, use a green candle; for love, a pink taper (see Appendix 1: Colors).

Light a candle of the proper color and hold the back of the spoon's bowl in its flame, barely touching the wick. After leaving it there for, say, 30 to 45 seconds, the flame will have covered the spoon with a black coating. Remove the spoon from the flame and hold it over a small bowl. Carefully scrape off the lampblack into the bowl using a small piece of cardboard or cardstock, such as a three-by-five-inch card.

Ensure that the lampblack actually does fall into the bowl. It's lighter than air and will happily fly all over the table or carpet if you don't watch it carefully.

Repeat this process 30 to 60 times (which will take from 30 minutes to an hour) until you've acquired a generous amount of the flimsy, dark black soot. If you're making an ink for a specific magical goal, visualize it constantly throughout the lampblack gathering.

Your hands will be dirty by this time, and hopefully, the spoon handle won't be too hot.

(If for some reason you're trying Magical Ink #2, collect the soot from smoldering frankincense and myrrh.)

Then make the following recipe. No amounts are given in this formula because lampblack is difficult (impossible!) to measure. One warning though—the longer you collect lampblack, the less miniscule the amount of resultant ink.

MAGICAL INK #3

Lampblack
Distilled Water
Gum Arabic

To the bowl of lampblack add warm or hot distilled water *one drop at a time*. Stop adding water before you think you should. Mix the soot and water with a finger until the soot has completely dissolved and the water is inky black. This isn't easy, as lampblack likes to float on top of the water.

If you've added too much water (i.e., if the water is a dull grey), add more lampblack until the dense hue is achieved.

Next, add a small amount of ground gum arabic, and mix with your finger (or a spoon if making a large quantity) until the gum has been dissolved in the warm liquid. The mixture should be as thick as commercially prepared ink. Study a bottle of ink to determine its correct thickness.

Judging the proper proportions of lampblack, water and gum arabic is difficult, but if you follow these instructions you should produce useable magical ink on your first try. After mixing, store in a small bottle and wash your hands—they'll need it.

Simple Magical Inks

Many of these were included in the previous edition of this book. Try out a few if you wish. If the liquid is too thin to write with, add a bit of gum arabic.

MAGICAL INK #4

Saffron essence makes a fine magical ink, but the price is exorbitant.

MAGICAL INK #5

Fresh pokeberries, when crushed, produce a purple ink. In fact, one of the names of poke is "inkberry." The seeds are poisonous, so as usual, keep this ink out of your mouth.

MAGICAL INK #6

Beet juice makes a reddish ink. Add gum arabic to thicken if necessary.

MAGICAL INK #7

Try blackberry, boysenberry or grape juice.

MAGICAL INK #8

"Invisible" inks are easily made, as any Boy Scout knows. Milk, lemon juice and so on are all used, written with a clean dip pen on white paper. This is useful in many types of spells; use your imagination. To make the invisible writing appear, hold the paper carefully over a candle flame (close enough so that the flame heats the paper but doesn't burn it) until the writing appears.

An example of the ritual uses of invisible inks: Write or draw an image of your magical goal with invisible ink. Do this with power, with visualization. When it has dried, stare at the paper and see—nothing. This represents your life without your need. Next, hold it near the candle flame, and as the image slowly appears, send energy into it knowing that the need will manifest in your life as well.

Using Magical Inks

It's simple. Here are a few ideas:

• Write or draw an image of your magical goal on a piece of appropriately colored paper. Visualize the letters glowing with energy as you write them, or the picture shimmering with power.

• Anoint the paper with oils in harmony with your need and burn it to ashes. As it burns, see the energy you've poured into it streaming out to manifest your need.

• Create a low-cost scrying tool: At night, burn a psychism-inducing incense. Add several drops of black ink to a small, round bowl of water. When the water has darkened, turn off the lights, light a yellow or white candle and gaze into the water. Relax your conscious, doubting mind and allow yourself to contact your psychic mind. Open yourself to receiving information relating to possible future trends.

NOTE: Some old spells call for ink to be taken internally. This may entail drawing an image on a piece of paper, dissolving this in water and downing the liquid. Most commercially prepared inks are poisonous, as are many home-prepared ones, so *do not drink or eat ink!* Keep modern knowledge in mind when performing old rituals.

Tinctures

OILS ARE WIDELY used in magic to stimulate ritual consciousness through our sense of smell, as well as to add their own energies to spells. The scented liquids known as tinctures are just as effective as oils. In magical perfumery, a tincture is created by soaking dried plant materials in alcohol, which captures the odor. This process is fairly quick and easy, and creates wonderful products that can be used much as oils are in magic.

However, there is a problem. The alcohol used in magical tincturing is *ethyl alcohol*, also known as ethanol or grain alcohol. Isopropyl, or rubbing alcohol, is distilled from petroleum products; its sharp odor makes it unsuitable for capturing fragrances, so don't try to use it. Ethyl alcohol is a completely natural product distilled from grain, sugar or grapes.

Unfortunately, ethyl alcohol is sometimes difficult to find. It is usually expensive. While "Everclear," a 192-proof alcohol, is sometimes available in the United States, it is quite costly. (192-proof alcohol indicates that it contains 96 percent alcohol.) Since I live near the U.S.–Mexican border, I usually buy my ethyl alcohol in Tijuana. Adults are allowed to bring one quart of liquor across the border.

For tincturing you need an alcohol of at least 70 percent strength, or 140 proof. Vodka, which is pure ethyl alcohol, is only 90 proof, or 45 percent alcohol, so it isn't strong enough to produce the best scent. Check liquor stores, supermarkets and drug stores for sources of ethyl alcohol. Once you've found it, you're ready to start making magical tinctures.

The process is almost unbelievably easy. Begin with a good supply of dried plant materials. Fresh herbs won't work due to their water content. Some plants aren't soluble in alcohol—that is, their scents won't transfer to the ethyl and so won't produce highly scented tinctures. Consult the list of recommended herbs in this section or experiment on your own.

Most sources say to use 70 percent alcohol, but I've had good results with 96 percent. If you wish to be adventurous (and also to stretch your alcohol supply), dilute the ethyl with distilled water. This will help capture certain plant scents that aren't fully soluble in water.

Creating Tinctures

Grind the dried herbs that are to be tinctured in your mortar and pestle. Reduce to the finest possible powder. This is especially important with woods such as sandalwood; you may wish to consider buying them pre-ground.

Next, empower the herb, keeping in mind the magical goal of the tincture you're about to make. Pour the herb into a small bottle with a tight-fitting lid. Using a small funnel, pour just enough ethyl alcohol into the bottle to wet and cover the herb. Cap tightly. Shake the bottle vigorously every day for a week or two. Every time you shake, visualize the tincture's magical goal.

Then, using a coffee filter (or a piece of cheesecloth laid in a strainer), strain the alcohol. The scent may be strong enough at this point—it usually is with gums such as frankincense and myrrh. If not, add more herb to the bottle and pour the alcohol over it. Do this quickly; alcohol evaporates when exposed to air.

Let this sit again and repeat the process, shaking every day. The alcohol should become heavily scented and colored. (In fact, this may happen soon after you add the alcohol to the herbs.) If it doesn't you're using a plant that isn't readily soluble in alcohol. Add a bit of water to the alcohol and try again, or select one of those herbs mentioned in this section.

To correctly determine whether the tincture is properly scented, apply a drop or two to your wrist. Wait until the alcohol has evaporated and then sniff. Many tinctures won't smell "true" in the bottle.

When the plant's scent has completely overpowered the sickly-sweet alcohol odor, filter it one last time, bottle, add a few drops of castor oil or glycerine to stabilize the fragrance, and label and store in a cool place out of direct sunlight until needed.

Now that you've made your magical tincture, what do you do with it?

Using Tinctures

Under no circumstances drink a magical tincture! Many of the plant materials used in magical tincturing can be harmful if swallowed. The 192-proof alcohol certainly isn't very healthy for you, either. However, there are other uses. One of these was mentioned in the Incense section: scented incense papers. This seems to work best with gum and resin tinctures or with any heavily fragranced tinctures.

Some tinctures can be used to anoint the skin, to bring the plant's power within you, but try this out on a small area of the skin at first. The alcohol will quickly evaporate, leaving the plant's scent. Some tinctures can be irritating to the skin, while others leave rather nasty stains or gummy, sticky residues. This is often the case with frankincense and copal tinctures. Lavender, clove, patchouly and many other tinctures are fine for anointing purposes, but all alcohol-based tinctures can dry sensitive skin.

Tinctures can also be used to anoint magical tools, sachets, candles and jewelry; added to bath water; mixed in with oils; added to ointments and so on. Virtually all ritual uses of oils also apply to tinctures.

Following are some herbs that I've tinctured with good results. Also included are some sample recipes for you to try. You may find, as I have, that tincturing is far more reliable in capturing certain plants' scents than is any other do-it-yourself method.

A few quick notes: ethyl alcohol will quickly "take" scents from such spices as clove and star anise. Gums such as frankincense, myrrh, benzoin and copal also work well, though the results, as mentioned above, can be rather gummy. Other herbs are rather hit-and-miss affairs. Experiment!

Recommended Tincturing Materials

BENZOIN—This dark brown, translucent tincture is cleanly antiseptic-smelling, and is perfect for increasing business success and sharpening mental powers. It is used in purificatory rituals such as anointing and then burning a white candle. A few drops of benzoin tincture can be added to scented oils and to ointments to preserve them.

CAMPHOR—Use only real camphor, of course. This produces a clear tincture with a penetrating, cool odor. Sniff it to lessen sexual desire. Use it to anoint healing amulets (sachets) or add to Full Moon baths.

CINNAMON—A gorgeous, rich scent. Anoint money sachets, add to money baths, sniff to develop psychic powers, add to protective blends. The tincture is a deep red, almost brownish black hue.

CLOVE—Another incredible scent. Use in protection and exorcism formulas. Anoint money with clove tincture before spending. Use for love. Makes a transparent, light brown tincture.

COPAL—This fine gum from Mexico produces a light yellow, translucent tincture that feels tacky on the skin. Its scent is reminiscent of a combination of frankincense and lemon. Anoint for protection and use in spirituality formulas.

DEERSTONGUE—A warm vanilla scent. Sniff to increase psychic powers. The light green tincture is also used to attract men.

FRANKINCENSE—One of the first tinctures I ever made, frankincense produces a beautiful golden-colored tincture with a full frankincense scent. Once you've smelled this, you'll realize that most frankincense oil is purely synthetic. Anoint tools, sachets or the body (if you don't mind sticky skin). Use for spirituality, exorcism, purification, luck and protection rites. This is one of the best tinctures to use in scenting incense papers.

GALANGAL—This rootstock produces a light yellow tincture smelling of ginger and camphor. Use for luck, money, protection, exorcism and psychic development.

LAVENDER—This light green tincture can be used to attract love; to produce sleep by anointing your forehead and pillow; to purify by adding to baths, and to promote chastity and peace.

MYRRH—A bittersweet brown tincture. Myrrh is used for spirituality, healing and protection purposes. The scent recalls ancient times and is evocative when mixed with frankincense. Another tincture well suited for use with incense papers.

NUTMEG—A translucent, reddish-orange tincture. Sniff to increase psychic powers, or anoint money, health and luck amulets (sachets).

PATCHOULY—This heady, earth-scented herb makes an evocative green tincture. It is useful for money, love and fertility purposes.

PEPPERMINT—Though slow-going, the results are worth your efforts. This mint-green tincture is used in money, purification and love rituals. Anoint sleep pillows. Try spearmint, too.

ROSEMARY—A rich, resinous tincture, yellowish green in color. It can be used for nearly every magical goal: love, healing, protection, exorcism, sleep, lust and so on.

SAGE—I use the local white sage for this tincture, which produces a powerful, greenish-brown tincture. Its scent is somewhat similar to camphor with a strong "green note." It is used in healing, purification, obtaining wisdom and protection, and can also be used to anoint wishing amulets or sachets.

SANDALWOOD—This is another herb that is slow to tincture. Be sure to use *ground* sandalwood for this and give it a try. This tincture seems to take the longest to "cook," but when finished, smells like sandalwood with a slight cedary odor. Use for protection, spirituality, healing and exorcistic purposes.

STAR ANISE—This spicy, star-shaped herb produces a sassafras-smelling tincture. Sniff to improve psychic awareness, especially before working with tarot cards, rune stones and other divinatory tools.

TONKA—A rich vanilla scent with a slightly bitter after-note. Anoint money, love, courage and wish amulets (sachets), but do not take internally. Tonka beans are poisonous and, therefore, are becoming harder to obtain.

VANILLA—This familiar culinary herb makes a rich, warm-smelling tincture. It is useful to attract love, to promote physical energy, and to stimulate mental processing.

WOOD ALOE—This Malaysian bark produces a tincture smelling of ginger and pepper, highly resinous. It is perfect for anointing sacred tools, the altar, luck and spirituality amulets and talismans.

To reiterate: Don't sniff tinctures until after the alcohol has evaporated from them—after anointing. Once the alcohol evaporates, the herb's scent will blossom before your nose.

The above list is short, but it is a good starting point for those interested in magical tincturing.

Following are a few formulas for tinctures that you can try. They are combinations of some of the herbs mentioned above. All of these are safe for anointing on the skin, but their alcohol content does make them drying. Gum-based resins, again, can be sticky. (Don't say I haven't warned you!)

For proportions, use equal parts unless your psychic awareness tells you otherwise. Mix them exactly as you would oils.

Remember that when using tinctures (as with all magical herb products), do so with visualization and power.

The Recipes

GUARDIAN TINCTURE

Cinnamon
Sandalwood
Clove

Anoint yourself or objects for protection.

HEALTHY MIND, HEALTHY BODY TINCTURE

Sage
Myrrh
Rosemary

Anoint your body, healing amulets (sachets), blue candles and so on to speed healing or to retain good health.

LOVE TINCTURE

Lavender
Rosemary
Patchouly

Anoint your body or love sachets to attract a love and to expand your ability to give and to receive love.

MONEY TINCTURE

Patchouly
Clove
Nutmeg
Cinnamon

Anoint money before spending; anoint money amulets, your purse or wallet, cash register and so on.

SACRED TINCTURE

Frankincense
Myrrh
Benzoin

Anoint yourself to increase your involvement with spiritual activities, especially prior to meditation and religious rituals of all kinds.

THIRD EYE TINCTURE

Star Anise
Clove
Nutmeg
Deerstongue

Anoint your pillow for psychic dreams (careful though; this will probably stain—use one pillowcase just for this purpose). Also anoint the wrists and forehead before using your natural psychic abilities.

Herb Baths

A BAG OF HERBS rests in a tub of warm water. As they soak, the plants emit tinted, scented water. The magical bath begins.

Adding herbs to the bath is certainly one of the easiest forms of magic. In essence, a tub of water containing a bath sachet is little more than a huge pot of herb tea in which the bather brews. When herbs are placed in warm water they release their energies as well as their scents and colors. As such, baths are powerful tools in gaining psychic awareness, drawing love, speeding healing and granting personal protection.

Making the Sachets

Choose to follow one of the recipes included in this section, or create your own. Each bath mixture may be prepared in advance and saved until needed if kept in an airtight jar.

Once you've assembled all ingredients, add them to your mixing bowl. Mingle the herbs with your fingers, pouring your power into them and visualizing your magical goal. When mixed, place about a handful or so in the center of a large square of cheesecloth. Tie up the ends and add this to the bath. If you don't have any cheesecloth, simply use an old washcloth.

To save time in the future, make up several bath sachets. Place them in a jar with a tight-fitting lid and store.

Using the Sachets

This is simple. Fill the clean tub with warm water. Place the sachet in the tub and let it steep until the water is colored and scented.

If you don't have a bathtub, or if you simply prefer showers, make up a sachet in a washcloth and scrub your body with this after your normal shower, just before toweling.

A third method of utilizing the sachets is a bit more complicated. Heat two cups water until boiling. Pour this over one or two sachets in a heat-proof container. Cover and let the herbs steep for ten to thirteen minutes. Remove the sachets, squeeze out the last drops of scented water from them, and pour the infusion into the bath.

Some natural magicians prefer to add the flowers, herbs and barks directly to the water without first enclosing them in cloth. This is almost certain to leave you with petal-covered skin and clogged plumbing if you don't spend ten minutes or so picking herbs out of the water after your bath.

As you step into the tub, feel the herb's energies mixing with your own. Visualize your magical goal. Don't make the herbs do all the work—invite their energies inside you and send them out to the universe (through your visualization) to bring your need into manifestation. Repeat the bath for as many days as you feel is necessary.

I've had people write to me asking how long they should repeat magical baths. There are no rules in this area. As I just said, continue the baths until you feel that they've done their work. That's it!

If you wish, burn an appropriate incense and perhaps some candles in the bathroom while you soak.

The Recipes

ANTI-HEX BATH

4 parts Rosemary
3 parts Juniper
2 parts Bay
1 part Mugwort

Soak in this mixture at night to purify you of all ills.

APHRODISIAC BATH

3 parts Rose petals
2 parts Rosemary
2 parts Thyme
1 part Myrtle
1 part Jasmine flowers
1 part Acacia flowers

Add three drops of musk oil to the tub. Bathe before meeting a lover, or bathe with a friend!

BEAUTY BATH

3 parts Lavender
3 parts Rosemary
2 parts Spearmint
1 part Comfrey root
1 part Thyme

Place a hand mirror next to the tub. Lie back, smell the scented water, and close your eyes. Relax. Be at peace. Visualize yourself as you wish to appear, then open your eyes. Hold the mirror before your face and see the new you.

"BREAK THE HABIT" BATH

2 parts Rosemary
1 part Lavender
1 part Lemongrass
1 part Lemon Verbena
1 part Sage

To rid yourself of negative, baneful habits as well as their root causes: Place the sachet in the tub. After it has colored the water, step into it. Lie back in the water and visualize yourself happily avoiding the habit or other negative condition—smoking, drinking, drugs, depressions, obsessions and so on. Visualize the water absorbing your desire and need for the habit. See in your mind's eye all the energy you've been giving to this negative condition seeping out into the water. When you've visualized all that you can, pull the plug and sit in the tub until the water has drained out. Splash fresh water onto your body, washing away all traces of the taint. Repeat daily.

DIETER'S MAGICAL BATH

2 parts Rosemary
2 parts Fennel
1 part Lavender
1 pinch Kelp

For best results, repeat this bath morning and night. While in the tub, visualize yourself as possessing complete control over your eating habits. See yourself eating sensible foods in sensible quantities. For symbolic associations, begin this bath regime two days after the Full Moon and continue until the New Moon. On the last day of the two-week period, visualize yourself as you wish to be—slim, fit, healthy.

DIVINATION BATH

3 parts Thyme
2 parts Yarrow
2 parts Rose
1 part Patchouly
1 part Nutmeg

Bathe in this mixture directly before practicing any form of divination, to relax the conscious mind and to stimulate psychic awareness.

ENERGY BATH

3 parts Carnation
2 parts Lavender
2 parts Rosemary
2 parts Basil

Use when fatigued or depressed. Gives a lift, especially if you let the water cool slightly before bathing. Visualize the water sparkling with fiery droplets of energy that melt into your body, lending you vitality and power.

EXORCISM BATH

2 parts Basil
2 parts Rosemary
1 part Yarrow
1 part Cumin
1 pinch Rue

Bathe in this mixture to cleanse yourself of negativity, especially when you feel that someone (or some*thing*) is out to get you. Visualize the energy-packed water absorbing the negative energies from your body. Splash fresh water over your body after this bath to remove all traces of the negativity.

HEALING BATH

3 parts Rosemary
2 parts Lavender
2 parts Rose
1 part Peppermint
1 part Cinnamon

To be used, of course, in conjunction with conventional medical attention. This bath speeds the healing process. To help shake off a cold, add two parts eucalyptus to this formula. (Avoid bathing if your doctor so informs you.)

LOVE BATH

3 parts Rose petals
2 parts Lovage
1 part Dill

Bathe in this mixture daily to bring a love into your life. Visualize yourself as a loving, caring person seeking another of like mind.

LOVE BATH #2

3 parts Rose petals
2 parts Rose Geranium
1 part Rosemary

Another like the above.

LOVE BATH #3

3 parts Orange flowers
2 parts Lavender
1 part Gardenia petals
1 part Cardamom
1 part Ginger
1 part Rosemary
1 part Rose petals

A third like the above.

MONEY BATH

3 parts Patchouly
2 parts Basil
1 part Cinnamon
1 part Cedar

Bathe in this mixture to increase your finances.

MONEY BATH #2

3 parts Clove
2 parts Cinnamon
1 part Galangal

Another like the above.

PEACE BATH

2 parts Catnip
2 parts Hops
1 part Jasmine
1 part Elder flowers

Bathe to stem anger and to relieve stress. Visualize yourself releasing the anger or stress into the water as you sit in it. Feel it floating out and the water absorbing the hurt, pain, nerves and wrathful feelings. Splash fresh water onto your body after the bath.

PROTECTION BATH

4 parts Rosemary
3 parts Bay
2 parts Basil
2 parts Fennel
1 part Dill

To strengthen your psychic armor, bathe in this mixture daily until you feel strong.

PSYCHIC BATH

3 parts Lemongrass
2 parts Thyme
2 parts Orange peel
1 part Clove
1 part Cinnamon

Use before working with your psychic awareness. Or, repeat this bath daily to become increasingly aware of psychic impulses. Visualize.

RITUAL PURIFICATION BATH

4 parts Lavender
4 parts Rosemary
3 parts Thyme
3 parts Basil
2 parts Fennel
2 parts Hyssop
1 part Mint
1 part Vervain
1 pinch Valerian root

This recipe, adapted from *The Key of Solomon*, is ideal for use before all types of magical rituals, or when you simply wish to feel clean and free of impurities. If you add more than a pinch of valerian, you'll be sorry. It smells—well, trust me; it smells!

SUMMER MAGICAL CLEANSING BATH

3 parts Marjoram
3 parts Thyme

Use this mixture during the spring and summer to wash away the chills of winter and to "spring clean" yourself.

WINTER MAGICAL CLEANSING BATH

3 parts Pine needles
2 parts Bay
1 part Rosemary

Bathe in this blend during the winter months to refresh and revitalize your magical energies.

WITCH'S BATH

3 parts Rosemary
3 parts Carnation petals
2 parts Galangal
2 parts Cinnamon
1 part Ginger

While bathing in this mixture, visualize yourself possessing perfected abilities to rouse, direct and release personal power. Use prior to all types of positive magical rituals for extra potency.

Bath Salts

BATH SALTS ARE an easily prepared alternative to bath herbs, and are to be preferred to the caustic mixtures now on the market. Most of these chemical-ridden formulas are almost guaranteed to irritate your skin.

Creating Bath Salts

The basic ingredients are table salt, baking soda (sodium bicarbonate) and Epsom salts (magnesium sulfate). Some herbalists also use borax. Add the salts to a large bowl in these proportions:

3 parts Epsom salts
2 parts baking soda
1 part table salt (or Borax)

Mix thoroughly. This is now the base from which you can create a wide variety of bath salts. With this you can make up a large quantity of one type of bath salt. If two or three types are preferred, simply divide the base and set aside those portions to be separately fragranced and colored.

It's wise to add the power of colors to bath salts. Use plain food coloring for this purpose, letting it fall drop by drop onto the salt base. If two or more colors are required to mix an exotic hue (such as purple), mix these in a spoon first and then add to the salts to avoid creating a two-toned product. Recommended colors for all bath salt mixtures are included in the recipes. For those that read "Color: White," simply leave them untinted.

Add many drops for a darker colored salt; fewer for a lightly hued salt. Mix the color into the salts with a spoon until it is evenly distributed.

Now add the essential oils drop by drop, one ingredient at a time, until the scent seems right. Mix with a spoon until all salt particles are moistened. Be prepared to spend some time doing this, perhaps a half hour or so. As you mix, visualize the energies within the oils merging with each other and with the salt. Keep the salt's magical goal in mind while you stir.

Empower the mixture according to the basic ritual in Chapter 3. Use or store until needed.

As to proportions: Though each recipe lists relative proportions (two parts almond oil; one part mint), rely on your nose to determine the exact quantities (such as one tablespoon or 30 drops). The more potent the finished product's scent, the less will have to be used for each bath. Bath salts should be strongly scented.

To use, add from two tablespoons to one-half cup of the ritual bath salts to a full tub. Mix with your hands, feeling their energies merge with the water.

While sitting in the tub, soak up the power. Allow yourself to receive it, or alternately, to release specific negative energies from yourself into the water.

Directly after every ritual bath (and before, if necessary), clean your tub, either with a commercial cleanser or with a damp cloth covered with baking soda. Ritual baths taken in unclean bathtubs won't have the desired effects!

The proportions here, though for essential oils, are by parts. One part may equal six drops. Generally speaking, there shouldn't be more than ten total drops of essential oil per half-cup of bath salts. Experiment to find what works best, and please use only genuine essential oils.

The Recipes

AIR BATH (ELEMENTAL)

3 parts Lavender
2 parts Rosemary
1 part Peppermint
1 part Bergamot Mint Bouquet
Color: Yellow

Use to attune with the powers of Air, for divination, theorization, aiding the memory, concentration, clear thinking, visualization and study.

CELIBACY BATH

4 parts Lavender
2 parts Camphor
Color: White

Add to a tub of tepid water—not hot. Bathe in this blend when you wish to cool down.

CIRCLE BATH

3 parts Rosemary
2 parts Myrrh
2 parts Sandalwood
1 part Frankincense
Color: Purple

Bathe in Circle Bath before any form of magical working to strengthen, purify and prepare yourself for ritual.

EARTH BATH (ELEMENTAL)

4 parts Patchouly
3 parts Cypress
1 part Vetivert
Color: Green

For use in attuning with the Earth, or for spells involving money, foundation, stability, creativity, fertility, ecology and so on.

EXORCISM BATH

3 parts Frankincense
3 parts Sandalwood
2 parts Rosemary
1 *drop* Clove
Color: White

Bathe in this mixture for a heavy psychic cleansing. Splash fresh water over your body after the bath. NOTE: Do not add more than one drop of clove essential oil—it can irritate the skin.

FIRE BATH (ELEMENTAL)

3 parts Frankincense
2 parts Basil
2 parts Juniper
1/2 part Orange
Color: Red

For use in attuning with the element of Fire, or for rituals involving strength, courage, passion, lust and so on.

FLOWERY LOVE BATH

3 parts Palmarosa
2 parts Lavender
1 drop Rose
Color: Pink

Bathe in this mixture to attract love and to expand your ability to give and to receive love. NOTE: I've specified one drop of rose because of its high cost. More can be added if desired; indeed, rose absolute can be used in place of palmarosa, which is much less expensive.

HEALING BATH

3 parts Niaouli
2 parts Eucalyptus
1 part Sandalwood
Color: Dark Blue

For use in speeding healing. Release the ailment into the water. Splash fresh water over your body before toweling. And don't bathe, of course, if your condition doesn't allow it.

HIGH AWARENESS BATH

3 parts Cedarwood
2 parts Sandalwood
1 part Frankincense
Color: Purple

Bathe in this mixture to direct your consciousness toward higher things, to promote spirituality and to combat Earth-obsessions such as uncontrolled spending, overeating, sluggishness and all forms of unbalanced materialism.

LOVE BATH

3 parts Rosemary
2 parts Lavender
1 part Cardamom
1 part Yarrow
Color: Pink

For promoting and attracting love. Use with visualization, as with all of these formulas.

LUST BATH

3 parts Sandalwood
2 parts Patchouly
1 part Cardamom
Color: Red

For promoting lustful desires.

PROTECTION BATH

3 parts Rosemary
2 parts Frankincense
1 part Lavender
Color: White

Bathe in this mixture daily to strengthen your psychic armor and to stave off all manner of attacks—physical, mental, spiritual, psychic and emotional.

PSYCHIC BATH

4 parts Yarrow
1 part Bay
Color: Light Blue

Use this blend in baths to strengthen your psychic awareness.

PURIFICATION BATH

3 parts Geranium
2 parts Rosemary
1 part Frankincense

Bathe in this blend to purify body, spirit and soul.

SEA WITCH BATH

3 parts Lotus Bouquet
2 parts Lavender
1 part Rosemary
Color: Dark Blue

Add a bit of sea salt to the salt base. Bathe in Sea Witch Bath for a gentle purification prior to magical works.

SPIRITUAL BATH

4 parts Sandalwood
2 parts Myrrh
1 part Frankincense
1 *drop* Cinnamon
Color: Purple

Use to increase your awareness of the divine, especially before religious rituals. NOTE: Use only one *drop* of cinnamon essential oil.

WATER BATH (ELEMENTAL)

2 parts Camomile
2 parts Yarrow
1 part Ylang-Ylang
1 part Palmarosa
Color: Dark Blue

Use for attuning with the element of Water, or for love, psychic awareness, friendships, healing and so on.

WATER BATH (ELEMENTAL) #2
(a less expensive version)

2 parts Palmarosa
1 part Sandalwood
1 part Myrrh
1 part Geranium
Color: Dark Blue

Another like the last.

Brews

MIDNIGHT. LIGHTNING SLASHES the stormy sky. Three haggard figures on a lonely hill lean over a huge cauldron. They throw noisome ingredients into the boiling water—poisonous herbs, noxious reptiles, snake venom—and cackle as steam rises and the wind howls like tortured demons.

So goes the standard brew-making scene, thanks in large part to authors such as William Shakespeare. They vividly captured and firmly implanted such powerful but absurd images in our minds.

Brews (also known as potions) may be as prosaic as herb tea, or as mystical as rainbow infusion. They stem from early magical, ritual and medicinal preparations, and are as effective today as they were thousands of years ago.

In herb magic, brews are little more than herbal infusions or teas. They needn't be prepared over an open fire in a forest clearing; your own stove or backyard will do nicely.

The brews in this chapter answer a variety of needs and are utilized in various ways. Some are drunk, others added to the bath, and still others prepared to release fragrant steam into the air, infusing the area with the sum total of the herb's vibrations.

It's the Water

The type of water used in brewing is of some importance. Well, spring and distilled waters are preferred over that which pours from the tap. You can buy these bottled or collect them from the source, so long as it's unpolluted and free running. Rain water is ideal for use—except when gathered in smoggy areas. Tap water can be used as a last resort, but consider purchasing the bottled variety in the future.

In the last edition of this book I mentioned that distilled water is used for medicinal preparations, "which is fine, but *not* for magical operations, for it is inert." Why this change of heart? If you're going to drink the brew (or even if you're not), distilled water is definitely better than chlorinated, fluoridated, bacteria-filled tap water. If it's all you have, use it.

Sea water and mineral water aren't recommended due to their high mineral content.

Brewing

The Heating

Fire, gas flame or stove coils will do for the heat source. I suppose you could prepare a brew in a microwave oven, but this isn't the best idea. If nothing else, it reduces some of the *magic* of the process.

If you're the old-fashioned kind, try making a brew in a fireplace or outdoors over a blaze.

The Vessels

It's best if the water and herbs don't come into direct contact with metal while brewing. There are few exceptions to this in herbalism. One is cauldron brewing, which is little-practiced today. Herbal products prepared with double boilers may also require metal pots. But in general, avoid metal.

Clear glass jars work well for Solar infusions. Simply place the water and herbs into the jar and set this in direct sunlight, preferably outdoors. Leave it there for most of the day. Some brews included here are made with glass jars of various colors.

The Brew

Not every brew included in this section is made in the following manner; use specific instructions where given.

For a basic brew: Gather, grind and mix the herbs. For brews to be drunk, use a separate culinary mortar and pestle for grinding, not the one used for heavy-duty magical herbs.

Empower the herbs with your magical goal.

Heat about two cups water to boiling. Place about one handful of mixed, empowered herbs in a teapot or some other heat-proof, non-metallic container. Pour the water over the herbs. Cover with an equally nonmetallic, steam-tight lid. Let the herbs brew for about 13 minutes. Strain through cheesecloth or a bamboo strainer, and use as directed.

Brews should be used as quickly as possible. If necessary, they can be stored in the refrigerator for three or four days. After this time return them to the Earth and create a new brew.

A note regarding "love" potions. There are no drinks that will emotionally enslave another person to you, no brews that will cause love. However, some brews have long been celebrated for relaxing inhibitions and mellowing the emotions. Also, a few have been used to smooth over difficulties during long-term relationships and marriages. A few of these are included here, but they're definitely not love potions!

The Recipes

APHRODISIA: A PASSION DRINK

1 pinch Rosemary
2 pinches Thyme
2 tsp. Black Tea
1 pinch Coriander
3 fresh Mint leaves (or 1/2 tsp. dried)
5 fresh Rosebud petals (or 1 tsp. dried)
5 fresh Lemon tree leaves (or 1 tsp. dried Lemon peel)
3 pinches Nutmeg
3 pieces Orange peel

Place all ingredients into teapot. Boil three cups or so of water and add to the pot. Sweeten with honey, if desired. Serve hot.

APHRODISIA #2

5 parts Rose petals
1 part Clove
1 part Nutmeg
1 part Lavender
1 part Ginger

Make in the usual way, preferably in an earthen pot. Add this mixture to tea, or serve alone to increase the passions.

CAULDRON OF CERRIDWEN BREW (*caution!*)

Acorns*
Barley
Honey
Ivy*
Hellebore*
Bay

Boil water in a cauldron over an open fire. Place all ingredients into the cauldron. Sit before it and entrance yourself by watching the flames. Smell its mystic scent and receive wisdom. (*Do not drink. Why? It's poisonous, that's why!*)

CAULDRON OF CERRIDWEN BREW (nontoxic)

1 part Bay
1 part Tobacco
1 part Damiana
1 part Mormon Tea
1 part Broom

Use according to the above directions.

CLAIRVOYANCE BREW

3 parts Rose petals
1 part Cinnamon
1 part Nutmeg
1 part Bay
I part Mugwort

Place in teapot, fill with boiling water, let steep, covered, for a few minutes. Remove cover, sniff steam (not so that you burn your nose) for a few moments, visualize the mystic scent opening your psychic awareness, then lie down and prophesize. If you wish, drink a bit of the brew as well, and let the steam continue to rise as you stretch your psychic awareness.

DREAM TEA

2 parts Rose petals
1 part Mugwort
1 part Peppermint
1 part Jasmine flowers
1/2 part Cinnamon

Mix, add one teaspoon to a cup. Pour boiling water over this and let steep, covered, for a few minutes. Drink before going to bed to produce psychic dreams.

EXORCISM BREW (*caution!*)

3 parts Rosemary
1 part Bay
1 pinch Cayenne*

Mix, add one teaspoon mixture to a cup, pour boiling over the herbs and let steep for nine minutes, covered. Drink a few teaspoons a day, or add to the bath.

(Cayenne pepper is marked here with a *caution!* because it is a strong herb. Use with care and respect.)

ISIS HEALING BREW

1 part Rosemary
1 part Sage
1 part Thyme
1 part Cinnamon

Half fill a blue-glass bottle with fresh water. Add the ground, empowered herbs to it and let this sit in the Sun all day. If by sunset the water has been colored by the herbs, it is ready for use. If not, store in the refrigerator overnight and steep in the Sun the following day. Strain. Anoint the body or add to bath water while visualizing yourself as being in perfect health.

KERNUNNOS PROTECTION BREW

1 part Pine needles
1 part Caraway
1 part Bay
1 part Basil
1 part Anise

In a red-glass bottle half-filled with water, steep the herbs in the Sun for a day. Strain and add to bath water, or anoint your body for personal protection. Also, anoint protective amulets and talismans.

LOVE WINE

3 tsp. Cinnamon
3 tsp. Ginger
1 one-inch piece Vanilla bean
2 cups Red Wine
2 tsp. Rhubarb juice (optional)

Score the vanilla bean along its length. Add herbs to the red wine with the vanilla bean. Add two teaspoons rhubarb juice (if available), and let sit for three days. Serve.

MONEY BREW

3 parts Sassafras
2 parts Cedar
1 part Allspice
1 part Clove
1 part Dill
1 part Vetivert
1 part Calamus

Half fill a green-glass bottle with fresh water. Add about a handful or so of the mixed, empowered herbs. Cap tightly and leave in full sunlight all day. At dusk, sniff the water. If the scent is strong, strain and add to baths, wash hands, anoint money charms and so on. If it isn't strong enough, chill overnight and return to the Sun the following day.

MOON BREW

Set a silver container filled with water out on the night of the Full Moon just as it rises (which will be at sunset). Allow the water to soak up Lunar rays all night. Just before dawn, rise and retrieve the water. Place in an earthen jug and cork tightly. (Never expose to the rays of the Sun.) Add to the bath for love; anoint money to increase wealth; touch to the brow to promote psychic awareness; place in the bath to attune with the spiritual planes or prior to Lunar rituals.

PROTECTION BREW (*caution!*)

3 parts Rue
2 parts Rosemary
1 part Vetivert
1 part Hyssop
1 part Mistletoe*

Brew as usual, strain and anoint each window and door of the house. Pour the rest down the drains to safeguard them. *Do not drink!*

PSYCHIC TEA

3 parts Rose petals
2 parts Yarrow
1 part Cinnamon

Brew, strain and drink a cup before or during divination and psychic work to enhance your psychic awareness.

PURIFICATION BREW

Collect any nine sacred plants, such as vervain, rue, rosemary, oak, pine, acacia, rose, carnation, thyme, basil, jasmine and so on. Place in a nonmetallic pot or bowl. Add rain water (or fresh water) and let the herbs soak, covered and away from light, for three days. Strain. Use for asperging the house, others, or yourself for purification. (See A Miscellany of Recipes for instructions on creating aspergers.)

PURIFICATION BREW #2

1 part Lemon Verbena
1 part dried Lemon peel
1 part Camomile

Brew, drink for purification prior to ritual. If desired, add a splash of lemon juice, a teaspoon of honey or sugar. (Sugar is used by Peruvian shamans in purification ceremonies.)

RAINBOW BREW

When it rains, wait for the clouds to break somewhere and look for a rainbow. If you find one, put a saucer or some other nonmetallic pan outside where it can catch rain. If it rains while the rainbow is still present, save the water for ritual uses. It has been blessed by the rainbow's appearance. Because the rainbow contains all colors, this "brew" is useful for all types of magic. Bottle and label. Add to baths or anoint the body and hands while visualizing your magical goal.

SLEEP BREW

1 part Rose petals
1 part Myrtle leaves
1 part Vervain

Soak rose petals in a pot of water for three days. Add more rose petals each day. On the third day, add myrtle and vervain at sunrise and let soak all day. That night, just before going to bed, bathe your forehead with three handfuls of the brew. Your sleep should be free from nightmares. Use the brew until gone, then make another batch if needed.

SOLAR CLEANSING BREW

2 parts Fern
2 parts Juniper
2 parts Rosemary
1 part Cumin
1 part Yarrow
1 part Pepper
1 part Rue

Place the ground, mixed and empowered herbs in a red bottle half-filled with water. Set this in the Sun, let steep, strain. For a gentle cleansing, sprinkle the brew around the house at sunrise for three or four days every month.

SUN WATER

Set a glass or crystal container of pure water outside just at dawn, in a place where the Sun's rays will shine on it all day. At sunset, bottle and cork the water. Keep it in a sunny place. Add to baths for energy, sprinkle around the home to remove evil, anoint yourself for purification and so on.

Ritual Soaps

BY THE LIGHT of a candle's flame, you're lying in a tub of herb-scented water, preparing yourself for magic. Incense smoke drifts on the air as you form a perfect mental image of your magical goal. Steam rises, laden with the fragrance and energies of flowers, seeds, roots and leaves.

Then, nearing the end of your bath, you reach for the soap—and it's sickly sweet, artificially perfumed. Your concentration is destroyed, pulling your attention from your ritual preparations.

Has this happened to you? It has to me. Although soaping isn't necessary in magical baths, a ritually correct soap can be a boost to any spell's effectiveness. Even if you don't bathe before ritual, it is wise to wash your hands. Even such a minor purification ritual can trigger the state of ritual consciousness. Therefore, spell soaps would be ideal for such uses.

Where can we obtain them? Don't try the supermarket. Make them at home. Not many people know how to do this today, but it's a lot of fun.

Most commercial soaps are formulated with caustic chemicals. They can be quite irritating to the skin, and are usually obnoxiously perfumed. Ritual soaps (of varying quality) are occasionally available at occult stores, but why not try making your own?

Don't worry—you won't have to get a fire crackling under your cauldron out in the countryside to do this. And unless you want to upset your neighbors with nasty smells and risk burning your hands with lye, it's best to start out with pure, natural castile soaps. These can be purchased at most drugstores and markets. Oils or herb brews are then added to the soap. The magic is in the scent and in your empowerment of the soaps.

Pure castile soap is usually made of coconut oil. Kirk's, a coconut castile made in the Phillipines, is ideal. Castile soap (named after Castile, Spain) is also made from olive oil, but I haven't had good results using this variety.

Any castile soap can be drying to the skin. If you have problems in this area, try adding one to two teaspoons apricot, almond or coconut oil to the water prior to mixing (see the below recipes), reducing the amount of water accordingly.

There are two types of ritual soaps: sphere and liquid. Here are complete directions for creating both forms.

Ritual Soap Spheres

Using a very sharp, thick-bladed knife, cut a four-ounce bar of castile soap into very small pieces no larger than 1/4-inch square—the smaller (so long as they're cubes) the better. Place these in a heatproof nonmetallic container.

Heat slightly less than 1/3 cup water until nearly boiling. Pour the still-hot water over the cut-up soap. Let it sit until the water has cooled sufficiently to allow you to handle it. Mix the soap and water with your hands. This will moisten the soap chips, but they shouldn't be floating on the surface of the water. If they are, add more soap.

Let the soap and water sit for about nine minutes until mushy. If the soap cubes are still hard, set the bowl in a pan of water and reheat it gently until the soap is soft.

While the soap is melting, mix together the oils and empower them with your magical need. Then add 20–50 drops of the combined oils to the soap/water mixture. Very warm water evaporates the oils, so wait until the water has cooled. Mix them in thoroughly. The scent should be strong; if not, add more oils.

The quality and strength of the oils you use determines the quantity needed to overpower the natural, rather antiseptic scent of genuine castile soap. Just add them until you can smell the oils.

Divide the scented soap mass into three or four parts. Form these into spheres with your hands. Place each on a nine-inch-square piece of cotton cheesecloth. Pull the ends tightly around the sphere, gather thom at the top and twist together. The cloth should be tightly wrapped around the soap sphere. Tie the ends closed with strong string. Repeat with each sphere.

Hang the soap spheres in a warm place for three days, or until the soap is completely hard. When the spheres won't give to finger pressure, remove the cloth wraps. The soaps are ready to be used in ritual baths. Or, they can be wrapped in clean cheesecloth, labelled, and given as gifts to friends who would appreciate them.

Liquid Ritual Soap #1

Liquid soaps are a new trend today, thanks to aggressive advertising by major manufacturers. These soaps, however, are actually detergents, and aren't the best substances to put onto your hands.

While ad agencies trumpet liquid soaps as if they were brand-new, the idea is actually as old as soap. American Indians agitated yucca and other suds-producing plants in water to create cleansing solutions. Ancient Hawaiians used the flowers of a wild ginger plant for the same purpose. Many saponin (soap-producing) plants grow throughout the world and were often the only source of soap for various peoples.

But we'll use castile as the basis of liquid ritual soaps. Here's the method:

Grate castile soap into a large bowl. Pack this into a measuring cup until you have exactly one cup. Remember to pack that soap!

Heat three cups water until almost boiling. Add the soap chips to the water. Turn off the heat and whip with a wooden or (if you have nothing else) metal whisk until the soap is completely melted.

Let sit until cool, then add 50–60 drops of the mixed, empowered oils. Once again, the exact amounts vary. You'll know it's time to stop adding oils when the soap is heavily scented.

Using a funnel, place the liquid soap in a jar. Cap and shake vigorously to mix in the oils. Label and use as needed.

Liquid Ritual Soap #2

You can also try making liquid spell soaps with brews. To the three cups hot water add five to six tablespoons mixed, dried, ground and empowered herbs rather than the oils mentioned in the following recipes. Take off the heat, let steep for 10 to 13 minutes and strain. Gently reheat the water, add one cup castile soap shavings, whisk and allow to cool. It is ready for use.

Unfortunately, when herb brews are mixed with castile soap the scent changes dramatically. If you try it, you'll understand what I mean. If you don't like the results, fortify the scent with a few drops of the oil form of one of the included herbs.

To use liquid soaps, simply wet your hands and apply a few drops of the soap. It foams easily and leaves your skin clean and scented.

The recipes follow. As you can see, there are endless varieties of soaps waiting to be concocted. Most of the oil recipes in this book can be used in scenting soaps. Once you've mastered the basics, make up a few types and keep them on hand in case of ritual need.

Some of these recipes suggest using rose water or orange flower water in place of plain water in making the soap/water mixture. This can be used or not, but use only water scented with genuine orange flower essential oil or rose essential oil.

Store unused soaps in your altar if it is designed with cupboards or shelves below it. Or, simply place them in your herb cupboard.

Remember—use ritual soaps *with power*. Visualize your magical goal as you wash.

The Recipes

ISIS SOAP

3 parts Myrrh
2 parts Frankincense
1 part Lotus Bouquet

Use before any Egyptian or Isian ritual. Also, wash with this soap to develop spiritual awareness. If you wish, substitute rose water for the water in which the soap chips are melted.

LOVE SOAP

4 parts Geranium
3 parts Palmarosa
2 parts Neroli
1 part Ginger

Wash with this soap to attract love, or prior to love rituals. And again, rose water may be used in the same proportions as plain water in preparing the soap.

LUCK SOAP

2 parts Vetivert
1 part Orange
1 part Nutmeg

Wash to change your "luck" or to bring positive energies into your life. Orange flower water may be used in place of plain water during soap manipulation.

MONEY SOAP

3 parts Patchouly
2 parts Peppermint
1 part Basil
1 part Pine
1 part Cinnamon

Wash your hands daily with this soap to attract money, or use prior to money-drawing rituals.

MOON SOAP

3 parts Sandalwood
2 parts Camphor
1 part Lemon
1 part Eucalyptus

Use before rituals on the Full Moon to attune with its energies.

PROTECTION SOAP

4 parts Rosemary
3 parts Basil
1 part Frankincense
1 part Bay
1 part Mint

Wash daily with this soap when you feel the need for protection, or before such spells.

PSYCHIC SOAP

3 parts Lemongrass
2 parts Bay
1 part Cinnamon

Wash with this soap to increase your psychic awareness, especially prior to divinatory or psychic workings.

SABBAT SOAP

4 parts Sandalwood	1 part Myrrh
3 parts Rosemary	1 part Bay
2 parts Patchouly	1 part Lemon
1 part Cinnamon	1 part Ginger

Use during ritual baths prior to the Sabbats (see Glossary) or as a general magical cleanser.

WITCH'S SOAP

3 parts Rosemary
2 parts Pine
1 part Cinnamon
1 part Orange

Wash with this soap before rituals of all kinds to increase your personal power.

Sachets or Herbal Charms

MAGICAL SACHETS—ALSO known as herbal charms (or amulets and talismans)—consist of herbs and other materials tied up in bits of cloth.

Some sachets ward off certain energies and disease; others draw specific situations or powers to you. In this new edition I've included astrological sachets for use by those wishing to stress the positive aspects of their Sun sign. They can be worn every day as a personal power booster or placed on the altar to magically represent you.

Sachets are easily made and have a long history. Cloth hasn't always been used. Herbs have been carried in horns, seashells, leather, fur and lockets. Magical rings were made into sachets by placing an appropriate herb below the jewel. Thus, the energies of both gem and herb worked toward the magical goal. Herbs were also sewn into clothing for protective purposes.

Creating Sachets

For most sachets, a handful or less of the empowered herb mixture is more than enough, depending on its desired size. Household sachets tend to be larger than ones designed to be carried on the person.

First, mix the herbs. Empower them with your magical need. *Know* that the herbs are pulsating with specific, programmed energies that are being released toward your goal.

Next, select the properly colored cloth. Choose a natural fiber material such as felt, wool or cotton. Synthetic materials such as polyester seem to disturb the herb's frequencies. Cut the cloth into a square from four to nine inches across. Place the empowered herbs on the center of the cloth, gather up the ends and tie them firmly together. You've trapped the herbs within the cloth. Use a natural cord such as wool yarn or cotton twine to shut the sachet.

A large stock of yarn and cloth in a wide array of colors is helpful. Felt works well and is available in many shades.

Using Sachets

If it is a personal charm, hold it in your hand, squeeze it gently to release its fragrance, and carry with you at all times.

If the sachet is designed for the house or car, squeeze and place it in the most appropriate spot.

Replace with freshly made sachets every three months or so, disassembling and burying the old ones.

The Recipes

ANTI-SORCERY SACHET

1 part Dill seed
1 part Flax seed
1 part Peony root

Tie up in white cloth, wear or carry, suspend over doors and windows.

ANTI-SORCERY SACHET #2

1 part Trefoil (Clover)
1 part Vervain
1 part St. John's Wort
1 part Dill

Tie up in white cloth and wear. To guard your home, hang in a window.

ANTI-THEFT SACHET

2 parts Rosemary
1 part Juniper
1 part Caraway seeds
1 part Elder
1 pinch Garlic

Tie up in white cloth and hang over the front door to protect the home and its contents. If you don't enjoy the strong garlic odor, use a pinch of crumbled garlic skins.

ANTI-TOOTHACHE SACHET

1 tbsp. Salt
1 Bread crumb
1 small piece Coal

Tie up in a piece of red silk and carry when pains begin. See a dentist to ensure that the sachet works!

AQUARIUS SACHET

3 parts Lavender
2 parts Patchouly
1 part Benzoin
1 part Mace
1 part Mint

Mix, tie up in gray or some other dark-colored cloth that appeals to you. Wear or carry to strengthen the positive aspects of your sign.

ARIES SACHET

3 parts Carnation
2 parts Juniper
1 part Frankincense
1 part Fennel
1 part Cumin

Blend the empowered herbs, tie up in red cloth and wear or carry to strengthen the positive aspects of your sign.

CANCER SACHET (MOONCHILDREN)

3 parts Sandalwood
2 parts Myrrh
1 part Gardenia
1 part Lemon Balm
1 part Gardenia petals

Tie up in white cloth and carry with you to strengthen the positive aspects of your sign.

CAPRICORN SACHET

3 parts Vetivert
2 parts Cypress
1 part Vervain
1 part Mimosa blossoms
1 part Comfrey

Mix, tie up in indigo, gray or any other dark cloth you prefer. Wear or carry to enhance the positive aspects of your sign.

CAR PROTECTION SACHET

2 parts Rosemary
2 parts Juniper
1 part Mugwort
1 part Comfrey
1 part Caraway
1 small Quartz Crystal point

Tie up in red cloth. Secrete somewhere in the car where it won't be found. And drive safely—this sachet won't guard against the driver's mistakes.* After a few months, take the sachet apart, save and cleanse the crystal (using Crystal Purification Incense, perhaps) and use again in the new sachet.

---

*See *The Magical Household* for more car protection rituals.

CAR PROTECTION SACHET #2

3 parts Rosemary
2 parts Juniper
2 parts Basil
1 part Fennel
1 part Mugwort
1 part Vervain
1 pinch Salt

Another like the above.

GAMES OF CHANCE SACHET

3 parts Patchouly
2 parts Nutmeg
1 part Jasmine flowers
1 part Cloves
1 part Cinquefoil
1 small Lodestone

Tie up the empowered herbs in green cloth and carry with you when risking your money for possible future return—investments, gambling, speculation.

GEMINI SACHET

3 parts Lavender
2 parts Mint
2 parts Gum Mastic
2 parts Clover
1 part Dill seed
1 part Anise

Tie up in yellow cloth and carry with you to enhance the positive aspects of your sign.

HEALING SACHET

2 parts Cinnamon
2 parts Sandalwood
1 part Rose petals
1 part Cayenne
1 part Ginger
1 part Rue

Mix, tie up in blue or purple cloth. Anoint sachet with Eucalyptus oil and wear or place near the bed at night.

HOME PROTECTION SACHET

3 parts Rosemary
3 parts Basil
2 parts Fennel seed
2 parts Dill seed
1 part Bay
1 part Fern
1 pinch Salt

Tie up in red cloth. Situate the sachet in the highest place inside the home.

HOME PROTECTION SACHET #2

1 part Fleabane
1 part St. John's Wort
1 part Capers (dry them before using)
a few grains Whole Wheat

This formula, from ancient Middle Eastern magic, should be tied up in red cloth and hung over the front door.

Victoria ©89

LEO SACHET

2 parts Orange peel
2 parts Cinnamon
1 part Frankincense
1 part Nutmeg
1 part Juniper
1 pinch Gum Arabic

Tie up in orange, gold or red cloth and carry with you to enhance the positive aspects of your sign.

LIBRA SACHET

2 parts Spearmint
2 parts Catnip
2 parts Rose petals
1 part Marjoram
1 part Thyme
1 part Mugwort

Tie up in yellow cloth and carry with you to enhance the positive aspects of your sign.

LOVE SACHET

3 parts Lavender
2 parts Rose petals
1 part Orris root

Tie up in pink cloth. Place the sachet among your clothing to infuse it with the scent of love. Or, wear to attract a love.

LOVE SACHET #2

3 parts Rose petals
2 parts Orange flowers
1 part Jasmine flowers
1 part Gardenia flowers

Another like the above.

LOVE "SPECIAL" SACHET

4 parts Rose petals
1 part Orange peel
1/2 part Carnation petals
1 pinch Baby's Breath

Mix, tie up in pink cloth and wear.

MONEY SACHET

3 parts Patchouly
2 parts Clove
1 part Oakmoss
1 part Cinnamon

Tie up in green cloth and carry to attract money.

NIGHTMARE CURE (*caution!*)

1 part Lupine
1 part Helenium (Heliotrope or Sunflower)
1 part Marshmallow
1 part Dock
1 part Elder
1 part Wormwood
1 part Strawberry leaves
1 part Yew berries*

Tie up in light blue or white cloth. Hang on bedpost near your head. This ancient formula also cures "water elf disease," as well as mischief caused by goblins! No guarantees are made for this formula's effectiveness.

PISCES AMULET

3 parts Sandalwood
2 parts Sage
1 part Eucalyptus
1 part Anise
1 part Lemon

Tie up in a purple cloth and wear or carry to enhance the positive aspects of your sign.

PROTECTIVE SACHET

3 parts Dill seed
2 parts Caraway seed
1 part Flax seed
1 pinch Salt

Tie up in white or red cloth and carry for protection.

PROTECTIVE SACHET #2

2 parts Marjoram
1 part Angelica root
1 part Dill seed
1 part Clove

Tie up in white cloth; place in a window.

SACRED BUNDLE SACHET

3 parts Cachana root
1 dried Chile pepper
1 kernel Corn
1 pinch powdered Turquoise

Wrap in white cloth and bury near your front door (or in a flowerpot) to guard your home and to bless it with power.

SAGITTARIUS SACHET

3 parts Sassafras
2 parts Cedar
2 parts Clove
1 part Star Anise
1 part Dragon's Blood
1 part Juniper

Tie up in purple cloth and wear or carry to strengthen the positive aspects of your sign.

SCORPIO SACHET

3 parts Pine
3 parts Myrrh
2 parts Galangal
1 part Allspice
1 part Violet flowers
1 part Basil

Tie up in bright red (or blue, if you prefer) cloth. Wear or carry to strengthen the positive aspects of your sign.

SPICY ROSE SACHET

1 part Rose—for love
1 part Rosemary—for remembrance
1 part Hibiscus—for delicate beauty
1 part Clove—for dignity
1 part Camomile—for energy in adversity

Tie up in pink cloth and give to one you love.

TAURUS SACHET

3 parts Patchouly
2 parts Oakmoss
1 part Cardamom
1 part Rose petals
1 Vanilla bean, crushed

Tie up in yellow or blue cloth and wear or carry to strengthen the positive aspects of your sign.

TRAVEL PROTECTION SACHET

1 part Mustard seed
1 part Comfrey
1 part Irish Moss
1 part Bladderwrack (also known as Kelp)

Tie up in white or yellow cloth. Carry with you when travelling, and tuck one into each suitcase and garment bag as well.

TWELVE-HERB YULE SACHET

7 parts Juniper	2 parts Rosemary
4 parts Cinnamon	2 parts Lemon peel
4 parts Allspice	2 parts Orange peel
4 parts Ginger	1 part Clove
4 parts Caraway	1 part Bay
2 parts Nutmeg	2 pinches Orris root

Tie up in green or red cloth and give as gifts on Yule or Samhain.

VIRGO SACHET

3 parts Lavender
2 parts Patchouly
2 parts Cypress
1 part Caraway
1 part Fern
1 part Mint

Tie up in a clear yellow cloth and wear or carry to enhance the positive aspects of your sign.

WEALTH SACHET

2 parts Cinnamon
2 parts Lemon Balm
1 part Cinquefoil
1 part Clove
1 whole Vanilla bean
1 whole Tonka bean

Crush the vanilla bean and mix all together. Empower. Tie up in purple or green cloth. Carry to increase riches and to establish a positive cash flow.

WEATHER PROTECTON SACHET (*caution!*)

1 part Mistletoe*
1 part Cedar
1 part Broom
1 part Bryony

Tie up in white cloth and hang near the chimney, in the attic, or elsewhere high in the house to protect it and its occupants against the ravages of the weather.

WITCH-FINDER TALISMAN

1 part Rue
1 part Agrimony
1 part Maidenhair fern
1 part Broomstraw
1 part Ground Ivy

Tie up in purple cloth and wear to know other Witches, if you are lonely and seek others of the Old Ways.

Powders

POWDERS HAVE LONG been an integral part of folk magic. They consist of ground herbs which are sprinkled to release their powers. A powder is an incense never burned, a sachet never worn.

I included two powder recipes in the last edition of this book (in Chapter 12: A Miscellany of Recipes), and devoted a portion of the video *Herb Magic* to this subject as well. I've also used them sporadically over the years. Still, I questioned the necessity of including this section.

After reviewing this expanded edition, I realized that the 10 distinct types of magical compounds already discussed, not to mention the hundreds of recipes, were bordering on overkill. Just how many forms of herb magic is anyone willing to practice, or at least, read about?

But I decided that if this book hoped to be a complete introduction to magical perfumery, a section on powders was necessary. Additionally, many of the ritual uses of powders are unique to this form. Hence, this section.

Making Powders

Simply grind herbs as finely as possible. To save time you can buy ground herbs, but doing so cheats you of really getting in touch with them.

While mortaring the herbs, during the whole long process, visualize ... imagine ... *see* your magical goal. Perhaps I haven't emphasized the need for *empowering* herbal products often enough in this book. To reiterate, the power lies within herbs and within ourselves. If we don't empower powders, incense or oils, if we don't accurately "program" them with our magical goals through visualization and concentration, such mixtures will have only slight effects. If you forget the empowerment, you might as well forget the magic!

Now that I've stepped down from my soapbox—once the herbs are powdered, mix them together. Empower them and the powder is ready for use.

Using Magical Powders

The easiest method is to simply scatter them when and where you need their energies. Other methods are also available:

• Sprinkle the powder in a circle around you, beginning and ending in the East and moving clockwise. Sit within this circle and absorb the powder's energies.

• Those who work with crystals and stones can add powders to their rituals. Sprinkle the appropriate powder around the crystal (or crystals) as it lays on the altar to increase its power.

• Sprinkle powders around candles before being burned to boost their energies.

• Scatter a ritually appropriate powder over the altar before spells.

• Sprinkle on the altar in specific shapes to use as focal points for visualization: protection powder in pentagrams; love powder in hearts; psychic powders in circles. It doesn't matter if the powder remains in the shape for long. And so on, as your imagination teaches you.

But remember—do this solely for positive purposes, to affect your possessions, yourself or others from whom you've obtained permission. *All manipulative magic is negative magic and will rebound on the magician.*

One note: some powders, particularly those that contain dragon's blood, will stain carpets, bedsheets, clothing and other materials. Be aware of this when sprinkling.

Happy powdering!

The Recipes

ASTRAL TRAVEL POWDER

2 parts Sandalwood
1 part Mugwort
1 part Cinnamon

Sprinkle on the bedsheets and pillow before sleeping to encourage consciously directed astral travel.

EXORCISM POWDER

3 parts Basil
2 parts Frankincense
2 parts Rosemary
1 part Yarrow
1 part Rue

Sprinkle throughout the house, or in any place needing a strong purification and protection.

HAPPINESS POWDER

2 parts Lavender
1 part Catnip
1 part Marjoram

When you wish to lift your spirits, sprinkle this powder in a circle on the floor or ground and sit within it, drinking in the powder's energies. Visualize them surrounding you and infusing you with joy.

HEALTH POWDER

2 parts Eucalyptus
1 part Myrrh
1 part Thyme
1 part Allspice

Sprinkle in the sickbed or in the recovery room to speed the body's healing process. Or scatter on the altar and burn blue candles.

LOVE POWDER

3 parts Yarrow
3 parts Lavender
2 parts Rose petals
1 part Ginger

For use in attracting love. Be sure to sprinkle the bedsheets or bedroom.

LUCK POWDER

2 parts Vetivert
2 parts Allspice
1 part Nutmeg
1 part Calamus

Use to bring positive changes into your life.

MONEY POWDER

2 parts Cedar
2 parts Patchouly
1 part Galangal
1 part Ginger

To attract money, sprinkle in your place of business, in your wallet or purse. Rub onto money before spending. Or, sprinkle in a dollar sign on the altar and burn green candles over the symbol.

PROSPERITY POWDER

3 parts Sassafras
2 parts Cinnamon
1 part Pine

To attract wealth in all its forms.

PROTECTION POWDER

2 parts Dragon's Blood
2 parts Sandalwood
1 part Salt

Mix and sprinkle outside around your property to dispel and stave off negativity.

PROTECTION POWDER #2

2 parts Mugwort
2 parts Frankincense
1 part Dill
1 part Juniper
1 part Cumin

Sprinkle where you need protection, inside or out. For personal protection, sprinkle in a circle and stand within it until you're charged with the herb's energies. Do this daily to lend protective energies to yourself at all times.

PSYCHIC POWDER

2 parts Yarrow
1 part Rose petals
1 part Lemongrass
1 part Eyebright

Sprinkle before exercising your innate psychic awareness.

SPIRITUALITY POWDER

2 parts Wood Aloe
1 part Frankincense
1 part Myrrh
1 part Sandalwood

Sprinkle in room prior to meditation or religious rituals to turn your awareness to higher things. Also, sprinkle in circles around blue candles for this purpose.

WISHING POWDER

2 parts Sage
1 part Sandalwood
1 part Tonka

In a lonely place, hold the powder in your right hand (if right-handed). Feel its energies and visualize your wish with perfect clarity. Rouse the power within you and send it into the powder. When it is jumping with energy, fling it as far from you as you can. As the powder touches the Earth, it releases its energy and goes to work to bring your wish into manifestation.

A Miscellany of Recipes

THESE RECIPES DON'T seem to fit anywhere else, and so have been grouped here under this convenient heading.

ASPERGER

Mint
Rosemary
Marjoram

Use sprigs of these fresh herbs. Tie the stem-ends together with white thread or string and use to sprinkle brews on yourself, on others or throughout your house. Visualize while utilizing the asperger. Also use for sprinkling salt water around the home to dispel negativity. Aspergers are used in Wiccan and magical ceremonies. Make a fresh asperger for each use.

ASPERGER #2

Vervain
Periwinkle
Sage
Mint
Ash
Basil

Use sprigs of the fresh plant materials. Tie to a handle of virgin hazelwood (i.e., from a tree that has not yet borne fruit) and use for sprinkling as in the above.

BALEFIRE (a magical fire)

Cypress
Laurel
Oak

Make a fire of the above woods and branches while visualizing its flames purifying and empowering all those near it. Use for any occasion when meeting with others for magical or ritual rites. It is purificatory and power-enhancing in its effects.

FRANKINCENSE PROTECTIVE NECKLET

Several ounces of Frankincense "tears"
(small, rounded lumps)

Empower the frankincense tears with protective energies. Thread a short, thin needle with yellow cotton thread. Heat the needle in a gas flame, in hot water or in a candle flame. (If using a candle flame, quickly wipe off the lampblack—if any—that forms on the needle.) Push the hot needle through the center of a frankincense tear and move it down onto the thread. Repeat the heating and threading process until you've created a necklet of frankincense "beads" that you can slip over your head. Knot the ends well and wear for protection or during magical rituals.

MEXICAN HEALING RUB

1 handful Yellow Daisies
1 handful Violets
1 handful Poppies
1 handful Rosemary

Mix together these fresh plant materials. Empower. Place in a large ceramic bowl. Wet the herbs thoroughly with vodka or some other nonodorous alcohol. If you don't wish to use alcohol, substitute apple cider vinegar. Rub the ill person's body with the wetted herbs, visualizing them absorbing the disease.

When finished, bury the herbs and wash your hands.

MONEY PENTACLES

4 tbsp. ground Cloves
4 tbsp. ground Cinnamon
4 tbsp. ground Nutmeg
4 tbsp. ground Ginger
a few drops Cinnamon oil
a few drops Clove oil
a few drops Nutmeg oil
2 tbsp. ground Gum Tragacanth (or Gum Arabic)
4 tbsp. Water

Combine the spices. Add the oils to them and mix well. Empower. Add the gum tragacanth to the water and mix thoroughly. Let it sit until it has absorbed the water. Add the ground, empowered spices to the gum/water mixture and blend well with your fingers. This should produce a stiff, dough-like mixture. If the mixture is too mushy, add a bit more of the ground spices. With your hands, form into flat, one-inch circular shapes. Using a sharp knife, trace a pentagram (five-pointed star) onto each flat circle. Let sit in a warm place out of the Sun to dry. When dried to a rock-hard consistency, carry in the pocket or purse to attract money. Or, place on the altar between two green, flaming candles that have been anointed with patchouly or cinnamon oil. If you wish, make a larger pentacle of the spices and ring with green candles to speed money your way. After four weeks bury the pentacle in the Earth with thanks and use a new one.

PILLOW, ASTRAL TRAVEL

3 parts Mugwort
2 parts Vetivert
1 part Sandalwood
1 part Rose petals
1 Vanilla bean, crushed
1 pinch ground Orris root

Make into a small pillow. Sleep on it to promote astral travel during sleep.

PILLOW, DREAM

2 parts Rose petals
2 parts Lemon Balm
1 part Costmary
1 part Mint
1 part Clove

Sew up into a small pillow and sleep on it to have vivid dreams.

PILLOWS, MAGIC

Use each herb individually, or mix for several purposes. Make these pillows small, about five inches square. Set them on top of your regular pillow.

Anise: halts nightmares
Bay: pleasant dreams
Camomile: restful sleep
Eucalyptus: healing
Hops: sleep, healing
Mugwort: dreams, psychic dreams
Peppermint: if used fresh, it induces sleep; replace daily
Thyme: happiness (eases depression)
Verbena: aphrodisiac
Yarrow: dreams of loved ones

POMANDER LOVE CHARM

1 large, perfect, fresh Orange or Lemon (see below)
2 tbsp. ground Cinnamon
2 tbsp. ground Coriander
2 tbsp. ground Ginger
1 tbsp. ground Orris
Whole Cloves

If you wish to attract a man, use an orange. If a woman, a lemon. Choose a fruit that is free of bruises or discoloration, which is firm and nearly ripe.

Grind the herbs. Place in a small bowl, mix together and empower with your need for love.

Hold the orange or lemon and visualize yourself in a loving relationship. Place an empty bowl or plate below the fruit to catch dripping juice. Push one of the cloves into the fruit. Now, retaining the visualization, push another clove as close as possible to the first one but slightly to one side. Continue adding cloves until you've formed a rough heart shape on the surface of the lemon or orange. Still visualizing, add more cloves until the orange is completely studded with them. You'll probably get some juice on your hands.

When the fruit is so covered with cloves that little of its skin shows, place it in the bowl of mixed, empowered spices. Roll it in the mixture until it is completely covered with the loving spice mixture. Leave it in the bowl for one to two weeks. Every day or so, roll the pomander over the spice mixture.

After a few weeks remove the pomander. Empower the pomander with your magical need. Place it on your altar. Anoint six pink candles with a love oil such as rose, jasmine, palmarosa or one of the blends suggested in this book. Set the candles in a circle around the pomander. Light the candles and let them flame for nine minutes or so while visualizing yourself in a relationship.

Tie the pomander with a pink cord, string or piece of yarn and hang it up where you'll see it, and smell it several times a day. Let the candles burn out.

The pomander will do its work.

PURIFICATION BLEND

1/2 cup Apple Cider Vinegar
1 handful fresh Eucalyptus leaves
1 handful fresh Rue leaves
3 pinches Salt
1 quart Water

Add the herbs to the vinegar and let sit overnight. Strain through cheesecloth and add to the water with the salt. Use the mixture to wash objects to be purified, such as jewelry, amulets or magical tools. Or add a half-cup amount to your bath. This is actually a very weak, diluted tincture.

ROSE LOVE BEADS

1 part fresh Rose Geranium leaves
2 parts fresh Rose petals—the more fragrant the better
Rose Water

Remove the white stem-ends from the rose petals. Empower the fresh herbs with your need for love. Cover the petals and leaves with rose water in a nonmetallic pan. Simmer, covered, for 30 minutes. Ensure that the mixture doesn't actually boil. Turn off the heat and let soak until the next day. Repeat the simmering again for a half hour. Repeat this for three days in all, adding rose water when necessary. On the last day squeeze out all water until you have a fragrant mess. The mixture should be dry enough to hold its shape. Form into small, round beads with your hands, each about 1/4 inch long. Push a large needle or stiff wire through each bead while it's still wet to form holes for stringing. Let dry for a week or so, moving them around to ensure even drying. String on pink thread, yarn or ribbon. The beads are ugly and black, but when worn on the body they release a delicious rose scent. Wear these for love, or add to sachets, place in purses and so on.

WITCHES' LOVE HONEY

1 cup pure, light Honey
2 broken Cinnamon sticks
1 tsp. whole Cloves
1 dime-sized piece of Sugar Ginger*
1 inch-long piece dried Lemon peel
1 inch-long piece Vanilla bean
1 pinch ground Cardamom

Empower all herbs and the honey with your magical intent. Pour the herbs into a jar with a tight-fitting lid. Add the honey and shake until all herbs are moistened. Cover it tightly with the lid and place the jar on your herbal altar between two pink candles. Light the candles and let them burn out. Let the honey sit in a dark place for three weeks. Add small portions to food and hot beverages to promote good feelings and love.

---

* Look for sugar (or crystallized) ginger in Asian food markets, herb stores and gourmet food shops.

Part III
Substitutions

Introduction

YOU MAY BE ALL set to mix up a batch of incense and then discover that, to your dismay, you're lacking one or two ingredients. Might as well put everything back and wait until you can obtain the proper herbs. Right?

Wrong!

The recipes in this book are truly suggestions, examples of mixtures that have proven to be effective. This doesn't mean that you can't alter them to fit your stock at hand, or simply change them to your liking.

If you lack some of the ingredients (wood aloe, for instance, is difficult to obtain today), simply substitute an herb with the same basic energies.

I'm amazed at how many people hesitate to substitute. Here's a slightly exaggerated example of a conversation that I have with alarming regularity:

"Have you got any gum assagraxanathicthon?" Great Herbal Magician asks me.

I snap my fingers. "Fresh out. What're you making?"

"An *ancient* incense for spirit manifestation," Great Herbal Magician says, lifting an eyebrow.

"Hmmm. Why don't you substitute gum mastic or dittany of Crete?"

"No! It *has* to be gum assagraxanathicthon!" G.H.M. huffs. "This 25,000-year-old recipe plainly states that if I don't use gum assagraxanathicthon, *evil spirits* will carry me off to the *Burning Sands of Araby!*" His lower lip trembles.

"Oh, it's for protection. Then you have three choices: substitute asafoetida, don't make that particular recipe—or pack for hot weather."

A far-fetched conversation? Not really. I've spruced it up a bit to make my point: magical recipes needn't be slavishly followed.

Before I get any requests for it, there isn't any "gum assagraxanathicthon." Nor are there are 25,000-year-old recipes floating around.

Substitutions are not only encouraged, they're often mandatory. While most of the ingredients mentioned in this book are available somewhere, at some price, none of us can stock them all. Therefore, anyone who makes up more than a few of these recipes will need to substitute.

Many recipes mentioned in other, more sensationalistic books (such as any of the spurious "Necronomicons" currently in circulation) list unknown, unidentified, long-extinct or nonexistent herbs. These are included for the following reasons:

1. To impress the reader with the author's "scholarship" and access to obscure magical textbooks (many of which are so obscure that they've disappeared).

2. To test both the reader's knowledge of the subject and her or his ability to disregard such false information and to substitute an ingredient with the same properties.

3. Because the author simply didn't know any better.

Therefore, it's impossible to compose some of these recipes without substituting.

True, I've included a few formulas in this book with unknown herbs—*selenetrope* in Moon Incense #2 and *Tapsus barbatus* in Spirit Incense #2. In the first instance I suggested substitutes; the latter recipe isn't recommended for use anyway, and so I have left it intact.

I'm not of the old school to which so many authors seem to belong: "Write to obscure; write to confuse."

So when you're out of sandalwood or come across an empty jar of lavender oil in your cupboard, refer to this section and determine the best substitute. The same is true if you find a recipe somewhere that includes selenetrope, *Tapsus barbatus* or even "gum assagraxanathicthon," as well as any poisonous substances.

How do you do this? It's best to know the missing ingredient's magical powers. With this in mind you can determine why it has been included in that particular recipe, and can substitute a plant with similar energies. Even if you're not sure why lemon oil was included in a purification blend, you can at least look under Purification in the tables and find some other oil to use in its place.

A few examples: Say you're creating a Fast Money Oil composed of mint, patchouly, pine and cinnamon. Then you remember that the last patchouly oil you saw cost $10 a bottle, and you only had a few bucks on you. You decided not to buy any.

So you look at the Money and Riches table in this section and study it, finally deciding on vetivert oil. It has a somewhat similar scent, is ritually appropriate, and you have a bottle on hand. Presto! You've successfully substituted vetivert oil for patchouly oil.

It can be that simple. If you wish to ensure that your substitution is the best possible choice (keeping in mind your in-stock selection of herbs), research each of the possibilities in books. Look at their backgrounds, their basic energies and their recommended magical uses. From this knowledge, choose the most appropriate herb.

When trying to compound formulas found in other sources, many problems can arise. Say you're reading Agrippa's *Three Books of Occult Philosophy*, originally published in English in 1651 (see Bibliography). For some reason you've decided to mix up the "fume," or incense, of Mars. Here are the ingredients—no amounts are given.

> Euphorbium
> Bdellium
> Gum Armoniak
> Roots of both Hellebors
> Loadstone
> a little Sulphur
> Brain of a Cat, or blood of a Bat*

Hmmm. Quite an incense, but for some reason, you decide to try to produce it.

First off, you decide to omit the brain or blood—for, um, *obvious* reasons. Such ingredients were used in earlier days to bind the incense

---

* According to the 1651 English edition. A 1974 edition (see Bibliography) listed this line of ingredients as "the brain of a hart, the blood of a man and the blood of a black cat." This lurid change seems suspicious to me.

together, as well as to add their supposed energies to the completed product.

If you wish to substitute something for the brain or blood, try egg white—an ancient symbol of life and a good binder.

Now, to euphorbium. This is the poisonous, milky juice of any of 4,000 species of the common *Euphorbiaceae* family, which grows worldwide. Perhaps the best-known member is the poinsettia. In ancient times euphorbium (the milky secretion of any species of *Euphorbia*) was used in medicine and magic. Its virulently poisonous nature probably contributed to its inclusion in this recipe.

Not wishing to commit suicide-by-incense, you look at the Mars table in this section for possible substitutes. How about tobacco? Though it's poisonous, adding a pinch of pipe tobacco to an incense won't kill you. Fine. You settle for tobacco.

Now gum bdellium. This is a rare substance gathered from several species of the *Buseraceae* family, which grows in India and Africa. Although known for at least 6,000 years, gum bdellium is virtually unobtainable today.

However, copal, the gum resin which has been used in New World rites since Mayan times, is obtained from a *Bursera* spp. tree. It is—at least distantly—related to gum bdellium. Additionally, gum bdellium is said to have a cedar-like aroma. Some types of copal could, I suppose, be described this way. The fact that both are gums (and that you have two ounces of the stuff in your herb cupboard) seems to indicate that it is a fine substitute. So, copal. You won't find this under the Mars heading but it is acceptable.

Using closely related plant materials is a valuable method of determining substitutions. You don't have any copal? Not to worry. The Mars list includes dragon's blood and pine resin. One of these could be used to replace gum bdellium. Where possible, substitute similar substances—oils for oils, gums for gums, barks for barks, leaves for leaves and so on.

The third ingredient, gum armoniak, is today termed gum ammoniac. This is a gum resin obtained from both an Iranian tree as well as a species of *Ferula*. It is, again, impossible to find but you're still determined to create some form of Agrippa's Mars incense.

So you look up *Ferula* in *Cunningham's Encyclopedia of Magical Herbs* and discover that the common asafoetida is one species of *Ferula*. Asafoetida is also listed under the Mars table in this part. Success! But you know that asafoetida has an overpowering scent. Just a pinch should do.

Roots of both hellebors. "Hellebor" was a common spelling of hellebore during the 17th century. "Both" probably refers to *Helleborus niger*, black hellebore, as well as to white hellebore, a common folk name that was applied to several different plants. Such a poisonous ingredient was probably included in this formula simply because it was poisonous. It is commercially unavailable today, and it would be an unwise magician who burned it in the censer. What else can you use? Look at the Mars listing. What about nettle? Sure, it isn't poisonous, but anyone who has touched a nettle knows that it stings. Such symbolism would make it a perfect candidate for an incense devoted to the "stinging" planet Mars. Nettle it is.

Loadstone. Maybe you have one of these natural magnets lying around the house. Lodestone (an alternate spelling) is traditionally attributed to Mars and/or Venus, so this inclusion fits. If you don't have a lodestone, just place a small artificial magnet into the finished product. Leave it there for a week or so and then remove before using. This will "magnetize" the incense with Martian powers.

Sulphur? No problem there. It's easily obtainable. If you don't have any, why not substitute a pinch of club moss (*Lycopodium clavatum*), or some other species of that common, primitive plant. Why is this plant used? One of its common names is "vegetable sulfur," due to its explosive nature. If you can't find club moss, decide that the asafoetida you've already included will do for the sulphur as well.

And finally, myrrh. If you have some, simply add it to the recipe. If not, substitute pine pitch or dragon's blood.

So, here's the original recipe with these suggested substitutions placed side-by-side:

AGRIPPA'S MARS INCENSE	NEW MARS INCENSE
Euphorbium	Tobacco
Gum Bdellium	Copal/Pine resin/Dragon's Blood
Gum Armoniak	Asafoetida
Roots of both Hellebors	Nettle
Loadstone	Lodestone/Magnet
Sulphur	Sulphur/Club Moss/Asafoetida
Myrrh	Myrrh/Pine resin/Dragon's Blood
Brain of Cat/Blood of Bat	Omit *or* Egg White

There! You've got a brand-new Mars incense built along the lines of a 16th-century recipe, which was either an adaptation or a recording of a much earlier formula. And you've successfully substituted every ingredient called for, no matter how strange or unavailable.

If you were to actually make this incense, it would be best to use several parts each of myrrh (or pine resin/dragon's blood) and copal, and a very slight amount of pipe tobacco, nettle and sulfur. The tiniest pinch of asafoetida—believe me—would be sufficient. A glob of egg white can also be added, but since you're probably not compounding a combustible incense, it can be omitted.

Whew! That's a good example of magical substitution. You probably won't need to work with such a difficult formula often, but if you do, you'll know the procedure.

Magical substitution isn't dangerous (remember the *Burning Sands of Araby?*) or against all magical tradition; nor will it render your herb compounds powerless so long as you follow these basic rules.

Don't fight substitution; work with it and enjoy it. It's a necessary and important aspect of magical herbalism.

Tables of Magical Substitution

Specific Substitutions

In order to increase the practicality of this book, I've devised this list of specific substitutions for several common and unusual herbs. It can be consulted when you lack an ingredient for an herbal mixture, as can the more general lists that follow.

Here are some additional guidelines:

• Rosemary can be safely used for any other herb.

• Rose for any flower.

• Frankincense or copal for any gum resin.

• Tobacco for any poisonous herb.

For other substitution ideas (particularly for oils), see Chapter 4.

Unless otherwise noted, all listings refer to plant materials, not oils.

ACACIA: Gum Arabic
ACACIA, GUM: Gum Arabic
ACONITE: Tobacco
ARABIC, GUM: Frankincense; Gum Mastic; Gum Tragacanth (for binding wet ingredients, not for incense use)
AMMONIAC, GUM: Asafoetida
ASAFOETIDA: Tobacco; Valerian
BALM OF GILEAD: Rose buds; Gum Mastic
BDELLIUM, GUM: Copal; Pine resin; Dragon's Blood
BELLADONNA: Tobacco
BENZOIN: Gum Arabic; Gum Mastic
CACHANA: Angelica root
CAMPHOR OIL: Eucalyptus oil; Lavender oil
CARNATION: Rose petals anointed with a few drops Clove oil

213

CASSIA: Cinnamon (Cinnamon sold in the U.S. is actually the less expensive cassia)
CASTOR BEAN: A few drops Castor oil
CEDAR: Sandalwood
CINQUEFOIL: Clover; Trefoil
CITRON: Equal parts Orange peel and Lemon peel
CLOVE: Mace; Nutmeg
CLOVER: Cinquefoil
COPAL: Frankincense; Cedar
COWBANE: Tobacco
CYPRESS: Juniper; Pine needles
DEERSTONGUE: Tonka bean (not for internal use); Woodruff; Vanilla
DITTANY OF CRETE: Gum Mastic
DRAGON'S BLOOD: Equal parts Frankincense and Red Sandalwood
EUCALYPTUS OIL: Camphor oil; Lavender oil
EUPHORBIUM: Tobacco
FRANKINCENSE: Copal; Pine resin
GALANGAL: Ginger root
GRAINS OF PARADISE: Black Pepper
GUM AMMONIAC: Asafoetida
GUM BDELLIUM: Copal; Pine resin; Dragon's Blood
HELLEBORE: Tobacco; Nettle
HEMLOCK: Tobacco
HEMP: Nutmeg; Damiana; Star Anise; Bay
HENBANE: Tobacco
HYSSOP: Lavender
IVY: Cinquefoil
JASMINE: Rose
JUNIPER: Pine
LAVENDER: Rose
LEMONGRASS: Lemon peel
LEMON PEEL: Lemongrass; Lemon peel
LEMON VERBENA: Lemongrass; Lemon peel
MACE: Nutmeg
MANDRAKE: Tobacco
MASTIC, GUM: Gum Arabic; Frankincense
MINT (any type): Sage
MISTLETOE: Mint; Sage
MUGWORT: Wormwood

NEROLI OIL: Orange oil
NIGHTSHADE: Tobacco
NUTMEG: Mace; Cinnamon
OAKMOSS: Patchouly
ORANGE: Tangerine peel
ORANGE FLOWERS: Orange peel
PATCHOULY: Oakmoss
PEPPERMINT: Spearmint
PEPPERWORT: Rue; Grains of Paradise; Black Pepper
PINE: Juniper
PINE RESIN: Frankincense; Copal
RED SANDALWOOD: Sandalwood mixed with a pinch of Dragon's
  Blood
ROSE: Yarrow
ROSE GERANIUM: Rose
RUE: Rosemary mixed with a pinch of Black Pepper
SAFFRON: Orange peel
SANDALWOOD: Cedar
SARSAPARILLA: Sassafras
SASSAFRAS: Sarsaparilla
SPEARMINT: Peppermint
SULFUR: Tobacco; Club Moss; Asafoetida
THYME: Rosemary
TOBACCO: Bay
TONKA BEAN: Deerstongue; Woodruff; Vanilla bean
TREFOIL: Cinquefoil
VALERIAN: Asafoetida
VANILLA: Woodruff; Deerstongue; Tonka Bean
VETIVERT: Calamus
WOLFSBANE: Tobacco
WOOD ALOE: Sandalwood sprinkled with Ambergris oil
WOODRUFF: Deerstongue; Vanilla
WORMWOOD: Mugwort
YARROW: Rose
YEW: Tobacco

Key to the Tables
> H = Herb, gum, flower, bark, root, leaf, fruit, seed
> O = Essential oil, absolute
> B = Bouquet
> S = Synthetic

Magical Goals

Not all magical goals are listed here. For those that are missing, see the following Planetary and Elemental tables, or check the Index. Use these lists for mixing your own blends or when substituting.

ASTRAL PROJECTION
Benzoin   H, O
Dittany of Crete   H
Cinnamon   H, O
Jasmine   H, O
Poplar   H
Sandalwood   H, O

COURAGE
Allspice   H
Black Pepper   H, O
Dragon's Blood   H
Frankincense   H, O
Geranium (Rose Geranium)   H, O
Sweet Pea   H, B
Tonka   H, B
Thyme   H

DIVINATION
Anise   H
Camphor   H, O
Clove   H, O
Hibiscus   H
Meadowsweet   H
Orange   H, O
Orris   H

EXORCISM
Angelica   H
Basil   H, O
Clove   H, O
Copal   H
Cumin   H
Dragon's Blood   H
Frankincense   H, O
Fumitory   H
Garlic   H
Heliotrope   H
Horehound   H
Juniper   H, O
Lilac   H
Mallow   H
Mistletoe   H
Myrrh   H, O
Pepper, Cayenne   H
Peppermint   H, O
Pine   H, O
Rosemary   H, O
Sagebrush   H
Sandalwood   H, O
Snapdragon   H
Thistle   H
Vetivert   H, O
Yarrow   H, O

HAPPINESS
Apple Blossom   H
Catnip   H
Hyacinth   H
Lavender   H, O
Marjoram   H
Meadowsweet   H
Sesame   H
Saffron   H
St. John's Wort   H

HEALING, HEALTH
Allspice H
Angelica H
Bay H, O
Calamus H
Carnation H
Cedarwood H, O
Cinnamon H, O
Citron H
Coriander H, O
Eucalyptus H, O
Fennel H
Gardenia H
Heliotrope H
Honeysuckle H
Juniper H, O
Lemon Balm H, O
Lime H, O
Mugwort H
Palmarosa O
Pepper, Cayenne H
Peppermint H, O
Pine H, O
Poppy seed H
Rose H, O
Rosemary H, O
Saffron H
Sandalwood H, O
Sassafras H
Spearmint H, O
Spikenard H
Thyme H
Violet H
Willow H
Wintergreen H
Yerba Santa H

LOVE

Apple Blossom H, B	Marjoram H
Apricot O (no scent)	Mastic H
Basil H, O	Mimosa H
Camomile H, O	Myrtle H
Catnip H	Neroli O
Chickweed H	Orange H, O
Cinnamon H, O	Orchid H
Civet S	Orris H
Clove H, O	Palmarosa O
Copal H	Peppermint H, O
Coriander H, O	Plumeria H
Cumin H	Rose H, O
Dill H	Rosemary H, O
Dragon's Blood H	Sarsaparilla H
Gardenia H	Stephanotis H
Geranium (Rose) H, O	Sweet Pea B
Ginger H, O	Thyme H
Hibiscus H	Tonka H, B
Jasmine H, O	Tuberose H, B
Juniper H, O	Vanilla H
Lavender H, O	Vervain H
Lemon H, O	Vetivert H, O
Lemon Balm H, O	Violet H
Lemon Verbena H, O	Yarrow H, O
Lime H, O	Ylang-Ylang O
Lotus B	

LUCK

Allspice H	Orange H, O
Calamus H	Poppy seed H
Fern H	Rose H, O
Grains of Paradise H	Spikenard H
Hazel H	Star Anise H
Heather H	Tonka H, B
Irish Moss H	Vetivert H, O
Nutmeg H, O	Violet H

LUST
Ambergris   S
Caraway   H
Cinnamon   H, O
Civet   S
Clove   H, O
Deerstongue   H
Ginger   H, O
Ginseng   H
Grains of Paradise   H
Hibiscus   H
Lemongrass   H, O
Nettle   H
Olive   H, O
Parsley   H
Patchouly   H, O
Peppermint   H, O
Rosemary   H, O
Saffron   H
Sesame   H
Stephanotis   H
Tuberose   H, B
Vanilla   H
Yerba Mate   H

MONEY AND RICHES
Allspice   H
Almond   H
Basil   H, O
Bergamot Mint   H, B
Calamus   H
Camomile   H, O
Cedarwood   H, O
Cinnamon   H, O
Cinquefoil   H
Clove   H, O
Clover   H
Dill   H
Elder   H
Galangal   H

Ginger   H, O
Heliotrope   H
Honeysuckle   H
Hyssop   H
Jasmine   H, O
Myrtle   H
Nutmeg   H, O
Oakmoss   H, B
Orange   H, O
Patchouly   H, O
Peppermint   H, O
Pine   H, O
Sage   H
Sassafras   H
Tonka   H, B
Vervain   H
Vetivert   H, O
Wood Aloe   H, O
Woodruff   H

PEACE
Cumin   H
Gardenia   H, B
Lavender   H, O
Lilac   H
Magnolia   B
Meadowsweet   H
Narcissus   H
Pennyroyal   H
Tuberose   H, B
Violet   H

POWER, MAGICAL
Allspice   H
Carnation   H
Dragon's Blood   H
Ginger   H, O
Gum Mastic   H
Tangerine   H, O
Vanilla   H

PROPHETIC (PSYCHIC) DREAMS

Camphor   H, O
Cinquefoil   H
Heliotrope   H
Jasmine   H, O

Marigold   H
Mimosa   H
Rose   H, O

PROTECTION

Angelica   H
Anise   H, O
Arabic, Gum   H
Asafoetida   H
Balm of Gilead   H
Basil   H, O
Bay   H, O
Bergamot Mint   H, B
Black Pepper   H, O
Calamus   H
Caraway   H
Carnation   H
Cedarwood   H, O
Cinnamon   H, O
Cinquefoil   H
Clove   H, O
Clover   H
Copal   H
Cumin   H
Cypress   H, O
Dill   H
Dragon's Blood   H
Eucalyptus   H, O
Fennel   H
Fern   H
Flax   H
Frankincense   H, O
Galangal   H
Geranium (Rose)   H, O
Heather   H
Honeysuckle   H
Hyacinth   H
Hyssop   H

Juniper   H, O
Lavender   H, O
Lilac   H
Lime   H, O
Lotus   B
Mandrake   H
Marigold   H
Mimosa   H
Mistletoe   H
Mugwort   H
Myrrh   H, O
Niaouli   O
Orris   H
Patchouly   H, O
Pennyroyal   H
Peony   H
Peppermint   H, O
Petitgrain   O
Pine   H, O
Rose   H, O
Rose Geranium   H, O
Rue   H
Sage   H
Sandalwood   H, O
Thistle   H
Valerian   H
Vervain   H
Vetivert   H, O
Violet   H
Wood Aloe   H
Woodruff   H
Wormwood   H

PSYCHIC AWARENESS
Acacia, Gum   H
Anise   H
Bay   H, O
Camphor   H, O
Cassia   H, O
Cinnamon   H, O
Citron   H
Clove   H, O
Flax   H
Galangal   H
Gardenia   H
Heliotrope   H
Honeysuckle   H
Lemongrass   H, O
Lilac   H
Mace   H, O
Marigold   H
Mastic, Gum   H
Mugwort   H
Nutmeg   H, O
Orange   H, O
Orris   H
Peppermint   H, O
Rose   H, O
Saffron   H
Star Anise   H
Thyme   H
Tuberose   H, B
Wormwood   H
Yarrow   H, O

PURIFICATION

Anise H	Lemon H, O
Arabic, Gum H	Lemon Verbena H, O
Bay H, O	Lime H, O
Benzoin H, O	Mimosa H
Calamus H	Musk S
Camomile H, O	Myrrh H, O
Camphor H, O	Parsley H
Cedarwood H, O	Peppermint H, O
Cinnamon H, O	Pine H, O
Copal H	Rosemary H, O
Eucalyptus H, O	Sandalwood H, O
Fennel H	Thyme H
Frankincense H, O	Tobacco H
Hyssop H	Valerian H
Lavender H, O	Vervain H

SPIRITUALITY

Arabic, Gum H	Lotus B
Cassia H, O	Myrrh H, O
Cinnamon H, O	Pine H, O
Copal H	Sage H
Frankincense H, O	Sandalwood H, O
Gardenia H	Wisteria H
Heliotrope H	Wood Aloe H
Jasmine H, O	

Planetary Substitutions

These lists are for use when compounding your own planetary blends or when substitution is necessary. Please note that all such correspondences are open to debate. I may change them from time to time as new information and insights into the nature of plants and the planets come to me. Broadly speaking, all are ritually appropriate. Some herbs appear in more than one section.

SUN

Recipes to promote healing, protection, success, illumination, magical power, physical energy, and to end legal matters.

Acacia H	Mastic, Gum H
Arabic, Gum H	Mistletoe H
Bay H, O	Oak H
Benzoin H, O	Orange H, O
Carnation H	Rosemary H, O
Cedarwood H, O	Sandalwood H, O
Cinnamon H, O	Tangerine H, O
Citron H	Wood Aloe H
Copal H	
Frankincense H, O	
Juniper H, O	

MOON

Recipes to promote sleep, prophetic (psychic) dreams, psychic awareness, gardening, love, healing, fertility, peace, compassion, spirituality. Also for blends concerned with the family.

Calamus H	Lemon Balm H, O
Camphor H, O	Lotus B
Coconut H	Myrrh H, O
Gardenia H	Poppy seed H
Grape H	Sandalwood H, O
Jasmine H, O	Willow H
Lemon H, O	

MERCURY

Recipes to promote intelligence, eloquence, divination, study, self-improvement; to help overcome addictions, break negative habits; for travel, communication, wisdom.

Almond   H
Bergamot Mint   H, B
Caraway   H
Dill   H
Fennel   H
Lavender   H, O
Lemongrass   H, O
Lemon Verbena   H, O
Peppermint   H, O
Thyme   H

VENUS

Recipes to promote love, fidelity, reconciliation, interchanges, beauty, youth, joy, happiness, pleasure, luck, friendship, compassion and meditation.

Apple Blossom H	Rose H, O
Cardamom H, O	Spearmint H, O
Crocus H	Stephanotis H
Daisy H	Sweet Pea B
Geranium (Rose) H, O	Tansy H
Heather H	Thyme H
Hyacinth H	Tonka H, B
Iris H	Tuberose H
Licorice H	Vanilla H
Lilac H	Violet H
Magnolia H, B	Willow H
Myrtle H	Ylang-Ylang O
Orchid H	
Orris H	
Plumeria H	

MARS

Recipes to promote courage, aggression, healing after surgery, physical strength, politics, sexual energy, exorcism, protection and defensive magic.

Allspice H
Asafoetida H
Basil H, O
Broom H
Coriander H, O
Cumin H
Deerstongue H
Dragon's Blood H
Galangal H
Ginger H, O
Nettle H
Peppermint H, O
Pine H, O
Tobacco H
Woodruff H
Wormwood H

JUPITER

Recipes to promote spirituality, meditation, money, prosperity, and to settle legal matters.

Anise H
Cinquefoil H
Clove H, O
Honeysuckle H
Hyssop H
Maple H
Nutmeg H, O
Oakmoss H, B
Sage H
Sarsaparilla H
Sassafras H
Star Anise H
Ti H

SATURN

Recipes to promote protection, purification, longevity, exorcisms, vision, and endings, especially when concerned with the home.

Amaranth   H
Bistort   H
Comfrey   H
Cypress   H, O
Mimosa   H
Pansy   H
Patchouly   H, O
Tamarisk   H

Elemental Substitutions

Before listing the herbs associated with each element, let's take a brief look at them.

The four elements (Earth, Air, Fire and Water) are the basic components of the universe. All that exists—or that has the potential to exist—is composed of one or more of these energies.

The most immediately recognizable manifestations of the elements are natural. A handful of dirt for Earth, a cloud moving in a breeze for Air, flame for Fire and a lake for Water. But the elements are much more than physical objects—*they are the energies behind all things,* manifest or unmanifest.

Many plants correspond to the elements. In turn, each element is associated with specific magical goals, as listed below. In burning an Air incense or anointing with a Fire oil we directly draw upon the element's energies to achieve her or his goal.

For the most potent effects, attune with the element before using one of its herbal products. Feel the heat of a fire when burning a Fire incense. Sense the purifying, moving energies of a stream when bathing in a Water bath. Imagine the rush of wind while anointing yourself with an Air oil. Smell the rich moistness of the Earth when using one of Her mixtures.

Elemental magic is one of the easiest forms to master, for it's all around us.*

Use these lists when compounding elemental mixtures, for creating your own recipes, or when substituting.

EARTH

Recipes to promote peace, fertility, money, business success, stability, growth (as in gardens), employment and so on.

Bistort H	Oakmoss H, B
Cypress H, O	Patchouly H, O
Fern H	Primrose H
Honeysuckle H	Rhubarb H
Horehound H	Vervain H
Magnolia H, B	Vetivert H, O
Mugwort H	
Narcissus H	

AIR

Recipes to promote communication, travel, intellect, eloquence, divination, freedom and wisdom.

Acacia H	Lemon Verbena H, O
Arabic, Gum H	Mace H, O
Almond H	Marjoram H
Anise H	Mastic, Gum H
Benzoin H, O	Parsley H
Bergamot Mint H, B	Peppermint H, O
Citron H	Sage H
Lavender H, O	Star Anise H
Lemongrass H, O	

---

* See *Earth Power* for more Elemental magic.

FIRE

Recipes to promote communication, defensive magic, physical strength, magical power, courage, will power, purification.

Allspice   H
Angelica   H
Asafoetida   H
Basil   H, O
Bay   H, O
Carnation   H
Cedarwood   H, O
Cinnamon   H, O
Clove   H, O
Copal   H
Coriander   H, O
Deerstongue   H
Dill   H
Dragon's Blood   H
Fennel   H
Frankincense   H, O
Galangal   H, O
Garlic   H
Grains of Paradise   H
Heliotrope   H
Juniper   H, O
Lime   H, O
Marigold   H
Nutmeg   H, O
Orange   H, O
Peppermint   H, O
Rosemary   H, O
Rose Geranium   H, O
Sassafras   H
Tangerine   H, O
Tobacco   H
Woodruff   H

WATER
    Recipes to promote love, healing, peace, compassion, reconciliation, purification, friendship, de-stressing, sleep, dreams and psychism.

Apple Blossom H
Balm, Lemon H, O
Calamus H
Camomile H, O
Camphor H, O
Cardamom H, O
Catnip H
Cherry H
Coconut H
Comfrey H
Elder H
Eucalyptus H, O
Gardenia H
Heather H
Hyacinth H
Iris H
Jasmine H, O
Lemon H, O
Licorice H
Lilac H

Lily H
Lotus B
Myrrh H, O
Orchid H
Orris H
Passion Flower H
Peach H
Plumeria H
Rose H, O
Sandalwood H, O
Spearmint H, O
Stephanotis H
Sweet Pea B
Tansy H
Thyme H
Tonka H, B
Vanilla H
Violet H
Ylang-Ylang O

Astrological Substitutions

Use these lists for creating your own blends or for substituting. If none of these herbs are available when you need to substitute, look to the sign's ruling planet for further suggestions.

ARIES (ruled by Mars)

Allspice H	Dragon's Blood H
Carnation H	Fennel H
Cedarwood H, O	Frankincense H, O
Cinnamon H, O	Galangal H
Clove H, O	Juniper H, O
Copal H	Musk S
Cumin H	Peppermint H, O
Deerstongue H	Pine H, O

TAURUS (ruled by Venus)

Apple Blossom H	Patchouly H, O
Cardamom H, O	Plumeria H
Daisy H	Rose H, O
Honeysuckle H	Thyme H
Lilac H	Tonka H, B
Magnolia H, B	Vanilla H
Oakmoss H, B	Violet H
Orchid H	

GEMINI (Ruled by Mercury)

Almond H	Lavender H, O
Anise H	Lemongrass H, O
Bergamot Mint H, B	Lily H
Citron H	Mace H, O
Clover H	Mastic, Gum H
Dill H	Parsley H
Horehound H	Peppermint H, O

CANCER (MOONCHILDREN; ruled by the Moon)

Ambergris S	Lilac H
Calamus H	Lotus B
Eucalyptus H, O	Myrrh H, O
Gardenia H, B	Rose H, O
Jasmine H, O	Sandalwood H, O
Lemon H, O	Violet H
Lemon Balm H, O	

LEO (ruled by the Sun)

Acacia H	Juniper H, O
Benzoin H, O	Musk S
Cinnamon H, O	Nutmeg H, O
Copal H	Orange H, O
Frankincense H, O	Rosemary H, O
Heliotrope H	Sandalwood H, O

VIRGO (ruled by Mercury)

Almond H	Lavender H, O
Bergamot Mint H, B	Lily H, O
Cypress H, O	Mace H, O
Dill H	Moss H
Fennel H	Patchouly H, O
Honeysuckle H	Peppermint H, O

LIBRA (ruled by Venus)

Apple Blossom H	Plumeria H
Catnip H	Rose H, O
Lilac H	Spearmint H, O
Magnolia H, B	Sweet Pea B
Marjoram H	Thyme H
Mugwort H	Vanilla H
Orchid H	Violet H

SCORPIO (ruled by Mars, Pluto)

Allspice H	Gardenia H
Ambergris S	Ginger H, O
Basil H, O	Myrrh H, O
Clove H, O	Pine H, O
Cumin H	Vanilla H
Deerstongue H	Violet H
Galangal H	

SAGITTARIUS (ruled by Jupiter)

Anise H	Honeysuckle H
Carnation H	Juniper H, O
Cedarwood H, O	Nutmeg H, O
Clove H, O	Orange H, O
Copal H	Rose H, O
Deerstongue H	Sage H
Dragon's Blood H	Sassafras H
Frankincense H, O	Star Anise H
Ginger H, O	

CAPRICORN (ruled by Saturn)

Cypress H, O	Oakmoss H, B
Honeysuckle H	Patchouly H, O
Magnolia H, B	Vervain H
Mimosa H	Vetivert H, O

AQUARIUS (ruled by Saturn and Uranus)

Acacia H	Mace H, O
Almond H	Mastic, Gum H
Benzoin H, O	Mimosa H
Citron H	Patchouly H, O
Cypress H, O	Peppermint H, O
Lavender H, O	Pine H, O

PISCES (ruled by Jupiter and Neptune)

Anise H	Mimosa H
Calamus H	Nutmeg H, O
Catnip H	Orris H
Clove H, O	Sage H
Eucalyptus H, O	Sandalwood H, O
Gardenia H	Sarsaparilla H, O
Honeysuckle H, O	Star Anise H
Jasmine H, O	Sweet Pea B
Lemon H, O	

Glossary

MANY OF THESE definitions are exclusive to magic, magical herbalism and perfumery. Naturally, these definitions are my own, based on deduction and personal experience. **Luck, Good** is a prime example. Italicized terms refer to other related entries in the Glossary.

Akasha: The fifth element, the omnipresent spiritual power that permeates the universe. It is the energy out of which the *Elements* formed.

Amulet: A magically *empowered* object that deflects specific, usually negative, energies. Generally, a protective object. (Compare with *Talisman*.)

Anaphrodisiac: A substance, such as camphor, that reduces sexual desires.

Aphrodisiac: A substance that produces sexual excitement.

Asperger: A bundle of fresh herbs or a perforated object used for purificatory purposes to sprinkle water during or preceding ritual.

Astral Projection: The act of separating the consciousness from the physical body and moving it about at will.

Bane, Baneful: That which destroys life. Poisonous, dangerous, destructive. Herbs such as henbane, hellebore and aconite are examples of baneful substances.

Banish: The magical act of driving away evil or negativity. A strong purification, sometimes associated with the removal of "spirits."

Beltane: A *Wiccan* festival celebrated on April 30th or May 1st. Beltane celebrates the symbolic union of the Goddess and God (the

Wiccan deities). It links in with the approaching Summer months.

Bouquet: In perfumery, a blend of natural or synthetic scents which reproduces a specific odor, such as rose or jasmine. Also known as a compound or a blend.

Brew: *See Infusion.*

Censer: A heat-proof container in which incense is smoldered; an incense burner or any similar object.

Circle, Magic: *See Magic Circle.*

Combustible Incense: Self-burning incense containing potassium nitrate; usually in cone, block or stick form.

Conscious Mind: The societally controlled, intellectual, theorizing, materialistic half of the human mind that is at work in everyday activities. Compare with *Psychic Mind.*

Consecration: A *ritual* of sanctification or purification. A ritual of dedication.

Curse: A conscious direction of negative energy toward a person, place or thing.

Divination: The magical act of discovering the unknown by interpreting random patterns or symbols through the use of tools such as clouds, tarot cards, flames, smoke. Divination contacts the *psychic mind* by tricking, or "drowsing," the *conscious mind* through *ritual* and observation of, or manipulation of, tools. Divination isn't necessary for those who can easily attain communication with the *psychic mind*, though they may practice it.

Elements, The: Earth, Air, Fire and Water. These four essences are the building blocks of the universe. Everything that exists (or that has potential to exist) contains one or more of these energies. The elements hum within ourselves and are also at large in the world. They can be utilized to cause change through *magic*. The four elements formed from the primal essence, or power—*Akasha.*

Empower, Empowering: The movement of personal energies into herbs, stones or other objects. The empowered objects are then used in *magic*. In *herb magic*, empowering aligns the energies within herbs with magical goals.

Enfleurage: A French perfumery term describing the process of extracting essential flower oils with purified fat. Also known as *pommade.*

Esbat: A Wiccan ritual occasion celebrating the Full Moon. Compare with *Sabbat. See also Wicca.*

Evocation: Calling up spirits or other nonphysical entities, either

to visible appearance or invisible attendance. Compare with *Invocation*.
Exorcism: Traditionally, the magical process of driving out negative entities. In *herb magic*, a powerful purification.

Grimoire: A magical workbook with information on *rituals*, magical properties of natural objects, preparation of ritual equipment. Many include "catalogues of spirits." The most famous of the old grimoires is probably *The Key of Solomon (see* Bibliography under Mathers). Most were first committed to paper in the 16th and 17th centuries, though they may be far older.

Handfasting: A *Wiccan, Pagan* or Gypsy wedding. More broadly, any wedding or solemn betrothal.

Herb: A plant used in magic. Herbs are usually strongly scented and are prized for their specific energies. Includes trees, ferns, grasses, seaweeds, vegetables, fruits and flowering plants.

Herbalism: The practice of cultivating, gathering and using plants for medicinal, cosmetic, ritual and culinary purposes. *See Herb Magic.*

Herb Magic: The practice of directing energies found within plants to create needed change. A branch of *magic.* Practitioners utilize *personal power* as well as other forms of energy, such as colors, candles, stones, sounds, gestures and movements.

Hex: *See Curse.*

Imbolc: A *Wiccan* festival celebrated on February 2nd. Imbolc marks the first stirrings of Spring and is a traditional time to practice magic.

Incubus: A male demon or spirit that was believed to sexually tempt and abuse women. Compare with *Succubus*.

Infusion: A liquid produced by soaking herbs in very hot (but not boiling) water. A brew or potion.

Invocation: An appeal or petition to a specific conception of Deity. A prayer. A request for a deity's appearance or attendance during a *ritual.* Also, a mystical practice that produces an awareness of Deity within. Compare with *Evocation*.

Luck, Good: An individual's ability to make timely, correct decisions, to perform correct actions and to place herself or himself in positive situations. "Bad luck" stems from ignorance and an unwillingness to accept self-responsibility.

Lughnasadh: A *Wiccan* festival celebrated on August 1st. Lughnasadh marks the first harvest and the symbolic ebbing of the Sun's energies.

Mabon: A *Wiccan* festival celebrated on or around September 21st, the Autumnal Equinox, which marks the second harvest. Autumn transmutes into Winter. A time of thanks and reflection.

Magic: The movement of natural energies (such as *personal power*) to create needed change. Energy exists within all things: ourselves, plants, stones, colors, sounds, movements. Magic is the process of "rousing" or building up this energy, giving it purpose, then releasing it. Magic is a natural, not supernatural, practice, though it is little understood. *See Herb Magic.*

Magic Circle: A sphere constructed of *personal power* in which *Wiccan* or magical rituals are often enacted. The term refers to the circle that marks the sphere's penetration of the ground, for it extends above and below the ground. It is created through *visualization* and *magic.*

Meditation: Reflection, contemplation, turning inward toward the self or outward toward Deity or nature. A quiet time in which the practitioner may dwell upon particular thoughts or symbols, or allow them to come unbidden.

Midsummer: The Summer Solstice (on or around June 21st), one of the *Wiccan* festivals and an excellent night for magic. Midsummer marks the point of the year when the Sun is symbolically at the height of its powers.

Noncombustible Incense: Incense which is compounded without potassium nitrate, and which requires heat to release its scent. Compare with *Combustible Incense.*

Ostara: A *Wiccan* festival occurring at the Spring Equinox (on or around March 21st), which marks the beginning of true Spring. A Fire festival celebrating the resurgence of Earth fertility, and an ideal time for magic.

Pagan: From the Latin *paganus,* meaning country dweller. Today, used as a general term for followers of *Wicca* and other shamanistic, polytheistic and magic-embracing religions.

Pentagram: The basic five-pointed star, visualized with one point upward. The pentagram represents the five senses, the *Elements* (Earth, Air, Fire, Water and *Akasha*), the hand and the human body. It is a protective symbol known to have been in use since the days of old Babylon. Today it is frequently associated with *Wicca.* A symbol of power.

Personal Power: The energy which sustains our bodies, and which is available for use in *magic.*

Psychic Mind: The subconscious, or unconscious, mind in which we receive psychic impulses. The psychic mind is at work when we sleep, dream and meditate. *Divination* is a ritual process designed to contact the psychic mind. *Intuition* is a term used to describe psychic information that unexpectedly reaches the conscious mind. *Psychism* describes the state in which information from the psychic mind is available to the conscious mind.

Psychism: The act of being consciously psychic. *Ritual consciousness* is a form of psychism.

Reincarnation: The doctrine of rebirth. The process of repeated incarnations in human form to allow evolution of the sexless, ageless soul.

Ritual: Ceremony. A specific form of movement, manipulation of objects or inner processes designed to produce desired effects. In religion, ritual is geared toward union with the divine. In *magic* it produces a specific state of consciousness that allows the magician to move energy toward needed goals. A *spell* is a magical ritual.

Ritual Consciousness: A specific, alternate state of awareness necessary to the successful practice of magic. The magician achieves this through the use of *visualization* and *ritual*. It denotes a state in which the *conscious mind* and *psychic mind* are attuned, wherein the magician senses energies, gives them purpose and releases them towards the magical goal. It is a heightening of the senses, an expansion of the awareness beyond the physical world, an interlinking with nature and with the forces behind all conceptions of Deity.

Sabbat: A *Wiccan* festival. *See Beltane, Imbolc, Lughnasadh, Mabon, Midsummer, Ostara, Samhain* and *Yule.*

Sachet: A cloth bag filled with herbs. In *herb magic* sachets are used to contain herb mixtures while they slowly release their energies for specific magical goals.

Samhain: A *Wiccan* festival celebrated on October 31st. Samhain is a gathering up of energies before the depths of Winter. An ancient night upon which to perform magic.

Scry, To: To gaze at or into an object (a quartz crystal sphere, pool of water, reflections, a candle flame) to still the *conscious mind* and to contact the *psychic mind.* This allows the scryer to become aware of possible events prior to their actual occurrence, as well as to perceive past or present events through other than the five senses. A form of *divination.*

Spell: A magical *ritual,* usually nonreligious in nature and often accompanied by spoken works.

Succubus: A female spirit or demon once believed to sexually tempt and abuse men. It may have been a theological explanation of nocturnal emissions. Compare with *Incubus*.

Talisman: An object *empowered* with magical energy to attract a specific force or energy to its bearer. Compare with *Amulet*.

Tincture: A liquid produced by soaking plant materials in ethyl alcohol (or medicinally, in apple cider vinegar) to produce a scented liquid.

Visualization: The process of forming mental images. Magical visualization consists of forming images of needed goals during *ritual*. Visualization is also used to direct *personal power* and natural energies during *magic* for various purposes, including *empowering* and forming the *magic circle*. It is a function of the *conscious mind*.

Wicca: A contemporary *pagan* religion with spiritual roots in the earliest expressions of reverence for nature. Wicca views Deity as Goddess and God; thus, it is polytheistic. It also embraces *magic* and *reincarnation*. Some Wiccans identify themselves with the word *Witch*.

Wiccan: A follower of *Wicca*. Alternately, denoting some aspect of that religion.

Witch: Anciently, a European practitioner of the remnants of pre-Christian folk magic, especially *herb magic* and *herbalism*. One who practiced *Witchcraft*. Later this term's meaning was deliberately altered to denote demented, dangerous, supernatural beings who practiced destructive magic and who threatened Christianity. This was a political, monetary and sexist move on the part of organized religion. The latter meaning is still currently accepted by many non-Witches. The term *Witch* is sometimes used by members of *Wicca* to describe themselves.

Witchcraft: The *craft* of the *Witch*—magic, especially magic utilizing *personal power* in conjunction with the energies within stones, *herbs,* colors and other natural objects. Some followers of *Wicca* use this word to denote their religion, producing much confusion on the part of outsiders.

Wort: An old term meaning *herb*. Mugwort preserves the word.

Yule: A *Wiccan* festival celebrated on or about December 21st, marking the rebirth of the Sun God from the Goddess. A time of joy and celebration during the miseries of Winter. Yule occurs on the Winter Solstice.

Appendix 1: Colors

THIS TABLE OF colors and their energies can be used when choosing candles for spells, for tinting bath salts, and for designing entire rituals around your herbal products. Though these ritual associations are generally accepted, some differences in thought do exist. Color is a magical system in and of itself.*

WHITE: Protection, purification, peace, truth, sincerity

RED: Protection, strength, health, vigor, lust, sex, passion, courage, exorcism

BLACK: Absorbing and destroying negativity, healing severe diseases, banishing

LIGHT BLUE: Tranquility, healing, patience, happiness

DARK BLUE: Change, flexibility, the subconscious mind, psychism, healing

GREEN: Finances, money, fertility, prosperity, growth, luck, employment

GRAY: Neutrality

YELLOW: Intellect, attraction, study, persuasion, confidence, divination

BROWN: Working magic for animals, healing animals, the home

PINK: Love, honor, morality, friendships

ORANGE: Adaptability, stimulation, attraction

PURPLE: Power, healing severe diseases, spirituality, meditation

---

* See Raymond Buckland's *Practical Color Magick* (Llewellyn, 1984).

Appendix 2: Sources

One of the regrettable omissions in the first edition of this book was a listing of reputable mail-order suppliers of herbs, essential oils, live herb plants and other materials. With my apologies, here it is.

APHRODISIA
264 Bleeker St.
New York, NY 10014
(212) 989-6440
Fax (212) 989-8027
A wide selection of dried herbs.

AROMA VERA INC.
5901 Rodeo Rd.
Los Angeles, CA 90016
(310) 280-0407
web site: aromavera.com
True essential oils.

COMPANION PLANTS
7247 N. Coolville Ridge Rd.
Athens, OH 45701
(740) 592-4643
Hundreds of rare and unusual herbs and plants. Live or seeds.

THE CRYSTAL CAVE
415 W. Foothill Blvd.
Claremont, CA 91711
www.merchantsmystic.com
Dried herbs, charcoal blocks, candles, censers and crystals, books.
Ask about availability of copal.

ENCHANTMENTS
341 E. 9th St.
New York, NY 10003
(212) 228-4394
Herbs, candles, charcoal blocks.

EYE OF THE CAT
3314 E. Broadway
Long Beach, CA 90803
(562) 438-3569
A huge stock of common and unusual dried herbs, charcoal blocks,
candles, books.

FIREWIND HERBAL PRODUCTS
P.O. Box 5527
Hopkins, MN 55343
(952) 543-9065
Firewindhp.com
Herbs, resins, charcoal, censers and more.

ISIS
5701 E. Colfax Ave.
Denver, CO 80220
(303) 321-0867
web site: www.ISISBOOKS.com
Dried herbs and oils, candles, charcoal blocks and books.

MAGICK BOOKSTORE
2306 Highland Ave.
National City, CA 91950
(619) 477-5260
e-mail: MAGICKBOOK@aol.com
Dried herbs, candles, books. Free catalog.

ORIGINAL SWISS AROMATICS
P.O. Box 606
San Rafael, CA 94915
(415) 479-3979
True essential oils.

Bibliography

THIS BOOK IS the product of personal experimentation, much of which was based on suggestions by friends and teachers. However, there are published sources that are of value to the student who wishes to further research the subject of magical perfumery. Some of these works contain only a fragment of magically oriented information. Others are magical textbooks. Distinction between these two extremes is made in the notes.

Additionally, many of these books print recipes not included in this work. I don't agree with all or even anything that the below authors have to say, but that doesn't mean that their books shouldn't be consulted.

The literature of magical herb products is even more limited than that of herb magic in general; hence, many of these works concentrate on the *processes* of herb magic—creating perfumes, soaps, incenses, ointments and so on—rather than on the magic itself.

Unfortunately, most of the classic books on this subject are out of print; but they can still be found in secondhand book stores, some libraries, or by mail from book-search services.

Utilize the information you find in them along magical lines. The processes described can easily be transferred to magical ends by choosing ingredients in harmony with your goal and by empowering the products once they're made.

Agrippa, Henry Cornelius. *The Philosophy of Natural Magic.* Antwerp, 1531. Reprint. Chicago: de Laurence, 1919. Reprint. Secaucus NJ: University Books, 1974.
This work contains the first volume of Agrippa's Three Books of

Occult Philosophy. Later additions, which are rather quaint, are also included. As I mentioned in Part III, some of the translations seem questionable. See the next entry.

Agrippa, Henry Cornelius. *Three Books of Occult Philosophy*. 1533. English translation first published in London, 1651. Reprint. London: Chthonios Books, 1986.
This is the first publication of Agrippa's complete magical work in over 300 years. These books gathered together much of the magical lore of his time—particularly that concerning plants, animals, stones, the planets and the elements. Of special interest are his "fume" recipes and his planetary attributions of plants. A classic work.

Aima. *Ritual Book of Herbal Spells*. Los Angeles: Foibles, 1976. A book of herb magic culled from a wide variety of sources, this good book includes many formulas for incenses (some of which are quite complex in the range of ingredients). A worthwhile book.

Arctander, Steffen. *Perfume and Flavor Materials of Natural Origin*. Elizabeth, NJ: Published by the author, 1960.
A scholarly look at essential oils—their manufacture, properties and the materials used. No magical information.

Bailes, Edith G. *An Album of Fragrance*. Richmond, Maine: Cardamom Press, 1983.
A delightful booklet of herbal recipes and processing techniques for creating incenses, oils and sachets. The author includes detailed instructions for *enfleurage* using purified fat, but includes no ritual information.

Barrett, Francis. *The Magus: A Complete System of Occult Philosophy*. Secaucus, NJ: University Books, 1967.
This book contains most of the standard incense formulas used in ceremonial magic of earlier centuries. Barrett compiled these in the late 1700s and was heavily influenced by Agrippa. *The Magus* is now available in an oversize paperback edition.

Conway, David. *Magic: An Occult Primer*. New York: Bantam, 1972.
Mr. Conway includes many interesting formulas for flying ointments and similar dangerous substances, but he fails to warn the reader of the attendant hazards of using them. Interesting, but I wouldn't recommend trying them.

Conway, David. *The Magic of Herbs*. New York: Dutton, 1973.
This book includes a few ancient formulas and a section on herb-

al narcotics, as well as a look at herbalism and astrology.

Devine, M. V. *Brujeria: A Study in Mexican-American Folk-Magic.* St. Paul: Llewellyn Publications, 1982.

Ms. Devine includes several incense and oil recipes here, some of which I've reproduced in this book with her permission. A wonderful, witty work.

Duff, Gail. *A Book of Potpourri: New and Old Ideas for Fragrant Flowers and Herbs.* New York: Beaufort Books, 1985.

This beautifully illustrated book contains a wealth of formulas and ideas for incense, scented inks, soaps and many other herbal products, though the focus here is on cosmetic rather than ritual magic.

Fettner, Ann Tucker. *Potpourri, Incense and Other Fragrant Concoctions.* New York: Workman, 1977.

This delightful book contains a section on incense, including directions for fashioning cone incense. Complete recipes are given for creating non-occult mixtures.

Griffith, F. L. and Herbert Thompson, eds. *The Leyden Papyrus: An Egyptian Magical Book.* New York: Dover, 1974.

This third-century Egyptian magical papyrus contains some curious herbal magic, much of which is barely comprehensible.

Hansen, Harold A. *The Witch's Garden.* Santa Cruz, CA: Unity Press, 1978.

A look at the flying ointments of days past. Not a practical book, though I've seen it touted as such. The emphasis is on the heavily negative aspects of herbalism (poisons, drugs). A depressing, biased book. Not recommended unless you're interested in such things.

Hayes, Carolyn H. *Pergemin: Perfumes, Incenses, Colors, Birthstones: Their Occult Properties and Uses.* Chicago: Aries Press, 1937.

This wonderful little booklet, now unfortunately long out of print, contains an excellent incense section as well as much interesting information about oils, with many recipes.

Huson, Paul. *Mastering Herbalism.* New York: Stein and Day, 1974.

This book contains a good chapter on perfumes (oils) and incense composition, offering several interesting recipes.

Junius, Manfred M. *Practical Handbook of Plant Alchemy.* New York: Inner Traditions International, 1985.

An advanced treatise regarding the "lesser work" of laboratory alchemy.

Leyel, C. F. *The Magic of Herbs.* New York: Harcourt, Brace and Company, 1926. Reprint. Toronto: Coles, 1981.

Truly a classic work, *The Magic of Herbs* contains a wonderful chapter on perfumes and perfumers, including many, many recipes from ancient sources. A must book for the serious magical herbalist!

Malbrough, Ray. *Charms, Spells and Formulas.* St. Paul: Llewellyn Publications, 1986.

An authentic guide to Louisiana Hoodoo magic, containing many great incense, oil, powder and wash recipes. Real Cajun magic.

Maple, Eric. *The Magic of Perfume.* New York: Weiser, 1973. This short introduction to the world of magical scents is curiously comprehensive—and well worthwhile.

Mathers, S. Liddell MacGregor, ed. and trans. *The Key of Solomon the King (Clavicula Salomonis).* 1888. Reprint. New York: Samuel Weiser, 1972.

This work, a translation of perhaps the most famous of all grimoires, contains some ink exorcisms, an asperger formula and a bit of other herbal information.

Meyer, David. *Sachets, Potpourri and Incense Recipes.* Glenwood, IL: Meyerbooks, 1986.

This booklet is a compilation of recipes and processes. It includes a short section describing materials used in herbal perfumery. No magical information.

Moldenke, Harold N. and Alma L. *Plants of the Bible.* Waltham, MA: Chronica Botanica Company, 1952.

A scholarly look at the herbs, barks and resins used in religion and magic in the Near East nearly 2,000 years ago.

Paulsen, Kathryn. *Witches' Potions and Spells.* Mount Vernon, NY: Peter Pauper Press, 1971.

A charming compendium of spells culled from ancient sources, this book contains many brew recipes, although some of them include the usual nasty substances.

Poucher, William A. *Perfumes, Cosmetics and Soaps.* 3 Vols. Princeton, NJ: D. Van Nostrad and Co., Inc., 1958.

An intelligent, in-depth look at the ingredients in, and the blending of, perfumes and cosmetics. Unfortunately, this work lacks magical information.

Salat, Barbara and David Copperfield, eds. *Well-Being: Advice from* the *Do-It-Yourself Journal for Healthy Living.* Garden City, NY: Anchor Press/Doubleday, 1979.

An excellent introduction to herbalism, containing much information on creating your own herbal remedies, cosmetics, and so on, with soap recipes. No magical lore is included.

Slater, Herman ed. *The Magical Formulary.* New York: Magickal Childe, 1981.

This work concentrates on Voodoo-type formulas for incenses, oils and powders, with a healthy sampling of Wiccan and ceremonial magic formulas as well. Pass over the hexing recipes, which were unfortunately included.

Tarotstar. *The Witch's Formulary and Spellbook.* New York: Original Publications, n.d.

An assortment of recipes for incenses, oils, inks and so on, much of it "black-arts" (i.e., negative, cursing, hexing) formulas. A good basic sourcebook if you can overlook the negative information.

Thompson, C. J. S. *The Mysteries and Secrets of Magic.* New York: The Olympia Press, 1972.

This fascinating work includes a chapter concerned with incenses, as well as much magical information otherwise unavailable.

Thompson, C. J. S. *The Mystery and Lure of Perfume.* Philadelphia: J. B. Lippincott, 1927.

A fabulous book devoted to perfumes, incenses and other scented goods of ancient times. Several recipes are given.

Traven, Beatrice. *The Complete Book of Natural Cosmetics.* New York: Simon and Schuster, 1974.

A chapter on creating natural perfumes is included in this work, but again, no magical information is given.

Verrill, A. Hyatt. *Perfumes and Spices.* New York: L. C. Page and Co., 1940.

A detailed account of perfumery, with many interesting tips on blending oils and recipes as well (though non-magical in nature). Much of this information seems to have come from Poucher (see above).

Vinci, Leo. *Incense: Its Ritual Significance, Use and Preparation.* New York: Weiser, 1980.

A useful little book with many recipes and hints, as well as directions for making cone incense.

Botanical Index

COMMON NAMES ARE just that—common. They vary from country to country and even from district to district. The variety of common names is confusing. Therefore, I've included the following list of plants mentioned in this book together with their Latin names to facilitate identification.

Exact identification for some plants is difficult due to a number of factors. In these cases only the genus is given.

Plants have been marked according to their safety. Plants labeled (*x*) should never be ingested. Plants labeled (~) should be used with caution, since they may adversely affect some people due to their specific health problems (i.e. diabetes, using MAO inhibitors, kidney disease, etc.). Plants labeled (*P*) should not be used when pregnant or nursing.

```
   Acacia, Gum—Acacia senegal
x  Aconite—Aconitum napellus
~  Acorn (fruite of the oak)—Quercus alba
   Agrimony—Agrimonia eupatoria
   Allspice—Pimenta officinalis or P. dioica
   Almond—Prunus dulcis
   Aloe, Wood—Aquilaria agollocha
   Amaranth—Amaranthus hypochondriacus
   Ambrette—Hibiscus abelmoschus
~P Angelica—Angelica archangelica
   Anise—Pimpinella anisum
   Apple—Pyrus spp.
   Apricot—Prunus armeniaca
   Arabic, Gum—Acacia vera
   Asafoetida—Ferula asafoetida
   Ash—Fraxinus excelsior; F. americana
   Avens—Geum urbanum
```

255

    Baby's Breath—*Gypsophila paniculata*
x Balm of Gilead—*Commiphora opobalsamum*
    Barley—*Hordeum* spp.
P Basil—*Ocimum basilicum*
    Bay—*Laurus nobilis*
    Bayberry—*Myrica* spp.
    Bdellium, Gum—*Bursera* spp.
    Beet—*Beta vulgaris*
x Belladonna—*Atropa belladonna*
    Benzoin—*Styrax benzoin*
P Bergamot—*Mentha citrata*
    Betony, Wood—*Betonica officinalis*
    Birch—*Betula alba*
    Birthwort—*Aristolochia clematitis*
    Bistort—*Polygonum bistorta*
    Blackberry—*Rubus villosus*
x Black Hellebore—*Helleborus niger*
x Black Nightshade—*Solanum nigrum*
    Black Pepper—*Piper nigrum*
    Black Tea—*Thea sinensis*
~ P Bladderwrack—*Fucus visiculosis*
    Broom—*Cytisus scoparius*
x Bryony—*Bryony* spp.
P Buchu—*Agathosma betulina or Baromsa betulina*

    Cachana—*Liatris punctata*
    Calamint—*Calamintha* spp.
x Calamus—*Acorus calamus*
P Camomile—*Anthemis nobilis*   German Camomile okay for P
x Camphor—*Cinnamomum camphora*
    Caper—*Capparis spinosa*
    Caraway—*Carum carvi*
    Cardamom—*Elettario cardamomum*
x Carnation—*Dianthus carophyllus*
    Cassia—*Cinnamomum cassia*
    Castor—*Ricinus communis*
P Catnip—*Nepeta cataria*
    Cayenne—*Capsicum frutescens*
    Cedar—*Cedrus libani or Cedrus* spp.
    Chicory—*Chicorium intybus*

Chrysanthemum—*Chrysanthemum* spp.
Cinnamon—*Cinnamomum zeylanicum*
Cinquefoil—*Potentilla canadensis* or *P. reptans*
Citron—*Citrus medica*
Clove—*Syzygium aromaticum* or *Carophyllus aromaticus*
~ P Clover—*Trifolium* spp.
Club Moss—*Lycopodium clavatum*
Coconut—*Cocos nucifera*
  x Comfrey—*Symphytum officinale*
Copal—*Bursera* spp.
Coriander—*Coriandrum sativum*
Corn—*Zea mays*
Costmary—*Balsamita major*
Costus—*Aplotaxis lappa*
Crocus—*Crocus vernus*
Cubeb—*Piper cubeb*
Cucumber—*Cucumis sativus*
Cumin—*Cumimum cyminum*
  P Cypress—*Cupressus sempervirens*

Damiana—*Turnera diffusa* or *T. aphrodisiaca*
  x Deadly Nightshade—*Solanum* spp.
  x Deerstongue—*Frasera speciosa* or *Liatris odoratissimus*
Dill—*Anethum graveolens*
Dittany of Crete—*Dictamus origanoides*
Dock—*Rumex* spp.
Dogwood—*Cornus florida*
Dragon's Blood—*Daemonorops draco* or *Draceaena* spp.

Elder—*Sambucus canadensis*
  x Eucalyptus—*Eucalyptus* spp.
  x Euphorbium—*Euphorbia spp.*
Eyebright—*Euphrasia officinalis*

Fennel—*Foeniculum vulgare*
  x Fern—various plants
  ~ Flax—*Linum usitatissimum*
Fleawort—*Inula conyza*
Frankincense—*Boswellia carterii*
Fumitory—*Fumaria officinalis*

Galangal—*Alpina officinalis* or *A. galanga*
Gall nuts (Oak galls from *Quercus alba?*)
Gardenia—*Gardenia* spp.
Garlic—*Allium sativum*
x Geranium (scented varieties)—*Pelargonium* spp.
Ginger—*Zingiber officinalis*
Grains of Paradise—*Aframomum melequeta*
Grape—*Vitis vinifera*
Grapefruit—*Citrus paradisi*
Ground Ivy—*Nepeta hederacea*
Gum Acacia—*Acacia senegal*
Gum Ammoniac—*Ferula* spp.
Gum Arabic—*Acacia vera*
Gum Bdellium—*Bursera* spp.
Gum Mastic—*Pistachia lentiscus*
Gum Scammony—*Convolvulus scammonia*
Gum Tragacanth—*Astragalus gummifer*

Hazel—*Corylus* spp.
Heather—*Calluna* spp. or *Erica* spp.
x Heliotrope—*Heliotropium europaeum* or *H. arborescens*
x Hellebore, Black—*Helleborus niger*
x Hemlock—*Conium maculatum*
~ Hemp—*Cannabis sativa*
x Henbane—*Hyoscyamus niger*
Hibiscus—*Hibiscus* spp.
Holly—*Ilex aquifolium* or *I. opaca*
Honeysuckle—*Lonicera caprifolium*
~ Hops—*Humulus lupulus*
P Horehound—*Marrubium vulgare*
x Hyacinth--*Hyacinthus orientalis*
Hyssop—*Hyssopus officinalis*

Iris—*Iris* spp.
Irish Moss—*Chondrus crispus*
x Ivy—*Hedera* spp.

Jasmine—*Jasminum officinale* or *J. odoratissimum*
~ P Juniper—*Juniperus communis*

Kava Kava—*Piper methysticum*
Kelp (sea plants including Bladderwrack)—*Fucus visiculosis*
Knotgrass—*Polygonum aviculare*
Lavender—*Lavendula officinale* or *L. vera*
Lemon—*Citrus limon*
Lemon Balm—*Melissa officinalis*
P Lemongrass—*Cymbopogon citratus*
Lemon Verbena—*Lippia citriodora*
~P Licorice—*Glycyrrhiza glabra*
Lilac—*Syringa vulgaris*
Lily—*Lilium* spp.
Lime—*Citrus limetta*
Lotus—*Nymphaea lotus*
Lovage—*Levisticum officinale*
Lupine—*Lupinus* spp.

~ Mace—*Myristica fragrans*
Magnolia—*Magnolia* spp.
P Maidenhair fern—*Adiantum pedatim*
Mallow—*Malva* spp.
x Mandrake—*Mandragora officinale*
Maple—*Acer* spp.
Marigold—*Calendula officinalis*
Marjoram—*Origanum majorana* or *O. vulgare*
Mastic, Gum—*Pistachia lentiscus*
Meadowsweet—*Spiraea filipendula*
Mimosa—*Acacia dealbata*
Mimulus—*Mimulus moschatus*
Mint—*Mentha spicata* (Spearmint); *M. piperita* (Peppermint)
x Mistletoe, American—*Phoradendron flavescens*
x Mistletoe, European—*Viscum album*
Mormon Tea—*Ephedra* spp.
Moss, Club—*Lycopodium clavatum*
P Mugwort—*Artemisia vulgaris*
Mullein—*Verbascum thapsus*
x Mums—*Chrysanthemum* spp.
Musk Thistle—*Carduus nutans*
Mustard—*Brassica* spp.
P Myrrh—*Comniphora myrrha*
Myrtle—*Myrtus communis*

x Narcissus—*Narcissus fazetta*
Neroli (essential oil of the Bitter Orange)—*Citrus aurantium*
Nettle—*Urtica dioica*
Niaouli—*Melaleuca viridiflora nigrum*
x Nightshade—*Solanum*
~ Nutmeg—*Myristica fragrans*

Oak—*Quercus alba*
Oakmoss—*Evernia prunastri* or *E. furfuraceae*
Olive—*Olea europaea*
Orchid—*Orchis* spp.
P Opoponax—*Comniphora erythraceae;* var. *glabrescens*
Orange—*Citrus sinensis*
Orris—*Iris florentina*
P Osha—*Ligusticum porteri*

Palmarosa—*Cymbopogon martini*
Pansy—*Viola tricolor*
Parsley—*Petroselinum sativum*
Passion Flower—*Passiflora incarnata*
Patchouly—*Pogostemon cablin* or *P. patchouli*
Peach—*Prunus persica*
P Pennyroyal—*Mentha pulegium*
Peony—*Paeonia officinalis*
Pepper, Black—*Piper nigrum*
Pepper, Chile—*Capsicum* spp.
Peppermint—*Mentha piperita*
Pepperwort—*Lepidium latifolium* or *Polygonum hydropiper?*
~ Periwinkle—*Vinca major*
x Pine—*Pinus* spp.
Plumeria—*Plumeria acutifolia*
Pokeberry—*Phytolacca americana*
Pomegranate—*Punica granatum*
Poplar—*Populus tremuloides*
Poppy—*Papaver* spp.
Primose—*Primula vulgaris*

x Ranunculus—*Ranunculus* spp.
~ Red Sandalwood—*Sanicula marilandica*
Red Storax—*Styrax* spp.

~ P Rhubarb—*Rheum* spp.
Rose—*Rosa* spp.
Rose Geranium—*Pelargonium graveolens*
Rosemary—*Rosmarinus officinalis*
P Rowan—*Sorbus acuparia*
P Rue—*Ruta graveolens*

Saffron—*Crocus sativus*
Sagapen—??? (See Spirit Incense #2)
Sage—*Salvia officinalis*
Sagebrush—*Artemesia* spp.
St. John's Wort—*Hypericum perforatum*
~ Sandalwood—*Santalum album*
Sarsaparilla—*Smilax aspera*
Sassafras—*Sassafras albidum*
Selenetrope—??? (See Moon Incense #2)
Sesame—*Sesamum orientale*
Solomon's Seal—*Polygonatum officinale* or *P. multiflorum*
Spearmint—*Mentha spicata*
Spikenard—*Nardostachys jatamansi*
Star Anise—*Illicum verum*
~ Stephanotis—*Stephanotis florabunda*
Storax—*Liquidambar orientalis*
Strawberry—*Fragaria vesca*
Sumbul—*Ferula sumbul*
Sunflower—*Helianthus annuus*
~ Sweet Flag—*Acorus calamus*
Sweetgrass—*Hierochloe odorata*
Sweet Pea—*Lathrys odoratus*

Tamarisk—*Tamarix* spp.
Tangerine—*Citrus reticulata*
P Tansy—*Tanacetum vulgare*
Tapsus barbatus—Unknown. Perhaps *Taxus baccata* (Yew) faultily transcribed over the centuries. *Barbatus* means "barbed or bearded" but this isn't much of a clue. I truly don't know.
Tarragon—*Artemesia dracunculus*
Tea, Black—*Thea sinensis*
Thistle—*Carduus* spp.
Thyme—*Thymus vulgaris*

Ti—*Cordyline terminalis*
~ Tobacco—*Nicotiana* spp.
x Tonka—*Dipteryx odorata*
Tragacanth, Gum—*Astragalus gummifer*
x Trefoil—*Trifolium* spp.
Tuberose—*Polianthes tuberosa*

Valerian—*Valeriana officinalis*
Vanilla—*Vanilla aromatica* or *V. planifolia*
Vervain—*Verbena officinalis*
P Vetivert—*Vetiveria zizanioides*
Violet—*Viola odorata*

x Water Parsnip—*Sium latifolium?*
Wheat—*Triticum* spp.
White Willow—*Salix alba*
Wintergreen—*Gaultheria procumbens*
x Wisteria—*Wisteria* spp.
x Wolfsbane—*Aconitum napellus*
Wood Aloe—*Aquilaria agallocha*
Wood Betony—*Betonica officinalis*
~ Woodruff —*Asperula odorata*
x Wormwood—*Artemesia absinthium*

P Yarrow—*Achillea millefolium*
Yellow Daisies—perhaps *Chrysanthemum leucanthemum*
Yerba Santa—*Eriodictyon californicum*
x Yew—*Taxus baccata*
Ylang-Ylang—*Canaga odorata*

General Index